ADVENT
CHRISTMAS

A Guide to the Eucharist and Hours

The Liturgical Seasons

ADVENT
CHRISTMAS

A Guide to the Eucharist and Hours

Kevin W. Irwin

PUEBLO PUBLISHING COMPANY

New York

Design: Frank Kacmarcik

ISBN: 0-916134-80-6

Printed in the United States of America.

To the memory of Kenneth F. O'Connell

Contents

Preface

Advent and Christmas are seasons of promise and fulfillment, expectation and accomplishment, hope for Christ's coming and joy at his incarnation. In the Advent liturgy, we listen once again to the words of Isaiah calling us to recognize our need for God. We experience the piercing challenge of John the Baptist, whose words and way of living call us to make straight the way for the Lord. It is John, most especially, who reminds us of the justice and peace of God's kingdom, incarnated in Jesus and experienced when and where we live the values of the gospel.

In the Christmas liturgy, we are drawn into God's love through Christ's taking human flesh and sharing our human condition. The Emmanuel for whom we long in Advent has never left us. Through the Christmas liturgy, we commemorate his incarnation and are thus drawn into God's infinite love once more.

The Epiphany liturgy reminds us that the Messiah came to set all peoples free and that the Lord's mission is now accomplished through us. The commemoration of the Lord's baptism is a reminder that through our baptism we share in the work of the Messiah.

The Advent liturgy is stark and reflective in its simplicity. Christmas and Epiphany are festive and exuberant in their solemnity. These seasons mark the turning of the calendar year. They are intended to help us to turn again and again to Christ each time we celebrate a "year of our Lord" until we are called from this life to share what the liturgy foreshadows and prefigures—eternal union with God in the kingdom forever.

In completing this book, I am deeply aware of many people whose insight and example have helped me to delve into the many levels of meaning contained in the liturgy of these seasons. I want to acknowledge the members of the monastic community of St. Anselm's Abbey, Manchester, New Hampshire. I wrote the first part of this book at that monastery where I was privileged to share in their reverent celebration of the eucharist and hours in Advent and Christmas, especially in 1984–1985. I want to acknowledge the students at The Catholic University of America who heard some of what is contained here in my class lectures in the fall of 1985. In addition, I want to acknowledge the community that gathers for daily eucharist at St. Andrew the Apostle Church, Silver Spring, Maryland, where I reside. Some of the material contained here was used in preparing and celebrating liturgy with them. For three of the reflections, I have drawn on ideas of friends: Patrick Hennessy, Joan Vail Thorne, and Kathleen Hodges. I want to thank them for their ideas (which they may well have forgotten they gave me); I also ask their indulgence if what they offered is presented here in less recognizable fashion.

Finally, a word about the man to whom I dedicate this work. Monsignor Kenneth O'Connell was a priest of the archdiocese of New York. Through many of my formative years and through the years we shared together in the ordained ministry in New York, he served as an inspiration and example. He died in November, 1984 after several months of suffering with incurable cancer. His example of gentleness and patience, characteristic of him throughout his life, were an inspiration to all as he faced death through terminal illness. The weekend before he died I was able to visit with him and his devoted family at St. Vincent's Hospital in New York. We spoke briefly a few times that weekend. The last time I spoke with him I was able to thank him for his life and for the way he faced his death. He died a few days before Advent, 1984 when I began writing this book. The references in it to death and to facing the mortality of human life are written with this friend and mentor in mind. His untimely death taught me a great deal. It has changed my perspective on life. Ken's death taught me that all life is terminal. Cancer took Ken's life; it did not take his spirit. The way he lived life and the way he died taught me that what matters is how we live the life God gives us and how we reflect his life and love with each other.

The death of a loved one helps us see that death is the last barrier, a threshold through which the Christian walks to meet God finally and fully. In the meantime, we believers need the Advent–Christmas liturgy to remind us of these core truths of Christianity.

On Wednesday of the First week of Advent, we hear these consoling words of Isaiah:

"On this mountain the Lord of hosts
   will provide for all peoples
A feast of rich food and choice wines,
   juicy, rich food and pure, choice wines.
On this mountain he will destroy
   the veil that veils all peoples,
The web that is woven over all nations;
   he will destroy death forever.
The Lord God will wipe away
   the tears from all faces. . . .
On that day it will be said:
   'Behold our God, to whom we looked to save us!
   This is the Lord for whom we looked;
   let us rejoice and be glad that he has saved us!'"
(Is 25:6–9)

I gratefully dedicate this book to a friend whose life and death have taught me a fuller meaning of the prayer we pray daily after the Lord's Prayer: "In your mercy keep us free from sin and protect us from all anxiety as we wait in joyful hope for the coming of our Savior, Jesus Christ."

Solemnity of Pentecost
The Catholic University of America
May 18, 1986

ADVENT

CHRISTMAS

A Guide to the Eucharist and Hours

First Week of Advent

FIRST SUNDAY OF ADVENT

Liturgical Context

On the first day of Advent, we begin to prepare for the annual celebrations of Christ's incarnation at Christmas, his manifestation at Epiphany, and the beginning of his mission at the feast of the Baptism of the Lord. Advent means "coming." We are to prepare for the coming of God among us as a child who is a king, as an infant who is a savior, as one born at a given time and place yet who is a Messiah for all ages and peoples.

But, even though Advent heralds the birth of Jesus, it turns our hearts and minds toward the future when Christ "will come again in glory to judge the living and the dead." Advent begins by preparing us to meet the Lord at the end of our earthly lives, at death, and when he returns at the end of time to bring time to an end. The *General Norms for the Liturgical Year and the Calendar* state:

"Advent has a twofold character: as a season to prepare us for Christmas when Christ's first coming to us is remembered; as a season when that remembrance directs the mind and heart to await Christ's Second Coming at the end of time. Advent is thus a period for devout and joyful expectation." (no. 39)

Of the four Advent Sundays, it is the first that emphasizes Christ's second coming, a theme which is sustained throughout the weekdays of the first half of the season until December 16.

The liturgy this Sunday emphasizes the eschatological—"Christ will come again"—aspect of all liturgical prayer and helps us to "wait in joyful hope for the coming of our Savior." Our devout and joyful expectation is for the Lord to come again and take us to his kingdom forever.

VS. FRUSTRATION EXPRESSED IN 'B' CYCLE THAT HE hasn't COME YET!

Advent is a season of moods and senses. Its liturgy is stark, simple, and sober. Unlike Lent, it does not have initiation and penitential themes running through it which culminate in the celebration of baptism. Advent speaks of Messianic hopes and expectations, which will not be fulfilled completely until Christ comes in glory and we finally enter the kingdom of heaven. (While communal celebrations of penance during Advent are certainly appropriate and a communal baptism on the feast of the Baptism of the Lord is most suitable, it is clear that the theology and spirituality of Advent did not develop in the Roman rite with the same baptismal and penitential aspects as did Lent.)

Advent prepares us for the birth of an infant Messiah and for the return of the Lord of heaven and earth. In fact, it is his Lordship and power that is proclaimed in the gospels today (under the title "Son of Man" in the "A" and "C" cycles).

Our waiting and watching are hopeful, however, since we have been graced by Christ's incarnation and saved by his unique act of redemption. Through baptism, we have been incorporated into his body, the church, which encourages his people to wait for their Lord to return and bring them to the fullness of eternal happiness. We rejoice when we sing, "O Come, O Come Emmanuel," because Emmanuel has come and remains with the church until the end of time. Until Christ comes again we pray:

"Deliver us, Lord, from every evil,
and grant us peace in our day.
In your mercy keep us free from sin
and protect us from all anxiety
as we wait in joyful hope
for the coming of our Saviour, Jesus Christ."
   (Embolism after the Lord's Prayer)

The scripture readings for the Sundays of Advent are structured in the following way:

"Each gospel reading has a distinctive theme: the Lord's coming at the end of time (First Sunday of Advent), John the Baptist (Second and Third Sundays), and the events that prepared immediately for the Lord's birth (Fourth Sunday).

"The Old Testament readings are prophecies about the Messiah and the Messianic age, especially from Isaiah. The readings from an apostle serve as exhortations and as proclamations, in keeping with the different themes of Advent." (Lectionary for Mass Introduction, no. 93)

The fact that the first Sunday continues the eschatological theme begun on the thirty-third Sunday of the year indicates how these weeks are joined liturgically. Even though one can say that today is the first Sunday of the liturgical year, its continuity with the last Sundays of the year reminds us that the present arrangement of a four-week Advent before Christmas on December 25 was not always the case. Liturgical tradition attests to a six-week Advent before Christmas in some parts of Gaul.

Theologically, this first Sunday looks forward to Christ's second coming and encourages us to prepare for the final judgment spoken of in the readings of the past two Sundays. Structurally, "Advent begins with Evening Prayer I of the Sunday falling closest to 30 November and ends before Evening Prayer I of Christmas" (*General Norms for the Liturgical Year and the Calendar*, no. 40).

The first part of Advent is more about endings (the final judgment) than about beginnings (a new liturgical year). This part of the liturgical cycle is not designed to present a series of distinct themes from the life and ministry of Jesus in logical succession. What the liturgy does provide are emphases and themes derived from the one mystery of Christ who "has died . . . is risen . . . [and] will come again."

Cycle "A"

The first reading this Sunday from the prophet Isaiah (2:1–5) speaks of the Lord who will gather all nations to himself and in his kingdom. This same text appears as the first reading at the eucharist on the Monday of the First Week of Advent (except in Year "A"). The short scripture reading at morning prayer on Advent Mondays consists of verse 3 of this text. Verses 1–5 also form one of the suggested readings for a votive mass for the spread of the gospel. Clearly eschatological in tone and universal in outlook, the text relates Isaiah's vision for Israel "in days to come." The "mountain of the Lord's house" recalls the giving of the Law at the mountain of

Sinai, the prominence of the city of Jerusalem (which is also reflected in the responsorial psalm: "I rejoiced because they said to me, 'We will go up to the house of the Lord' " (Ps 122:1)), and the eschatological banquet described by Isaiah (25:6) as taking place "on this mountain [where] the Lord of hosts will provide for all peoples. . . ." What was originally intended for Israel will be extended to encompass "all nations [who] shall stream toward [this mountain]" (vs. 2). Just as the Lord revealed his law on Sinai, so will he reveal his word (vs. 3) to a new and universal community. Further, verse 4, "he shall judge between nations," looks forward to a time of peace which will be the work of the Lord. Armaments will be destroyed. No crafted implement will be used for war for all nations will come to know the Lord as source of harmony and lasting peace: "they shall beat their swords into ploughshares and their spears into pruning hooks" (vs. 4). The prophet invites his listeners to heed, believe in, and welcome this revelation. He asks them to respond to it by walking in the "light of the Lord" (vs. 5).

The fact that we are still living in a time of conflict and division is evidence enough that our lives are incomplete and unfulfilled. We yearn for an end to conflict and division, especially in Advent, and pray that the Lord will come to us here and now through the liturgy to "instruct us in his ways" and to enable us to live in his peace.

This hope-filled attitude is reflected in the responsorial psalm (Ps 122). This text is often used in Christian liturgy where "Jerusalem" (vs. 2) and the "city of peace" (vss. 6–8) can be understood to refer in hope and expectation to the peace the Messiah's kingdom will bring. In Advent, we look forward in "joyful expectation" to the coming of our Savior at Christmas and at the end of time.

The second reading from Romans (13:11–14) is a text frequently repeated in Advent. The natural symbolism of diminishing light at this time of year is introduced here. St. Paul states: "the night is far spent; the day draws near . . . let us cast off deeds of darkness and put on the armor of light" (vs. 12). We are to put "off" carousing, drunkenness, and lust; we are to put "on" the Lord Jesus Christ (vs. 14). This occurs for the first time at baptism; it recurs every time the Christian seriously turns again to the Lord. Baptism takes away original sin but it does not take away our ability to choose between good and evil. During Advent, we are exhorted to reaffirm the choices that lead to God.

Today's gospel acclamation, used in all three lectionary cycles this Sunday, prays that the Lord will grant us his kindness and his salvation (see Psalm 85:5). Although we are sinners who need to prepare for Christ's second coming, the Lord whom we worship and the God to whom we pray is our Savior and Redeemer who extends to us infinite and redeeming love.

The text of Matthew 24:37–44 refers to the Genesis story of Noah and the flood (chaps. 6–9). The point Matthew makes is that the people of Noah's day were totally unconcerned about what really matters—their relationship with God as they lived their careless lives. Unfortunately, this same attitude marks those of us in our day who do not respond to God's revelation. When the "Son of Man" comes, the definitive separation between the saved and the damned will occur. Until that day, we are to prepare by staying awake and being attentive to the Lord (vs. 42). We are assured that the Lord will come, but we do not know when (vs. 44). To be ready for that day and hour, we should scrutinize ourselves to determine how well we live according to the gospel and to do what is necessary to reform and change our lives.

CHOOSE LIGHT – RM
WALK IN NIGHT – IS

Cycle "B"

The first reading today is from a section of the book of Isaiah (63: 16–17, 19; 64:2–7). This text is actually a prayer for guidance and direction uttered by those who are close to God and who call him "father" and "redeemer" (vs. 16). The degree of intimacy with God and familiarity with his revelation evident here makes this a very comforting passage with which to begin Advent. (It is repeated near the end of the Christmas cycle at the office of readings on the Wednesday and Thursday after Epiphany.) The author inquires why God allows us to wander, we who have heard his call and have agreed to his covenant. Why do we "harden our hearts" (see Psalm 95:8, "harden not your hearts," the familiar invitatory to the hours) so that we no longer fear the Lord (vs. 17)? Because God's people are estranged from him and separated from his ways, the prophet asks (begs, really) for a most dramatic demonstration of God's power: "that [he] would rend the heavens and come down." The cosmic imagery of the quaking mountains and the torn heavens symbolizes the power of the Lord.

The second section of the text (Is 64:2–3) uses the flashback technique where the author recalls God's deeds performed out of love for his people whose hearts remained cold. The prophet urges his hearers to acknowledge their sin and evil (vss. 4–6). As we hear the moving words of the prophet: "Yet, O Lord, you are our father; we are the clay and you the potter: we are the work of your hands" (vs. 7), we are invited to surrender ourselves to be shaped and formed by God, the author and sustainer of all life.

Our desire to reform our lives is reflected in the responsorial psalm: "Lord, make us turn to you, let us see your face and we shall be saved" (Ps 80:4). We call on God's power as "the Lord of hosts" (vs. 15) to "once again . . . take care of this vine" and "protect what your right hand has planted" (vs. 16). When the scriptures speak of God's "right hand," it can mean God's power, and in other cases it can mean a place of honor where those who have been God's worthy followers will enjoy everlasting happiness. St. Matthew alludes to this when describing the final judgment (Mt 25:31–46). Here the chosen are called to the right hand of the Son of Man.

We who pray this psalm and reflect on the Isaiah reading in Advent must allow ourselves to be the clay that the Lord shapes, as we wait in hope for his coming in glory.

The second reading (1 Cor 1:3–9) relates St. Paul's greeting to and thanksgiving for the community at Corinth. This particular passage refers to the Lord's final coming, thus making it a most appropriate Advent text. "You lack no spiritual gift as you wait for the revelation of our Lord Jesus Christ" (vs. 7) is meant to strengthen the wavering Corinthians as they await the end time when the Lord will bring to completion the work he began in them. They are not to be afraid for "he will strengthen you to the end, so that you will be blameless on the 'day' of the Lord's coming" (vs. 8).

In Advent, we acknowledge our in-between status—between Christ's incarnation and his second coming. Like the Corinthians, we are to be confident because we have been richly endowed with spiritual grace and blessings. Like them, we are exhorted today to live fully the life God has given us and in this way prepare for his final coming.

The text from Mark's gospel (13:33–37) reflects the strong eschatological note of this first Advent Sunday. It urges us to "be constantly on the watch" and to "stay awake" (vs. 33), that is, to be ready for the Lord to come again. The parable of the master leaving his servants in charge of his household (vss. 34–35) describes our situation today for we too await the return of our saving Lord. Trying to speculate when we will die or when the Lord will in fact "come again" is futile. What matters is the extent to which we live in God's presence everyday and reflect his life in our lives. When we are called from this life, we will be judged on how we lived God's justice and mirrored his love in this world.

Cycle "C"

Today's first reading from the prophet Jeremiah (33:14–16) is taken from a section that is likely postexilic in origin. The author proclaims that the Lord will "raise up for David a just shoot" who "will do what is right and just in the land" (vs. 15). This verse helped to inspire the evangelists to speak about Jesus as a descendant of the tribe of David (as seen, for example, in the gospel used at the Christmas Vigil, Matthew 1:1–25). The prophet's words refer to a future king who will make Judah "safe" and Jerusalem "secure." He is "our justice" (vs. 16). Christians see this prophecy as referring to Christ who is "just in all ways" and who is the source of justice for his people.

The promise of a redeemer expressed in this reading leads the assembled community to utter the poignant words of the responsorial psalm: "To you, O Lord, I lift up my soul" (Ps 25:1).

During Advent, we make the psalmist's words our own: "you are God my savior . . . for you I wait all the day" (vs. 5). We wait in joyful expectation for the Lord's coming into our lives today, at Christmas, at death, and at his second coming.

Our prayer must be one of humility before God for the psalmist tells us that "he guides the humble to justice, [and] teaches the humble his way" (vs. 9). It is the spiritually poor and the contrite of heart who are the Lord's friends. Our friendship with the Lord is based on his enduring and sustaining love, which covenant love enables us to love as he loved and to live as he taught us to live.

The second reading from First Thessalonians (3:12–4:2) fits into the pattern of Advent readings by exhorting and instructing us on how we should live. We are to love one another with the love of Christ (vs. 12) and open ourselves to the very holiness of God which will make our hearts "blameless and holy . . . at the coming of our

Lord Jesus Christ" (vs. 13). Paul urges even greater effort when he says: "we beg and exhort you . . . to conduct yourselves in a way pleasing to God . . . you must learn to make still greater progress" (4:1). This verse is particularly appropriate for us who in Advent are urged to deepen our commitment to the Lord and to open our hearts for the promised Redeemer to fill us with his love.

The gospel from Luke (21:25–28, 34–36) concerns Christ's second coming and our preparation for it. When Luke speaks about the "Son of Man" coming on a cloud with great power and glory (vss. 25–28), he is recalling the passage from Daniel 7:13ff. where the author describes a vision of "one like the son of man coming on clouds of heaven," that is to say, "of one coming from above, from God." Luke speaks in this way to urge his community to prepare for Christ's return in glory. To prepare for that day, Luke warns us to put away overindulgence (vs. 34), be constantly on the watch, stand secure in our commitment to the Lord and to "pray constantly" (vs. 36). For Luke, the end times will not involve a "war of the worlds" catastrophe. For those prepared for his coming, it will be the final and all important reunion of God and humanity when Christ will draw all things to himself.

On this first Advent Sunday, the really important question is not "getting into heaven" so much as it is living here and now with the awareness that our lives are in God's hands and that our deeds do matter in witnessing to his love in our world.

Sacramentary Texts

The eucharist today begins with the traditional entrance antiphon from Psalm 25 (vss. 1–3): "To you, my God, I lift my soul. . . . No one who waits for you is ever put to shame." (This same psalm has already been commented upon as the responsorial psalm in the "C" cycle.)

With confidence and hope, we begin Advent by stating that we long for the Lord to come and that we wait for him who even now supports and sustains us.

The absence of the *Gloria* throughout Advent demonstrates the sobriety of this season and marks it as one of promise; its return at Christmas marks it as a season of fulfillment.

The Latin text of the opening prayer is taken from the old Gelasian Sacramentary and is rich Advent theology and spirituality, which unfortunately is not so evident in the present English translation.

In this prayer, we ask God to give us the strength and determination to perform works that are just and right in this life so that when Christ comes again, we may be worthy to be called to his right side and possess everlasting life in heaven.

The alternative prayer offers a number of images and expressions that reflect the spirituality of Advent, especially "our longing for Christ our Savior," "the light of [his] Word," and the petition "that the dawn of his coming may find us rejoicing in his presence."

Both the prayer over the gifts and the prayer after communion, taken from the Leonine Sacramentary, are also assigned to the Mass formulas for Mondays and Thursdays during the first three weeks of Advent. The Latin text of the prayer over the gifts asks the Father to accept the bread and wine now presented and offered. We also ask that our devotion in this life may reap the reward of redemption. This prayer fittingly leads to the eucharistic prayer by referring to the bread and wine presented and offered. The reference to life eternal is particularly appropriate because of this Sunday's stress on the second coming and our being reunited with Christ forever.

The prayer after communion asks that the Eucharist may teach us to yearn for and love the things of heaven and may, through "its promise and hope, guide our way on earth."

Celebration of the Eucharist

The assembly can experience the starkness and simplicity of Advent even before the liturgy begins, provided care is taken with the sanctuary decor. Eliminating unnecessary sanctuary clutter (extra candlesticks, baptismal font, chairs, kneelers, tables, etc.) and providing hangings, covers for gospel book and lectionary, and vesture in shades of violet, gray, and blue can help the assembly to immerse itself in the liturgical mood of watching and waiting.

If an Advent wreath is used, it should not detract from the primary symbols of the liturgy (lectern, altar, chair) and it should be large enough that the assembly can see it especially when being lighted, if this is part of the entrance rite.

Since the Sundays of Advent are named first, second, third, and fourth in the *General Norms for the Calendar* (no. 41), it would seem unnecessary to stress the third Sunday as different by the use of rose vesture and a pink candle for the wreath. The joy and rejoicing that was formerly associated with the third Sunday is now understood as integral to the whole season of quiet waiting.

Other aspects of church decor during Advent might include a Jesse tree and/or a "giving tree" containing sketches of gifts needed by the poor. Where possible, the symbols on the Jesse tree should coincide with the colors used in the hangings and the vesture for the season.

A well-placed entrance procession and recession of ministers, accompanied by a simple musical refrain for the congregation (entrance) or organ music only (recessional), could help foster a sober and reflective atmosphere.

Simple settings for the eucharistic acclamations can help to unify these four Sundays. A sung *Kyrie, eleison* (either in Greek or English) to a chant-like melody can also help establish the atmosphere appropriate for Advent.

The use of the second greeting by the presider today ("the grace and peace of God our Father") would be a subtle reiteration of Paul's greeting to the Corinthians found at the beginning of the second reading in the "B" cycle. If the rite of blessing and sprinkling with holy water is used today, it could be introduced by a comment about Advent as a season of renewal and reaffirmation of our commitment to the values of the kingdom of God. The prayer that concludes this introductory rite is especially apt at this season because it clearly emphasizes the eschatological aspect of the eucharist:

"May almighty God cleanse us of our sins,
and through the eucharist we celebrate
make us worthy to sit at his table
in his heavenly kingdom."

If the third form of the penitential rite is chosen, the use of the second sample formula (ii) would be especially appropriate today since it refers to the three comings of Christ: in history "to gather the nations into the peace of God's kingdom," in the present "in word and sacrament," and in the future "in glory with salvation for your people."

Since Advent is a special time for listening to the Word of the Lord in preparation for receiving the good news of his coming at Christmas, it might be well to emphasize the proclamation of the Word on Advent Sundays by a gospel procession. For this action, the deacon (or priest) would carry the gospel book in procession to the lectern accompanied by two ministers with candles. Such a procedure would allow for a more elaborate gospel procession to occur at Christmas with additional ministers, lights, and incense.

The third sample formula for the general intercessions (see Appendix I) is for Advent. It should be borne in mind that this and all these sample formulas are to be adapted for local use.

The introduction to this formula is particularly wordy and should be reduced. As it stands, the suggested text contains three thoughts that can be developed individually: asking for God's mercy; Christ's mission to the poor, sick and hungry; and prayer that he may find us "watching and ready at his coming."

Advent preface I, taken from excerpts in the Leonine Sacramentary, is assigned for use today. It carefully balances the two aspects of the season, incarnational and eschatological, when it states:

"When he humbled himself to come among us as a man
[Christ] fulfilled the plan you formed long ago
and opened for us the way to salvation.
Now we watch for the day,
hoping that the salvation promised us will be ours
when Christ our Lord will come again in his glory."

The use of the third eucharistic prayer would be especially appropriate today because it refers to Christ's second coming and our being "ready to greet him when he comes again." The second and third memorial acclamations are most explicit about waiting for the Lord to come in glory, thus making them appropriate choices today. It should be noted that the second is more of an appeal ("Lord Jesus, come in glory"), thus adding a certain poignancy and urgency to this part of the liturgy.

The Lord's Prayer could well be introduced by the use of (or a variation on) the fourth sample text: "let us pray for the coming of the kingdom as Jesus taught us." Should the Lamb of God be extended beyond three strophes, the addition of Christological titles that appear in the Advent scriptures would be appropriate (for example, Son of Man).

At the invitation to communion, the text as presented should be underscored since it is an instance in the present Roman rite when the eschatological notion of sharing in the sacrament is expressed. Derived from Revelation 19:9 ("Happy are they who have been invited to the wedding feast of the Lamb"), this text refers to the eucharist as a foretaste and pledge of what we will share at the wedding feast in the kingdom of God. Therefore, it would be improper, especially in Advent, to make it refer to sharing in the eucharistic elements only. The eucharist is our privileged yet provisional share in the life of God which we will share fully in the kingdom forever.

The solemn blessing for Advent is provided in the mass formula this Sunday and might well be used on all Advent Sundays as another way of unifying these liturgies. Appropriately, it refers to us as those who "believe that the Son of God once came" and who "look for him to come again." The hopeful aspect of Advent is reiterated in the last section which states:

"You rejoice that our Redeemer came to live with us as man.
When he comes again in glory,
may he reward you with endless life."

Should a simpler conclusion be desired, the use of numbers 1 or 16 of the prayers over the people containing explicit references to "the everlasting life you prepare for us" (1) and to "the life to come" (16), would be fitting.

Liturgy of the Hours

Advent begins with Evening Prayer I on Saturday evening. The prescribed hymn in the Latin breviary is *Conditor alme siderum* ("Creator of the Starry Skies"), which focuses on Advent's many varied images and themes in a poetic way. The regular four-week psalter is followed in Advent, but the antiphons change at the major hours on Sundays to reflect the meaning of the season.

The first antiphon at Evening Prayer I speaks about the "good news" that "our God will come to save us." The second declares that the Lord "is coming" on a day that "will dawn with a wonderful light." The third states that "the Lord will come with mighty power." These examples show that the eschatological aspects of the Advent liturgy dominate as we begin the season.

In the scripture reading from 1 Thessalonians 5:23–24, St. Paul prays that God will make his people "perfect in holiness" and "irreproachable at the coming of the Lord Jesus Christ" (vs. 23). As we wait for Christ to come again, he consoles and strengthens us to be less unworthy and less imperfect as we journey to his kingdom.

The antiphon to the Canticle of Mary evokes the eschatological aspect of Advent by stating: "see the Lord coming from afar; his splendor fills the earth." Mary's canticle speaks of the lowly being raised up, and of the good things with which the Lord has filled the hungry. It is this same Lord who raises us up as we await his final coming.

The intercessions provided are brief and direct and offer a marked change from the sometimes overly wordy texts found in the breviary.

The invitatory refrain used in this first part of the season refers to the second coming: "Come, let us worship the Lord, the King who is to come."

For the four Advent Sundays, the antiphons to the psalms at the office of readings all refer to the King who is to come. He will come with "power and might to save the nations" (first), and will cause rejoicing for his people because in his presence they will not fear any longer (second). The last text exhorts us: "let us cleanse our hearts for the coming of our great king, that we may be ready to welcome him."

The first reading from Isaiah (1:1–18) begins a semicontinuous reading of this prophetic book that will extend through Advent to Christmas on most days until the Baptism of the Lord. Today's selection is a summary of Isaiah's message, a direct challenge to his hearers to reform coupled with the assurance of divine mercy as they turn again to God. The name "Isaiah" itself means "Yahweh is salvation," an appropriate title for a prophet whose people were facing threats of invasion by the Assyrians and whose spiritual life was at a low ebb. The prophet begins by urging the people to "hear" and to "listen" to the voice of the Lord (vs. 2). They have "spurned the Holy One of Israel" and must face up to the destruction which has resulted (vss. 5–8). Yet, God has left a remnant who will be saved, thereby showing that despite their infidelity, he would never forget them or allow them to be destroyed (vss. 5–9). The faithful remnant and the unfaithful sharers in the covenant must, however, respond to God's abiding fidelity. They must cleanse themselves by putting away misdeeds, doing good, and redressing the wronged (vss. 16–17). Those who admit their sin and who turn to the Lord will be forgiven:

"Come now, let us set things right,
   says the Lord:
Though your sins be like scarlet,
   they may become white as snow;
Though they be crimson red,
   they may become white as wool." (vs. 18)

This text offers a most appropriate reflection with which to begin Advent. We are invited to reflect on the Word of God in this season and thus are welcomed into God's presence. The Word has become flesh and that Word is with us in the proclaimed word of scripture, read at the liturgy. Like Isaiah's hearers, we are to trust in the Lord's mercy for us and to accept the challenge to live in conformity with that word.

Today's patristic text, from the catechetical instructions of St. Cyril of Jerusalem, deals with the second coming of Christ as judge. Cyril states:

"At his first coming he was wrapped in swaddling clothes in a manger. At his second coming he will be clothed in light as in a garment. In his first coming he endured the cross, despising the shame; in the second coming he will be in glory. . . . The Savior will not come to be judged again, but to judge those by whom he was judged."

The eschatological aspect of Advent thus clearly stated reminds us that this season concerns not only the coming of God's Son in innocence and infancy, but also his return as Lord and King of all the earth.

The antiphons at morning prayer reflect the theology of Advent. The first is taken from the particularly hopeful Isaian text (25:6–10): "On that day sweet wine will flow from the mountains, milk and honey from the hills, alleluia." Significantly, this antiphon introduces Psalm 63 (the first in the psalter for Sunday week I), which deals with our longing for God, a central Advent theme.

In the second antiphon, the cosmic dimensions of waiting for the Lord are noted: "the mountains and hills will sing praise to God . . . for he is coming, the Lord of a kingdom that lasts forever." This antiphon is an appropriate introduction to the canticle from Daniel (3:57–88, 56), which praises the Lord for all of creation.

The third antiphon, introducing the psalm of praise (Ps 149), speaks about Jesus as "a great prophet [who] will come to Jerusalem; of that people he will make a new creation."

After the scripture reading from Romans (13:11–12, noted above under the readings for the "A" cycle at the eucharist), the antiphon to Zechariah's canticle is particularly striking because it emphasizes the incarnational aspects of Advent: "The Holy Spirit will come upon you, Mary; you have no need to be afraid. You will carry in your womb the Son of God, alleluia." Fittingly, this text is used at that point of morning prayer when we stand up, make the sign of the cross, and sing the canticle of John the Baptist's father. This text and these gestures signal our welcoming of the new covenant in Jesus.

Both the eschatological and incarnational aspects of Advent are found in Evening Prayer II. As used in the Christian liturgy, the first and third antiphons are understood in the light of our anticipation of Christ's second coming. "Rejoice, daughter of Zion; shout for joy, daughter of Jerusalem" (first), and "I am coming soon, says the Lord; I will give to everyone the reward his deeds deserve" (third). The first antiphon is taken from Revelation (22:20); the third makes direct reference to the Lord's judgment.

The second antiphon: "Christ our King will come to us: the Lamb of God foretold by John," hints at the ministry of John that will be emphasized on the second and third Sundays of the season.

The Magnificat antiphon reiterates the Marian emphasis of today's morning prayer: "Do not be afraid, Mary, you have found favor with God; you will conceive and give birth of a Son, alleluia." This particular text is taken from the section of Luke's gospel (1:3–31), which is part of the text proclaimed on the Fourth Sunday of Advent in the "B" cycle.

Among the petitions presented at evening prayer, we find a number of titles for Christ and names of people associated with the birth of Jesus: the angel Gabriel, John the Baptist, Joseph, Simeon, and Zechariah. Last evening, the intercessions emphasized the implications of Christ's second coming; today's texts concern how the events leading to the incarnation still affect us.

Celebration of the Hours

At Evening Prayer I, if the hymn *Conditor alme siderum* is not used in one of its many English translations, a substitute should be chosen which reflects the subtlety of the Latin text in emphasizing the eschatological and incarnational aspects of Advent.

As Advent begins, it may be well to determine whether, in singing or reciting the psalms, a slower pace and longer pauses between psalms might be appropriate. The psalm prayers provided are the standard ones assigned through the year; composing others with greater emphasis on Advent themes (without making them "theme" prayers) would be appropriate.

If a longer scripture reading is desired at evening prayer, the text of 1 Thessalonians can be expanded from verses 23–24 to verses 16–24, or even verses 12–24. The Canticles of Zechariah and Mary directly relate to the theology of the Advent-Christmas season; thus, it would be appropriate to emphasize their importance by singing them with suitable musical settings.

Petitions at morning and evening prayer may be added to the ones provided in the text, or others may be substituted in their place. However, the liturgical structure should be adhered to and the universality of this prayer should be respected.

At evening prayer, the singing of the Our Father and the solemn blessing of Advent would be most appropriate.

If the invitatory is joined to the office of readings, the singing of Psalm 95 with the assigned antiphon would be a good way to begin the hour.

The last verses of the first reading are used as its responsory today (vss. 16–18). This is a particularly helpful text (despite its length) for evoking our response to the Lord's invitation to us in this season. The response after the patristic text poses still more of a problem because of length. If the first responsory is sung (as intended), then remaining silent after this text would be a fitting option. This is especially true if the *Te Deum* is sung to complete the hour.

At morning prayer, the use of an Advent hymn that fuses incarnational and eschatological themes would be a fitting introduction to this hour.

If a longer scripture reading is desired, the text from Romans 13 could be expanded to include verses 8–14. (It should be noted that in the "A" cycle, verses 11–14 are assigned as the second reading at the eucharist.)

The intercessions at morning prayer are comparatively few in number (four); using them as they stand or adápting them, but retaining their structure would be a good way of maintaining a certain sobriety of expression in Advent.

Should a more seasonal dismissal be desired for this hour, the use of either number 1 or 16 of the prayers over the people from the Sacramentary would be fitting options. The use of such a simple prayer (instead of the solemn blessing, for example) would not detract from the priority of the Sunday morning eucharist when the solemn blessing would be most appropriate.

The suggestions made above for Evening Prayer I should be consulted for Evening Prayer II. The use of Philippians 4:4–5 as the scripture reading at this hour indicates that a certain quiet joy is now understood to be part of the whole season. Expanding this reading to include verses 4–7 would be a way of giving it more emphasis. (The fact that this is also the second reading on the third Sunday in the "C" cycle should pose no conflict because of the two-week separation.) The use of the optional responses to the intercessions: "come, Lord, and do not delay" (Evening Prayer I) and "come, stay with us, Lord" (Evening Prayer II) would be appropriate since they capture succinctly the theology of Advent.

Reflection—"Do We Wait in Joyful Hope?"

It is at least curious, if not downright mysterious, that most of our reminders of the end of the world come from commentators speaking about the arms race or from self-appointed "prophets" with placards in air terminals and bus stations. Yet, if we really were to listen to the texts we use at the liturgy, we would realize that what we celebrate each time we come together concerns the end of time: "Let us pray for the coming of the kingdom in the words our Savior gave us;" and "as we wait in joyful hope for the coming of our Savior . . . [who] will come again in glory to judge the living and the dead."

Perhaps one of the reasons we "turn off" these parts of the liturgy is that they seem far-fetched. The time of the end of the world is surely unpredictable and so we tend to live life each day as it comes (or as we try to plan it!), forgetting about the urgency of Christ's second coming. We are challenged by the liturgy today to evaluate the extent to which we live out the values of God's kingdom here and now and how we set our hearts on what really matters—God's word, ways, and kingdom.

The reference in Matthew's gospel to the uncaring people of Noah's time should make us ask ourselves what it is we spend time on and what we really value in life. Are we planning vacation to vacation, or party to party (especially in this holiday season)? Do we realize that there are urgent world, national, and personal issues that need addressing as we preoccupy ourselves with pursuits that are largely trivial? Do we realize the urgency in the texts of St. Paul about not conforming ourselves to this age? Are we willing to accept responsibility to live here and now the life that God gave us at baptism?

What makes our celebration of the liturgy today hope-filled and positive, however, is that we face these issues in the presence of the Lord, Emmanuel, who has never left us. Yes, the Emmanuel for whom we long and to whom we pray has come among us and has never abandoned us.

Our task today is not to predict the second coming. Rather we are invited to draw strength, hope, and guidance from the Lord we worship. When we pray, "thy kingdom come," we need to open our hearts to the kingdom that is already among us in Christ and to long with equal confidence "for the [second] coming of our Savior, Jesus Christ."

MONDAY OF THE FIRST WEEK OF ADVENT

Liturgical Context

In the present reform of the Advent liturgy, each weekday has its own mass formula (chants for the entrance and communion processions, opening prayer, prayer over the gifts, and prayer after communion) and carefully selected readings.

"There are two series of readings: one to be used from the beginning of Advent until 16 December; the other from 17 to 24 December.

"In the first part of Advent, there are readings from Isaiah, distributed in accord with the sequence of the book itself and including salient texts that are also read on Sundays. For the choice of the weekday gospel, the first reading has been taken into consideration." (Lectionary for Mass Introduction, no. 94)

Careful attention to these texts and to the eschatological emphasis of this first part of Advent can help in appreciating, planning, and celebrating today's liturgy.

Liturgy of the Eucharist

The eucharist is introduced by an entrance antiphon comprised of Jeremiah 31:10 and Isaiah 35:5. The combined texts urge us to "hear" the message of the Lord which will eventually be made known to the "ends of the earth." As we begin the season of Advent, we are urged to allow the word to take root in our hearts.

The opening prayer from the old Gelasian Sacramentary exhorts us to be vigilant and watchful for the Lord's second coming, waiting for him "in joyful prayer."

Two passages are assigned for the first reading today. The first, Isaiah 2:1–5, is used when the "B" and "C" Sunday cycles occur because this text is the first reading on the "A" Sunday (see commentary above). The second text, Isaiah 4:2–6, is used only when the "A" cycle of Sunday readings is proclaimed. This text is also found in the office of readings tomorrow (Is 2:6–22, 4:2–6) and verses 2–3 are assigned for morning prayer on December 31. The positive aspects of the second coming are noted: "Over all his glory will be shelter and protection" (vs. 6). When that last day comes, "The branch of the Lord will be luster and glory" (vs. 2); as God protected his chosen ones on their journey to the promised land, so will he protect his elect with a "smoking cloud by day" and a "flaming fire by night" (a reference to God's presence to Israel during the Exodus).

Today's responsorial psalm was also used yesterday in the "A" cycle (see above for comment).

The gospel text is from Matthew (8:5–11). Just after performing the miracle of cleansing a leper (Mt 8:1–4), Jesus meets a centurion who says to him" "Sir, my serving boy . . . is paralyzed, suffering painfully." Jesus tells the centurion that he will come and heal the servant (vs. 7). The centurion, however, humbly states, "I am not worthy to have you come under my roof. Just give an order and my boy will get better" (vs. 8; the RSV translation has the more familiar phrase "but only say the word"). Jesus is amazed to see such extraordinary faith especially since he had not found its like in Israel (vs. 10). Jesus cured the servant because of the centurion's trust in Jesus (see Mt 8:13). This text reminds us that we, as followers of Christ, should not merely trust in his power, but have an active unquestioning faith that he will give us the grace to do whatever God wills for us, especially in this holy season.

The prayer over the gifts and the prayer after communion were both used at mass yesterday (see above).

The communion antiphon prays meditatively and confidently: "Come to us, Lord, and bring us peace. We will rejoice in your presence and serve you with all our heart" (see Ps 106:4–5; Is 38:3).

Celebration of the Eucharist

At the introductory rites, a brief introductory comment by the presider (or other minister) followed by a deliberate pause can foster a reflective spirit.

A simple chant-like setting for the *Kyrie* as the response to the second set of invocations in the third form of the penitential rite (ii) would continue this prayerful atmosphere.

The use of number 1 of the verses before the gospel (Lectionary, no. 193): "Come and save us, Lord our God; let us see your face, and we shall be saved" (see Ps 79:4) could underscore the centurion's trust in Jesus proclaimed in the gospel as well as our own faith in the power of God's revealed word.

Among the intercessions today, petitions for a deepened faith in God's word during Advent, for those who preach and teach the word, and for those who hoped in God's word while on earth who now await the fullness of his revealed glory in the kingdom would be appropriate. At this season, one should evaluate the intercessions lest they become too wordy. The starkness of the Advent liturgy lends itself to simpler prayers.

Advent preface I is prescribed today. The use of the second or third memorial acclamation would continue the eschatological emphasis of this part of the season.

The use of the former introduction to the Lord's Prayer would be useful since it refers to our awe before God (first reading) and to the importance of the word (gospel): "Taught by our Savior's command

and formed by the word of God we dare to say . . ." The wording of the response to the invitation to communion should be noted today because of its obvious resonance with the gospel: "Lord, I am not worthy to receive you, but only say the word and I shall be healed." This might be mentioned in a homily which links the readings with the celebration of the eucharist.

Should a prayer over the people be selected to conclude the liturgy, the use of number 2, asking for the Lord's "protection and grace" and "health of mind and body" would coincide with today's gospel.

Liturgy of the Hours

The first reading at the office of readings, Isaiah 1:21–27; 2:1–5, continues the section of Isaiah begun yesterday. In the first verses, a lament over Israel, the prophet uses the image of adultery to dramatize the people's apostasy. Instead of allowing justice, mercy and peace to flourish in her, Jerusalem becomes the home of those who do not even care for orphans and widows. Because of unfaithfulness, God's city itself needs renewal and reform (vss. 21–23). The prophet assures his hearers that God will avenge the disobedient, those who do not observe his ways. Then he will intervene to raise up worthy leaders so that Jerusalem will once again be worthy of its name "city of justice, faithful city" (vs. 26). Those who repent will receive God's justice once more (vs. 27). The more encouraging aspect of the prophet's message (2:1–5) has already been described (see above, First Sunday, "A" cycle).

The words of Isaiah are particularly important to us at the start of Advent for our obligations in justice and in sharing the peace of the Lord are no less real than they were for Jerusalem's inhabitants in Isaiah's time. The response to the reading reflects our waiting for the Lord who "will teach us his ways and we will walk in his paths" (Mi 4:2).

In the second reading from a pastoral letter of St. Charles Borromeo, the saint reminds us that "Christ's coming was not only for the benefit of his contemporaries; his power has still to be communicated to us all." This is accomplished by the Holy Spirit who teaches us to prepare our hearts for Christ's coming through the liturgy. The response, based on brief passages from the prophet Joel (2:15), Isaiah (62:11), and Jeremiah (4:5) underscores the Advent character of

St. Charles' letter: "our God and Savior is coming: proclaim the good news, let it be heard."

At morning and evening prayer on Advent weekdays, the customary antiphons from ordinary time are used for the psalmody. The scripture readings assigned for these hours today are repeated on the other Mondays of Advent. Today's morning prayer text, Isaiah 2:3, has already been discussed (above, "A" cycle on Sunday).

The text for evening prayer, Philippians 3:20–21, reminds us that when the Lord comes he will remake our bodies "according to the pattern of his glorified body, by his power to subject everything to himself" (vs. 21). We will be made totally new when we meet the Lord for whom we longed during our earthly life.

The responses to the scripture readings at morning and evening prayers are repeated daily thoughout Advent (except on Sundays). At morning prayer, the theme of light is stressed: "Your light will come, Jerusalem, the Lord will dawn on you in radiant beauty . . . you will see his glory within you." At evening prayer, the urgency of our need for God is emphasized: "Come and set us free, Lord God of power and might . . . let your face shine on us and we shall be saved."

The antiphons to the Canticles of Zechariah and of Mary change daily. Today's antiphon to Zechariah's canticle stresses our preparation for the Lord to come as "Savior to set [us] free." As we raise our voices in this prayer, we are invited to "lift up your eyes . . . [to] see the great power of your king." The antiphon to the Canticle of Mary is explicitly incarnational as it speaks of Mary who "conceived by the power of the Holy Spirit." Once again, it is this antiphon (as seen yesterday) which provides an incarnational note during this first and more eschatological part of Advent.

The intercessions provided at these hours will appear again on Monday of the third week. At morning prayer, the theme of light is important: in the introduction, Christ is called light from light, and the first petition calls upon his light which never fades. The second and third petitions appropriately dedicate the day to God in general terms. The fourth petition reflects the Advent theme of "a new earth for us—where there will be justice and peace." At evening prayer, the intercessions speak more about our need for Christ the savior to "save us" (first petition) and to "free us from the sin of the world" (second). Other petitions refer to Christ's birth from the Virgin through the Holy Spirit, and ask that Christ will free our bodies from corruption.

Celebration of the Hours

For the invitatory (whether used at the office of readings or at morning prayer), the use of the text before the readings at the office of readings: "Lord, show us your mercy and love.—And grant us your salvation" would be an option that would be a change from the daily use of the seasonal refrain. The use of Psalm 24 as the invitatory psalm would be appropriate with its reference to our climbing the mountain of the Lord (vs. 3) "with clean hands and pure heart" (vs. 4).

At the office of readings, the responsory to the Isaiah text might well be sung or recited meditatively. However, this should not take the place of silence, so necessary to help create and sustain the prayerful and sober Advent atmosphere.

The hymns to introduce morning and evening prayer should deal with the second coming of Christ and the cosmic dimensions of our expectation of him. Hymns about John the Baptist, for example, should only be introduced after the second Sunday, and those leading directly to the incarnation should be used after December 17.

The use of scripture readings other than Isaiah 2:3 at morning prayer would be a suitable option today since that passage occurs in the office of readings. If it is retained, then extending it to verses 1–5 would help provide a more adequate reflection of the author's message.

At evening prayer, the text from Philippians could be extended to include some of the preceding verses, for example, verses 17–21. Another option would be to devise a continuous series of readings from some Pauline epistles dealing with the second coming and to read them in a semicontinuous way at evening prayer. Such texts could be taken from 1 and 2 Thessalonians and Philippians.

At the intercessions at both morning and evening prayer, the use of either alternative response: "Come, Lord Jesus," or "Come, Lord, and save us" would reflect the theology of the season in a direct and laconic way. Adapting the presented petitions, perhaps to reflect the needs of the local community as well as the church universal, is always an option, as is introducing the Lord's Prayer with a brief comment. At evening prayer, it could appropriately mention our need for the Savior's forgiveness in our lives.

Reflection—"I Give You My Word"

How often do we attest to the truth of a statement by saying, "I give you my word?" Or how often do we commit ourselves by saying, "I give you my word?" The very fact that we use such a phrase may be an indication that to state something is not enough; we need to prove that we say what we mean and mean what we say.

The Advent liturgy is filled with instances when God gives us his word and in giving that word effects what it means. In today's gospel, the centurion affirms that Jesus' saying the word would be enough to cure his servant. He trusted in the power of Jesus to do as he promised. Unlike ourselves who often ask for reassurance and guarantees, this man exemplified the kind of trusting attitude we ought to have before God as we start Advent.

The message of God to us is all-sufficient and summarized in the coming of his son among us. His words and deeds are the means God uses to communicate with us. God has given us his word in scripture and the unique Word made flesh in Jesus. We worship this Lord at the liturgy; it is his word that we ponder. It is appropriate that at the beginning of Advent, we realize the essential role which the revealed word plays in this season and should play in our lives. It is through the word that we, like the servant, are healed.

TUESDAY OF THE FIRST WEEK OF ADVENT

Liturgical Context

The words of Isaiah dominate both at the office of readings and at the eucharist. Our preparation for the Messiah requires that we not grow weary of experiencing his saving presence here and now as we celebrate the liturgy in his memory.

Liturgy of the Eucharist

Today's entrance antiphon, derived from Zechariah (14:5, 7), uses typical prophetic language and Advent imagery to describe our situation as those who wait for the Lord to come with all his saints. "Then there will be endless day," the prophet assures us, for all will be revealed, and we will stand in his illuminating and warming presence. The obvious coincidence between the imagery of this text and the cold of winter and the fainting warmth of the sun's rays should not be lost today.

The first reading is taken from the very significant text of Isaiah (11:1–10), describing the Messianic king of Israel whom we acknowledge to be the Lord Jesus. The importance of this text in Christian worship is seen in its proclamation at mass on the Second Sunday of Advent ("A" cycle) and at the office of readings on Christmas day. In its original setting, it probably referred to the qualifications of the ideal king who would be a second David. Just as David was an unlikely choice because of the relative insignificance of Jesse's family, so the ideal ruler would be insignificant were it not for the gift of God's spirit with which he was endowed. This new king will judge wisely and rule in the presence of the God he knows and loves. The gifts of wisdom, prudence, and counsel will enable him to look beyond physical appearances to judge justly (vs. 3). The poor and downtrodden will receive his special care (vs. 4). Through the king, God's reign will be established. The ideal and peaceable kingdom of Eden will be restored (vss. 7–8) where wild beasts are wild no longer and innocent children need not fear snakes and animals. The whole earth will be blessed in him and his reign will extend to all nations.

Proclaimed in the Christian assembly, this text refers to Emmanuel whose attributes and gifts establish the universal rule of God among us. Through the mystery of the incarnation, all creation is restored and renewed. But even the incarnation can only establish a new reality; it cannot guarantee its fulfillment. Hence, we must still pray for the Lord to come again in the fullness of power and might to complete humanity's redemption and to bring us to his kingdom forever. In the meantime, our communal hearing of and reflection on this text reminds us that hostility and division have been overcome in Christ, and that he is the Lord who empowers us to live in his peace and to spread his justice on the earth.

The responsorial psalm affirms that "justice shall flourish in his time, and fullness of peace for ever" (Ps 72:7). The text refers to the "king" (vs. 1), to his reign extending to the ends of the earth (vss. 8, 17), and to the salvation given to the poor and lowly (vss. 12–13), thus making it a most appropriate prayerful reflection on the reading.

The gospel text from Luke (10:21–24) joins the vision of Isaiah with our present situation by assuring us that the fullness of divine revelation has come in Jesus. While many in the history of Israel "wished to see what you see but did not see it, and to hear what you hear but did not hear it" (vs. 24), we are privileged witnesses to the presence of Christ in our day. Our present participation in word and sacrament helps us see his power at work in our lives and in the world, a power that we still hope and pray to be brought to completion when "Christ will come again."

That the liturgy involves God acting among us and our responding to him in Christ is emphasized in the prayer over the gifts. We admit that we cannot merit anything without God's grace and we pray that he will be pleased with the prayers and gifts we present.

The prayer after communion summarizes the liturgy of Advent by asking that we who share in the mystery of the eucharist be strengthened "to judge wisely the things of earth" and "to love the things of heaven." (Both these texts are used again on the Second Sunday and on Tuesdays and Fridays in the second and third weeks of Advent.)

The communion antiphon refers to today's readings by acclaiming that "the Lord is just" and that "he will award the crown of justice to all who have longed for his coming" (2 Tm 4:8). We who celebrate these sacred mysteries are hereby challenged to prepare for the coming of the Just One at the end of time. In the meantime, we welcome him in word, sign, and symbol at the eucharist.

Celebration of the Eucharist

A fitting introduction to the liturgy would include a sung "Lord have mercy" with the third set of sample invocations (iii), referring to the "Son" and to the "splendor of the Father," an interplay noted in the gospel.

The use of number 14 of the alleluia verses (Lect., no. 193) about the Lord coming to save and the blessedness of "those prepared to meet him" would fittingly introduce this gospel concerned with our seeing in Christ the fullness of revelation.

For the general intercessions, the sample formula in the Sacramentary appendix for Advent could be used as a guide. Additional intercessions could concern the gift of judging according to God's standards not our own (as in the Isaiah text), the renewed gift of the

Spirit of the Lord on all believers in Advent, and the importance of ministry to the marginal and unchurched since the Lord has come for all.

Advent preface I is assigned for use today. It could be accompanied by the third eucharistic prayer because of its reference to the universality of the Lord's mission (reflected in the first reading): "from age to age you gather a people to yourself." The Lord's Prayer could be suitably introduced by the second introduction about praying to the Father in the words our Savior gave us; it is through the Son that we are able to call God "our Father." The use of number 13 of the prayers over the people would be an appropriate conclusion to the liturgy because of its reference to seeking the Lord with all our hearts, a theme frequently repeated in Advent.

Liturgy of the Hours

The reading from Isaiah at the office of readings (Is 2:6–22; 4:2–6) exemplifies a pattern often seen in prophetic speech: confrontation with evil yet hope coming from trust in God. The first section (Is 2: 6–22) deals with just such a confrontation. Instead of trusting in God's revelation and promises, God's chosen ones have consorted with "soothsayers" and "fortunetellers" (vs. 6) and have worshiped idols. Isaiah reminds Israel that the Lord will "have his day" when he will overcome "all that is proud and arrogant."

The second part of the reading (Is 4:2–6) offers a hope that God will come again for the sake of his people to make them pure and holy. The prophet sees the Lord overshadowing his people's "place of assembly" with a cloud reminiscent of the cloud that led the people through the desert—a sign of God's protection. In Advent, this reading reminds us of God whose word recreates and renews those who trust in its power.

The passage from a sermon of St. Gregory Nazianzen is rich in paradoxes that surround Jesus' incarnation. The Word of the Father becomes like us in all things except for sin; he who is rich becomes poor, "he takes on the poverty of my flesh, that I may gain the riches of his divinity."

Through the liturgical celebration of Christ's incarnation, we share fully in his divinity now as we await our complete union with him in the world to come. The responsory, derived from Galatians, Ephesians, and Romans, highlights the virginal incarnation of Jesus which takes place "at the appointed time" for our redemption. These

Advent weeks lead to the celebration of the glorious day of Jesus' birth and of our re-creation in Christ.

The scripture reading at morning prayer from Genesis 49:10 is used on all Advent Tuesdays. This text refers to the tribe of Judah from which the promised Messiah will come. The Son of God from all eternity becomes incarnate in a particular time and place to redeem all peoples of all times and places. The beginning of this mystery lies in the rather insignificant tribe of Judah.

Jesus' origins in Israel are reaffirmed in the antiphon to Zechariah's canticle which refers to the "root of Jesse" from which the flower will blossom and all creation will see the saving power of God. Jesse, a man from Bethlehem, was David's father and Jesus was a descendant of David. From this "root" has come the Messiah and Lord of all.

The intercessions at morning prayer speak of our "works of penance" in Advent. Although Advent is not a penitential season like Lent, it is a time to "bring low the mountains of our pride" and to "prepare a path in our hearts" for the coming of Christ as we draw closer to him, especially through celebrating the liturgy and working toward the justice and peace he established.

At evening prayer, the scripture reading based on 1 Corinthians 1: 7b–9 states that we are to live now as we await Christ's second coming ("the revelation of Jesus Christ") in such a way "that we will be found blameless" on that day.

This same note of preparing ourselves for the parousia is woven into the antiphon to Mary's canticle (taken from Isaiah 55:6): "seek the Lord . . . while he is near." This nearness of God to us is noted in each of the intercessions that follow.

Celebration of the Hours

For today's invitatory, either the seasonal antiphon or the verse before the readings about preparing the way for the Lord could be used as the refrain.

Both psalm prayers provided at this hour, after Psalms 10 and 12, are the customary ones assigned throughout the year. Yet they have a relevance to Advent, for they speak of God as our comfort and security and of the light that comes from God's saving word. This latter image is particularly striking in Advent.

If a longer reading is desired at morning prayer, verses 11–12 may be added to the present text of Genesis 49:10. If additional petitions are added to the intercessions, they should be composed in the spirit of those given in the text because of their clear Advent emphases. At the Lord's Prayer, the invitation "with longing for the coming of God's kingdom" would underscore the theology of Advent.

At evening prayer, if a longer form of scripture reading is desired, the use of 1 Corinthians 1:3–9 (also used as the second reading last Sunday in the "B" cycle) would be appropriate. Should the continuous reading of other Pauline letters be followed during Advent, any passages suggested in the breviary would be superseded. If petitions are added to the intercessions, they should reflect the balance between the nearness of God to us and our need for him as exemplified in those provided.

Reflection—"A World Renewed"

In today's liturgy, Isaiah envisions a world free from hostility and filled with God's peace. What is "really real" for the prophet is a world renewed in God's image and likeness. Because of the fall and our distance from God, we need prophets and visionaries to remind us of how life can be in God's hands. The force of the Advent liturgy today moves us to examine how firmly we trust in God, pray for reconciliation with enemies, and long for the ultimate union of all peoples in Christ. The reconciliation and harmony we pray for may have to take place within ourselves. With God's help, we must bridge the gaps we have made between work and prayer, the secular and the sacred, the human and divine elements of life. With Christ as the source and foundation of all of life, these apparent anomalies can be overcome.

Clearly, reconciliation is a difficult task. Advent is a time to break down those barriers that separate us from God, from others, and from our best selves. The harmony and reconciliation, envisioned by the Advent prophets, can and will be achieved. In Christ, all things are possible.

WEDNESDAY OF THE FIRST WEEK OF ADVENT

Liturgical Context

Today's eucharist contains a strong eschatological emphasis together with the promise of the Lord's healing those in grave need.

Wednesday of the First Week of Advent 29

The liturgy of Advent deepens today and invites us to self-examination and honest preparation for the Lord's coming to us now and at the end of time.

Liturgy of the Eucharist

The eschatological emphasis in the eucharist begins with the entrance antiphon, a combination of Habakkuk 2:3 and 1 Corinthians 4:5. We are reminded that "the Lord is coming . . . [and] will not delay." This text means that the Lord's final coming will surely take place but at a time known only to him. When he does come all will be brought "to light" and he will reveal himself "to every nation."

In the opening prayer, taken from the old Gelasian Sacramentary, we pray that the Lord would make our hearts ready to receive him by giving us divine help and strength. This help, when we accept it, will lead us "to share in the banquet of heaven." The combination of drawing strength from the eucharist and longing for the Lord's final coming make this prayer a most appropriate Advent text with which to introduce the first reading, Isaiah 25:6–10.

This reading contains language and imagery which has been incorporated into the section of the third eucharistic prayer used at liturgies for the dead about that day, "when every tear will be wiped away." The prophet begins by referring to the "mountain" (vss. 6, 7, 10) where "the Lord of hosts will provide for all peoples a feast of rich foods. . . ." In the Old Testament, the mountain of God had a special meaning as a place where all peoples would one day meet. In the New Testament, the mountain is the site of Jesus' giving the beatitudes and of his crucifixion.

In the messianic age, the Lord "will destroy death forever" (vs. 8); the chosen will understand the plan of God and will say, "This is the Lord for whom we looked; let us rejoice and be glad that he has saved us" (vs. 9). In the meantime, however, we Christians celebrate our firm faith in Christ's love present to us at the eucharist. Yet, just as Israel's passover meals looked to be fulfilled in Christ, so do our eucharists look for their completion in the banquet of the Lord in his kingdom.

The eschatological aspect of this reading is reflected in the response to the familiar Psalm 23, today's responsorial psalm: "I shall live in the house of the Lord all the days of my life" (vs. 6). This aptly describes our situation as those who feed now on the eucharist and yet who long for that of which it is a pledge, our future glory in God's kingdom.

Today's gospel reading from Matthew (15:29–37) depicts Jesus as going "up onto the mountainside," where "the large crowds of people come to him," an echo of the mountain theme in today's reading from Isaiah. It is on this mountainside that Jesus cures the crippled and multiplies loaves and fish for the four thousand. Other sections of Isaiah should be recalled here about healing the deformed and curing the sick as signs that the kingdom has come. The juxtaposition of the healings (vss. 29–31) and the feeding miracle (vss. 32–39) is useful for our reflection as we gather for the eucharist. The Lord, who healed and sustained his first followers, heals and sustains us by the bread of life and the cup of eternal salvation.

The prayer over the gifts and the prayer after communion today speak about our present share in the eucharistic sacrifice and the coming feast of Christmas. They will be repeated on Wednesdays and Fridays until December 17 and are used on the Third Sunday of Advent.

The communion antiphon is inspired by Isaiah 40:10 and 35:5, and declares that the Lord "comes in strength." He does so in the eucharist and will do so in glory at the end of time.

Celebration of the Eucharist

After a brief introduction, the presider or other minister could use the second set of sample invocations from the third penitential rite (ii), which acclaim Christ's coming.

Number 9 of the alleluia verses (Lect., no. 193) would be appropriate since it speaks about the Lord coming in power to "enlighten the eyes of his servants."

The introduction to the sample formula for the Advent general intercessions (Appendix I in the Sacramentary) speaks of our need for "salvation," and one of the petitions refers to the gospel by asking, "that the Lord Jesus may heal the sick, [and] rid the world of hunger." These and related petitions would be most suitable, as would explicit use of the imagery of the first reading when praying for the dead (always a last petition).

Another way of reiterating the eschatological character of the first reading would be to use the third eucharistic prayer, which asks God to "strengthen in faith and love [his] pilgrim church on earth."

Introducing the Lord's Prayer with the fourth invitation about the coming of the kingdom would continue this emphasis.

If the Lamb of God is extended beyond three strophes, addition of titles of Christ, such as "Paschal Lamb" and "Word made flesh," would be appropriate. The first reiterates the imagery of the first reading; the second subtly refers to the feast of the incarnation (noted in the prayer after communion).

The use of number 18 of the prayers over the people speaking of the "mystery of the eucharist" and of being "reborn to lead a new life" would be a fitting conclusion to the liturgy.

Liturgy of the Hours

The text of Isaiah 5:1–7, which is the first reading at the office of readings, is about a vineyard, an image for Israel; "the vineyard of the Lord of hosts is the house of Israel," says the prophet (vs. 7). But the vineyard did not bring forth good grapes. Since the Lord found no justice in Israel, he will intervene to "make it a ruin" (vs. 6).

When proclaimed in Advent, this text reminds us that there will be a judgment for each of us when good and evil will be accounted for. The present season is the time given us to determine where we stand as we wait for the Lord to judge us.

The text from St. Bernard speaks about what he calls the "middle coming of the Lord" in "spirit and in power." St. Bernard states that we Christians behave appropriately in Christ's presence (the "middle coming") by keeping God's word. "Let it enter into your very being, let it take possession of your desires and your whole way of life." The sustenance so clearly emphasized in today's liturgy is the proclaimed word that mediates the Word Incarnate to us.

At morning prayer, the scripture text is from Isaiah (7:14b–15), which will be used on Wednesdays until December 17. In this text, Isaiah foretells the coming of Immanuel, the great descendant of King David, and reminds us that the Immanuel for whom we long in Advent is the Lord who always remains with us.

The antiphon to Zechariah's canticle uses John the Baptist's own words: "The One who is coming after me is greater than I; I am not worthy to untie the straps of his sandals." This theme will dominate the liturgy later in Advent; it is introduced here to prepare us for his prophetic ministry.

The intercessions at morning prayer speak about us "rejoicing in hope" as we pray. The important Advent themes of the justice and peace of God and the Lord's power and might are reflected here. The optional response, "Emmanuel, be with us," recalls the reading from Isaiah.

At evening prayer, the reading is from 1 Corinthians (4:5) about the return of the Lord, whose coming will lay bare the intentions of our hearts. What is hidden in darkness will be brought to light when Christ comes again as Lord and judge of all the earth. Hence, the eschatological aspect of this season and of the whole Christian life is reiterated once more.

The antiphon to Mary's canticle speaks about the law coming forth from Zion and the "word of the Lord from Jerusalem." As we abide by God's law and word in Advent, we need not fear his coming again "to judge the living and the dead."

The optional response to the intercessions reiterates the pilgrim church's constant prayer: "Lord, your kingdom come."

Celebration of the Hours

At the invitatory today, the seasonal verse or the verse before the readings, "Turn back to us, O Lord, our God,—show us your face and we shall be saved," fittingly reflects the themes of the season. The use of the classic invitatory psalm (Ps 95), with its recounting of Israel's history and the important verse "listen to the voice of the Lord," makes this especially fitting as the beginning of the office of readings. The fact that only Psalm 18 is used at this hour offers the possibility of praying the psalm straight through rather than separating its sections with doxologies and antiphons. A generous pause for silence after would be a good way of leading to the first reading from Isaiah.

The responsory, Psalm 80:14ff., could well be used in celebration to bring out the fact that the vineyard is the Lord's own possession.

While both psalm prayers provided at morning prayer are used through the year, they nonetheless coincide well with Advent. Should a longer reading from Isaiah 7 be desired, verses 10–15 would be a logical unit to use.

Since the scripture reading refers to "Immanuel," the use of the alternate response to the petitions using "Emmanuel" would be appropriate.

At evening prayer, 1 Corinthians 4:1–5 would be a longer text to use to expand on the text provided. Especially if the alternate response to the petitions is used, "Lord, your kingdom come," the third introduction to the Lord's Prayer, "with longing for the coming of God's kingdom let us offer our prayer to the Father" would be an appropriate introduction to this prayer.

The addition of local needs and some more particular concerns in the intercessions at both morning and evening prayer can help adapt the liturgy to particular situations.

Reflection—"To Be a Pilgrim"

Cardinal Basil Hume's most recent book is entitled *To Be a Pilgrim*. The cardinal states in the preface that his book is a message from one pilgrim to another as we all travel the earthly journey to heaven.

The liturgy of Advent and in particular today's liturgy contains strong messages for pilgrims—for us who believe that God has called us to live his life on earth and who will call us to his kingdom forever. In the meantime, however, we continually need messages "from one pilgrim to another" to help, guide, and inspire us as we journey to the kingdom. These messages come in many forms. At the eucharist, we recall the messages of prophets and evangelists to fellow pilgrims to console and inspire them to trust more deeply in the Lord. We recall these same messages as we pray at the liturgy of the word. We trust in their enduring power to reshape and to rekindle in us deepening faith and trust in God. Yet the context of the eucharist assures us that the Lord is present not in word only but through the eucharistic meal. Just as he fed Israel in the desert and Jesus multiplied bread to feed the multitude, so we who gather for the eucharist receive the sacrament of his presence among us in food and drink.

To be a pilgrim means to share faith with others who see beyond the things in this life and who look to eternal life with God. In the meantime, we can share in the messages of other pilgrims to us and in the sustenance of heavenly food with other pilgrims as we journey to the Kingdom.

Liturgical Context

Today's liturgy contains strong eschatological characteristics, especially in the first reading at eucharist and in the passage from St. Ephrem in the office of readings. The emphasis is on vigilance as we wait for the Lord to "come again," when he will take us to himself forever. To watch and wait for Christ is by no means to waste time, but to put time into its proper perspective.

Liturgy of the Eucharist

The entrance antiphon contains an acclamation of faith in the Lord who is near and in his commands which are just (see Psalm 119:151–152). For us to live by God's commands is to show our dedication to him and reverence for his ways.

The opening prayer is a recasting of the one formerly used on the Fourth Sunday of Advent. There is an urgency in the Latin original (not reflected in the present translation) that asks God to rouse his power and to rescue us by his great might. Our sins impede us from turning fully to him. Hence, we need the Lord to renew his saving love in us to strenghthen us against temptation. Our task is to open ourselves to the Lord to whom we pray and from whom we seek forgiveness.

The first reading from Isaiah 26:1–6 continues the section proclaimed yesterday. Using vivid eschatological language and imagery, the prophet envisions "a strong city" (Jerusalem) where God will dwell with his people and make them holy. God's people are to "trust in the Lord forever" because he is "an eternal rock" (vs. 4). This image for God establishes the imagery used in the gospel today about building on rock, not sand (Mt 7:24, 26). Because God is as strong as a rock, he has the power to do mighty deeds for the weak and the poor and "humble those in high places" (vs. 5).

In the responsorial psalm, we acclaim as "blessed" "he who comes in the name of the Lord" (Ps 118:26). We pray in our need that we will be admitted to the city of God when we say: "open to me the gates of justice."

In the gospel, we are challenged to base all our hopes on God alone, not on sandy foundations (vs. 26). The gospel begins with the reminder that it is not those who *cry out* "Lord, Lord" who will enter

God's kingdom; it is they who *do* the will of the Father (vs. 21). We can claim the Lord as our Lord and savior only when we base everything on him as our rock and foundation.

Today's readings challenge us to lead lives of integrity based on Christ as the bedrock of our lives. This is reflected in the communion antiphon taken from Titus (2:12–13, which verses form part of the second reading for Christmas Midnight Mass). As we approach the altar to receive the eucharist, we pray that our lives will be honest and holy "in this present age, as we wait for the happiness to come when our great God reveals himself in glory."

The importance of the eucharist in our lives here and now as we await the second coming is reflected in the prayer over the gifts and the prayer after communion (as found on the First Sunday of Advent).

Celebration of the Eucharist

After a brief introduction about Christ as the rock and foundation of our lives, the third form of the penitential rite using invocations of Christ as "the rock of our salvation," "the source of life and holiness," and "Emmanuel, God with us" would appropriately reflect today's scripture readings.

Of the alleluia verses offered for this first part of Advent, number 6 (Lect., no. 193) would point to our need to "seek the Lord while he can be found" (from Isaiah 55:6). Even though we know he is always in our midst, during Advent we are to be particularly attentive to his presence among us.

The eschatological character of the readings is reflected in Advent preface I used today ("hoping that the salvation promised us will be ours when Christ our Lord will come again in his glory"). This motif can be sustained by using either the second or third memorial acclamation and the fourth invitation to the Lord's Prayer ("Let us pray for the coming of the kingdom . . ."). The use of either number 1 or 16 of the prayers over the people would provide a fitting conclusion to the liturgy since each refers specifically to the consolation of the life to come.

Liturgy of the Hours

The reading from Isaiah at the office of readings (Is 16:1–5; 17:4–8) presents two oracles: one dealing with God's justice extended to Israel's enemies, and the other dealing with hope in God amid seemingly hopeless situations. The first oracle was probably very difficult for Israel to hear because the prophet tells them that even the Moabites, their enemies, would receive God's favor and share in his justice (vss. 4–5). Israel is told not merely to tolerate them but to welcome them and be their shelter.

For us who hear this first oracle, the bite of the reading is no less real. How do we react when we realize that we are to love our enemies?

The second oracle offers Israel hope despite situations that seem to be hopeless. Despite the history of humankind's dealing with one another, the Lord will always be there to guide and free his people: "On that day man shall look to his maker, his eyes turned toward the Holy One of Israel" (Is 17:8). We can do nothing less than to have resolute trust in God, the maker of all and Lord of our lives.

The second reading at this hour is taken from the writings of St. Ephrem about the need for vigilance before the Lord who comes. The author reminds us that even though we know that Christ will come again, we do not know when or where. "He has kept those things hidden so that we may keep watch, each of us thinking that he will come in our own day." For us, as for second century Christians, what is at issue is not a date or a time—it is an attitude of expectation and welcome.

At morning prayer, the reading is from Isaiah 45:8, that part of Deutero-Isaiah where the author cries out that the Lord's justice will descend and his salvation will bud forth on the earth. Once again, we are reminded that in Advent, we long for the fulfillment of the Lord's justice. In the meantime, we who have already experienced his justice are to respond by living just and honorable lives.

The antiphon to Zechariah's canticle recalls the vigilance theme of Advent when it states: "I shall wait for my Lord and Savior and point him out when he is near." By his preaching, Zechariah's son, John the Baptizer, prepared the way for the coming of the long-awaited Savior.

The intercessions reflect Advent themes, especially the first and fourth petitions referring to the "glorious kingdom" of God and to "the day of [Christ's] coming."

At evening prayer, the reading is from the letter of James (5:7–8, 9b) about patience and not losing heart as we wait for the Lord's coming. (James 5:7–10 will be used as the second reading on the Third Sunday of Advent in the "A" cycle.)

The antiphon to Mary's canticle recalls the incarnational aspects of Advent by quoting Elizabeth's greeting to Mary (Lk 1:42). We too acclaim Jesus as "blessed" who is the fruit of her womb.

The structure of the petitions today is familiar. The Christological titles used are particularly rich and can be used when adapting the penitential rite at Mass or extending the Lamb of God: Word of God, true light, only-begotten Son, and Christ Jesus. The nuptial imagery in the last petition should be noted; it reflects the intimacy with God that is ours through the incarnation.

Celebration of the Hours

At the office of readings, the use of the verse "Hear the word of the Lord, all you nations—Proclaim it to the ends of the earth" would be an appropriate way to begin the liturgy on a note of Advent vigilance and universality.

This universality is most clearly reflected in Psalm 67, which is a fitting invitatory psalm. The psalmody assigned for this hour continues Psalm 18 begun yesterday. These verses can be combined into one lengthy psalm with the first antiphon used at the beginning and end. The use of a period of silence after the psalmody and after the readings is especially important during Advent.

At morning prayer, the hymn chosen should reflect eschatological aspects of the season. The psalm prayers provided can also be adjusted to be more reflective of the season.

Should a longer scripture reading be desired, the use of Isaiah 45:4–10 would provide the context within which the assigned verse is found.

At the intercessions, the addition of some petitions about how the activities of the coming day should be filled with the spirit of Advent would be appropriate.

At evening prayer, an expanded scripture reading from James 5 would include verses 7–10.

The singing of Mary's canticle would be especially appropriate today since the antiphon has an incarnational tone.

If additional intercessions are composed, they should imitate the style reflected in those presented, acknowledging an aspect of Jesus' ministry or a title of Christ on which to base our prayer.

Reflection—"How Firm a Foundation?"

An eighteenth-century hymn entitled "How Firm a Foundation" refers to the faith that is established in us through the "excellent Word of God." God has revealed himself to us through Jesus, the Word incarnate. He continues to reveal himself in the word proclaimed at the liturgy. In the light of today's readings at Mass, we might turn around this hymn title and make it a question: How firm is the foundation of God's word in our hearts?

Who of us would not choose a rock over sand as a foundation for a house, or integrity over hypocrisy as a way of life? These choices are clear and obvious. Yet the real test comes in living out these verbal professions. How do we show that Jesus is the rock and foundation of our lives? Do we pray as we should, especially in Advent? Do we "go all out" at an occasional retreat or holy hour, but neglect day-to-day reflection on God's word? All of the greats in the history of Christian spirituality speak of daily application to prayer and holy reading as the means to a deeper spiritual life. How firm in the foundation of prayerful reflection on the Word of God is this Advent?

FRIDAY OF THE FIRST WEEK OF ADVENT

Liturgical Context

The strong eschatological themes in today's readings remind us that even though Christ has fulfilled the promises made to Israel, we still await their final completion in his kingdom. The liturgy we celebrate is a pledge of Christ's love that will be fulfilled in the kingdom. The liturgy is thus a manifestation of the kingdom of God among us.

Liturgy of the Eucharist

Today's entrance and communion antiphons firmly situate the liturgy as an Advent celebration. At the entrance, we proclaim that the

Lord "is coming from heaven in splendor to visit his people . . . to bring them eternal life." The Lord's act of visiting us means that he will abide with and sustain those who celebrate the liturgy in his name.

The communion antiphon affirms that one day the Lord Jesus "will transfigure our lowly bodies into copies of his own glorious body" (Phil 3:20–21). At death, we shall come face to face with God and be drawn into his eternal love forever. Fittingly, we use this text as we share in Christ's body and blood, itself a pledge of the future glory that awaits us at the heavenly banquet.

Today's opening prayer was formerly used on the First Sunday of Advent. It reflects the theology of the season by pleading that the Lord would stir up his power and come to save us.

The readings speak of signs of the coming reign of God. In the reading from Isaiah (29:17–24), the prophet declares that "on that day" when the Lord comes, the deaf will hear, the blind will see (vs. 18), the lowly will experience joy, and the poor will rejoice in the Holy One of Israel (vs. 19).

When the prophet first proclaimed this message, he called upon Israel to have hope and to be patient until the Lord would accomplish his promises. This attitude is reflected in the responsorial psalm, Psalm 27:

"Wait for the Lord with courage;
  be stouthearted and wait for the Lord." (vs. 14)

The gospel text from Matthew (9:27–31) tells of one of the Lord's healing miracles. This particular passage coincides well with the first reading since it shows Jesus accomplishing signs which Isaiah promised would accompany the coming of God's kingdom—"the eyes of the blind shall see."

What is particularly significant in Matthew's narration, however, is that the blind call Jesus by his Messianic title, "Son of David." Matthew recounts that Jesus "touched their eyes and said, 'Because of your faith it shall be done to you' " (vs. 29). It is by words and a gesture that Jesus healed the two blind men. Patristic authors often point out that it is by word and gesture in the sacraments that the Lord continues his healing among us. Through words and gestures, signs and symbols, we experience anew the presence of God in our midst in sacraments, especially the eucharist.

The importance of the sacraments as present experiences of God's love is brought out in the prayer after communion which speaks of "food from heaven" that gives us a share in the "things of heaven." (Both this and the prayer over the gifts were already used on Tuesday this week with a slightly different translation for the prayer after communion.)

Celebration of the Eucharist

If the third form of the penitential rite is used, the selection of the fifth set of sample invocations (v) about the dead being raised to life, sinners receiving pardon and peace, and the Lord bringing "light to those in darkness" would coincide with the readings.

For the alleluia verse, number 9 (Lect., no. 193), about the Lord coming with power to enlighten the eyes of his servants, would be most appropriate.

In composing the general intercessions, it would be helpful if the introduction noted our need for God (both spiritual and physical), and that in our need we turn to God in prayer. Petitions could include that the terminally ill would receive hope and strength from God, that the weak in faith might imitate the men in the gospel and come to deep faith in Christ, and that the dead might come to enjoy the fullness of life in the kingdom of heaven.

The first introduction to the Lord's Prayer would be a fitting choice today because it notes our trust in God as "we pray with confidence . . . in the words our Savior gave us."

The use of number 2 of the prayers over the people would be a fitting conclusion to the liturgy, since it asks for health of mind and body and that we might always be faithful to the Lord.

Liturgy of the Hours

The text from Isaiah (19:16–25) in the office of readings speaks of the peace that would exist between Egypt and Assyria when they unite in worshiping the true God of Israel. This passage presents the prose section of what otherwise is a poetic description of turning to God: "Although the Lord shall smite Egypt severely, he shall heal them; they shall turn to the Lord" (vs. 22). They will "cry out to the Lord against their oppressors," and he will send them "a savior to defend and deliver them" (vs. 21). For us who read this passage in Advent, the prediction of Egypt's conversion offers comfort and consolation. Even those who are farthest from God can return by admitting their sin and receiving his mercy and forgiveness.

But, lest this seem to be "cheap grace" or an easy way out, the text implies a deeper level of forgiveness. Where formerly these nations were enemies, in the Lord they are to become friends. We who confess our misdeeds must turn to each other in forgiveness and reconciliation—Christian attitudes that reflect God's grace at work in our midst. The ideal of harmony and universality often seen in the Advent liturgy requires the hard work of forgiveness leading to reconciliation in Christ. It is this universality that is reflected in the responsory (taken from Luke 13:23 and Isaiah 19:21) to this text. When the kingdom comes "East and West [will be] seated at the feast in the kingdom of God."

The second reading from the *Proslogion* of St. Anselm describes our need for God and our destiny as a people who are made to see God. Anselm states: "Teach me to seek you, and when I seek you show yourself to me . . . let me seek you in desiring you and desire you in seeking you." Like the blind men in today's gospel, we come before the Lord as those who have never seen the Lord but who yearn to see him in heaven. Like Anselm, we pray now that we will gain deeper insight into the mystery of God revealed to us in his Son as we long for him to come among us again at Christmas and at the end of time. Today we pray (in the responsory, Psalm 106:4) that the Lord would come and bring us salvation.

At morning prayer, the reading from Jeremiah (30:21, 22) recalls the covenant formula, "You shall be my people, and I will be your God" (vs. 22), used repeatedly in the Old Testament. It also refers to a "leader" from Jacob (vs. 21) which, when read in the Christian assembly, means the promised Messiah. It is he who will bring the old covenant to an end and become the passover sacrifice establishing the new covenant in his blood.

The antiphon to Zechariah's canticle, "Our God comes, born as man of David's line, enthroned as king forever," refers to the paradox of the incarnation which is celebrated throughout the Christmas season.

The Advent theme of "glory" is reflected in the introduction to the intercessions today and in the first petition. The last petition asks that despite our sins the Lord will sanctify his chosen ones and bring them to eternal happiness."

At evening prayer, the reading from 2 Peter (3:8b–9) refers to the coming of the Lord, to his faithfulness in keeping his promises, and to the patience he shows to all who need to repent. This is a reflection on a prime aspect of the Advent liturgy.

The power of the coming Lord is reflected in the antiphon to the Canticle of Mary: "Out of Egypt I have called my Son; he will come to save his people." Jesus was incarnate because of our need for a savior; he continues to live and act among us because of our need for complete redemption. The petitions this evening call upon Christ as our shepherd and guardian. It is he who leads us to the kingdom of heaven.

Celebration of the Hours

At the office of readings, the regular Advent invitatory or the verse, "Let your compassion come upon me, Lord—Your salvation, true to your promise," used with Psalm 67, would be a fitting introduction to the hours.

Since the single Psalm 35 is assigned as the psalmody at this hour, singing it or reciting it as a unit would allow for a significant pause before the readings. If a psalm prayer is composed, it might well deal with our situation in Advent as a people who await a renewed experience of the Lord as Savior.

At morning prayer, the first psalm prayer (following Psalm 51) could acknowledge our sin and our longing for the coming of Christ who forgives sins and leads us to the joy of the kingdom. Following the canticle from Isaiah (45:15–25), a psalm prayer could speak of the amplitude of the Lord's covenant and the unity of all peoples in Christ.

If a longer scripture reading is desired, the expansion of Jeremiah 30 to include verses 12–22 would offer a more logical unit.

If the intercessions are rewritten, the third petition could well be rephrased as a more positive statement about those who seek the Lord (like that in the fourth eucharistic prayer about all who seek God "with a sincere heart").

At evening prayer, a psalm prayer following Psalm 41 could note our need for salvation in Christ, and a prayer following Psalm 46 could speak of God as our refuge and strength, the hope of all who trust in him. If a longer version of the text of 2 Peter is desired, it could be expanded to include verses 8–13.

As an introduction to the Lord's Prayer, the presider could speak about our openness to the Lord's will being done in our lives as a way to prepare for the coming of the kingdom.

Reflection—"Faith to Miracles or Miracles to Faith?"

How do we regard the miracles stories in the gospels? We may instinctively assume that these prove Jesus was God as he came among us as a man. Such has often been a conventional apologetical gambit. Christ's miracles proved his divinity.

Today's gospel, however, offers another approach reflected repeatedly in the New Testament—from faith to miracles. In healing the blind men, Jesus responds to their faith-filled request, not just to a request to him as the wonder-worker. They call him "Son of David," saying, in effect, we believe that you are the promised one of God and we adore you. It is on the basis of this conviction and in response to their obvious need that Jesus does indeed act in a way that reveals his power over all creation. He cures their blindness so that they can now see what is around them physically and also perceive the depth of what they know Jesus to be in faith—Messiah and Lord. This approach is clearly from faith to miracles.

What about us who already believe? Do we bring the same confident faith to prayer and to the liturgy? We may not need physical cures, but each of us, as long as we live on this earth, needs to be converted completely to the Lord. We must bring to prayer and liturgy those areas in our lives that need forgiveness (our vices) and those things that need strengthening (our virtues). No one of us will ever be made perfect until we meet God in the kingdom. In the meantime, when we pray and worship in faith, we open ourselves to the healing power of God to remake, refashion, and renew us in his grace and in his peace.

SATURDAY OF THE FIRST WEEK OF ADVENT

Liturgical Context

The tension inherent in the Christian life, of being faithful to the incarnate Lord and awaiting his return in glory, is a dominant theme in today's liturgy. This tension is to be translated into patience, says St. Cyprian, a virtue which especially marks the Advent Christian.

Liturgy of the Eucharist

Today's entrance antiphon prays: "Come, Lord . . . let us see your face, and we shall be saved" (Ps 80:4, 2). Here, we invite the Lord to be the center of our lives, replacing those things that so often become too central—our possessions, accomplishments, or status.

In the opening prayer, we ask the Father, who has sent his only Son to free us from "the ancient power of sin and death," to help us as we wait for his coming in glory. It is the work of his grace alone that gives us "true liberty." We do not pray for an escape from the struggles of this earthly life. Rather, we ask for God's grace to sustain us now and to lead us to the joys of heaven.

The first reading from Isaiah 30 (vss. 19–21, 23–26) assures us that despite present trials, the Lord will answer all our needs and eventually bring us home to his kingdom. These verses (actually, verses 18–26, as will be used at the office of readings on Monday of the third week of Advent) challenge Israel to greater faith in the Lord even as they reaffirm God's patience as he deals with his people. The key here is taken from verse 18 (not read today): "the Lord is waiting to show you favor, and he rises to pity you; For the Lord is a God of justice: blessed are all who wait for him." (Fittingly, this last phrase will be used today as the response to the reading.)

Isaiah assures Israel of God's response to their need (vs. 19) by recalling his past kindness when they wandered in the desert. As he taught them to follow his call and fed them during their desert journey (vs. 20), so will God intervene on their behalf to instruct and sustain them in God's ways.

Another important image found in this reading (vs. 26) is the light that will come for the people's illumination. The diminishing daylight at this time of year coincides with this image to exemplify our need for God who came as a light into the darkness of sin and death. This text reminds us that to receive the light means letting go of spiritual darkness that results from sin.

The responsorial psalm (Ps 147) uses the text from Isaiah 30:18 as the refrain: "Happy are all who long for the coming of the Lord." Verses of the psalm that coincide well with the first reading acclaim the Lord who "heals the brokenhearted," "binds up their wounds," and "sustains the lowly" (vss. 3, 5).

The gospel text continues the section proclaimed yesterday from Matthew (9:35–10:1, 6–8). The reading begins with the summary statement that Jesus preached the "good news of God's reign" and "cured every sickness and disease" (vs. 35). Jesus is pictured as one "moved with pity" for those in need. The weary and wounded find solace and comfort in him. In summoning the twelve and sending them forth (Mt 10:1), Jesus requires that they imitate him in showing compassion and in extending his mercy to "the lost sheep of the house of Israel" (vs. 6). This mission was entrusted not only to the twelve, but also to all Jesus' later followers. The task of the church in Advent is to bear witness to the presence of God in our day and to proclaim the coming of the kingdom. In this way, we bear witness to the hope and compassion of Jesus.

Another Advent theme is reflected in the communion antiphon: "I am coming quickly, says the Lord, and will repay each . . . according to his deeds" (Rv 22:12). Fittingly, these Advent themes are stressed as we receive the eucharist, our food for the journey to final union and communion with the Lord.

Celebration of the Eucharist

Today's liturgy should be relatively simple compared with the Sunday eucharist to be celebrated tomorrow. The third form of the penitential rite with the first sample set of invocations (i), acclaiming Christ as the one who heals the contrite, calls sinners, and pleads at the Father's right hand, would be an appropriate introduction to the liturgy.

For the alleluia verse, number 2 of the options (Lect., no. 193), "Lord, let us see your kindness, and grant us your salvation" (from Psalm 85:8), would appropriately introduce the gospel and would indirectly reflect our situation as those who need the Lord's kindness as we await his final coming.

The intercessions today could be especially simple with a brief introduction (for example, a variation on the Eastern use: "In peace, let us pray to the Lord") and four or five simply worded petitions with "Come, Lord Jesus" as the response. Among the needs mentioned should be those of the physically and emotionally ill who may despair of God's help.

After Advent preface I, the use of the second eucharistic prayer would be fitting. The introduction to the Lord's Prayer could address our need for God as we confidently pray to him.

Liturgy of the Hours

The first reading at the office of readings from Isaiah 21:6–12 speaks of the assured ruin of Babylon. The watchman spoken of may be the prophet himself addressing his contemporaries (vs. 6). His message interprets what he sees in the light of God's revelation to him. There is no answer to the rhetorical question, "how much longer the night?" (vs. 11) for we can never know when the Lord will come again. In its original setting, this may have been a reference to the suffering Israel was undergoing. Even though suffering would likely endure (vs. 12), the people are encouraged to draw hope from the presence of God with them in their need. Ultimate vindication for the just is assured, however, and these must not take part in the sins of many of the chosen (see the responsory, Revelation 18).

The coming judgment we look to in Advent is not meant to make us cower before God; it is a simple reminder that our actions in this life do matter for life eternal.

The second reading from St. Cyprian takes up the important Advent theme of patience. In addressing his third-century audience, Cyprian assures them that the final judgment will take place and they should conduct themselves worthily in the present. "We must endure and persevere if we are to attain the truth and freedom we have been allowed to hope for; . . . but if faith and hope are to bear their fruit, patience is necessary."

In a world that lives on instant communication and is peopled by so many who strive for instant success, this text appears to run counter to the assumption that "time is money." Cyprian's message is, therefore, all the more important. It is by the almost imperceptible daily efforts we make at preparing for and awaiting the Lord's coming, that we usher in God's kingdom. What we do in this life prepares for its final revelation. The responsory from Habakkuk 2:3 assures us that "He will appear at last; he is true to his word;—keep watching for him. . . ."

The reading at morning prayer from Isaiah (11:1–2) was discussed above, since verses 1–10 have already been proclaimed at mass on Tuesday of this week.

The antiphon to Zechariah's canticle exhorts us to watchfulness: "Banish your hearts, O people of Zion; God, your God, is coming to you, alleluia." This attitude of watchfulness is reflected in the intercessions, especially the final one: "Strengthen us to the last—until the day of the coming of Jesus Christ our Lord." Until that day, we pray that God's justice will flourish in the church and that we will be attentive to his word.

Celebration of the Hours

For the invitatory today, the use of the verse at the office of readings reflects the position of Israel as the chosen who have received the word: "the Lord proclaims his word to Jacob—his laws and decrees to Israel." The use of Psalm 100 as the invitatory psalm would be appropriate since it reflects the presence of the Lord with us and it reminds us of his "eternal and merciful love" (vs. 5).

Since Psalm 105 is assigned for this hour, reciting or singing it straight through with the first antiphon at the beginning and end would be an option today. This would allow for a significant period of silence before the readings. The text of the antiphon, "Sing praise to the Lord; remember the wonders he has wrought," fittingly introduces the psalm which recounts God's dealings with Israel.

At morning prayer, the hymn should continue to stress the Lord's second coming and the cosmic imagery of this first part of Advent. If a longer reading than Isaiah 11:1–2 is desired, the addition of verses 3–10 would be an option (although these verses were used at Mass on Tuesday). The use of an alternate response to the intercessions, "Lord, protect your people," would be fitting as would the use of the first introduction to the Lord's Prayer from the eucharist: "Let us pray for the coming of the kingdom. . . ."

Reflection—"We Are the Weak and Weary"

The temptation to dismiss sacred scriptures as archaic or as merely recounting what happened long ago and far away is a very real one. When we hear that Jesus cures the sick or feeds the multitude, we can tend to dismiss these deeds as having happened once and for all without any relevance to us as having been accomplished and hence do not have an effect on us.

Yet, in terms of today's gospel, we should be aware that we who are weak and weary experience the same compassion Christ lavished on those in need during his lifetime. This comes to us through other people and through the liturgy.

Until we are called to God's kingdom, we need each other to reveal God's love to us here and now. The Lord who gathered the outcasts to himself and who healed the sick comes to us where two or three are gathered in his name and when bread is broken and eaten and wine poured and shared. We do these things in his memory; we ask him to heal and cure us in our time of trial and suffering. The liturgy is food for the journey for us who are the weak and the weary. When we live the love we celebrate at liturgy, we make Christ known and are thus strengthened and confirmed in love— God's love for us and our love for each other.

Second Week of Advent

SECOND SUNDAY OF ADVENT

Liturgical Context

Today's liturgy of the eucharist introduces the important Advent figure of John the Baptizer. By design, the scriptures deal with Messianic prophecies (first reading), moral exhortations about how to conduct ourselves as we await the second coming (second reading), and the call of John the Baptizer (gospel).

The liturgy of the hours, however, emphasizes John the Baptizer only in the second reading at the office of readings; the other hours reflect other appropriate and predominantly eschatological Advent themes.

Cycle "A"

Today's first reading from Isaiah (11:1–10) has already been proclaimed on Tuesday of the first week of Advent (see above for commentary) and will be used at the office of readings on Christmas day. The vision of the prophet should guide our prayer in Advent as we await the One who will "decide aright for the land's afflicted" (vs. 4b).

The response, Psalm 72:7, about justice flourishing and peace being established forever echoes the Isaian reading. This psalm was also used last Tuesday; it will be used on December 17 and on the solemnity of the Epiphany. This latter use points to the universal reign of justice and peace in Christ.

The second reading from Romans 15:4–9 concerns the demands placed on believers to deepen their "harmony with one another" in order to "glorify God, the Father of our Lord Jesus Christ" (vs. 5). In Advent, we are to ponder the scriptures more faithfully to experience the Lord who is the "source of all patience and encouragement" (vs. 5), and as the One who is the source of unity among Christians, no matter what their origin or race.

Christ calls all people to unity with him, for, as the gospel acclamation says: "All mankind shall see the salvation of God (Lk 3:4, 6)."

The gospel text from Matthew 3:1–12, about John's ministry as preacher and baptizer, is also used in the sample communal penance service for Advent in the revised liturgy of penance. John declares that merely saying "Abraham is our father" (vs. 9) is not "evidence that you mean to reform" your way of life. We must show our fidelity to God by our deeds.

Matthew speaks here of the separation of the chaff from the grain (vs. 12), a concept he develops later (Mt 13:24–30) under the metaphor of the weeds and wheat, to show that bad and good coexist in the church. On this Advent Sunday, however, we can direct our thoughts to the way each of us is giving real evidence of a new, reformed life. Are we to be barren chaff or grain that will grow into new life?

Cycle "B"

The first reading from Isaiah (40:1–5, 9–11) will also be used on Tuesday of this week and as the new optional reading on the feast of the Baptism of the Lord, "C" cycle. The author begins by repeating the word "comfort" (vs. 1) to all in Jerusalem who are God's chosen (vs. 2). He expands on the Exodus motif when he refers to the "desert" (vs. 3). The new exodus will be larger and universal in scope—"all mankind shall see it together" (vs. 5). Israel is once again reassured that the Lord's word to her will stand forever and that he will stand by her despite her infidelity (vss. 7–8). Whereas in the first reading in the "A" cycle (Is 11), paradise will be reestablished after the Fall (Genesis), this text speaks about a new and even more glorious exodus for those who trust in God's word. These instances show how Isaiah draws on the traditions of the Pentateuch to instruct and inspire Israel during her exile.

Today's text is especially appropriate because all the synoptics use Isaiah 40:3 to describe John the Baptist's ministry: "A voice cries out: in the desert prepare the way of the Lord! Make straight in the wasteland a highway for our God." Alongside images of comfort and consolation are the demanding words and ascetical example of John the Baptist—the central figure in the liturgy this Sunday.

In the responsorial psalm, we ask to share in the Lord's comfort with the fitting response: "Lord let us see your kindness, and grant us your salvation" (Ps 85:8). We are reminded that "near indeed is his salvation to those who fear him" (vs. 10), and that "justice shall walk before him, and salvation along the way of his steps" (vs. 14).

The second reading from 2 Peter (3:8–14) deals with the coming judgment of God despite the delay of Christ's second coming. Delay does not mean it will not occur. Thus, he urges his hearers to prepare for it. The author is careful, however, not to frighten his hearers. He assures them that the Lord does not delay in keeping his promises (vs. 9), and that he wants no one to perish but all to come to repentance (vs. 9). (This text is used in the concluding prayer in the sample set of intercessions for Advent in the Sacramentary appendix.) Precisely because the Lord wants all to be saved, it is imperative that Christians prepare for his second coming by being holy in conduct and devotion (vs. 11) and to be found without stain (vs. 14).

Today's gospel reading from Mark (1:1–8) states simply: "here begins the gospel of Jesus Christ, the Son of God" (vs. 1), and then narrates the appearance of John as the messenger sent to herald the coming of the Messiah. Unlike the other synoptics, the gospel of Mark contains no narrative of the birth or infancy of Jesus.

The gospel is indeed the good news of our lives when we respond to its challange to "make ready the way of the Lord, clear him a straight path" (vs. 3). The people of Jerusalem and of "the Judean countryside" came to hear the preaching of John as he proclaimed the nearness of the kingdom (vs. 5). To demonstrate their commitment to repent, they were baptized in the Jordan "as they confessed their sins" (vs. 5). This water bath signified their sincere preparation for the coming Messiah—one more powerful than John (vs. 7) who will baptize with the Holy Spirit and with fire (vs. 8). Here Mark paints a striking portrait of John as one who effaces himself so that the Lord may be recognized as savior to all.

Cycle "C"

The first reading, Baruch 5:1–9 (who was known as Jeremiah's secretary), comes from a section dealing with a prophecy that Jerusalem's captivity in Babylon will end soon and that God will vindicate his own. Using typical prophetic imagery, Baruch states that God commands every lofty mountain to be made low so that "Israel may advance secure in the glory of God" (vs. 7). In God alone will Israel find true mercy, justice, glory, and joy (vs. 9). When the people abide by the prophet's word, Israel will receive God's abundant blessings.

Today's responsorial psalm, Psalm 126, helps contemporize this text when we pray: "The Lord has done great things for us; we are filled with joy" (vs. 3). The mercy, justice, joy, and peace referred to by Baruch are ours when we live according to the word of the Lord. For the faithful believer, Israel's exile ended in union with God. For us "in exile" on earth, this prayer offers us hope and comfort.

The second reading from Paul's letter to the Philippians (1:4–6, 8–11) summarizes much of what Advent is about. What really matters in our living God's life here and now is choosing those things that will lead us to eternity. This is Paul's prayer for us:

"[may] your love . . . more and more abound, both in understanding and wealth of experience, so that with a clear conscience and blameless conduct you may learn to value the things that really matter, up to the very day of Christ." (vss. 9–10)

The gospel from Luke (3:1–6) introduces John the Baptist by stressing John's fulfillment of the role set forth in Isaiah 40. Luke recalls the Isaian passage which deals with God's highway (the new exodus) prepared in the wasteland of apparent destruction and devastation. Even the contours of the earth will be changed—valleys filled in, mountains made low—as the salvation of God is revealed to all. Luke's editorial plan is clear. With the coming of the church, all lands and peoples are welcomed into what was once reserved for Israel. Through the power of the Holy Spirit, all nations can now "see the salvation of God" (vs. 6).

In addition, Luke points to the fact that John's preaching and teaching inaugurated God's kingdom on earth at a specific place and time. This so-called historical interest in Luke can be appreciated as we hear the passages chosen for the Christmas-Epiphany cycle which detail events at Nazareth, Bethlehem, and Galilee. This gospel repeatedly points to Jerusalem, since it is there that Christ died and rose from the dead. What was the central sanctuary for the chosen of Israel now becomes the starting point for the evangelization of all nations.

Sacramentary Texts

The entrance antiphon is taken from the traditional introit of the Roman Missal (see Isaiah 30:19, 30). In it we are invited to take the place of the "people of Zion" and to wait for the Lord to come and save "all nations." We who are redeemed in Christ's blood are to listen to "his majestic voice" spoken through his word in Advent until we hear his voice call us to his eternal kingdom.

Today's opening prayer is a traditional Advent text taken from the old Gelasian Sacramentary. In it we call upon the God of power and mercy with a sense of urgency as we await the coming of Christ (not clearly expressed in the present translation). We pray that God would remove from our hearts the sins that impede Christ from coming into our lives. We ask this so that we can be the better prepared for the second coming ("and become one with him when he comes in glory"). This prayer indicates that each of us needs a change of heart and a more radical turning to the Lord; thus, it reflects the message of the Baptist.

The sustenance we receive in the eucharist is noted in the prayer over the gifts and the prayer after communion (already described above in the commentaries for Tuesday and Friday of the first week of Advent). The communion antiphon quotes Baruch 5:5, part of the first reading in the "C" cycle today, and 4:36, about the "joy that is coming to you from God." This joy is indeed ours when we receive the body and blood of Christ, a pledge of our living with Christ in the kingdom.

Celebration of the Eucharist

The decor and gestures utilized last Sunday should be repeated today and for the next two Sundays to establish continuity through Advent. The atmosphere and sense of the liturgy should reflect the quiet joy and hopefulness of the season.

The rite of blessing and sprinkling with holy water would coincide well with the ministry of John the Baptist who called for reform and acknowledgment of sin, symbolized in the water bath of baptism. Although we renew our commitment to Christ and renew our baptismal profession of faith at every eucharist, to emphasize this fact in today's celebration would be appropriate. (Any comments during the liturgy should avoid giving the impression that Christian initiation and John's preparatory baptism of repentance are the same.) The conclusion to this rite should include the prayer that speaks of the eucharist as leading to the eternal banquet in the kingdom.

Even though the Sacramentary provides optional comments after "Let us pray" at the opening prayer to direct our silent reflection, Advent might be a good time not to use them in order to emphasize the starkness and simplicity of the season.

Today the responsorial psalm and alleluia verses deserve special care in celebration because they summarize so much of what is contained in the readings.

The general intercessions today could pray for justice and peace in a world torn by dissension and violence. While these intentions should not be politicized, they should mention specific conflict areas in the world. As always, some petitions should reflect from the theme of the homily and some should reflect local needs, especially local Advent programs.

Even though the Advent solemn blessing does not appear with the Mass formula today, it is always possible to use it. Hence, repeating it (if used last Sunday, or repeating the prayer over the people that was used) would be another way of reinforcing the liturgical unity of these weeks.

Liturgy of the Hours

At Evening Prayer I, the antiphons to the psalmody, the antiphon to the Canticle of the Blessed Virgin and the intercessions are new this week. The first two antiphons mention how Christ comes as our King and God to save us; the third contrasts the old and new covenants by stating that the law came through Moses but grace and truth come through Jesus Christ. Hence, these antiphons note the three comings of Christ and emphasize the salvation granted us as we prepare for his coming at Christmas.

The Canticle of Mary expresses the quiet joy of Advent: "Come to us, Lord, and may your presence be our peace; with hearts made perfect we shall rejoice in your companionship forever."

The interplay between the comings of Christ and the salvation won for us is noted in the intercessions. The fourth petition refers to

Christ's second coming as judge; we pray that he will show us his mercy and forgive our weaknesses. The first and second refer to his being born of the Virgin Mary and coming as the messenger of the covenant. Strikingly, the references in the third and fifth petitions to the paschal mystery indicate clearly why Christ came to take on our humanity: "in your life on earth, you came to die as a man—save us from everlasting death." We also note (in the last petition) that it is by Christ's death that the dead receive hope. Such texts specify how the liturgy makes us sharers in the mysteries of Christ's incarnation and paschal mystery.

The text of Isaiah 22:8b–23 at the office of readings reflects the prophet's anger at the inhabitants of Jerusalem who were satisfied with halfhearted conversion and halfhearted virtues. Crafty enough to provide for their physical needs (vss. 10–11), they do not look to their maker in humility and gratitude. Instead of accepting the opportunity for conversion and reform, they prefer feasting and celebration: "Let us eat and drink for tomorrow we die" (vs. 13). (Paul uses this text in his treatment of death in 1 Cor 15:32.) The prophet then contrasts the loyal Eliakim (vs. 20) with the wicked Shebna (vs. 15). Because of Eliakim's loyalty and kindness to the inhabitants of Jerusalem, he will carry the "key of the house of David on his shoulder" (vs. 22), thus becoming an influential member of God's chosen servants. This text offers many avenues for reflection, not the least of which concerns the provisional nature of so many of the things we regard as essential in life. When the Lord comes again, even these "essentials" will fade away. What we will be judged on is our fidelity to him in faith and how we treat each other. Will we be like the wicked Shebna or the loyal Eliakim?

The second reading from Eusebius of Ceasarea's Commentary on Isaiah draws a parallel between the prophet's words about "the voice of one in the wilderness" and the message of John the Baptist: "Prepare the way of the Lord." Eusebius sees "the way of the Lord" as being prepared by the preaching of the gospel by the apostles. We prepare the way for Christ to come into our lives by our Advent prayers and reflections.

At morning prayer, the antiphons reflect a variety of Advent themes. The first antiphon states "our God is here among us" as a way of introducing Psalm 118. Verses of this psalm, which have often been commented upon in the Easter liturgy to reflect the power of Christ's resurrection, may well be understood to refer to the presence of God with us in Advent as we experience now the salvation of those who will one day be called to his right side in the kingdom:

"The Lord's right hand has triumphed;
his right hand raised me up.
The Lord's right hand has triumphed;
I shall not die, I shall live
and recount his deeds." (vss. 15b–17)

A later verse of this psalm (vs. 22), also used to refer to the resurrection, has been adapted as a psalm prayer. In it we acclaim the Lord who has become the cornerstone of the new edifice of God's people.

The second antiphon from Isaiah 55:1 invites us to drink from the waters, a rich symbol of the refreshment we receive from Christ's powerful word. This reference to an element of creation is an appropriate introduction to the canticle in praising God for his wonderful works (Dn 3:52–57). The third antiphon, introducing Psalm 150, assures us that "Our God will come with great power to enlighten the eyes of his servants. In Advent we praise him for his powerful deeds as we long for him to give us "eternal joy with [his] saints" (to use the words of the psalm prayer that follows).

The text from the prophet Malachi (3:1): "I am sending my angel before me to prepare the way for my coming," is the antiphon to the Canticle of Zechariah and refers to John as the final messenger to announce the Lord's coming. The canticle itself reminds us of the mission of John to prepare for the coming of the light of the world—"the dawn from on high shall break upon us" (Lk 1:78).

The more eschatological aspects of Advent reappear in the intercessions. We acknowledge that Christ will come again to "judge the living and the dead." Hence, we pray that he will show us his "power to save" (second petition) and give us "the revelation of your glory" (fourth petition). Even as we look forward to his coming in glory (third petition), we also pray that he will "protect us [now] in times of temptation" (first petition).

The eschatological aspects of Advent are reaffirmed in the antiphons at Evening Prayer II when we acknowledge that "the Lord will come on the clouds of heaven with great power and might" (first antiphon); even "if he seems to delay, [we are] to keep watch for him, for he will surely come" (second antiphon). We acclaim him as "our king and lawgiver [who] will come to save us" (third antiphon).

Unlike the Magnificat antiphon last evening, referring to the second coming of Christ, the text this evening refers to the birth of Jesus, specifically to the role of the Virgin Mary. This incarnational aspect is reiterated in the introduction to the intercessions and especially in the (third) petition about Christ assuming our human weakness. We pray now that we might receive new life by his coming (first petition) as we look for him to come again (third and fourth petitions). The image of the right side of the Father is used in the last petition when we pray for the dead: "You sit at the right hand of the Father—gladden the souls of the dead with your light."

Celebration of the Hours

At evening prayer in the Latin edition of the hours, the hymn *Conditor alme siderum* is used. With this as a guide, it would be appropriate to use a hymn that emphasizes Christ's second coming. The psalm prayers at first evening prayer are useful as presented because they refer to the importance of the word of God for our direction (first) and about the coming judgment (second).

The scripture readings at both Evening Prayer I and II and at morning prayer are the same for all Advent Sundays. The options recommended last week should be kept in mind when planning these hours. It should be noted that the suggested Sunday responses are not the same as those used on weekdays.

Singing the Canticle of the Blessed Virgin Mary would be especially appropriate at Sunday evening prayer to help solemnize the Advent season. This would be particularly appropriate at Evening Prayer II with its antiphon emphasizing the incarnation.

The addition of local needs in the intercessions at evening prayer would help to balance the universal needs noted in the proposed texts. To sing the Lord's Prayer and to conclude these evening hours with the solemn Advent blessing would enhance them even more.

The Advent invitatory, "Come, let us worship the Lord, the King who is to come," or the verse, "Lift up your heads and see.—Your redemption is now at hand," both reflect strong Advent themes, thus making either appropriate as today's invitatory. The use of the classic invitatory psalm, Psalm 95, would be especially appropriate on Sunday.

The singing or recitation of Psalm 104 at the office of readings can be done straight through or it can be broken into sections as presented. Should the psalm be done as a unit, any of the three antiphons provided would enhance its meaning since they all reflect appropriate Advent themes. However, the psalm prayer that follows is wordy and might be adjusted in favor of a more succinct prayer reflecting the theology of the season.

At morning prayer, it would be appropriate to sing the Canticle of Zechariah with the antiphon about John the Baptist as a way of underscoring his ministry so dominant in the eucharist today. The balance between the first and second comings of Christ seen in the intercessions today should be held to even if these are rephrased. To overemphasize the incarnational aspect of Advent is to miss a wealth of theology and meaning intrinsic to the season.

A sung Lord's Prayer can help enhance this celebration as would the use of number 1 or 16 of the prayers over the people from the Sacramentary. (While the solemn blessing for Advent is recommended for evening prayer, these shorter options are suggested for morning prayer because of the centrality of the Sunday eucharist which should not be eclipsed by this hour of prayer.)

Reflection—"The Lord's Messengers"

Statistics show that the holidays are particularly difficult times emotionally and psychologically. Suicide rates rise in December. Pre- or post-holiday "blues" are featured magazine and newspaper stories. This season has been so abused in our culture that it raises the expectation that an exhilirating Christmas season will take away all our troubles. It is not uncommon to fantasize about the perfect holiday and then to be depressed about the reality which is so imperfect, so human.

Added to this is the fact that in our society many families do not come together for holidays because of distance or, unfortunately, because of estrangement. What should be a time of unity and celebration often becomes a time for deeper sadness about the marital difficulties or family disputes.

How appropriate it is that today's hopeful liturgy tells us that John is the messenger who exemplifies what real holiday preparation is all about. True Christmas preparation requires that we search our souls to determine what areas of our lives need the healing and saving message of the Christ who comes. What are the areas in relationships that need the curing and illuminating light of Christ? Is this season of extra entertaining the time when I will finally choose to stop drinking to excess or to stop overeating?

What are the areas in our world that need the justice and peace of Christ, so frequently mentioned in the Advent liturgy? What countries practice oppression by allowing only the very rich to prosper? How do we express our concern for the poor? Is this the season when we help organizations that channel food to starving people? "Justice and peace" are meant to be hallmarks of those who follow him who came among us to establish the justice and peace of the kingdom of God.

Today's liturgy proclaims John the Baptist as the last messenger to prepare the way for the Lord. In our day, in our world, in our nation, and in our families, we are God's messengers.

MONDAY OF THE SECOND WEEK OF ADVENT

Liturgical Context

Despite the emphasis given to the life and ministry of John the Baptist yesterday, the liturgy for the weekdays this week returns to the more eschatological emphasis of Advent. The liturgy reminds us that we still await the full revelation of the kingdom, hence we continue to pray "Come, Lord Jesus."

Liturgy of the Eucharist

Except for the opening prayer, all of today's chants and prayers were used last Monday and will be used again next Monday. The opening prayer has been chosen from the Leonine Sacramentary because it coincides with the scripture readings. In it we pray that we may be purified during Advent to prepare for the celebration of the great mystery of the incarnation.

The first reading from Isaiah (35:1–10) names God as savior and reflects on our need for salvation. The prophet here lists many manifestations of God's power which signal the coming of the Messianic age. Examples from nature and human life indicate the greatness of the Lord who "comes to save you" (vs. 4). The "glory of the Lord" and the "splendor of our God" (vs. 2) often pictured in dramatic and even fearful ways are here given very positive meanings for it is God who strengthens the weak in body (vs. 3) and those whose hearts are frightened (vs. 4). The vindication and recompense which God will bring is pictured as saving and sustaining, not condemning or judging. Later, the prophet indicates that God's love and redemption require faith and correct conduct ("no one unclean may pass over [the Lord's] highway" (vs. 8)).

When proclaimed in the Advent liturgy, this text reminds us of the Lord's fidelity even when we grow weary of running life's course according to his will. The hopefulness of Advent is made all the greater when we admit our need for the Savior who comes to us at Christmas to be forever Emmanuel, God with us.

The responsory to Psalm 85 is a verse from the first reading, "Our God will come to save us" (Is 35:4). We are reminded in the consoling words of the psalm that "near indeed is his salvation to those who fear him." In him kindness, truth, justice, and peace converge (vs. 11); these virtues combine to give us his salvation (vs. 14).

The gospel from Luke, 5:17–26, recounts the healing of the paralytic and contains the important revelation that Jesus has the power to forgive sins as well as to heal physical ills. The paralytic's friends bring him to Jesus because they believe in his power ("seeing their faith Jesus said . . ." (vs. 20)). What caused a strong reaction from the Pharisees was that Jesus said, "Your sins are forgiven you" (vs. 20), thereby identifying himself with God. This healing miracle thus becomes a pointed confrontation whereby Jesus asserts his identity as God and man.

The liturgy at which these texts are read is itself a continual expression of God's forgiveness. Our hearts are disposed to the Lord through hearing the word and through preaching the gospel. Through the liturgy of the eucharistic table, we feed on the body and blood of the Lord given to us "so that sins may be forgiven." Although we acknowledge our unworthiness before God, we come to receive his body and blood to be strengthened in faith, especially during Advent, as we await the full revelation of God's power when Christ will come again.

Celebration of the Eucharist

After a brief introduction about our need for the coming savior and acknowledging our sins before him, the second form of the penitential rite would be appropriate. This short, yet pointed, acknowledgment, "Lord, we have sinned against you," aptly reflects the gospel today and would be an indirect introduction to it.

For the alleluia verse, number 1 (Lect., no. 193) would be suitable: "Come and save us, Lord our God; let us see your face and we shall be saved" (from Psalm 79:4).

Among the petitions in the prayer of the faithful, mention might be made of the violence in our world that cries out for the peace of Christ, of instances of terrorism that need God's reconciling love, and of apparently hopeless situations that need God's consolation. The petition for the sick and the dying could include a reference to the cure of the paralytic in the gospel.

That the eucharistic rite itself reflects its sin-forgiving aspects should be noted from the Lord's Prayer on. In the Our Father, we pray for forgiveness and reconciliation; in the sign of peace, we demonstrate our commitment to share the peace of Christ; and in the Lamb of God, we acclaim him who takes away "the sins of the world." This combination of prayer, gesture, and sharing in the eucharistic bread and wine demonstrates the truth and effect of what we hear proclaimed in the word today.

If a more elaborate dismissal is desired, the use of the solemn Advent blessing referring to the "Redeemer who came to live with us" would subtly relate to the notion of our need for a savior to redeem us and free us from our sins. Of the prayers over the people, number 2 speaks about the protection and grace we receive from the eucharist and "health of mind and body."

Liturgy of the Hours

The first reading at the office of readings continues the proclamation from Isaiah (24:1–18), containing vivid apocalyptic imagery about the final judgment by Yahweh. The coming day of the Lord will bring devastation on those who have violated God's commandments, not turned to him in faith, or whose actions do not reflect their belief. Referring to the imagery of Genesis 1:1, the prophet states that unlike "the beginning" when ordered creation came forth from chaos, on the "day of the Lord," ordered creation will return to chaos because of covenant infidelity (vs. 5). The prophet also states that "the city of chaos, symbolic of evil," will be "broken down" (vs. 10) in contrast with Jerusalem, the city of God and the city of peace, which will endure.

Yet, Isaiah ends on a positive note. Those who proclaim the "majesty of the Lord" (vs. 14), and give glory to the Just One (vs. 16) are those who will be saved. As we turn to the Lord during this Advent season, we pray that the chaos of our lives will be reordered into the creation God intended, according to his image and likeness.

The second reading from St. John of the Cross points out that God, "by giving us, as he did, his Son, his only Word, he has in that one Word said everything. There is no need for any further revelation." It is this word that forms us into his people when we gather for liturgy and prayer. We are to fix our eyes "on him alone for in him . . . you will find more than you could ever ask for or desire." The signs and wonders of former ages have now passed away to allow their author and source to be revealed in liturgy and prayer. The responsory to the reading (from Micah 4:2 and John 4:25) aptly summarizes the insight of John of the Cross: Christ will teach us everything.

The scripture reading, Isaiah 2:3b, at morning prayer is assigned for all Advent Mondays until December 17. The antiphon to Zechariah's canticle, "The Lord proclaims: 'Repent, the kingdom of God is upon you, alleluia,' " reinforces the urgency of repentance noted in the Isaiah text at the office of readings.

The introduction to the intercessions reflects the second coming of Christ; in the petitions, we pray that until that time the church would be the instrument foretelling his coming and a sign of salvation for all peoples. As we await this coming of the Lord, we pray that here and now he would "cleanse our hearts of every vain desire."

At evening prayer, the text of Philippians 3:20b–21 is used again to remind us of the "coming of our savior, the Lord Jesus Christ."

In the antiphon to the Magnificat, we look forward to the coming of the king who, as Lord of all the earth, takes away our present slavery.

The introduction to the intercessions reminds us that Christ will come again to judge the living and the dead. But first he will come to protect us with his own divine life.

Celebration of the Hours

The same invitatory and verse before the readings presented last Monday are provided today. Choosing the one not used last week would offer appropriate variety. The use of Psalm 95 as the invitatory psalm would reflect the first reading in the office of readings about abiding by the word of the Lord.

The psalmody at the office of readings, from Psalm 31, can easily be done in one unit with the first antiphon and the psalm prayer offering fitting Advent themes.

As already noted, the well-phrased response to the text of St. John of the Cross makes it a fitting option if a response is desired.

At morning and evening prayer, it would be important to choose hymns that reflect the second coming of Christ and its cosmic dimensions.

For the scripture readings at these hours, reference should be made to last week's suggestions. At both morning and evening prayer, the optional response to the petitions is "Come, Lord Jesus," which would fittingly reflect the Advent season.

At both hours, the introduction to the Lord's Prayer could emphasize our watching and waiting for the coming of the Lord.

If petitions are added to the intercessions at evening prayer, the balance and imagery used in the proposed texts should be imitated.

Reflection—"Two Sides of Advent"

Sometimes we experience dread in the face of violence, discord, and terrorism. We shudder at the apparent hopelessness of it all, and we wonder how God can allow this to happen. More personally, when we experience the loss of a loved one in death at an untimely age or when we ourselves endure a lingering illness, we sometimes wonder where a loving God can be in all of this. Today's texts tell us that it is when we are most in need, when things seem hopeless, that we come to know the many, and sometimes indirect ways that God is present with us. When we feel hopeless and helpless, in a world that seems fixed on perdition and self-destruction, Isaiah tells us that we ought turn to God and in him find hope and strength.

Also paradoxical is that we have to go through deserts in this life and through rough times to make us aware of the solace which Christ gives and that he came to reveal as Emmanuel. When we admit the dryness of our prayer, or the wasteland of our meditation, it may well be that these are the very means that God is using to make us hunger and thirst for him all the more. It is to the Lord who makes deserts lush and arid land fertile that we are to turn in Advent.

TUESDAY OF THE SECOND WEEK OF ADVENT

Liturgical Context

Today's first reading at the eucharist from the book of Isaiah is from a section commentators call the "Book of Consolation." When compared with other Isaian texts that have been proclaimed at mass during Advent, this text reflects a changed situation for the chosen people and a changed style reflective of the poetry of the psalms. Repetition of words and key concepts provides a more image-filled language that evokes as much as it informs. Such a style coincides well with Advent—a season of images, glimpses, and fore-shadowings.

Liturgy of the Eucharist

All the chants and prayers in today's Mass formula were used last Tuesday, except for the opening prayer which is taken from the Leonine Sacramentary. This text reflects the theology of Advent as it speaks about the salvation proclaimed to the ends of the earth (prophesied in Advent and celebrated especially at Epiphany) and the glory of the Lord's birth among us (commemorated at Christmas).

Today's first reading from Isaiah (40:1–11) is also read on the Second Advent Sunday in the "B" cycle (see above for commentary). The Lord who "comes with power" (vs. 10) is the same Lord who is also imaged as a shepherd tenderly leading his flock (vs. 11). The shepherd image provides a clear link between this reading and today's gospel from Matthew, (18:12–14), which speaks of the Lord's infinite compassion and mercy exemplified in the shepherd leaving ninety-nine in search of a single lost sheep. When seen in its wider context (vss. 10–14), however, this text challenges us to care for each other as Christ shepherds us.

A verse from the first reading is used as the response to Psalm 96: "The Lord our God comes in strength" (Is 40:9–10). The Lord for whom we wait in Advent is both the Lord of all creation and a helpless child, a mighty Lord clothed in the garments of salvation and an infant wrapped in swaddling clothes. It is to him that we sing a new song (vs. 1) and his salvation that we acclaim day after day (vs. 2). It is this Lord who will "rule the world with justice" (vs. 13).

Celebration of the Eucharist

After a brief comment to introduce the liturgy, it would be well to use the third form of the penitential rite with the second set of invocations of Christ (who "will come with salvation for his people") to prepare the assembly for the readings which speak so clearly of the comfort we receive from God and his assured salvation.

The use of number 4 of the alleluia verses (Lect., no. 193) would be appropriate since it is taken from Isaiah, 40:9–10 ("raise your voice and tell the good news: the Lord our God comes in strength"). (Generally speaking, the alleluia verse should not reflect the first reading, yet the close association today between this particular verse and the message of the gospel makes it an appropriate choice.)

Among the intercessions today, there could be a petition for Jewish believers, that they might experience the presence of God in their midst; for those marginal to the church, that they might feel welcomed by their fellow Christians; for the church, that it may always be a sign of Christ's compassion; and for the sick and dying, that they may experience God's presence with them in their need.

To introduce the Lord's Prayer, the first invitation stating that we pray "with confidence to the Father" would reflect the way God is imaged in today's scripture readings.

A brief introduction to the sign of peace could stress its meaning as a sign of God's love for us and our sharing that love with each other.

If additional invocations are used at the Lamb of God, the titles of Jesus as Good Shepherd, Mighty God, and Sovereign Lord would reflect today's readings.

Liturgy of the Hours

Today's reading from Isaiah (24:19–25:5) parallels yesterday's by describing the devastation wrought against unfaithful Israel (vss. 19–23) and offers a hymn of praise of Yahweh's victory over evil that will take place for the chosen in the reign of the Messiah (25:1ff.). Israel's rebellion was so blatant that the prophet envisions that "the

Lord will punish the host of the heavens . . . and the kings of the earth" (vs. 21), thus indicating that nothing and no one will be spared his purifying destruction. When all this happens, the Lord of hosts will then reign "on Mt. Zion and in Jerusalem" (vs. 23). The cosmic imagery here and the assurance of destruction for the faithless reiterates the familiar Advent notion that divine judgment will accompany the coming of the Lord. Like Israel of old, we are summoned to a definitive decision for God in faith or suffer the consequences of faithlessness. Yet, true to biblical tradition, the Lord pictured here is not a distant, omnipotent god, uncaring or unsparing of his people. The second part of this reading recalls that the Lord who will judge will do so with mercy and compassion. Besides recalling the mighty power of the Lord, the prophet reminds us that he is a "refuge to the poor [and] to the needy in distress" (25:4).

The second reading at this hour is from the Pastoral Constitution on the Church in the Modern World (no. 48). This text affirms the eschatological nature of the church and her role as "the universal sacrament of salvation." With one eye on the needs of this world and the other on the coming of the Lord in glory, the church must be true to her vocation as sign and instrument of salvation. In this sense, she is truly the pilgrim church on earth. The response to this reading is from Philippians (3:20–21), which is a portion of the reading assigned for yesterday's evening prayer.

At morning prayer, the reading from Genesis (49:10), used last Tuesday, is repeated, as is the text of 1 Corinthians 1:7b–9 for evening prayer. The Canticle of Zechariah is preceded by an antiphon emphasizing our joy in the Lord during Advent: " 'Rejoice and be glad. . . . I will come and make my dwelling in you,' says the Lord."

At evening prayer, the coming of God Incarnate is noted in the words of John the Baptist (proclaimed as part of the gospel in all lectionary cycles last Sunday): "Prepare the way of the Lord; make straight the path of God." Hence, even in this first part of the season, the liturgy subtly reflects both incarnational and eschatological themes.

At morning prayer, the intercessions reflect the theme of the coming of light in Christ in the introduction as well as in the first and third petitions (the latter noting the baptized who have been enlightened through this sacrament). Because of the obvious darkness of this time of year, the Advent liturgy uses the theme of waiting for the light of Christ to dawn at Christmas.

At evening prayer, we are invited to pray to Christ, "our Lord and Redeemer, who will appear . . . on the last day," a phrase clearly reflecting Advent theology. The first petition indicates how we participate in the mystery of the incarnation and thus share in Christ's divine life. The third petition characterizes our lives as lived by faith on earth until we share in glory in the kingdom of heaven.

Celebration of the Hours

Since both the regular Advent invitatory and today's verse before the readings were proposed last Tuesday for celebration, the one not chosen then should be used to begin the office today. The use of Psalm 24 as the invitatory psalm would be appropriate because it reflects our coming into the Lord's presence (vs. 3) whom we acclaim as the "king of glory" (vs. 10).

Since the psalmody for this hour is from Psalm 37, singing or reciting it as one unit with one antiphon and an adapted psalm prayer at its end would allow for a more significant period of silence before and between the readings. The responsory from Philippians (3:20–21) after the second reading helps to emphasize the biblical foundation for this teaching and reinforces the important Advent theme about the end of time.

At both morning and evening prayer, the choice of a hymn oriented toward Christ's second coming would be appropriate. The options for the readings at morning and evening prayer offered last week should be consulted. The fact that a text has already been used should not mean that it ought not be repeated. The liturgy itself encourages certain repetitions so that the many layers of meaning from one text can be uncovered and pondered.

At both morning and evening prayer, additions to the intercessions should be based on the helpful structure provided.

A sung Lord's Prayer today introduced by the simple phrase, "Let us pray for the coming of the kingdom," would suitably yet subtly emphasize our longing for the second coming.

Reflection—"Affirmation Not Endorsement"

A basic principle of healthy relationships (whether "working" or familial) is that we should praise or encourage others while at the same time we must correct or criticize them. Thus, the criticism is not preceived as a condemnation. Affirming another makes it easier for that person to "hear" our negative statement, to evaluate it, and then to act on it.

Today's first reading at Mass shows Isaiah comforting Israel, and in the gospel Jesus himself is pictured as the Lord who seeks out the lost to care for them.

However, in neither case is "affirmation" to be understood as "endorsement" of the *status quo*. Both Isaiah and Jesus affirm as they challenge and spur their hearers to greater fidelity to God and his ways. As the church continues the work of Jesus in our day, it stands ready to welcome those who have strayed. Yet, it cannot endorse patterns of life or ways of thinking incompatible with its nature. Today's message of comfort from Isaiah carries with it the challenge to be prepared for the Lord's coming. The example of Jesus calls the lost to rely on him for reconciliation, not an endorsement of prior wandering (and apparently faithlessness).

WEDNESDAY OF THE SECOND WEEK OF ADVENT

Liturgical Context

Beginning tomorrow, the weekday readings at the eucharist emphasize the preaching and ministry of John the Baptist. Therefore, in appreciating and celebrating the liturgy today, the eschatological features of the season and the import of the Isaian text should be underscored.

Liturgy of the Eucharist

Except for the opening prayer, today's chants and prayers are the same ones used last Wednesday. In the opening prayer, we acknowledge the incarnational aspect of Advent by stating that "we await the healing power of Christ your Son." Yet there is also a subtle reference here to the final coming of Christ. In citing "his coming," the Latin text speaks about our receiving grace from heaven to sustain us now as we look forward to that final day.

Today's first reading, Isaiah 40:25–31, continues the proclamation of Isaiah 40 begun yesterday. Here, second Isaiah emphasizes a dominant theme in his teaching—we believe in the Lord of creation and the Lord of history. The God "who has created all things" (vs.

26) is also the God who sustains all that he has made. This "eternal God" "gives strength to the fainting" (vs. 29). Some may well grow weary on their way to God (in fact each of us does at times), but the prophet assures us that "They that hope in the Lord will renew their strength" (vs. 31). The Advent virtue of hope is thus given a biblical orientation and focus.

Psalm 103, used as the responsorial psalm, is a hymn acknowledging this Lord whose grace and mercy extend to us now when he "pardons all your iniquities, [and] heals all your ills" (vs. 3). He alone can redeem us from destruction; his mercy and graciousness endure forever (vss. 4, 8). We can exclaim with the psalmist: "Merciful and gracious is the Lord, slow to anger and abounding in kindness" (vs. 8).

The brief gospel from Matthew (11:28–30) is an example of a text chosen to reflect the first reading. The comfort motif of Isaiah 40 is carried through in the liturgy's use of this section of Matthew (verses 25–30 are assigned as an option for masses for the dead). We are invited to come to the Lord, all of us who are "weary and find life burdensome" (vs. 28). Jesus assures us that he will refresh us for he is gentle and humble of heart (vss. 28–29). Even though we might experience difficulty in accepting the burden of living his gospel, the text assures us that his yoke is "easy" and his burden is light (vs. 30). This reading offers us another example of the way the Lord comes to us—both to challenge and to comfort, especially during Advent.

Celebration of the Eucharist

The introduction to the liturgy could mention the Lord's gentleness and compassion; then the third form of the penitential rite could be used with adapted invocations such as: "you are the Lord of all creation," "you call your people to more abundant life in you," and "you are gentle and humble of heart." A sung *Kyrie* to accompany the invocations would help set a prayerful tone for the liturgy.

For the alleluia verse, number 10 (Lect., no. 193) about the Lord's bringing us his peace would be an appropriate introduction to the gospel.

Among the intercessions, the needs of those (noted yesterday) who are estranged from the church or who have grown weary in professing the faith could be reiterated. Also, a prayer for peace in the Middle East would reflect a present concern about the land that was once home for Jesus' first followers.

To introduce the Lord's Prayer with the first invitation ("Let us pray with confidence") or a variation on this theme would recall the message of both readings today.

Since, by coincidence, the communion antiphon is from Isaiah (40:10), using it as a refrain to a communion psalm (for example, Psalm 23) would help bring out the central meaning of this chapter of Isaiah read yesterday and today.

The use of number 24 of the prayers over the people indirectly reflects the gospel and thus would be an appropriate conclusion to the liturgy.

Liturgy of the Hours

Today's first reading at the office of readings, Isaiah 25:6–26:6, has already been commented upon above (in two sections at the eucharist on Wednesday and Thursday last week). It reflects what have come to be Advent attitudes of hope and patience as we wait for the final coming of Christ.

The second reading from St. Augustine's discourse on the Psalms relates them to Christ, specifically to the themes of incarnation and redemption. While the paschal mystery will receive greater emphasis in the Christmas season, Augustine reminds us that as we commemorate God's Son taking flesh as one of us, we also commemorate his passage from this life through death and his glorious resurrection. St. Augustine states: "It was not enough for God to make his Son our guide to the way; he made him the way itself, that you might travel with him as leader, and by him as the way."

At morning and evening prayer, the scripture texts assigned for Advent Wednesdays recur. The Canticle of Zechariah is introduced by an antiphon emphasizing the Davidic descent of the Lord. At evening prayer, the antiphon to Mary's canticle also uses Old Testament imagery when it assures Zion that the promised Just One will come to those who await him.

The intercessions at morning prayer are introduced by a reference to the Lord "who came among us in his mercy" on the basis of which we now pray. Familiar Advent notions abound in the petitions about the Lord who came among us and will come again; and about his leading us into light so that we can witness to his justice in the world.

At evening prayer, the intercessions use familiar titles for the Lord that recall his paschal mystery. We pray to the "Lord," and to the "Lamb of God" who "came to recover what was lost," and to "take away the sin of the world."

Celebration of the Hours

Because Psalm 100 shows our relationship to the Lord as his people (vs. 5), it would be a good choice as the invitatory psalm; it fits well with either the Advent invitatory or the verse before the readings.

The first two sections of psalmody at the office of readings are from Psalm 39. Fittingly, they are introduced by an antiphon that uses 2 Corinthians 5:2 as its source: "We groan in pain as we await the redemption of our bodies."

The psalm prayer that follows Psalm 52 could be understood to refer to the separation of the good and evil at the end of the world (symbolized here by the separation of the fruitful and the unfruitful).

At morning and evening prayer, the scripture readings could well be adjusted as noted above for last Wednesday.

The text of the second petition at morning prayer could be rewritten to make its meaning clearer as an Advent text.

Since various titles of Jesus are used in the intercessions at evening prayer, other titles should be used in any additional petitions.

Since today marks the last day of a predominantly eschatological period of Advent, it would be fitting to conclude these hours of prayer with an invitation to the Lord's Prayer that mentions the coming of the kingdom and the use of either number 1 or 16 of the prayers over the people as the dismissal.

Reflection—"Come, Lord Jesus"

A frequent response to the intercessions in Advent is "Come, Lord Jesus." This same plea also marks many of the prayers of the Advent liturgy. When we make this appeal, we affirm the absolute priority of God's kingdom in our lives through Christ's incarnation and redemption. Often, we cry out, "Come, Lord Jesus," in times of personal crisis and despair. This plea becomes a prayer of hope and trust in the Lord's presence.

Yet, how willingly do we pray, "Come, Lord Jesus," when things are going well? Or, to use the imagery of the gospel, when our grain bins are full?

It is precisely when we think things are going the way we want them to go and when we feel that everything is under control that we forget to pray to the Lord. If we cry out for God only when we need him to relieve a burden, how true is our commitment to prepare for the coming of his kingdom?

THURSDAY OF THE SECOND WEEK OF ADVENT

Liturgical Context

Today marks the second phase of Advent weekdays as described in the Introduction to the Lectionary for Mass:

"On Thursday of the second week the readings of the gospel about John the Baptist begin. The first reading is either a continuation of Isaiah or a text chosen in view of the gospel." (no. 94)

This emphasis on John coincides with the second and third Advent Sundays. However, unlike the Sundays which emphasize his preaching and baptizing for repentance, the weekday texts emphasize John as witness, model believer, and the last of the prophets to prepare the way of the Lord. Thus, it is John's integrity and example that is stressed on these weekdays.

Liturgy of the Eucharist

Except for the opening prayer, the antiphons and prayers assigned for the eucharist today were all used last Thursday (and will be used next week if December 17 does not precede). The opening prayer has a certain urgency (reflected more strongly in its Latin original) as we ask the Father to give us his love to help us "prepare the way" for his Son. The deeds we do "to serve [God] and one another" show our openness to receive Christ as he comes to us in each other, especially in the poor and needy.

It is significant that the first Advent preface is still assigned for proclamation until December 17 even though the second explicitly mentions John. This first text clearly emphasizes the eschatological aspects of the season and our preparation for Christ to come in judgment. John's preaching prepares us for the coming of Christ in human flesh, and it urges us to evaluate how prepared we will be to welcome him when he comes at death and in glory at the end of time.

Today's first reading from second Isaiah (41:13–20) speaks about God's direct intervention on behalf of his people despite their unfaithfulness. Israel is told not to fear (vs. 13) since her "redeemer is the Holy One of Israel" (vs. 14). However, God's concern for his people did not mean that they could abuse his mercy. The terms "worm Jacob" and "maggot Israel" (vs. 14) indicate that, in fact, they were not always faithful to their Lord. Second Isaiah urges them to rely on the Lord, especially now that they are in turmoil. He assures them of God's abiding presence (vss. 13–16) and describes how powerful he is (vss. 17–20). He is able to overturn conventional expectations: the needy become the privileged (vs. 17), deserts become marshlands (vs. 18), and parched land becomes a spring of water (vs. 18). The prophet thus urges us to admit our need for God this Advent, to acknowledge the dry and arid parts of our lives that need the saving spring of Christ's life and love.

The response to Psalm 145 reiterates that "the Lord is kind and merciful, slow to anger, and rich in compassion" (vs. 8). We gather to "bless [his] name forever and ever" (vs. 1), since his kingdom is for all ages (vs. 13). The Lord we worship "is good to all and compassionate toward all his works" (vs. 9).

In the gospel, Matthew 11:11–15, Jesus states that John the Baptizer is to be exalted far beyond any other "man born of woman" (vs. 11) because of the way he witnessed to the coming of God in our midst. However, Jesus quickly adds that "the least born into the kingdom of God is greater than [John]" (vs. 11). Real status, dignity, and preeminence come about because of fidelity to the demands of the kingdom of God, not because of human generation or lineage. Greatness now is measured by fidelity to the kingdom's demands. Being faithful to the word leads us to the joys of the kingdom, where the least is greater than anyone on earth, even John the Baptist.

Celebration of the Eucharist

The introduction to the liturgy could speak about being faithful to the Word of God as John was in preaching and ultimately by suffering for the sake of the Word. The use of the second set of sample invocations for the third penitential rite would reiterate the Advent notions of the three comings of Christ, especially to us in the liturgy in "word and sacrament to strengthen us in holiness."

For the alleluia verse, number 14 (Lect., no. 193) about the Lord coming "to save his people; happy are those prepared to meet him" coincides well with our receiving the word in faith and then sharing in the kingdom of God.

Appropriate petitions today would be for those who witness the kingdom of God by caring for the poor, for those who have grown weary of responding to the Lord's word, and for the deceased who heard the word of God on earth that they may experience the fullness of God's presence in the kingdom.

The fourth introduction to the Lord's Prayer would coincide with the emphasis on the kingdom in the gospel. A fitting conclusion to the liturgy would be number 24 of the prayers over the people, in which we pray for protection from all harm, that we may never offend the Lord and may seek him in all that we do.

Liturgy of the Hours

The first reading at the office of readings from Isaiah (26:7–21) continues the eschatological reflection begun yesterday. It is to the Lord's ways and his judgments that we look (vs. 8). In faith, we can make the prophet's plea our own: "My soul yearns for you in the night . . . when your judgment dawns upon the earth, the world's inhabitants learn justice" (vs. 9). We ought not to presume on a sustained divine generosity, however, because the Lord who establishes his peace on the earth requires that we respond generously and lovingly to others. This will be the criterion of our final judgment.

The second reading from St. Peter Chrysologus offers a useful reflection on main figures of salvation history: Noah, Abraham, Jacob, and Moses. As we journey through Advent, we need to be reminded of "the flame of divine love" that was "enkindled" in their hearts by God's affection—a love that we yearn for as we await the coming of the Lord. Once we have tasted his love, we want it to take over our lives as it did the lives of these forefathers in the faith.

Thursday of the Second Week of Advent　　75

At morning prayer, the scripture reading from Isaiah (45:8) is presented (as it was last Thursday). This verse is also used as the traditional (and presently used) entrance antiphon on the Fourth Sunday of Advent.

The antiphon to the Canticle of Zechariah refers to the presence of God as the author of all that we do: "I will help you, says the Lord. . . . I am your Savior, the Holy One of Israel."

The intercessions begin with a reference to God "who sent his Son to save mankind," an indication of our need for divine help. In the petitions, we pray for the virtue of integrity (first), that we may hope in the Lord who will come in glory (fourth).

At evening prayer, the reading from James (5:7–8, 9b) is repeated from last Thursday.

The antiphon to the Magnificat uses the words of John the Baptist, "The one who is coming after me existed before me; I am not worthy to untie his sandals." This text clearly reflects the shift in the liturgy toward emphasizing the ministry of John. It also reminds us of John's humility.

The second petition refers to the incarnation of Jesus, which makes us brothers and sisters, and asks that we do not become "estranged" from him. The third petition prays that the Lord not judge harshly those he redeemed at great cost.

Celebration of the Hours

The Advent invitatory or the verse before the readings, "hear the word of the Lord . . . proclaim it to the ends of the earth," would be fitting introductions to the hours today, especially when combined with Psalm 95.

At the office of readings, Psalm 44 is presented in three sections; reciting it as a unit with any one of the proposed antiphons at beginning and end would be an option. The third antiphon, "Rise up, O Lord, and save us, for you are merciful," is particularly appropriate since it reflects the theme of the psalm and our situation in Advent, waiting for Christ the Savior.

At morning prayer, both psalm prayers could be rewritten to draw out more clearly the implications of the Advent season. The suggestions made last Thursday for the scripture readings should be recalled today. Further, at morning prayer, the petitions could be expanded to speak of the particular needs of the community as we await the coming Savior. A sung *Kyrie, eleison* as the response (with a simple, haunting tone) would help emphasize our longing for God.

At evening prayer, the antiphons effectively set up the text by referring to "light" and "salvation."

The psalm prayer at its conclusion could be adjusted to speak more effectively of the Advent mystery and our longing for the fullness of light and salvation in Christ.

Among the intercessions presented, the last two could be reworded to deal more explicitly with Advent. The use of the optional response, "Come, Lord Jesus," would be appropriate.

Reflection—"Unprecedented Self-Effacement"

John the Baptist stands as a model of unprecedented self-effacement before God. Aware of the importance of his ministry and of the urgency of his mission to all Israel, John humbly stands aside when the Lord comes. As important as was his ministry, John was fully aware that he was not the Messiah. As important as was his preaching, it was the word of the Lord that really mattered. As significant as was baptism by John, it was the water bath in the Holy Spirit that would lead to salvation. John, this last and specially chosen prophet, leads us by word and example to realize that we too must be self-effacing before the Lord.

John's example functions as a most important Advent model for us, especially as we prepare for the coming holidays. There are cards to send, gifts to purchase, food to prepare, family to please, and neighbors to greet. But, in all this, we ought to remember why we do it—out of love for others and to spread the peace of Christ, the true gift of Christmas. We are to incarnate Jesus' love in our daily lives among those we love and especially among those who do not love us.

FRIDAY OF THE SECOND WEEK OF ADVENT

Liturgical Context

The scripture readings at today's eucharist continue according to the plan determined for this part of Advent: the gospel is about John the Baptist and the first reading complements it. The liturgy today invites reflection on the many facets of God's saving work among us—in the past, in the present, and still to come.

Liturgy of the Eucharist

The opening prayer today is the only text not used in last Friday's Mass formula. The Latin text, from the old Gelasian Sacramentary, asks God that we, his people, who await the coming of his only-begotten Son with the greatest vigilance, may hasten to meet him with lighted torches in expectation of his approaching salvation. The reference to torches recalls the imagery found in the parable of the wise and foolish virgins who carried torches to welcome the bridegroom (Mt 25:1–13). Watchfulness and preparedness for Christ's coming are the themes of this short Advent prayer.

The brief first reading, Isaiah 48:17–19, deals with the commands and ways of the Lord. The Lord reveals what is for our good and leads us along the paths we should travel (vs. 17). Once again, God's initiative is stressed here both in revealing his commands and in helping his followers to observe them. Using a traditional formula, the prophet speaks about the promised result: "If you would hearken to my commandments, your prosperity would be like a river, and your vindication like the waves of the sea" (vs. 18). In elaborating on the results of observing the law, Isaiah refers to the Abraham cycle in Genesis when he states, "Your descendants would be like the sands and those born to your stock like its grains" (vs. 19). Like Abraham and all those with whom God initiated and sustained the covenant relationship, we are invited to renew our commitment to the Lord, especially during this season of Advent.

The responsorial psalm, Psalm 1, takes up these important themes when it uses the text "Those who follow you, Lord, will have the light of life" (Jn 8:12) as its refrain. We are given a choice of living according to the Lord's ways or not. The blessed are those who delight in the law of the Lord and meditate on it day and night (vs. 2). The wicked, on the other hand, "are like chaff which the wind drives away" (vs. 4). "For the Lord watches over the way of the just, but the way of the wicked vanishes" (vs. 6).

Today's gospel, Matthew 11:16–19, continues the section of Matthew begun yesterday. John the Baptizer criticizes his contemporaries who spend their time playing and singing rather than being attentive to the Messiah in their midst (vs. 16). They were not active resisters; they passively and blithely let the revelation of the Lord pass them by. Such types criticize holiness in whatever guise it appears. John fasted, Jesus ate and drank, yet neither could please or persuade "this breed" to follow the ways of God (vss. 18–19).

When proclaimed for our reflection in Advent, this text challenges us to obey the commands of Jesus and to prepare for his coming. Even though fast and abstinence no longer bind under sin on Fridays, these might be appropriate ways to concretize our preparation for Christ's coming.

Celebration of the Eucharist

The introduction to the liturgy could emphasize John's exemplary behavior despite the reaction of his contemporaries. Such an example should serve for us as we seek to deepen our Advent preparation despite cultural expectations to the contrary. The use of the "I confess" formula would be one way of acknowledging that we have not always chosen the Lord's ways ("in what I have done and in what I have failed to do"). It is appropriate to stress the penitential rite on Friday, the traditional day of penance and reflection on Christ's passion. A sung "Lord have mercy" would help set a prayerful tone for this Advent liturgy.

The use of number 13 of the Advent alleluias (Lect., no. 193) with its invitation to "go out to meet him" recalls the opening prayer's petition that God would help us hasten to meet his Son with torches burning.

Among the petitions, one could refer to the Jewish people and their faith response to the covenant. Another could refer to those faced with the dilemma of serious moral choices. Another could mention our need for greater integrity of life.

Liturgy of the Hours

The first reading at the office of readings from Isaiah (27:1–13) returns to the vineyard imagery of Isaiah 5:1–7 (used on Wednesday of the first week of Advent). This vineyard, identified with God's chosen (vs. 6), is cared for by the Lord who calls himself "its keeper" (vs. 3); "lest anyone harm it, night and day I guard it." Yet, being a part of God's chosen is no guarantee of salvation. The good will be separated from the bad (vs. 13). There are obvious parallels for this text in the New Testament, the clearest of which is Matthew 25 used as the gospel on the solemnity of Christ the King ("A" cycle), the Sunday before Advent begins. Isaiah tells us that a "trumpet shall blow" (vs. 13) to gather the elect on the day of the Lord. This text also serves as background for Paul's texts about the end times (1 Thes 4:16, 1 Cor 15:52). Fittingly, a verse from Matthew (24:31) is used as the responsory depicting Jesus gathering the chosen from the four winds. This text reiterates much of the eschatological-judgment theme which began this Advent. However, it also recalls that the Lord cares for and sustains us who have been grafted into Christ, the true vine.

The second reading from St. Ireaneus compares and contrasts the old and new covenants, especially as they are personified in Eve and Mary. By using texts from Genesis and St. Paul (especially), the author offers a masterful synthesis of our need for a savior and of Mary's role in redemption. We inherit estrangement from God through Adam; through Christ, the second Adam, we are reunited with the Father.

At morning prayer, the reading from Jeremiah (30:21–22), assigned for last Friday, is repeated. The antiphon to Zechariah's canticle encourages our application and attention to Advent when it says: "Say to the fainthearted take courage! The Lord our God is coming to save us."

The notion of needing to be saved is implied in the introduction to the intercessions which states that we cry out with joy "to Christ, our Redeemer, who comes to save us from our sins." Both Advent themes of incarnation and eschatology are reflected in the petitions.

At evening prayer, the scripture reading (2 Peter 3:8b–9) is the same as the one assigned for last Friday.

The theme of rejoicing in hope characterizes the antiphon to Mary's canticle: "Rejoicing you shall draw water from the well springs of the Savior."

The title "Redeemer" is used again to introduce the intercessions, but this time it is specified that he "came to bring good news to the poor." Some of the proposed petitions refer to the incarnation of Jesus as the basis for asking that God act for us now (third), and to Christ's second coming which will bring eternal life to those who have died (fifth).

Celebration of the Hours

Since Friday is traditionally a day for more serious reflection on the passion, it might be appropriate to use Psalm 24 as the invitatory psalm today. It speaks about the Lord's entry into the temple to which only those without sin will be admitted. Christ's act of redemption has forgiven the sins of those who believe in him. The use of the verse before the readings, "Let your compassion come upon me, O Lord—Your salvation, true to your promise," would be an appropriate invitatory verse since it refers to our need for the coming Messiah.

Psalm 38 is assigned as the psalmody at the office of readings. It can conveniently be recited/sung as one unit with any of the antiphons offered. The psalm prayer reflects the nature of Friday as a day to commemorate the paschal death of Christ, an aspect that should not be neglected even though this text be edited for celebration.

At both morning and evening prayer, a general Advent hymn, noting the cosmic and eschatological themes of the season, would be appropriate. The psalm prayers offered at both hours are especially suited to Advent themes and might well be used as given. The one exception would be to eliminate the reference to the eucharist in the second prayer at morning prayer since the liturgy of the hours is a separate cycle and to note the eucharist here is out of place. The use of the optional response to the petitions, "Come, Lord Jesus" (especially if sung), would add to the prayerfulness of these hours. The Lord's Prayer could be introduced by referring to the coming of the kingdom.

Reflection—"Expectations of God"

What is our understanding of God's role in our lives? This seems to be a relatively simple question, and we can readily reply: "to save us," "to redeem us," "to love us," "to care for us," and "to be with us." The God we pray to in Advent and whom we ask to come into our lives is Savior, Redeemer, Incarnate Son, Only-begotten, and Emmanuel. But, does this get to the point of the question? Even knowing and using these titles does not automatically mean that we really want God to intervene in our lives because we know that when he does, he often requires us to make some radical changes.

To say that we want a savior means that we must admit the sin in our lives and our need for forgiveness. To admit that we need a redeemer means that we must admit those things that weigh us down and cause us to be locked into harmful patterns of life. To admit that we need Emmanuel means that there are times when in our self-sufficiency we do not act according to God's plan for us.

When we realize our need for savior, redeemer, and Emmanuel in Advent, the liturgy requires that we not only change our interior selves, but that we show that change by the way we treat others.

SATURDAY OF THE SECOND WEEK OF ADVENT

Liturgical Context

John the Baptist's witness to the Messiah is presented for our reflection today.

Liturgy of the Eucharist

Today's opening prayer (the single substitution in this Mass formula repeated from last Saturday) is from the Leonine Sacramentary. This prayer shares with many other Advent collects notions of expectation, hope, and pleading that God would come to us. We pray that the splendor of God's glory will shine in our hearts so that "we may be revealed as the children of light" when his Son comes. We receive this light especially at Christmas, the feast noted both in this text and (more literally) in the prayer after communion.

The reading from Sirach (48:1–4, 9–11) deals with Israel's infidelity and God's fidelity. Elijah is invoked as one who worked to reestablish the tribes of Jacob. The prophet's words are likened to a "flaming furnace" (vs. 1) whose power reflects the power of God's word that shut up the heavens three times (vs. 3). The creative power of God's word in Genesis is recalled to show that the prophets who speak the word of the Lord are charged to renew and recreate God's people. Elijah's particular mission is to "put an end to wrath before the day of the Lord" (the familiar description of the eschatological times).

When proclaimed as a prelude to the gospel about John the Baptist, this text recalls the important ministry of the prophets to turn hearts and minds each year to the coming of the Messiah among us.

The use of Psalm 80 as the responsorial psalm, with the refrain, "Lord, make us turn to you, let us see your face and we shall be saved" (vs. 4), underscores our trust in God's word as active and alive among his people. We ask the Lord, "to look down from heaven, and see" (vs. 15); to "take care of this vine" (vs. 15) (an important image for Israel in the Hebrew scriptures); and to "protect what your right hand has planted" (vs. 16). We are called to be sons and daughters of God's right hand; we live that way when we turn to him in prayer and reflect his love in our lives. We beg him to give us "new life" this Advent (vs. 19).

The gospel (Mt 17:10–13) follows the description of Jesus' transfiguration. It is important to recall that Jesus is joined by Moses and Elijah at his transfiguration, figures who represent the "law and the prophets." The apostles who had experienced Jesus' transfiguration now ask him about the belief that Elijah would return as the forerunner of the Messiah. Jesus tells them, "Elijah has already come." It is then that they realize Jesus has been speaking of John the Baptizer. Jesus says that just as some people rejected Elijah and his prophetic message, so Jesus will "suffer at the hands" of those who reject him.

Recognizing John as the fulfillment of Elijah, necessarily involves change and conversion. For us to respond to the proclaimed word means to acclaim the Lord present in the liturgy and to attest to his saving presence in our lives. If we do not respond this way, we are like those who rejected Jesus as the Messiah.

Celebration of the Eucharist

The tone of this liturgy should be simple and direct both because of the nature of Advent and as a contrast to the fullness of tomorrow's liturgy. The introduction to today's liturgy could address our being drawn into the mystery of Jesus' suffering and glory in this life. Our participation in his humiliation and glorification leads to complete union with him in the kingdom.

The use of the second form of the penitential rite with the phrases "we have sinned against you," "show us your mercy and love," and "grant us your salvation" would be a simple yet appropriate acknowledgment of our need for the coming Messiah, the Savior Christ.

For the alleluia verse, number 7 (Lect., no. 193) reiterates the message of John the Baptist: "Prepare the way for the Lord, make straight his paths" (Lk 3:4).

The model Advent intercessions could be used today with additional prayers for prophets among us who call us to deeper conversion to the Lord, for ourselves that we would put aside the things that hinder us from welcoming Jesus as our Messiah, and for those who suffer physically or emotionally that they might draw strength from the Lord who suffered so that we might be redeemed.

The use of the second eucharistic prayer (because of its brevity) and the fourth invitation to the Lord's Prayer (because it refers to the coming kingdom) would be appropriate today.

Liturgy of the Hours

Today's first reading at the office of readings from Isaiah (29:1–8) reflects the crisis Israel faced during Hezekiah's reign. Jerusalem is about to be besieged and the prophet's task is twofold: to call the chosen to renewed conversion, and to remind them that the Lord will not desert them in their time of need.

The responsory, part of which is taken from Isaiah 54:4, puts it succinctly: "fear not, you shall not be put to shame; for the Lord of hosts will visit you."

The second reading from Blessed Isaac of Stella (a twelfth-century Cistercian abbot) is a reflection on the place of both Mary and the church in the work of redemption, and thus emphasizes the incarnational aspect of Advent. The responsory draws out the new covenant implications of the formula "I shall be your God and you will be my people" (Lv 26:11–12) by adding the important text from St. Paul "you are the temple of God" (2 Cor 6:16).

The scripture reading at morning prayer from Isaiah (11:1–3a) is the same as last Saturday's. The antiphon to the Canticle of Zechariah points to the coming of the Lord at the end of time: "The Lord will set up his standard in the sight of all the nations, and gather to himself the dispersed of Israel." This is a particularly helpful antiphon for a canticle that speaks of the renewal of the covenant in the coming Messiah. It was because he assumed our human condition and appeared in human flesh that all nations now share in the relationship with God that was once unique to Israel. The remnant of Israel, so often spoken about in Isaiah, will share in the fullness of the Lord's promises.

The introduction to the intercessions and three petitions recall the second coming of the Redeemer, "who will come again in glory with great power." The Lord Jesus is hailed as "the good news for mankind." Jesus Christ *is* the gospel.

Celebration of the Hours

The verse before the readings would be an appropriate invitatory today since it reflects the important place of the word through which we come to know God. Psalm 100 would be a fitting invitatory since it is joyful and reflects our relatedness to God (vs. 3).

The significant text of Psalm 106 is prayed at the office of readings and may be recited or sung as one unit. The use of the first antiphon with it would be particularly appropriate at this Advent time since it asks the Lord to come with his "saving help."

It should be recalled that the use of psalm prayers is optional. Not to use them at morning prayer would allow more time for silent reflection between the psalms.

The use of the optional response to the petitions would be fitting.

Because the intercessions sustain the Advent emphasis on waiting for the second coming, any additional petitions should be composed according to the pattern proposed.

Reflection—"From Incarnation to Redemption"

Even though the creche tradition did not start until the thirteenth century (usually accredited to St. Francis of Assisi), it has taken firm hold. This tradition emphasizes the reality of Christ's human birth among us, and so the creche contributes to our appreciation of what it means when we say that the Word became flesh.

However, it must be remembered that the central mystery of faith is paschal. Christ took on human form in order to suffer, die, and rise to glory with the Father. The gospel today reminds us that the Son of Man had to suffer and so enter into a glory that is previewed in the transfiguration. There can be no salvation without the dying and rising of Christ. There can be no resurrection without humiliation, passion, and death. There can be no passion and death without the coming of Jesus in human form.

Even as creches begin to appear again this year and as we send and receive Christmas cards depicting the human birth of Jesus, we ought to bear in mind that the incarnation feast leads to the paschal victory.

Third Week of Advent

THIRD SUNDAY OF ADVENT

Liturgical Context

Popular piety, influenced by medieval trappings (e.g., rose-colored vestments) tended to emphasize the uniqueness of this Sunday as a day for rejoicing in an otherwise heavily penitential season. The present liturgy, however, emphasizes continuity during the Advent Sundays of "devout and joyful expectation" by making today's readings complement last week's about John the Baptist and by making the use of rose-colored vesture optional.

However, certain elements of today's liturgy remain from the former Roman usage, for example, the entrance and communion antiphons about "rejoicing" and looking forward to the coming salvation. These indicate that there is a certain heightened expectation today which carries through until Christmas. Thus, today's liturgy builds toward Christmas by emphasizing the ministry of John the Baptist as the one who prepared the way for the Lord.

Cycle "A"

Today's first reading from Isaiah (35:1–6, 10), proclaimed at the eucharist last Monday (see above for commentary), expresses in familiar scriptural imagery God's glory reflected in nature and his power in the lives of his chosen. Isaiah tells how the Lord's glory will be shown as he comes in power to heal the blind, the lame, the deaf, and the dumb. This text invites us to reflect on our need for the saving grace and power of Christ to change our lives.

Psalm 146, today's response, was also used last Monday with the slightly different refrain: "Our God will come to save us." Today's more urgent text, "Lord, come and save us" (vs. 4), indicates that the coming of the savior is drawing ever nearer, not only at Christmas, but at the end of time.

Part of the second reading from the letter of James (5:7–10) is used as the scripture reading at evening prayer on the Thursdays of Advent. When understood in its original context, this passage refers to people who are dealt with unjustly by the dominating rich. Because of this unfortunate, but unalterable circumstance, James urges his followers to see in the prophets "models of suffering hardships" (vs. 10). Even though this community experienced rejection for speaking "the word of the Lord," James urges them to persevere in the ways of the Lord.

Using agrarian imagery, James stresses patience as an essential virtue. The farmer knows that the dormancy and stillness of winter must occur if planted crops or perennials are to bud forth in spring. When the earth is frozen cold and the land is barren, the farmer must wait patiently for days of longer sunlight to make the soil tillable and the rains of spring to make the crops grow. As sure as they are that winter will flow into spring (vs. 7), so must they (and we) be patient for the Lord's coming (vs. 8). Yet, even this time of expectation requires a response from us. James maintains that the sign of the truly expectant community is the patience it shows to each other (vs. 9). This exhortation sharpens what is woven through the whole Advent liturgy—we are part of a remnant people who long to see the fullness of the Lord and yet who are to manifest in this time and place the love that is already incarnate in him.

The alleluia verse used today is found in all three lectionary cycles and is taken from the opening verse of the first reading in the "B" cycle (Is 61:1), which text is found in the gospel in the "C" cycle.

The gospel from Matthew (11:2–11) recounts John's question whether Jesus is the expected One and Jesus' statements to the crowd about John. Jesus avoids a direct answer; instead, he summarizes much of what the prophet Isaiah proclaimed (see today's first reading). This text would have been well known among John's contemporaries and it would assure them that indeed Jesus was the "long-expected" One.

The outcasts whom Isaiah says will one day be exalted are mentioned as those cured by Jesus—the blind see, cripples walk, lepers are cleansed, the deaf hear, the dead are raised to life, and the poor have the good news preached to them (vs. 5). But, even physical well being and health will pale when compared with the saving news proclaimed and actualized in Jesus. As the Messiah, Jesus is

God's presence to his people and offers salvation in the Father's name for the forgiveness of sins. Just as those in Isaiah's time had to wait and trust that the Lord would deliver them (exemplified in physical infirmity), so we who live in the present age must wait and trust that the Lord will indeed "come again" to take us to his kingdom forever. By indirectly answering John's question about his identity, Jesus indicates the depth of his saving mission (beyond physical healing) and he shows that it is his saving word that will both challenge and guide us until his kingdom comes in its fullness.

In the second part of the text (vs. 7–11), Jesus describes John as the messenger who prepares the way of the Lord. This text is taken from Malachi (3:1) and was used by Mark in last Sunday's gospel ("B" cycle) to emphasize John's role as the last and definitive prophetic voice preparing for the Messiah. Jesus states forcefully: "I assure you history has not known a man born of woman greater than John the Baptizer" (vs. 10). Yet, the concluding verse (vs. 11) contrasts John's greatness with the greatness of those who experience the fullness of the kingdom of God. Jesus maintains that as important as is human life, our allotted span of years to live and love on earth pales in comparison with being called to the kingdom for all eternity. In that kingdom, there will be no more sick or well, maimed or agile, poor or rich, blind or seeing, deaf or hearing, lepers or cleansed, marginal or mainstream. There will only be one community gathered in the name of the Lord whose Lordship all will share. It is this kingdom for which we long and whose final coming we invite in our Advent prayer.

Cycle "B"

Isaiah 61 (from which verses 1–2, 10–11 are used as today's first reading) is used a number of times in the reformed liturgy: as the first reading at the Chrism Mass on Holy Thursday (vss. 1–3, 6, 8–9), as an option for confirmation (same verses), as an option for the common of the Blessed Virgin, the common of the consecration of virgins and the religious profession (vss. 9–11), and in the Christmas-Epiphany cycle as the first reading in the office of readings on the Monday between Epiphany and the Baptism of the Lord (vss. 1–11). Originally spoken as an oracle about the restoration of Zion, this text was used by Luke (4:18ff.) to refer to Jesus, a usage often found in the liturgy. Today's liturgy emphasizes the eschatological importance of this text as we look forward to the "year of favor from the Lord" and the "day of vindication" (vs. 2). The Spirit-inspired mission of announcing good news to the lowly, healing the broken-hearted, and offering liberty to captives (vs. 1) is reflected in the fourth eucharistic prayer:

"To the poor he proclaimed the good news of salvation,
to prisoners freedom,
and to those in sorrow, joy."

What is particularly instructive about this text is that it joins these manifestations of the coming kingdom with the kingdom's universality and its nuptial imagery. The prophet states that "justice and praise [will] spring up before all the nations" (vs. 11) and that the salvation promised will be revealed as the newly married reveal themselves to each other in love (vs. 10). What the prophet experiences of the Lord's salvation and justice will be the possession of all who follow his ways. That this experience of salvation is likened to nuptial intimacy reiterates the important Advent theme of the intensity of God's self-revelation through his son. All that is promised and foreseen in this text has been accomplished in Jesus.

The responsorial psalm is taken from the familiar Canticle of the Virgin Mary used daily at evening prayer (Lk 1:46–48, 49–50, 53–54). This particular text is a continual reminder of what is emphasized on this Advent Sunday—in Christ, the world's standards of success and prosperity are overturned for the hungry are given every good thing while the rich are sent away empty. The accompanying refrain is taken from the first reading, "My soul rejoices in my God" (vs. 10). The rejoicing and exaltation experienced by God's prophet, Isaiah, was also experienced by the Lord's servant, Mary. It can be experienced by us in Advent when we admit our emptiness, our poverty, and our need for the richness of God's grace to come to us. The reversal of expectations in this canticle and the overturning of our culture's ways of judging success should mark our lives as Christians, especially during this season when we cry once again for the Lord to come and be with us.

Part of the second reading from 1 Thessalonians (5:16–24) has already been used in Advent as the reading for Sunday Evening Prayer I (vss. 23–24). The context of this passage is Paul's consideration of the second coming; its contents concern virtuous conduct and the importance of a hopeful spirit with which to greet the Lord. Paul tells the Thessalonians to "rejoice always" (vs. 16), to pray always, and to render constant thanks (vss. 17–18). Concerning their community life, Paul urges that they not stifle the inspirations of the Spirit, nor despise prophecies (even though they should test them). They are to "avoid any semblance of evil" (vs. 22) as they live the Christian life. Yet the apostle reminds them that it is not by their own efforts that they will be saved or are able to do what the Lord asks of them.

The gospel is from John (1:6–8, 19–28). The verses proclaimed today concern John the Baptist and will be used again on January 2. The use of John's gospel today is an exception to the principle that Mark is read in the "B" cycle. The fact that Mark has so little about John the Baptist shows the need for a supplement, amply provided by the gospel of John.

The major point of these verses is that John is not the Messiah (vs. 19) and that this mission was to come "as a witness to testify to the light" (vs. 19). As important as his mission was, he himself repeatedly states that he was not the light (vs. 18) and that he was "a voice in the desert, crying out: make straight the way of the Lord" (vs. 23). The force of his preaching about the Messiah and his baptizing in preparation for Christ's coming was to prepare them to receive the Lord. Themes already seen and which characterize John's ministry are reiterated here: his unworthiness (vs. 26), his act of baptizing, and his preaching to prepare for the Messiah (vs. 27). Yet, particularly significant Johannine features are inserted which give today's text a heightened urgency. That Christ is referred to as the light is repeated in John's gospel to demonstrate that Christ the light is pitted against Satan and the forces of darkness.

Here John gives testimony about Jesus' identity; later on in this gospel, Jesus gives testimony on behalf of the Father. He came to bear witness to the Father and to testify to the enduring power of his truth and love. That John testifies on behalf of Jesus here helps to set up the drama of Jesus bearing witness and giving testimony at his trial before Pilate. John's words challenge us today to seek and discover the Christ already in our midst. It is he who is saving Lord and our light.

The fact that some of these same verses will be used again at Christmas (Jn 1:1–14) indicates a subtle interplay between the darkness of the world at this time of year and the birth among us of him who is acclaimed the light of the world. When proclaimed today, the emphasis is on our discovering signs of the light of Christ in our midst. Unlike the crowds to whom John speaks, we should be able to recognize him (vs. 16) and to grow in an awareness of his presence even amidst the deepest darkness within us and around us in the world.

cf p-93

Cycle "C"

The verses from the prophet Zephaniah used as today's first reading (3:14–18a) comprise the alternate first reading on December 21. Some of the verses are found in other places in the Lectionary: verses 14–18 for the Visitation, verses 14–15 for Masses for Thanksgiving, and verses 18–21 for Masses for the Unity of Christians. The text assigned for today concerning the judgment to come on the day of the Lord is rather atypical of Zephaniah. Rather than continue the prophet's chastisement of Jerusalem, these verses offer promise, hope, and joy for those who expect the Lord to come. The prophet urges his audience to "shout for joy" (vs. 14) and to look for the Lord's coming since then they will no longer fear or be discouraged (vs. 16). The "mighty savior," God, "will rejoice over you . . . [and] renew you in his love" (vs. 17).

This attitude of joy and gladness is reiterated in the response from Isaiah (12:2–3, 4, 5–6) with the refrain, "Cry out with joy and gladness; for among you is the great and Holy One of Israel" (vs. 6).

The second reading from the letter to the Philippians (4:4–7) was traditionally used in the Roman rite as today's epistle, with certain verses appearing in the introit. The first word of the Latin introit gave the title *Gaudete* (rejoice) to this Sunday. Part of this text has also been assigned as the reading at Evening Prayer II on Advent Sunday (vss. 4–5). Two concerns addressed by Paul surface in the reading today. The first deals with a dispute in the community between Evodia and Syntyche, who are mentioned in verse 7. Paul advises them to "dismiss all anxiety" and to come to "mutual understanding in the Lord" (vs. 6). Nothing should disturb the peace of the community for as Paul states, "the Lord is near" (vs. 5), and our conduct before this coming should be unselfish and free from both quarreling and jealousy. The petty disputes that mark every human life should be appraised for their true worth, especially during Advent.

The gospel from Luke (3:10–18) about the mission of John the Baptist completes this Sunday's three-cycle emphasis on his preaching and work. (Some of these verses will be used on the feast of the Baptism of the Lord in the "C" cycle, verses 15–16, 21–22.)

This text may be divided into two sections. The first deals with the required response of particular groups to the question "what ought we to do?" to prepare for the Lord's coming (vs. 10). We must respond in deed as well as in word. Tax collectors and religious officials, for example, must be content with what is their just due and not exact any additional payment (vss. 12, 14). Both Paul's instruction to the Philippians and John's teaching here challenge us not to let this day go by without serious and prayerful reflection on what needs to be purged and eliminated from our lives.

The second part of the gospel deals with the peoples' anticipation of the coming Messiah (vs. 15). In Luke's gospel, John does not fulfill a precursor role. Rather, he is the last of the prophets. His message is to be heeded as were the messages of all the other prophets in Israel's history. Yet, unlike the other prophets, his mission includes the act of baptizing with water (vs. 16), a direct preparation for the one who is mightier. Luke is clear to underscore John's significant place in salvation history as the one whose words and baptism should affect the chosen as they await the Messiah. When the Lord comes, he will separate good from evil, wheat from chaff (vs. 17). The reality of this final judgment should affect us throughout our lives and help us make proper and just choices for the kingdom of God. Luke's text ends with the important summary: "using exhortations of this sort [John] preached the good news to the people" (vs. 18).

Sacramentary Texts

The entrance and communion antiphons today follow the traditional usages of the Roman Missal. They confirm the notions of quiet joy and rejoicing associated with this season. Advent is an important time to help us discover our need for God year after year.

The communion antiphon from Isaiah (35:4), "Say to the anxious: be strong and fear not, our God will come to save us," continues the hopeful atmosphere of today's liturgy. Even as we stand in need of the Savior and have to admit the things that distance us from him, the liturgy invites us to be tranquil and confident before him.

The opening prayer, from the Leonine Sacramentary, reflects the growing anticipation of Christmas evident in the rest of the liturgy. In it we admit our situation as those awaiting the feast of the birth of the Lord, which event gives us great joy.

The prayer over the gifts and the prayer after communion have already been discussed since they are used on Wednesdays and Saturdays in Advent. Their unique contribution here is to show the importance of the eucharist in our lives as we celebrate this season, look to Christmas, and ultimately to the eternal banquet in the kingdom.

The Sacramentary notes that either Advent preface may be used today. The text for the second, from the Leonine Sacramentary, is somewhat less eschatological than the texts of the previous Advent texts and mentions John specifically:

"His future coming was proclaimed by all the prophets.
The virgin mother bore him in her womb
   with love beyond all telling.
John the Baptist was his herald
and made him known when at last he came.
In his love Christ has filled us with joy
as we prepare to celebrate his birth,
so that when he comes he may find us watching in prayer,
our hearts filled with wonder and praise."

Celebration of the Eucharist

The basic options, gestures, and symbols that have been chosen for Advent Sundays should continue today. The music program could include a prelude and/or a postlude to indicate the heightening anticipation of Advent as we move toward Christmas. These should not be overpowering, however, and should retain the sense of watching and waiting.

The rite of blessing and sprinkling with holy water today would be a fitting introduction to the eucharist, the sacrament that renews our baptismal commitment and covenant.

The refrain for the responsorial psalm can be the same for all Advent Sundays, but the texts of the psalms themselves should change each week. This is particularly true in the "B" and "C" cycles today, since these verses come from canticles in Luke and Isaiah.

The sample formula of Advent intercessions should be reviewed when composing those to be used today.

The choice of Advent preface I or II should be made in the light of whether eschatological or incarnational themes dominate in this celebration. If the intent is to emphasize the ministry of John the Baptist, then the second would be the more fitting choice.

Because of its directness, the second eucharistic prayer would be a useful option today. Its brevity would also allow for a more deliberate proclamation by the presider.

The solemn blessing found in today's Mass formula is appropriate, especially if it has been used on the other Sundays.

After the prayer after communion, it might be well to announce a communal penance service to be celebrated this week. Scheduling such a service now instead of right before Christmas makes sense to give the liturgy of penance an emphasis it deserves separate from the Christmas eucharist. As the community's moment of reconciliation and forgiveness, this service should not repeat the readings proclaimed at the eucharist on the Sundays of Advent.

Liturgy of the Hours

Should this Sunday occur on December 17, the hymn, readings, antiphons to the Canticles of Zechariah and Mary, and the intercessions assigned to that day are used instead of the ones assigned for this Sunday. (See below for commentary.) This adjustment reflects liturgical tradition which gives special emphasis to the days immediately preceding Christmas from December 17 to 24.

At Evening Prayer I on this third Sunday, the antiphons to the psalmody reflect the Advent themes of joy and hope. What is striking this evening is their intensity: "Rejoice . . . your savior will come to you" (first) and "I, the Lord, am coming to save you; already I am near; soon I will free you from your sins" (second). The third antiphon reflects imagery found in the Advent scriptures when it pleads: "Lord, send the Lamb, the ruler of the earth, from the rock in the desert to the mountain of the daughter of Zion." Our longing for the coming savior builds as Advent progresses; these texts foster anticipation.

That we await the only God who can save us is reflected in the antiphon to Mary's canticle: "There was no god before me and after me there will be none; every knee shall bend in worship and every tongue shall praise me." This text, taken in part from Philippians (2: 10–11), used as the Christological canticle at this evening prayer, invites us to single-minded trust in the coming of our one Lord and Savior.

The intercessions provided this evening are the same as the ones for the First Sunday of Advent.

As the office of readings, the first reading from Isaiah (29:13–24) reveals the perversity and superficial religiosity of the chosen people. Isaiah first excoriates Israel's shallowness (vs. 13). "This people draws near with words only and honors me with their lips alone, though their hearts are far from me," says the prophet, in phrases reminiscent of Psalm 51:12, "a clean heart create for me, O God, and a steadfast spirit renew within me."

Since true conversion is interior, the alleged wisdom of the people will be exposed for what it is—shallow and baseless (vs. 14). Their "perversity" is so severe that the relationship between creator and creature is confused; the chosen now think they can determine their destiny (vs. 16).

To submit to the Savior who comes at Christmas implies our acceptance of him as the origin and destiny of all that we do. We are clay in his hands, not our own. This means that we surrender our wills and talents to the Lord who made them in the first place, so that how we use them is properly ordered to the glory of God, not to self-glory.

Yet, true to prophetic tradition, Isaiah concludes this passage with the statement that the redemption of the people is assured in spite of their apostasy (vss. 17–19) if they but turn to the Lord. Signs of this redemption are seen in overcoming physical blindness and deafness (vs. 18), which images are used in the responsory from Matthew (11: 4, 5), referring to Jesus' power.

The second reading from St. Augustine relates to the gospel from the eucharist about John's life and mission. Here the author speaks about John as the voice and Jesus as the Word. The ministry of John was to prepare for the coming of the mightier one, for the Word made flesh. It is John who is the last prophetic voice to prepare the way for the Lord.

At morning and evening prayer, the only new elements are the antiphons for the psalmody and for the Canticles of Zechariah and Mary. The scripture readings and intercessions are repeated from the First Sunday.

At morning prayer, the antiphons to the psalms reflect the urgency of our Advent preparation. "The Lord is coming without delay. He will reveal things kept hidden and show himself to mankind" (first). This fittingly introduces Psalm 93 about the relationship between creator and creature. The second section of psalmody (Dn 3:57–88, 56) praising the Lord of all creation is introduced by a fitting Advent text: "Mountains and hills shall be level, crooked paths straight, rough ways smooth. Come, Lord, do not delay, alleluia." The promises made to the chosen of Israel now passed on to us are reflected in the third antiphon (used with Psalm 148 in praise of creation): "I will enfold Zion with my salvation and shed my glory around Jerusalem, alleluia."

The antiphon to Zechariah's canticle is taken from today's gospel of the "A" cycle, where John has others inquire whether Jesus is the expected one. Although we might regard this question as unnecessary and the answer cryptic, this text offers important food for thought. How often do we act as though the Messiah had not come and how frequently do we overlook the deeds he has worked to show his saving presence in our midst?

At evening prayer, the antiphons to the psalmody speak about the Lord who "will come" (first) to take his place as judge of all. In the second text, the mountains and hills prepare for the Lord who comes with power as Lord of all the earth. The third is taken from the second reading in the "A" cycle about patience: "Let us live in holiness and love as we patiently await our blessed hope, the coming of our Savior."

The antiphon to Mary's canticle coincides with that used with Zechariah's canticle about signs of the Messianic era.

Celebration of the Hours

Because special emphasis is given to John the Baptist at the eucharist today, it might be well to choose general Advent hymns to introduce the hours, lest there be an overemphasis on this prophetic figure. Because so many elements of today's hours are repeated from the First Sunday, the suggestions made above should be reviewed.

The use of either the Advent invitatory or the verse before the readings, "Lift up your heads and see.—Your redemption is now at hand," would serve as an appropriate introduction to the hours especially when joined with Psalm 95.

Psalm 145 is assigned for use at the office of readings whose three sections can be combined into one for celebration. Whichever antiphon was not used last Sunday (with Psalm 104) could be used as the antiphon today. The psalm prayers presented at all hours today can be reworded to reflect more adequately themes appropriate to Advent. Yet, it should also be recalled that these are optional and can be replaced with longer periods of silence.

Reflection—"Crippled Inside"

It was during Advent, 1980 that the world awoke to the shocking news that John Lennon had been shot and killed. Acts of violence in such faraway places as El Salvador and the north of Ireland suddenly became real for Americans. This act of violence happened on the sidewalks of New York. Who would have foreseen that this incredible act would be followed by assassination attempts on John Paul II and President Reagan?

Paradoxically, in 1980, the Third Sunday of Advent followed Lennon's assassination, the day when the liturgy proclaims encouraging texts about Israel not losing hope during her exile and Isaiah's vision about the end of destruction for the chosen people. How fitting it was that these readings and images challenged and consoled Christian congregations as they tried to make some sense out of violence and bloodshed.

Interestingly, part of the imagery used in Isaiah is echoed in a Lennon lyric stating that we are all "crippled inside." Can we not say that we are all crippled, blind, lame, deaf, and dumb at times, perhaps all too many times in our lives? If we examine ourselves, our national priorities, and our society's values, is it not the case that we are sometimes blinded, struck dumb, and crippled by passing allurements rather than being insightful, attentive, and forceful in our defense of the gospel's values?

Are we spiritually lame because of our sins, faults, and temptations, or "crippled inside" because of those things that weigh heavily on our consciences? Does unnecessary guilt enslave us to self-doubt or even to doubts about Christ's love for us? How important it is to recall that Christmas is all about the coming of Christ to forgive our sins and to lead us to the joyful vision of God.

Do we get so busy at this time of year with all that "we have to do" that we become deaf by default? Do we allow any time in our busy lives for silence, prayer, and reflection on the astounding mystery of God made man, or word made flesh? Are we so comfortable with the level of noise pollution in our lives that we almost forget what a silent night can be like?

In a world that desparately needs the love of Christ and which suffers because of violence, hatred, and war, we come to pray today, aware that the only one who can free us from being "crippled inside" is the Lord whose love is incarnate again among us at Christmas. From him alone comes tranquility and peace—especially for us who are "crippled inside."

MONDAY OF THE THIRD WEEK OF ADVENT

Liturgical Context

Should the days from December 17 on occur this week, then the liturgies assigned to those days replace those of this third week of Advent. Except for the opening prayers, the Mass formulas each day are taken from those already used and commented above in the first week of Advent. Similarly, in the liturgy of the hours, the scripture passages at morning and evening prayer are the same as those used since Advent began and the intercessions repeat those used in the first week. Hence, the commentaries above should be consulted for these repeated texts and prayers.

Liturgy of the Eucharist

The opening prayer takes up the light theme that will be reiterated frequently through the Christmas-Epiphany season. We who experience darkness in nature at this time of year long for the light of Christ to come and shatter our physical and spiritual darkness. In this particular prayer, we ask the Lord to hear our voices raised in prayer and to send his light to illumine the shadows of our hearts and to drive out all darkness that results from evil and sin.

Today's first reading from Numbers (24:2–7, 15–17) mentions Balaam, employed by Balak, king of Moab. This wicked king, an enemy of Moses, wanted Balaam to speak against Israel; instead Balaam spoke in her favor. This message that God would triumph (as he did in the days of Moses) was continually read for Jewish believers who found insight and encouragement from Balaam's words. When proclaimed for us who share in the new covenant, the Messianic overtones of the text are brought into relief. The Davidic monarchy can refer to Chirst: "His king shall rise higher, and his royalty shall be exalted" (vs. 7).

The reference to the coming "star" is significant, for it situates our waiting in nature's present darkness for the brilliance that can only come upon us by an act of God. It is for his full revelation that we long in Advent.

In the responsorial psalm, we pray that the Lord would teach us his ways (Ps 25:4), yet in doing so we are aware that his ways often overturn the established ways of our society. Further on we pray: "he [the Lord] shows sinners the way. He guides the humble to justice, he teaches the humble his way" (vss. 8–9). We who use these words of the psalmist affirm our need for the Lord by calling him "God my savior" (vs. 5), which title figures prominently in the Christmas liturgy.

True to the plan of the Lectionary, today's gospel from Matthew (21:23–27) refers to the ministry of John the Baptist. Yet the text primarily concerns Jesus' authority. Matthew heightens the drama by casting "chief priests and elders of the people" (vs. 23) as Jesus' antagonists. They question Jesus, not so much about the fact that he taught (for such a function was commonly shared among the Jewish rabbis of his day), but on the intensity of his teaching. They ask, "On what authority" he does this. At a deeper level, we can read their question as an implicit rejection of Jesus as Messiah. Jesus "answers" them with a question about how they interpret John's baptism (vss. 24–25). The crux of the problem is faith. If they had believed in John, they would have accepted his baptism and thus would be prepared for Jesus' authoritative teaching. On the other hand, if they did not have faith, they would have perceived John's teaching as merely human. In order to evade the question, they say that they do not know on whose authority he acted. They hedged, since to affirm faith in John's message and in Jesus' teaching would have meant surrendering their teaching role to Jesus.

To surrender to Jesus' authority is sometimes hard, especially when we realize that any status and prestige we might lay claim to is nothing compared to his lordship over us.

Celebration of the Eucharist

The introduction to the liturgy could speak about our growth in faith in Advent as a privileged time to draw near to our Savior and Lord. The use of the third penitential rite with the second set of invocations and a sung *Kyrie, eleison* would reiterate Advent themes about the Lord's coming and set a meditative tone for the celebration.

Of the alleluia verses, number 14 (Lect., no. 193), stating, "The Lord is coming to save his people; happy are those prepared to meet him," would be a subtle introduction to a gospel about accepting Jesus as Messiah.

The Advent model for the general intercessions could be used as a source for the prayer of the faithful today. Additional petitions could be for bishops, priests, and deacons, that they may witness to the Lord by word and example; for the young, that they would deepen their faith as they mature; and for the understanding that being chosen requires us to live out our faith in deed as well as in word.

Advent preface I is still prescribed today even though preface II was offered as an option yesterday. It points to the dual function of Advent in preparing for the coming of Christ at Christmas and at the end of time.

A brief introduction to the Lord's Prayer about our growth in faith by calling on the Father would subtly reflect the gospel. The use of number 2 of the prayers over the people in which we pray that we might "always [be] faithful" would be an appropriate conclusion to the liturgy.

Liturgy of the Hours

The first reading at the office of readings from Isaiah (30:18–26) was already used as the first reading at eucharist on Saturday of the first week of Advent (see above). Its emphasis on the patience and mercy of God is most welcome at a time in this season when we are repeatedly challenged by the words and example of John. It is always with this understanding of God's mercy and love that we turn to him in deeper faith and trust.

The second reading from William of St. Thierry's *On the Contemplation of God* reflects some of the rich theology of the Greek fathers on the incarnation as summarized by this twelfth-century abbot. The crux of his presentation is found in the words:

"you first loved us so that we might love you—not because you needed our love, but because we could not be what you created us to be, except by loving you."

It is through the only-begotten Son that we have access to the Father and can call upon him in faith. This reflective passage reminds us of our situation before God (after the fall) and of our need for a redeemer to lead us to our true destiny in God.

At this hour, the text of Psalm 50 is introduced by an appropriate Advent antiphon: "Our God will be made manifest; he will not come in silence." During this season, we long for the revelation of God in Christ in both his words and deeds of love.

At morning prayer, the antiphon to Zechariah's canticle recalls the eschatological aspect of Advent: "From heaven he comes, the Lord and Ruler; in his hand are honor and royal authority." The Lord for whom we wait was born an infant, but he was also our savior and king.

At evening prayer, the Canticle of Mary is introduced by an antiphon (taken from the canticle itself) referring to Mary's role in the incarnation: "All generations will call me blessed; the Lord has looked with favor on his lowly servant."

Celebration of the Hours

Psalm 24 could serve as the invitatory psalm today because it refers to the important Advent themes of coming into the Lord's temple and praising him as the king of glory.

The psalmody at the office of readings from Psalm 50 can be prayed as a unit. The use of the first antiphon, "Our God will be made manifest; he will not come in silence," would be appropriate to begin and end this psalm. The psalm prayer given in the text could be reworded to reflect our need for the salvation promised us in Christ.

At morning and evening prayer, it would be important to choose hymns containing general Advent themes to begin these hours (rather than emphasize John the Baptist whose mission is noted at the eucharist).

At morning prayer, because of the importance of the text of Isaiah 2:2–5 as the second section of psalmody, the insertion of a psalm prayer here rather than after Psalm 84 would be fitting. The prayer following Psalm 96 is too rich and full as it stands; using those sections that apply more directly to Advent would be sufficient. The intercessions could be reworded to reflect our more intense preparation for Christmas at this point in Advent.

At evening prayer, the first psalm prayer following Psalm 123, about longing for God and his mercy, is most fitting. The second, however, following Psalm 124 might be better adjusted to reflect more specific Advent themes. The model intercessions are well done. They exemplify how such prayers can be structured and how such texts function in celebration.

Reflection—"Asking the Right Questions"

Often, we refer to a person who has the right answers to our questions as "smart" or "intelligent." We are impressed with his or her aptitude and performance. But, we do not necesarily call them "wise." In today's gospel, the people who questioned Jesus were intelligent, but they were not "wise." Wisdom is not amassing facts or having wide-ranging information on a variety of topics. In the light of the incident between Jesus and the chief priests, we could say that wisdom lies with the person who knows about the Messiah and freely accepts him in faith and submission. It is that link—submission—that joins knowledge and virtue. As presented the chief priests did not possess the humility to submit to the Messiah for whom they waited.

Are we very different? Do we find that we amass information about religion but tend to forget that this information is meant to lead us to God? Are we "smart" and "intelligent" when it comes to religion, but really unwise because we refuse to submit to God's will for us?

Today's liturgy, at which we hear this gospel, is for our instruction and formation, that we might not only grow in knowledge about God, but that we might grow in submitting ourselves to him.

Are we like the chief priests who ask, "on what authority" do you do these things, or are we the faithful who really mean what they pray in the Lord's Prayer, "thy will be done"?

TUESDAY OF THE THIRD WEEK OF ADVENT

Liturgical Context

If today occurs on or after December 17, everything assigned to that date is used today instead of what follows.

Liturgy of the Eucharist

Today's opening prayer reminds us that the liturgy inserts us into and makes us participants in Jesus' dying and rising. We pray that the Lord's coming may free us from the evil that enslaves us as a result of original sin. In hope, we pray that the coming celebration of the incarnation will renew the life of God within us.

The first reading from the prophet Zephaniah (3:1–2, 9–13) offers a contrast between the inhabitants of the "tyrannical city" (vs. 1), who no longer hear the voice of the Lord (vs. 2), and the *anawim*, the poor of Yahweh, who long for his coming to save them. The Lord assures us that despite rampant infidelity, he will "leave as a remnant . . . a people humble and lowly, who shall take refuge in the name of the Lord" (vs. 12). This remnant survives because they trust in the Lord's fidelity to them. In Isaiah, this remnant is described as the *anawim*, the poor, the lowly, the meek, and those who suffer because they believe in God's sustaining love and mercy. The Lord for whom we wait in Advent will come again to us who admit our weakness and sin and therefore need his holiness and strength.

The responsorial psalm with its refrain, "The Lord hears the cry of the poor" (Ps 34:4), confirms this emphasis on the *anawim* by exalting the lowly who will hear and be glad (vs. 3). When the afflicted call out, the Lord hears (vs. 7) and he is especially close to those whose hearts are broken (vs. 19). It is the Lord who will save those whose spirits are crushed (vs. 19) and in so doing fulfills the role promised to the prophets. He will exalt the *anawim*.

The gospel from Matthew (21:28–32) continues yesterday's confrontation between Jesus and the chief priests. In a "case study" to illustrate his teaching (vs. 28), Jesus asks which son really obeyed his father's will: the one who promptly promised to obey but did not, or the one who said "no" but later did as he was commanded (vs. 31). The latter son is clearly designated as the virtuous one. The lesson is clear—those who do the Father's will and surrender to him completely are saved, not those who (like the chief priests) say all the right things but do as they please.

Jesus then states that "tax collectors and prostitutes are entering the kingdom of God before you" (vs. 31), that is, before the priests who are consumed by ritual detail rather than by love for God and neighbor. God's poor will be admitted into the kingdom before such religious professionals. Once again, Matthew forcefully states that religious practice must go beyond formalism. We who hear John preaching "a way of holiness" (vs. 32) are invitied to "repent and believe" (vs. 32) in the coming Lord and to admit our need for him.

Celebration of the Eucharist

The introduction to the eucharist could speak about the virtue of integrity, examples of which are John the Baptist and the son in the gospel who repented and did his father's will. The use of the first form of the penitential rite, admitting that we have sinned "in what I have done and in what I have failed to do," would point to our need for God's forgiveness as it comes through the liturgy.

The use of number 8 of the alleluia verses (Lect., no. 193) would coincide well with our admission of sin and our need for the Messiah: "Come, O Lord, do not delay: forgive the sins of your people."

In the general intercessions, petitions for growth in integrity, for true humility before God, for the poor whom the Lord loves in a special way, and for the grace to accept the spiritual poverty in our own lives would coincide well with today's scriptures. The use of the third eucharistic prayer with the petition that the Lord will "strengthen in faith and love [his] pilgrim church on earth" would be appropriate.

All eucharistic prayers contain the Matthean text that the blood of the new covenant was shed "so that sins may be forgiven." This notion deserves special emphasis today. Ways of reiterating it would be to use a special introduction to the Lord's Prayer about being forgiven and forgiving others, and a special introduction to the sign of peace through which we experience anew and extend Christ's peace.

Liturgy of the Hours

The first reading at the office of readings from Isaiah (30:27–33; 31:4–9) deals with the Lord's judgment against Assyria and his defense of Jerusalem. The judgment theme reiterates that the Lord's "lips are filled with fury" against nonbelievers (vs. 27) and thus "his breath . . . will winnow the nations with a destructive winnowing" (vs. 28), an image often used to describe the fate of those who fail to obey the word of the Lord. The voice of the Lord will be heard, however, and the Lord's judgment will be obvious "in raging fury and [the] flame of consuming fire" (vs. 30). What was spoken of against Assyria may be applied to those who do not heed the Lord's voice or obey his commands.

The second part of the text shows God's favor for the chosen who heed his word. He promises to protect them in Jerusalem against their attackers (31:4–5); he will be their sustaining Lord. The following carefully phrased invitation to return to the Lord characterizes how the prophets describe God's dealings with his people:

"Return, O children of Israel, to him who you have utterly deserted. On that day each one of you shall spurn his sinful idols of silver and gold, which he made with his own hands." (vs. 6)

As we hear this text today, it is important that we hear and obey the Lord's word addressed to us. It is by hearing and abiding in that word that we are remade as the Lord's chosen.

The second reading from the *Imitation of Christ* comes from a section on humility and peace. This passage draws on the prior spiritual tradition, emphasizing humility as the way to experience God's peace. The *anawim* theme, so clearly enunciated in Advent, is obviously related to this text.

Part of the responsory (from Psalm 25:9–10) reminds us of the goal of all acts of humility: "The Lord leads the humble to justice; he teaches the meek his ways."

The antiphon to Zechariah's canticle deals with the eschatological aspect of Advent; that for Mary's canticle deals with the coming commemoration of the incarnation. The theme of urgency is clearly enunciated in the first text, "Arise, arise! Wake from your slumber Jerusalem. . . ." The incarnational theme is clear in the text: "before Mary and Joseph had come together, they learned that Mary was with child by the power of the Holy Spirit, alleluia."

The verse before the readings can be a very helpful invitatory today because of its emphasis on John: "A voice is heard, crying in the wilderness: Prepare the way of the Lord.—make straight his paths." The use of Psalm 95 containing a review of salvation history and emphasizing the importance of hearing the word of the Lord would also be most fitting.

The use of Psalm 68 about the Lord's entrance into his holy sanctuary is the psalmody at the office of readings today making it possible to recite or sing it as one unit with an antiphon at beginning and end. The second of the suggested antiphons is especially appropriate: "Our God is a saving God; he, the Lord holds the keys of death." Here, the liturgy once again indicates that one way we can appreciate the urgency of the coming reign of God is to see it in terms of our death. The proposed psalm prayer with its reference to the "holy meal" is better rewritten so that the themes appropriate to the eucharist and hours remain separate.

At morning prayer, the canticle from Isaiah (26:1–4, 7–9, 12), used as the second psalm, should be especially noted. Its accompanying antiphon is significant: "My soul has yearned for you in the night and as morning breaks I waited for your coming." This night/day motif fits in well with the important Advent theme of darkness/light.

At evening prayer, the psalm prayer following the first psalm (Ps 125) can be adjusted to reflect Advent themes more clearly. Also, the prayer following the second psalm (Ps 131) is wordy and can easily be condensed and adapted to reflect the theology of Advent.

At both hours, a sung Lord's Prayer with an invitation noting our awarensss of the coming of the kingdom would be appropriate.

Reflection—"Fidelity and Prostitution"

Because of their obvious definitions, the terms *fidelity* and *prostitution* do not go together very well. To be a prostitute in a spiritual sense can mean being unfaithful to the one God by whoring after images and likenesses of gods who promise ease, comfort, consolation, and riches. Fidelity, on the other hand, means exclusiveness in a deep love relationship and complete submission to God in faith. Fidelity and prostitution are clear opposites.

In today's gospel, Matthew pictures conversion as possible even for prostitutes. They can (and many will) turn to the Lord in faith despite misspent years of sexual promiscuity, once they know their need for God's forgiveness and love.

On the other hand, those who are faithful only to outward religious practices may not be truly faithful to God. Matthew paints a sorry picture of the chief priests and elders because they are satisfied with half-filled and half-converted lives.

Today, the scriptures invite us to ponder how truly converted we are to the Lord's ways and how much we truly need this season for deeper conversion to the Lord. The gospel plays on words today; this can be amusing and offer a twist on religious truth. But, Advent is no word game; it is about resolute conversion to the Lord.

WEDNESDAY OF THE THIRD WEEK OF ADVENT

Liturgical Context

In liturgical tradition, Wednesday, Friday, and Saturday this week were Ember days, days of fast, abstinence, and special preparation for Christmas.

Today's refrain to the responsorial psalm from Isaiah (45:8) was the Ember day introit, and the present opening prayer is a slight variation on the former first collect of two used today. The traditional first reading was Isaiah 2:2–5, which now plays such a prominent role in the early days of the season, and the gospel of the annunciation (Lk 1:26–38), formerly proclaimed on Ember Wednesday, is now the gospel on the Fourth Sunday, "B" cycle.

If today falls after December 16, then the liturgy assigned for that date is used instead of what follows.

Luturgy of the Eucharist

Today's opening prayer asks that we who prepare for the celebration of the coming of the Son of God among us might experience his saving help in this life and be led to our promised home in heaven. Hence, it links eschatological and incarnational aspects of Advent.

The first reading from Isaiah (45:6–8, 18, 21–25) deals with our relationship with God as creator and Lord. Verse 8, containing an urgent plea for the coming Lord, has had a significant place in the Advent liturgy, since it was the traditional entrance antiphon for the

Fourth Sunday: "Let justice descend, O heavens, like dew from above. . . ." This is part of a longer passage acclaiming God as "the creator of the heavens" (vs. 18) to whom we owe reverence and homage: "I am the Lord, and there is no other" (vs. 18). In this passage, the prophet speaks of God's promises as extending beyond Israel to "all you ends of the earth" (vs. 21).

The psalm response uses creation imagery to reiterate our need for God as savior and to admit "the Just One" into our lives (Is 45: 8). Many Advent themes combine in the psalm itself (Ps 85) to remind us of the nearness of salvation (vs. 10), the Lord's justice (vs. 12), and the benefits of true justice and salvation for those who trust in him (vs. 14).

The gospel from Luke (7:18–23) presents Luke's account of what was already seen on the Third Sunday ("A" cycle) from Matthew about the disciples of John asking whether Jesus is the Messiah. Luke's editorial additions reveal that God's power was at work through Jesus at the very time the disciples inquired whether he was the Messiah. The evangelist relates that: "[Jesus] was curing many of their diseases, afflictions and evil spirits; he also restored sight to many who were blind" (vs. 21). Once again, these examples of Jesus' power would cause a believing Jew to reflect back to the Messianic hopes of Israel and to see these miracles as evidences of the presence of the Messiah.

Especially significant is God's action among us in the present through liturgy as we long to experience the fullness of his saving presence in the kingdom. The signs of the messianic age recounted in the gospel demonstrate Jesus' role as savior; it is this savior to whom and through whom we pray at liturgy.

Celebration of the Eucharist

Today's introduction could note the many signs of God's love for us and how we experience it in the liturgy. The third form of the penitential rite, with acclamations of Christ who healed the sick, who preached the good news, and who is our saving Lord, would be appropriate in light of the gospel.

For the alleluia verse, number 9 of the Advent texts (Lect., no. 193), "Behold, our Lord will come with power, he will enlighten the eyes of his servants," would be an indirect reference to the gospel.

Among the intercessions today, petitions for the physically ill, for the spiritually needy, for God's justice to reign in our troubled world, and for a deeper faith in the mystery of Christ's love would be appropriate.

The first Advent preface is still assigned for today. To introduce the Lord's Prayer with a reference to our calling on God who sent us his Son as "savior" would reflect the title used in the first reading. Should the Lamb of God be extended beyond three strophes, using the titles Messiah, Word made flesh, and Emmanuel would reflect themes of today's liturgy.

Liturgy of the Hours

Today's first reading at the office of readings from Isaiah (31:1–3, 32:1–8) comes from the latter part of this book, describing an ideal future when leaders will implement the justice of God and all people will be cared for. The messianic overtones are especially clear when this is read in Advent, as we long for the fulfillment of our hopes in the kingdom to come. The first part of the text describes an oracle against Egypt and an exhortation for Israel to trust in the Lord alone, not its own devices (31:1–3). The king described in the second part of the text is indeed an ideal person compared with the nobles of the time (vss. 4–8, especially). The king to whom we look in Advent is the Lord Jesus himself and not to any other ruler or lesser god. This messianic understanding is reflected in the responsory to the reading (especially, Jeremiah 23:5 and Isaiah 32:3, 4).

The second reading from Irenaeus' *Against Heresies* is a careful exposition on the comings of Christ in history, in the present, and in the future. What we learn from this instruction is the interrelatedness of these comings and the hope we draw from them as we pray now for the coming of his kingdom.

At morning prayer, the antiphon to Zechariah's canticle draws on sections of Isaiah that deal with Jerusalem's receiving the Lord's comfort. This hopeful text is especially important because it accompanies the canticle about how John's birth is the sure sign of the coming of the Messiah, the fulfillment of Israel's hopes and desires.

At evening prayer, the antiphon to Mary's canticle can be understood to refer to the coming feast of Christmas and to the end of time. "You, O Lord, are the One whose coming was foretold; we long for you to come and set your people free," both discloses our need for the promised One to come and shows the urgency with which we pray for this to happen in our time. At this point in the season, the Advent liturgy almost bursts with expectation. The quiet joy of the season now builds to growing excitement of what is to be revealed at Christmas when we share in the mystery of God's love in our present lives.

Celebration of the Hours

For the invitatory today, the verse before the readings would be appropriate, since it acknowledges that our salvation comes from God alone: "Turn back to us, O Lord, our God.—Show us your face and we shall be saved." When accompanied by Psalm 100, which expresses our relationship to God, "we are his people, the sheep of his flock" (vs. 3), this prayer fittingly introduces the hours as our response in prayer to God's initiative toward us.

Psalm 89:2–38, as the psalmody at the office of readings, can be prayed as a unit with the second antiphon, which is especially fitting because of its Advent overtones: "When the Son of God came into the world, he was born of David's line." (This also coincides with the first reading at this hour from Isaiah.) The assigned psalm prayer is rather long and could be condensed to be a clearer reflection of this season.

At both morning and evening prayer, the hymns to begin the hour should reflect general Advent themes. The psalm prayer after Psalm 86 at morning prayer is suitable for Advent. The prayer following Psalm 98 contains insights into the passion of Christ, into our experience of redemption and the second coming. Additional intercessions could reflect the growing intensity of Advent and the response, "Come, Lord Jesus," would be another way of emphasizing our need for God. The use of either number 1 or 16 of the prayers over the people would be a fitting conclusion to this hour because of the Advent themes they contain.

At evening prayer, the prayer following Psalm 126 is adequate in content, but its style could be improved. The prayer following Psalm 127 is especially suitable since it expresses our need for God in this Advent-Christmas season. The Colossian hymn (1:12–20) prayed this evening is a good summary of the Christ event and our being newly created in him.

The use of "Come, Lord Jesus" as the response to the intercessions and either number 1 or 16 of the prayers over the people as the dismissal would parallel the options used at morning prayer.

Reflection—"The God of Revealed Religion"

Today's liturgy reminds us that Advent is a time to refocus our attention on who the Messiah is and the role he plays in our lives. The readings at Mass tell us that the Lord we worship is more than a creator or miracle worker—he is a God who draws us into relationship with him. The God of the logicians may well be called the "maker of all things," but it is the God of the scriptures who discloses himself as the ever-present God who loves and cares for all he has made.

St. Luke tells us of the signs and wonders Jesus worked that show the power of God at work in him. Yet this same evangelist takes pains to tell us that God is at work now in the Christian community which continues in time and space the incarnation of God. The Christ of revealed religion continues to reveal himself where two or three are gathered in his name. It is here that we meet God, ever present with us and among us, the God Emmanuel. We respond appropriately to this love by loving each other and respecting the origin of all relationships, love incarnate in Christ.

THURSDAY OF THE THIRD WEEK OF ADVENT

Liturgical Context

The liturgy prescribed for today is used when the date is before December 17; from December 17 to 24, the liturgy assigned to those days is used.

Liturgy of the Eucharist

In the opening prayer, taken from the old Roman Missal, we acknowledge the burden which our sin lays upon us. Hence, we pray for "courage and strength" that the coming of the Son of God will bring us the joy of salvation. This prayer is a humble yet confident plea. To admit our weakness is to admit our human condition before God, a condition embraced by Jesus in the incarnation.

The first reading from Isaiah (54:1–10) reiterates the intimate relationship between God and Israel. Using the example of a lack of physical descendants and the deprivation of a "deserted wife" (vs. 1), the author states that Israel's joy will be like the joy a "barren one" experiences who becomes the mother of many children. Israel's descendants "shall dispossess the nations and shall people the desolate cities" (vs. 3)—certainly an astounding promise considering the tiny remnant to whom this promise is made. The one to accomplish this is their "redeemer . . . the Holy One of Israel, called the God of all the earth" (vs. 5).

In addition to numerous progeny, the author uses the analogy of marital fidelity to describe Israel's relationship with God: "The Lord calls you back, like a wife forsaken and grieved in spirit" (vs. 6). This is an apt example to use in Advent, the season of our being called back again and again into God's love. The prophet maintains that even though God will have to discipline his people at times (vs. 7), it is his "enduring love" (vs. 9) that should sustain Israel. Despite natural disasters (like the flood in Noah's time) and calamities over the earth, the Lord promises Israel that "my love shall never leave you nor my covenant of peace be shaken" (vs. 10). Despite sin (admitted frankly in the opening prayer), we come before the Lord in Advent full of the same confidence that inspired Isaiah to write these words to strengthen the weary of the remnant Israel to recommit themselves to the Lord.

This general statement about fidelity and God's sustaining love is reflected in the responsorial psalm, Psalm 30. We recognize the psalmist's wisdom when he says, "At nightfall weeping enters in, but with the dawn, rejoicing" (vs. 6). We may well shed tears of regret for sin or of compunction because of the distance that separates us from God, but this prayer reassures us of God's merciful love: "His anger lasts but a moment, a lifetime his goodwill" (vs. 6). It is the Lord who "changed my mourning into dancing" and to whom we give thanks (vs. 12).

The gospel of Luke read yesterday continues today (7:24–30), recalling what was proclaimed on the Third Sunday of Advent, "A" cycle (Mt 11:7–11), about John's vocation to prepare the way of the Lord. The specific Lukan additions (especially verses 29–30) offer important insight into this evangelist's understanding of the Messiah. He states, "the entire populace that had heard Jesus, even the tax collectors, gave praise to God. . . ." (vs. 29) This phrase exemplifies Luke's emphasis on Christ's mission to all peoples, not just to

Israel. The fact that "tax collectors" would be invited to this relationship with God would shock Jesus' contemporaries and later generations of believers into realizing that submission to God's will is the only criterion for entrance into the kingdom.

Celebration of the Eucharist

The introduction to the liturgy could consider the importance of the eucharist as a privileged means for growth in faith. In the liturgy of the word, we are challenged to respond to ever new levels of God's revelation to us; through the eucharistic meal, we are strengthened to live the faith we profess. To acknowledge our need for God's "mercy and love" and his "salvation," the use of the second penitential rite would be useful.

For the alleluia verse, number 7 (Lect., No. 193) about John's ministry, would be appropriate: "prepare the way for the Lord, make straight his paths: all mankind shall see the salvation of God" (Lk 3:4, 6).

Among the intercessions, today prayers for those involved in missionary efforts throughout the world and in evangelization work in our country would emphasize the universality noted in Luke's gospel. A response to our sharing in God's love for us (proclaimed in the first reading) would be to pray for those involved in outreach programs, especially to those who will be the recipients of the community's charity at Christmas.

The fourth introduction to the Lord's Prayer, "for the coming of the kingdom," would be appropriate as would number 4 of the prayers over the people about "avoiding evil" and finding in God "the fulfillment of [our] longing."

Liturgy of the Hours

The first reading at the office of readings from Isaiah (32:15–33:6) is an oracle of the future when God's promised deliverance will be accomplished and his peace established. This new age will be signaled with the outpouring of the spirit (vs. 15); then deserts will become orchards and orchards become as dense as forests. When the people experience God's justice, peace, and security (vss. 16–18), they will know that the new age has come. However, even as we acclaim the Lord who "is exalted, enthroned on high; [who] fills Zion with right and justice" (33:5), we are aware that this has yet to be fully established among us. Hence, the prophet's prayer can be our own: "O Lord, have pity on us, for you we wait. Be our strength every morning, our salvation in time of trouble" (33:2). This text exemplifies what we yearn for in Advent—fulfillment in God alone and the fullness of his peace and justice.

The second reading from the Constitution on Divine Revelation (nos. 3–4) of Vatican II summarizes salvation history from the perspective of Christ as its center and as the one who brings it to perfection. For us who celebrate the liturgy, this Christ-centeredness is essential for appreciating what we experience in coming together for the memorial of Christ's paschal mystery.

The antiphons to the gospel canticles at morning and evening prayer offer hopeful and future-oriented prayers reflective of the many moods and themes of Advent: "Arise, arise, Lord; show us your power and might" (Zechariah) and "all you who love Jerusalem, rejoice with her forever" (Mary). In both, we yearn for God's power and might to be fully revealed.

Celebration of the Hours

The verse at the office of readings would be a useful invitatory verse today, "Hear the word of the Lord, all you nations,—Proclaim it to the ends of the earth," since it reflects the significant Advent theme of God's mercy and salvation extending to the ends of the earth. The use of Psalm 95 would be an appropriate invitatory psalm since it touches on so many significant instances in salvation history when God revealed himself to Israel.

At the office of readings, the first two psalms could be combined into one unit (since both are from Psalm 89:39–53). The use of the second antiphon, "I am the root and stock of David; I am the morning star," would coincide well with the theology of Advent. The psalm prayer following Psalm 90 subtly expresses the Advent theme of yearning for the kingdom to come: "until the day we gaze upon the beauty of your face."

At morning prayer, the use of Isaiah 40:10–17 as the second part of the psalmody coincides with the emphasis placed on Isaiah during Advent. The psalm prayer following Psalm 99 would be a more adequate reflection of Advent if it is reworded to emphasize the presence of the Word in our midst. Yet, the last part noting Christ's paschal sacrifice ("consecrate your people in his blood until our eyes see your face") is particularly significant because it ties together the incarnation and redemption.

At evening prayer, the psalm prayers following Psalm 132 and the canticle from Revelation 11–12 could be adjusted to reflect Advent themes more specifically, especially the latter since in praising Christ we also yearn for his salvation to come upon us in this season. At both morning and evening prayer, a sung Lord's Prayer would underscore the eschatological aspect of the coming of God's kingdom.

Reflection—"Over and Over Again"

In this season, we review the familiar stories of the manifestations of God among us. We hear the same readings and pray the same prayers we used last year and will use again next year. But, we do this as a people who need to experience their evocative and recreative force again and again because we ourselves change and are different each year. We bring to the liturgy new and varying needs—loved ones, relationships, jobs, crises—and seek to blend them with the liturgy we celebrate. When we pray at liturgy, our hopes, needs, conflicts, and setbacks are taken seriously, cherished, and embraced by God again and again.

Yet the stakes are high. When we come to liturgy, we must also be willing to be changed by the words we speak, by the texts we hear, and by the Lord we worship. Our search for him can be nothing short of ceaseless. The prize is the only really valuable thing on earth—the living God.

FRIDAY OF THE THIRD WEEK OF ADVENT

Liturgical Context

If today's date is December 17 or later, then the liturgy is taken from the texts assigned to that date. If not, then those assigned to today are used.

In liturgical tradition, this day was specially emphasized as an Ember day. Even though none of the texts assigned to that day remain, the penitential nature of Fridays throughout the year should make this a day of more intense preparation for Christmas.

Liturgy of the Eucharist

Today's opening prayer is taken from the old Gelasian Sacramentary; it reflects our present situation "as we await the coming of [the] Son." This text succinctly reflects God's initiative as we strive to do his will on earth and eventually be welcomed into his kingdom.

The first reading from Isaiah (56:1–3, 6–8) coincides with these themes for it too assures us of God's initiative in our salvation (vss. 7–8); yet, it reiterates how important it is that we respond and act according to his decrees. The prophet warns us that we should "observe what is right [and] do what is just" (vs. 1) for God's salvation is approaching. Yet, this invitation is not just for those of the family of Israel who have waited for this deliverance. The door of salvation is now open to all people, even to foreigners who did not share in God's promises to Israel (vss. 2–3). If we but turn to the Lord in true and honest conversion, we shall be heir to his promises and be made joyful in his "house of prayer for all peoples" (vs. 7).

The responsorial psalm, Psalm 67, is proposed as an option for the invitatory in the liturgy of the hours because of its sense of gathering all peoples to praise the Lord; this is seen in today's response, "O God, let all the nations praise you" (vs. 4).

The gospel, John 5:33–36, is the single text from John found on Advent weekdays. Jesus describes the Baptist as "the lamp set aflame and burning bright" (vs. 35) which leads all believers to the knowledge of the Messiah. Using another typical Johannine theme, the author has Jesus affirm, "I have testimony greater than John's, namely, the works the Father has given me to accomplish" (vs. 36). Jesus gives "testimony" by words and deeds which should lead us to him as the source of truth and the fullness of the Father's love.

Celebration of the Eucharist

The introduction to the liturgy could address the criterion of our doing the will of God to show that we live in the light of Christ, a light foretold by John and renewed in us through the liturgy. In the "I confess" form of the penitential rite, we acknowledge our sins ("in what I have done and in what I have failed to do") which have prevented our turning to Christ the light. A sung "Lord have mercy" would help establish a reflective tone to the liturgy.

The use of number 12 as the alleluia verse (Lect., no. 193) ("the day of the Lord is near: he comes to save us") reminds us to await the coming feast with longing and expectation. The intercessions might contain petitions for Jewish believers to remain faithful to the covenant God forged with them; for those involved in ecumenism to characterize their efforts with honesty and mutual charity; for a deeper appreciation of reflective prayer; and for a greater witness to Christ in our lives.

The eschatological emphasis of Advent preface I, prescribed for the last time today, could be supported by using the third memorial acclamation (ending in "until you come in glory").

The notion of God's initiative to his people, seen in the first reading and always operative in the liturgy, can be underscored by the proclamation of the third eucharistic prayer with the text, "Father, hear the prayers of the family you have gathered here before you."

To introduce the Lord's Prayer, the presider could note the importance of our calling God "Our" Father since liturgical prayer is communal by nature, thus a reflection of the covenant made first with Israel and now extended to us.

The sign of peace could be introduced as a gesture by which we acknowledge the communal nature of our faith.

The use of number 9 of the prayers over the people, about extending the love of God, would be an appropriate conclusion since part of the message of John's gospel is that we who have seen the light should reflect the light in our lives.

Liturgy of the Hours

In the first reading from Isaiah (33:7–24) at the office of readings, the prophet relates how the country is languishing and the social order is in upheaval (vss. 7–9); infidelity and turning away from God are rampant. What is needed is a "consuming fire" (vs. 14) to separate the good from the bad (a commonly used image for separation and purification). The virtuous will survive such a refining fire (vs. 15) and will see the coming Messiah (vs. 17). Even as they look to Zion, "the city of our festivals" (vs. 20), they are directed to see beyond rite and cult to the Lord who will come to save them. A Messianic interpretation of this text guides us to use the liturgy as important moments to acknowledge our need for God; when we do so, we will be like Israel preparing for the "king who will save us" (vs. 22).

The second reading from St. Augustine's treatise on the Psalms offers advice about prayer. He simply says that the desire to pray is itself a prayer (reflecting St. Paul's teaching in Romans 8). Augustine also uses Pauline ideas when he states, "if you wish to pray without ceasing, do not cease to desire." Before, during, and after set times for prayer, our lives should be marked by an openness to God and a willingness to receive what the Lord reveals to us in all circumstances of life. The noise pollution of our culture and the efficiency of managing every minute in life (both in business and in leisure) militate against this kind of pervading openness to God. For this reason, Augustine's teaching offers important insight and direction.

The antiphons to the New Testament canticles at morning and evening prayer bring out important Advent themes. At morning prayer, we are charged to "guard what is good and cherish what is true, for our salvation is at hand." At evening prayer, the mission of the Baptist is recalled: "This was the witness of John the Baptist: The One who comes after me existed before me." Hence, the truth of the gospel at Mass is reaffirmed; John came as a lamp to prepare the way for Christ, the enduring light of the world.

Celebration of the Hours

The fact that today is a Friday should be recalled when planning the hours so that in subtle ways a deeper seriousness about Advent preparation is made apparent. The use of the invitatory assigned to the first part of Advent ("Come, let us worship the Lord, the King who is to come") would be especially appropriate today since this text will be replaced tomorrow by another used until December 24. Psalm 24 would be an appropriate invitatory with its emphasis on seeking "the face of the God of Jacob" (vs. 6) and praising the "king of glory" who we pray will be manifest among us ("let him enter," vss. 7, 9, 10). Whatever psalm is used, it should not be Psalm 100, already assigned for morning prayer today.

At the office of readings, the praying of Psalm 69: 2–22, 30–37 in three sections can be merged together. The third antiphon is especially appropriate, "Seek the Lord, and you will live." The psalm prayer could be condensed, yet its clear reference to the passion should be retained as a way of indicating that this is a Friday in Advent.

The hymns selected to begin morning and evening prayer should be general (and eschatological) in contrast to the more incarnational emphasis that will begin tomorrow.

The prayer following Psalm 100 could be rewritten to reflect Advent themes more directly.

Among the intercessions, petitions about the penance we perform today (Friday) and the place of self-deprivation so that others may share in the goods of the earth would be appropriate.

At evening prayer, petitions acknowledging our sin and for those truly seeking God in Advent would be appropriate. Singing the Lord's Prayer and concluding the hours with either number 1 or 16 of the prayers over the people would reiterate the eschatological aspects of Advent, since by design these will fade in importance (but not be eliminated) with tomorrow's liturgy.

Reflection—"Deeds of Darkness and Deeds of Light"

At this time of year, nature provides us with a perfect setting for the texts and prayers we use at the liturgy. We experience the shadows of evening earlier and earlier each day, and we feel less warmth from the sun's rays. We are approaching that time of year when the sun is farthest from us, when the sun's rays tease rather than tan. The darkness of winter is upon us; we long for the brightness of spring and summer. The Advent-Christmas liturgy demonstrates that amidst the shadows of evening and the cold of winter, we can still experience a brightness and warmth that far exceeds what comes through nature.

This general Advent theme is specified for us in today's gospel. John is a lamp who makes us aware of our darkness and of our need for true brightness—for God. At Christmas, we experience the light of Christ in the deadest part of winter to strengthen and guide us from winter's death to an eternal spring in God's love.

Fourth Week of Advent

FOURTH SUNDAY OF ADVENT

Liturgical Context

The Advent liturgy today emphasizes Mary and Joseph this Sunday, the two people immediately involved in the birth of Jesus. This emphasis accords with the tradition of the Ambrosian liturgy which has always given special attention to Mary on this Sunday. In the former arrangement of the Roman rite, however, the gospel emphasized the ministry of John the Baptist (Lk 3:1–6), which coincided with the emphasis on John in the gospels on the second and third Sundays. Mary's place in our redemption is clearly emphasized in the present Advent-Christmas liturgy: this Sunday, on the Solemnity of the Immaculate Conception (Dec. 8) and the Solemnity of Mary, Mother of God (Jan. 1).

Today, the lectionary assigns three important infancy narrative texts from Matthew and Luke—Joseph's dream ("A"), the annunciation to Mary ("B"), and Mary's visitation to Elizabeth ("C"). Mary and Joseph are presented as model believers who did the will of God despite taxing, not to say confounding, circumstances. Yet this was God's plan for them. Because of their obedience, we all share in the divinity of Christ who humbled himself to share in our humanity.

Cycle "A"

Today's first reading from Isaiah (7:10–14), repeated on December 20, is used as the first reading on the Annunciation (March 25) and is offered as an option for commons of the Blessed Virgin. Originally written to reflect the historical situation of King Ahaz, who relied on himself rather than on the Lord, this text has traditionally been used in the Advent liturgy to describe our situation as a people looking for the definitive sign of God's favor to us in his Son. The response of Ahaz, that he would not tempt the Lord by asking for a sign (vs.

12), is really an ironic response for in fact the king preferred to rely on his own authority. The Lord says that there will be an important sign for Israel, the birth of an ideal king who will be called Immanuel (vs. 14). The original setting of this declaration should be recalled—God will intervene on Israel's behalf and give them a king (unlike Ahaz) who will lead them in God's ways and who will be the fulfillment of his promises to the house of David.

When read in the Christian assembly, these words have obvious Messianic overtones. The definitive sign of the fulfillment of God's promises is the birth of the Messiah. While the text's original intent does not refer to the birth of Jesus from a virgin mother, the church's use of this verse to refer to the virgin birth (in liturgy and patristic sermons) should not be overlooked.

The responsorial psalm reflects our expectation of God's dwelling among us at Christmas through the incarnation and our longing for him as we pray, "Let the Lord enter; he is the king of glory" (taken from verses 7c and 10b of Psalm 24). This particular psalm is used as an optional invitatory to the hours because it acknowledges the Lord of creation (vss. 1–2) who forgives our sins and purifies our hearts (vss. 3–4). We who "seek the face of the God of Jacob" (vs. 6) in Advent long to be united with him who is forever with us as Emmanuel.

The second reading from the beginning of the letter to the Romans (1:1–7) is a most significant text theologically for it speaks about the role and rule of Christ as a consequence of his human birth among us. Paul begins by acknowledging that his mission was to "proclaim the gospel of God" (vs. 1), a message that concerns the incarnation and paschal mystery of Christ (vss. 3–4). It is this mystery of faith that we celebrate at the liturgy, and it is this paschal relationship that compels us to continue Paul's apostleship to bring all to "obedient faith" (vs. 5) in Christ.

A clear example of the way the liturgy uses a scriptural verse to introduce the gospel is evident in today's gospel acclamation: "A virgin will give birth to a son; his name will be Emmanuel: God is with us." Taken from Matthew 1:23, this verse forms the link between today's first reading and the gospel of Joseph's dream.

The text of Matthew 1:18–24 is proclaimed today (and also on December 18) to help us realize who Jesus is and how his human birth came about so that we can be all the more prepared to wel-

Fourth Sunday of Advent   121

come him when he comes to us as the Incarnate One at Christmas. When proclaimed today, this text helps us see the power of God at work through Mary and Joseph, whose obedience to God's will is the virtue we should imitate. The obedience of the true disciple, seen throughout Matthew's narrative, is indicated here in the first chapter. Joseph stands as one who obeys the Lord's commands unhesitatingly. Mary and Joseph are thus models for all generations of believers who follow the Lord in faith.

Matthew uses the title "Emmanuel" here (vs. 23), whose significance ("God is with us") is used at the very end of the gospel (Mt 28:20) to assure the church of the enduring presence of God. Closely associated with the meaning of Emmanuel are the titles "Son of David" (vs. 20) and "Jesus" (vs. 21). Just as the titles Paul uses in the second reading reveal levels of understanding about who Christ is, so do Matthew's use of these titles to describe that Jesus is present with his people, that he is of royal lineage, and that he "will save his people from their sins" (vs. 21). This Christological emphasis and understanding is central to an appreciation of this text as the gospel of the Christmas vigil. When proclaimed on this Advent Sunday, this text discloses qualities of Joseph and Mary that offer examples for our imitation as we seek to deepen our awareness of what God asks of us who commemorate his incarnation. Like Joseph and Mary, we are to obey and do his will.

Cycle "B"

The first reading from 2 Samuel (7:1–5, 8–11, 16) reflects the latter section of today's gospel (Lk 1:26–38, at vss. 32–33), where the angel tells Mary that Jesus' dignity will be great and that "he will be called son of the Most High. The Lord God will give him the throne of David his father. He will rule over the house of Jacob forever. . . ." The first reading thus offers an old covenant counterpart to this act of divine intervention; the Lord promises to make the house of David secure forever. God's initiative in electing Israel and in sustaining her as his special possession is read on this last Advent Sunday as a way of summarizing the history of salvation that would lead to the final act of God's deliverance of his people—the birth of his Son of the "house of David" (Lk 1:27).

This notion of reviewing the salient moments of salvation history is reflected in the responsorial psalm (Ps 89) for in it we recall God's "faithfulness" and "kindness" (vss. 2–3) in establishing and confirming Israel in the covenant (vs. 4). The chosen house of David is specified, and David receives the word of the Lord: "forever will I confirm your posterity and establish your throne for all generations" (vs. 5). When used in the Advent liturgy, this text offers the important understanding that the Judaeo-Christian tradition stems from God's abiding love for his covenanted people.

The second reading from Romans (16:25–27) is the conclusion of what was proclaimed in the "A" cycle (from Rom 1:1–7). Paul preaches the good news ("gospel," vs. 25) revealing the "mystery hidden for many ages but now manifested . . ." (vs. 26) for all nations—the incarnation and paschal mystery of Jesus. Like Paul, we offer praise and thanks to the Father through him whose birth, life, death, and resurrection has given us new birth and a new relationship with God—the intimacy of union and abiding love through Christ.

The gospel acclamation (which will also be used in the "C" cycle) underscores the importance of Mary's obedience and acceptance of God's will for her (Lk 1:38) and is taken from the end of today's gospel.

The gospel is the annunciation text (Lk 1:26–38), used also on the Solemnity of the Immaculate Conception when it could be interpreted as another example of our being attentive to the Word of God as was Mary who accepted the message of the angel. When proclaimed today, just before we commemorate the birth of Jesus at Christmas, it is Mary's obedience and faith that stand out as qualities to be imitated. While in the "A" cycle it is the angel's message to Joseph that occasions his obedience, here it is Gabriel's message to Mary that causes her to place her trust in the Lord. Luke emphasizes the astounding character of the event by noting twice that Mary was a virgin (vs. 27) and that she was "highly favored" (vs. 28). Clearly, Mary was put off at first by this revelation; the evangelist says that "she was deeply troubled by his words" (vs. 29). Later, Mary continues her questioning by asking, "how can this be since I do not know man?" (vs. 34) In this way, the evangelist shows that Mary's trust and obedience were born of a definite act of the will, not a facile acceptance of what seemed logical and predictable. Mary submits and says: "Let it be done to me as you say" (vs. 38) which text is significant for it reflects a formula that will be used elsewhere (especially

Lk 8:19–21) where others are to respond to the Lord's word the way Mary did. The fact that the incarnation will be accomplished by the power of the Holy Spirit "who will overshadow you" (vs. 34) is significant for this same language is used at the transfiguration when God's power so overshadows Jesus that he is revealed as the Son of God. This divine instrumentality also reveals Luke's concern to draw attention to Mary's virginal conception (vs. 34), a fact already noted by the repetition of the word "virgin" in verse 27. Just as God created male and female in Genesis and intended them to come together to be one (Gn 2:24), so here God is acting within Mary by special intervention, and the child she will bear will recreate and restore humanity to its lost innocence. The active "spirit of God" over the waters in Genesis 1:2 prefigures that it is by the Holy Spirit that Mary will conceive and bear a son.

Among the many significant themes which emerge from reflecting on this text is the notion of Mary's humble submission to the Lord's will for her and her acceptance of his word despite obvious hardship. Even though she did not understand fully what was involved, she placed her trust in the Lord. Thus, Mary serves as a model for all believers.

Cycle "C"

The first reading from the book of Micah (5:1–4) is used in three other places in the liturgy, each time relating to the Virgin Mary: on the Nativity of Mary (September 8), as an option on commons of the Blessed Virgin, and as the reading assigned for morning prayer on the Solemnity of Mary, Mother of God. While originally part of the prophet's vision of the new Israel that will be rebuilt and restored through the Messiah, when read at Christian liturgy, the text emphasizes Jesus' Davidic descent. "Bethlehem-Ephrathah" is singled out as the tribe from which would come the "ruler in Israel" (vs. 1). This tribe, once noted only because of its insignificance, will now be remembered as the line from which the Messiah was born. This Messiah will bear the "strength" and "the majestic name of the Lord, his God" (vs. 3). It is he who "shall be peace" (vs. 4). The single verse that could have Mariological connotations speaks of "she who is to give birth" (vs. 2), clearly making the act of physical birth a point of reference for the liturgy today.

The responsorial psalm, Psalm 80, was already used on the First Sunday of Advent, "B" cycle; hence, its use today reiterates important Advent themes as much as it reflects the first reading. The references to Israel as the "vine" (vs. 15) of the Lord should not be ignored, and the reference to the one on the Lord's "right hand" (vs. 18) should be noted, since this location plays such an important part in the Advent liturgy.

The second reading from the letter to the Hebrews (10:5–10) is particularly significant because it combines a number of references to Jesus' doing the will of God: "I have come to do your will, O God" (vs. 7). When contrasted with other (ritual) sacrifices and offerings (vss. 5–6) and when seen within the context of the whole of Paul's letter contrasting old and new covenant sacrifices (with Jesus as their fulfillment), this emphasis on the will of God is a most significant point of instruction for Christ's followers. Like him, they are to follow the will of God as their self-offering, rather than to trust in ritual or cultic sacrifices alone. The author states that it was by this "will" that we have been sanctified once for all (vs. 10); thus, the paschal sacrifice of Christ is seen in relation to Jesus' attitude as he gave himself in life and in death as our ransom and redemption.

The gospel of the visitation proclaimed today (Lk 1:39–45) is also used on the feast of the queenship of Mary (August 22), as an option for the common of the Blessed Virgin, and on the Solemnity of the Assumption (August 15). The parallels between Mary and her cousin Elizabeth are clearly related; by extension, we can say that the parallels between the ministry of Jesus and John the Baptist are also indicated here. Once again, the ways of God confound the laws of nature for Elizabeth "who was thought to be sterile" (vs. 36) was now well along in her pregnancy. Significant Lukan motifs here include the statement that "she who trusted that the Lord's words to her would be fulfilled" (vs. 45), indicating the importance of living according to God's word. Then there are the parallels between Elizabeth's praise of Mary: "blessed are you among women and blessed is the fruit of your womb" (vs. 42), and the canticle that Mary utters in verses 46–55, the Magnificat. Clearly, the notion of obedience to God's will receives special attention in the very style in which this passage was written, a motif which should be especially noted today since Mary's place in redemption is emphasized in today's liturgy.

What is stressed is not so much the physical generation of Jesus as the attitude with which Mary and Joseph accepted the Lord's will for them and the way Jesus obeyed his Father's will for him.

Each of us is called to emulate and imitate these examples of obedience in the concrete circumstances of our lives, which certainly require other, but no less real, sacrifices and acts of obedience.

Sacramentary Texts

The entrance and communion antiphons are taken from today's traditional Mass formula from the Roman Missal. At the entrance, we use the words of Isaiah 45:8 and plead with God to "rain down" and "bring forth" the "Just One," "a Savior." These titles set the stage for reflection on images of Jesus which go beyond the birth of a baby. In Advent, we await the renewal of our identity in Christ and our being reunited with the Father through his paschal sacrifice; hence, we acclaim him as "Savior."

The communion antiphon is from Isaiah 7:14 (used in the first reading in the "A" cycle) to refer to the son to be born as "Emmanuel." This same Emmanuel feeds us with his body and blood; by these we are sustained to lead lives worthy of him and his redemption.

In the opening prayer, we ask the Lord to fill our hearts with his love, so that, as the angel revealed, "the coming of your Son as man, so lead us through his suffering and death to the glory of his resurrection." If we focus only on the human birth of Jesus, we lose perspective on the real heart of the way God deals with us—through the paschal mystery. Hence, the appropriateness of this text.

In the prayer over the gifts, we ask that the same "Spirit which sanctified Mary" may make holy the gifts we offer. Once again, this same Spirit who enabled Mary to become the mother of God is always active in the celebration of liturgy.

The prayer after communion (especially in its Latin original) is a strong statement that we who partake in the eucharist share even now in eternal redemption. Hence, we pray that we might be the more prepared to celebrate Christmas as a feast of our salvation.

Celebration of the Eucharist

Today's liturgy should reflect continuity with the other Advent Sundays in terms of gestures, symbols, and environment. Also, the musical settings of the acclamations should be the same as those used during the last three weeks. Some additional festivity could be introduced, however, because of the nearness of Christmas, such as a more joyful prelude and/or postlude with or without choir participation. However, music that is traditionally used at Christmas should not be anticipated in any way, whether this means carols or the texts of the Christmas liturgy itself. The pressures of our culture to anticipate Christmas should be firmly withstood. The day of Christmas is the feast of the incarnation, it does not occur anytime earlier. "Christmas masses" for special groups during Advent simply do not exist liturgically. There can be no anticipation of Christmas just as there is no anticipation of Easter.

The use of the second greeting ("the grace and peace of God our Father") would be appropriate today especially in the "A" cycle when these words form part of Paul's greeting to the church at Rome. The introduction to the liturgy could speak of Mary's and Joseph's obedience to the will of God and the challenge which today's readings offer in terms of our being obedient to God's will in our lives. We come to the eucharist to be strengthened in faith so that our trust in the Lord's will is more firm.

The titles of Jesus expressed in the third form of the penitential rite, example three ("Son of God," "Son of Man," etc.), make it a logical choice.

When planning the gospel acclamation for today, respect the difference between that assigned for the "A" cycle and that assigned for the "B" and "C" cycle.

The general intercessions should reflect Advent preparation as well as the scriptures of the day. The petitions could include reference to those seeking to know the will of God in their lives, those seeking reconciliation with the church or family members, and discovering the real values of Christmas as opposed to passing pleasures and things. For the conclusion to the intercessions, the collect offered in the sample intercessions for Christmas (which speaks directly of Mary as a model) would be appropriate.

The second Advent preface is prescribed today with its reference to Mary: "The virgin mother bore him in her womb with love beyond all telling."

The second eucharistic prayer with its simple structure and obvious brevity would reflect the starkness of Advent. It also contains a reference to Mary and the apostles and saints "who have done your will throughout the ages."

The introduction to the Lord's Prayer could contain a reference to the text, "thy will be done," and the example of Mary, Joseph, and Jesus himself as each of them did God's will.

At the Lamb of God, additional titles of Christ taken from the scriptures today (especially from Romans and Matthew) would be appropriate additions.

The solemn blessing of Advent would be a fitting conclusion to the liturgy as it would complete the unity established this Advent.

Liturgy of the Hours

At Evening Prayer I, the first antiphon accompanying Psalm 122 states, "He comes, the desire of all human hearts," reflecting our Advent longing for the Lord who will fill our hearts. The second antiphon heightens the sense of expectation: "Come, Lord, do not delay; free your people from their sinfulness." This text appropriately leads to Psalm 130, our cry to the Lord from the depths; yet it also indicates our need for the coming Savior to free us from sin and to reconcile us once again with God and one another. The third antiphon is adapted from the text of Galatians (4:4–5) and states "the fullness of time has come upon us at last; God sends his Son into the world." This text introduces the Philippians canticle (2:6–11), which appropriately reminds us of the price which Christ paid in the incarnation—of humbling himself, taking the form of a slave, and accepting death for our salvation. Thus, the liturgy reminds us that the coming feast of Christmas includes commemorating the birth of Jesus and his death and resurrection.

The remainder of this hour has already been commented upon above (scripture reading on the First Sunday and the intercessions on the Second Sunday). The antiphon to the Canticle of the Blessed Virgin is taken from whatever day between December 17 and 24 on which this Sunday falls.

The antiphons at the office of readings offer important images of the "heavenly King; [who] comes with power and might to save all the nations, alleluia." Once again, the notion of our need for the coming Messiah and his universal reign is noted along with the acclamation "alleluia" closely associated with the Easter season. This antiphon leads to Psalm 24, designated as an optional invitatory psalm for the hours. As we pray these verses about standing in the

Lord's holy place and having "clean hands and a pure heart" (vs. 4), we are reminded of the coming Savior who forgives sin and makes us worthy to come before God in prayer. The last antiphon shifts from acknowledging the Lord to exhorting us about what to do as we near the end of Advent: "Let us cleanse our hearts for the coming of our great King, that we may be ready to welcome him; he is coming and will not delay." (Both readings at this hour are chosen from the current day and are not proper to Sunday.)

At morning prayer, the first antiphon refers to the nearness of the "day of the Lord" who comes "to save us." The juxtaposition of this eschatological reference with the role of Jesus as savior conveniently combines both Advent themes. Psalm 118, which follows, contains many references which are associated with Advent, such as "the Lord's right hand has triumphed" (vs. 15). It also contains elements commonly used to refer to Christ's role as Messiah to Israel and then to all nations: "the stone which the builders rejected has become the corner stone" (vs. 22). The second antiphon contains strong eschatological references and incarnational emphases when it states that we should "go out to meet him" (as did the wise virgins whose oil supply was sufficient), and that the Lord is a "Strong God, Ruler of all, [and] Prince of Peace." The third antiphon, "Your all-powerful Word, O Lord will come to earth from his throne of glory," reminds us of Jesus' humble acceptance of our humanity, which is fully graced by Christ's divinity.

At Evening Prayer II, the antiphons reflect our need for the savior (first) and the proximate feast of the Incarnation when we say, "come, O Lord, do not delay" (second). The imagery of Isaiah is clearly reflected in the second antiphon when we note that as a result of the Lord's coming "crooked paths will be straightened and rough ways smooth." These cosmic results are expressed in the third text in which we affirm that "ever wider will his kingdom spread, eternally at peace, alleluia." What was imaged in nature about the power of the Messiah is now seen in the universality of his church.

At both morning and evening prayer, the rest of the hour is taken from the occurring weekday between December 17 to 24.

Celebration of the Hours

Taking the lead from the dominant role of the proper weekdays in the hours today, it would be most fitting to use general Advent hymns to begin morning and evening prayer. For the invitatory, the text assigned for this second part of Advent, "The Lord is close at hand; come, let us worship him," would be most appropriate, as would the use of Psalm 95. If another psalm is chosen in its place, it should not be Psalm 24 since it is already assigned for use at the office of readings.

At all the hours, the proposed psalm prayers could be adjusted to include more attention to Advent themes. However, it should also be recalled that these are prayers, not instructions. As such they should contain appropriate language, metaphor, and idiom proper to collect prayers which would suitably recall the eschatological and incarnational themes of Advent.

The Lord's Prayer at morning and evening prayer could be introduced by a subtle reference to doing God's will as exemplified by Mary and Joseph. Singing this prayer would also enhance its place in the liturgy.

The use of the solemn Advent blessing to conclude these hours would be appropriate, especially if this text has been used to conclude these hours on the other Advent Sundays.

Reflection—"No Laid-Back Heroes"

One of the most distressing examples of our contemporary malaise is the advent of the "laid-back" hero. Recognizable by his cool, disinterested demeanor, and unshakable reserve, the laid-back hero is unwilling to become involved, sauntering through life unimpressed and uncommitted. Whether he appears in the fiction of Hemingway or in a characterization by Bogart, we tend to idolize and emulate this icy species. Don Quixote becomes a fool in our eyes for caring too much, and Rhett Butler's line somehow becomes immortalized: "Frankly, Scarlett, I don't give a damn!"

Its contemporary forms are rarely so stark, but a modern translation is the slogan "be true to yourself" the opposite of which is being committed or loyal to another. Seeking fulfillment takes precedence over service. "Love" winds up meaning "never having to say you're sorry." Fidelity is only for one's mate.

Preoccupation with self is hardly a new phenomenon. But what is novel about its current manifestation is its social acceptability. Not too long ago being selfish was shameful; now it's trendy.

Disdaining to joust with windmills or to deal with what might be, our laid-back hero faces, instead, the more subtle demons of guilt and despair. Assuming the stance of being in control, the modern person has no one to turn to.

Today's gospel story reminds us (almost embarrassingly) that our life's destiny is, in fact, not in our hands, that the ethic for us who believe is "thy will be done," and that the real book of life comes from the Lord's word rather than shallow compositions that sell thousands of copies. *Looking Out For Number One* may have been a bestseller, but its thesis is clearly anti-gospel.

Despite the fact that Mary has few lines assigned to her in the scriptures, she takes her place in Advent with Isaiah and John the Baptist as an Advent hero; like them she is hardly laid back. Their example is important for us because they put such faith in God's promises and in God's revelation that they staked everything—life, prosperity and even social status to say and do what he wanted them to do.

We come to the liturgy today because we need to see things God's way and to live that way as well. For our instruction, the church gives us the heroes of Isaiah, John the Baptist, and Mary during this season—hardly examples of our culture's laid-back heroes.

DECEMBER 17

Liturgical Context

The norms for the liturgical year state: "the weekdays from 17 December to 24 December inclusive serve to prepare more directly for the Lord's birth" (no. 42).

This shift toward incarnational themes on December 17 is not new. In the former Roman usage, the "O" antiphons, beginning at evening prayer, emphasized titles of Christ whose coming we await at Christmas. These antiphons are retained in the present reform and are also found as the alleluia verses at the eucharist (Lect., no. 202). (In more popular usage, these antiphons comprise the verses to the familiar "O come, O come, Emmanuel" with their order reversed.)

The Introduction to the Lectionary describes the choice of readings at Mass:

"In the last week before Christmas the events that immediately prepared for the Lord's birth are presented from Matthew (Chapter 1) and Luke (Chapter 1). The texts in the first reading, chosen in view of the gospel reading, are from different Old Testament books and include important messianic prophecies." (no. 94)

And yet we are still celebrating Advent, not Christmas. As Advent comes to an end, our joy and anticipation grow, but they are still restrained until Evening Prayer I on Christmas (Eve). The use of Christmas decorations, a creche, or Christmas music is out of place until Christmas itself. Messianic prophecies, narratives about the human birth of Jesus, and patristic texts about this birth are meant to lead us to appreciate the full power and mystery of the incarnation as commemorated on Christmas.

Liturgy of the Eucharist

Unlike the first part of Advent, all elements in the mass formulas from December 17 to 24 have been carefully selected to reflect the day's scripture readings. Today's entrance antiphon from Isaiah (49: 13) reflects the shift from expectation to excitement at the Lord's coming. We pray in joy and thanksgiving that the Lord "will take pity on those in distress."

The opening prayer from the Leonine Sacramentary uses the important title "Word" to describe the birth of Jesus among us; hence, it subtly directs our attention to a key phrase in the gospel of Christmas morning from John 1:14, "the Word became flesh." The prayer also draws on the parallelism often seen in the liturgy of the humanity/divinity of Christ. This particular text reflects the prayer said when the deacon (or priest) pours water into the wine at the presentation of the gifts: "By the mystery of this water and wine may we come to share in the divinity of Christ, who humbled himself to share in our humanity." The collect acknowledges God as "creator and redeemer." We pray that he would re-create and redeem us through the eucharist we celebrate and through the approaching Christmas feast.

The first reading from the book of Genesis (49:1-2, 8-10) was obviously chosen to coincide with the genealogy from Matthew's gospel proclaimed today (Mt 1:1-17). This account of the destiny of the tribe of Judah coincides with Matthew's opening words concerning "Jacob the father of Judah and his brothers" (vs. 1). These particular verses from Genesis provide the context for the scripture reading assigned at morning prayer on Advent Tuesdays (Gn 49:10) described above. This "last will and testament" is proclaimed when Jacob gathers his sons together to "listen" to him (vs. 1). Judah, from whom Jesus descended, will be specially blessed and will receive special homage from the other tribes because the Messiah will be born from his family.

Psalm 72 is the responsorial psalm today and tomorrow. It was used on the Second Sunday of Advent, "A" cycle, on Tuesday of the first week of Advent, and will be used again on some of the weekdays after Epiphany. When read with a Messianic understanding, the "justice" and "fullness of peace" (vs. 7) noted are clearly incarnate in Jesus. It is he who is acclaimed as "the king's son: [who] shall govern your people with justice and your afflicted ones with judgment" (vss. 1–2). Such an interpretation complements the Messianic prophecies already proclaimed in Advent.

The gospel, tracing the human ancestry of Jesus from the early patriarchs to his birth from Mary, is proclaimed from Matthew 1. The author is concerned to identify Jesus as part of the history of Israel—one who both shares her history and fulfills her destiny. Once again, the use of titles for God and Christ are important to understand the meaning of this text and the full meaning of the incarnation of the "son of David" (vs. 1), "son of Abraham" (vs. 1), "Jesus" (vs. 16), and "Christ" (vs. 16). Matthew is concerned to point to the reality of the birth of Jesus and his role in our redemption. Part of Matthew's theological interest is to point out that the group of people he mentions forms a rather unlikely lot from whom Jesus drew his heritage. This is an "unlikely" group because their virtue was not always imitable; in fact, there were times when their conduct was scandalous (e.g., David's affair with Bathsheba disguised yet noted in vs. 6 "by the wife of Uriah").

That God could intervene through strange situations (such as this infidelity) is reflected in Matthew's use of four women's names (Tamar, Rahab, Ruth, and the wife of Uriah) who lead up to Mary (vs. 16). All these women had something irregular about their marital unions and all relied on God to intervene to accomplish his plan through them. The recounting of names (which can seem foreign to us) would be a sign to first-century Jews of how God acted in their history and how the birth of the Messiah reflected their election and special status. When proclaimed at the liturgy today, this text illumines even more strongly the reference to the humanity of Jesus in the opening prayer. It is precisely through his humanity that Jesus became Messiah and Lord; we who share in his humanity by our human birth can now share in divinity through him.

Both the prayer over the gifts and the prayer after communion are taken from the old Gelasian Sacramentary. In the prayer over the gifts, we ask that our offerings be blessed by the Lord and that the church might be strengthened by the eucharist, the bread from heaven. The prayer after communion emphasizes that the "light" of Christ, which we receive sacramentally, will make us radiant when the Lord comes to us at Christmas or at his second coming.

The communion antiphon (from Haggai 2:8) speaks of the "desired of all nations" whose coming will fill "the house of the Lord" with glory. We who receive the Lord's body and blood are ourselves a "house of the Lord."

Celebration of the Eucharist

The introduction to the liturgy could note the shift in emphasis toward a more urgent and fervent preparation for Christmas. If the third form of the penitential rite is used, titles of Jesus drawn from today's readings would be appropriate (such as "Son of Abraham," "Son of David," "Anointed One," and "Lord of all the nations").

The use of the first "O" antiphon ("O wisdom") as the gospel acclamation (Lect., no. 202) would be most fitting. (Even though this text is not required, the Latin Lectionary assigns the "O" antiphons in order as the alleluia verse beginning today.)

A brief introduction to the gospel about the fact that it emphasizes the humanity of Jesus (or another theme to be drawn from the text) would prepare the assembly for the proclamation of what can be a difficult text to listen to.

In the prayer of the faithful, petitions about respect for the unborn and for all life, for those of the Jewish faith, for Christians to prepare themselves more intensely for Christmas, and that the wisdom of God would enlighten world leaders would be appropriate.

The second Advent preface is prescribed for use today; it could well be followed by the second eucharistic prayer containing the text "with all the saints who have done your will throughout the ages." This could be a subtle reflection of those whose names are noted in the gospel who helped accomplish God's plan of salvation.

The third memorial acclamation, "until you come in glory,"

would serve as a reminder of the eschatological aspect of Advent (which should not be lost sight of during this second part of the season). Other ways of reiterating this theme would be to "pray for the coming of the kingdom" at the Lord's Prayer (fourth option) and using either number 1 or 16 of the prayers over the people as a dismissal.

Liturgy of the Hours

Beginning today, the readings at the office of readings, the antiphons to the Canticles of Zechariah and Mary, the intercessions at morning and evening prayer, and the concluding prayer are those assigned to the dates of December 17 through 23. The psalmody and accompanying antiphons are taken from the current weekday; hence, there is no direct relation between these separate sources for the hours. In the commentaries that follow, only the texts proper to the above-mentioned dates are noted.

At the office of readings, the shift toward incarnational themes is seen in the first reading from second Isaiah (45:1–13) originally addressed to the Israelites in exile. The chosen people long for a time when their present misfortune will end. Hence, notions of comfort and hope dominate here and in the passages read until Christmas. Today's text is a hymn addressed to the foreigner Cyrus who is named the "anointed one" (vs. 1). The victories ascribed to him are really the Lord's (vss. 2–3), who does such deeds to reveal his identity and to assure Israel of his presence with them (vs. 3). The promised victory is not due to Cyrus' ingenuity; it is accomplished because the Lord is with them (vs. 5). This Lord requires a commitment of faith as opposed to dabbling in the worship or works of any other god: "I am the Lord, there is no other" (vss. 5–6). Curiously, it is the outsider, Cyrus, who will be the instrument for rebuilding Jerusalem and freeing the exiles (vs. 13); yet it is really the Lord who saves them.

Verse 8, "Let justice descend . . . ," appears in the Advent liturgy as the entrance antiphon on the Fourth Sunday. Originally, it referred to the advent of justice and salvation; when used in Christian worship, its reference to the "Just One" can rightfully be understood to carry important Messianic overtones. (This same verse is also part of the responsory that follows.)

The patristic text from St. Leo the Great provides a commentary on the genealogy read at the eucharist. The humanity of Jesus is stressed clearly in this passage. In taking on our human nature, the Lord has graced our human condition so that we who live this human life can share in his divinity. The divine plan that saved Israel from the Egyptians and which guided them to safety through the exile is the same divine plan that established from all eternity that the Son of God would reunite us with the Father from whom we were separated.

At morning prayer, the urgency of these Advent days is reflected in the antiphon to Zechariah's canticle, which states that the kingdom of God is "at hand" and that the Savior "will not delay his coming."

Appropriate Advent themes are found in the petitions (repeated from Saturday of the first week) which speak of the "seed of justice" planted among God's people, about listening to the Word of God to "persevere in holiness," about the "Son who is to come," and about being strengthened "until the day of the coming of Jesus Christ our Lord."

At evening prayer, Mary's canticle is introduced by the first "O" antiphon: "O wisdom, O holy Word of God, you govern all creation with your strong yet tender care. Come and show your people the way of salvation." By combining the Old Testament notion of God's wisdom and the New Testament revelation about Jesus as the life-giving Word of God who governs and rules all creation, this text succinctly summarizes traditional Advent images.

The intercessions at evening prayer (already used at Evening Prayer I on the First and Third Sundays) are interesting both structurally and textually, and the responses are all variations on the "Come, Lord Jesus" motif already seen. The help of the Lord is sought as we affirm that he is the savior and redeemer who will free us from sin and bring us to everlasting life, where we shall finally see God "face to face."

Celebration of the Hours

The invitatory assigned to the days between December 17 to 24 is, "The Lord is close at hand; come let us worship him." When accompanied by Psalm 100, this part of the liturgy can help reflect the urgency and eagerness with which we celebrate these latter days of Advent.

With regard to the choice of appropriate hymns at morning and evening prayer, it should be noted that the Latin Breviary offers texts that emphasize the coming feast of the incarnation. At morning prayer, *Magnis prophetae vocibus* is used about Christ as the eternal light and about our desire to see God. At evening prayer, the hymn is *Verbum salutis omnium*, about the coming of the Word of God from Mary at which all peoples exult for they see in it the final and fullest manifestation of God's love. Since the texts of the Canticles of Zechariah and Mary will be emphasized in the readings at Mass just before Christmas and because these texts refer to the incarnation, it would be helpful to sing them as a normal part of these hours from now until Christmas.

If the intercessions are adapted today, the importance of eschatological themes at morning prayer and the simpler structure of petitions at evening prayer should be retained.

Extra lighted candles at evening prayer, and subdued electric light would help underscore the liturgy's message—we who live in the darkness of the world need the light and illumination that comes from God. The singing (or careful recitation with musical background) of the "O" antiphons in such an atmosphere could help draw out some of the many levels of interpretation associated with the coming of the Light of the world among us who "dwell in darkness and the shadow of death."

Reflection—"The Human Face of God"

Roman Catholicism has never neglected the importance of the body in theology, spirituality, and liturgy. Even when certain tendencies pointed to a kind of spiritism or disdain for the things of the flesh, traditional Catholic doctrine affirmed the importance of our flesh as the instrument of salvation (to paraphrase St. Augustine).

Part of the enchantment of Christmas comes from retelling the story of how Jesus was born in a manger at Bethlehem. Inherent in this story is the affirmation that God's Son assumed human flesh so that we who are made in flesh and blood can share his divine life here on earth. We share in this divine life not by forsaking our humanity or by ignoring our bodies; rather, we do it by appreciating and accepting the presence of God among us and within us.

St. Matthew's genealogy can seem to be a list of names (unpronounceable for some) with little or no obvious meaning to us who are so far removed from their time and place in history. And yet an important lesson here is that the God we worship and adore sent his Son into human history and that his lineage goes back to the patriarch Abraham.

But, this is only part of the story, its ancient part. The modern part of the story concerns how we experience the presence of God in our lives and how others come to know God through us. Because we communicate with words and deeds through our bodies, we can say that we, like the men and women in the genealogy, have to put our lives in service to God's divine plan. Part of that plan means that we manifest to others the presence of God as the Lord who is among us still.

The real human face of God may well be our face as we show compassion and love to one another—particularly when we reveal his forgiving love. The only God many people may ever come to know in this world is the God we make known to them.

DECEMBER 18

Liturgical Context

The shift in emphasis in the liturgy begun yesterday continues with the second "O" antiphon today and the continuation of the gospel of Matthew (1:18–25). The antiphon, formerly addressed to "Adonai," reminds us of the relationship established between God and his chosen people through the covenant, which is fulfilled and fully realized in the incarnation.

Liturgy of the Eucharist

Today's entrance antiphon contains the significant titles of Christ as "King" and "Lamb" whose coming is acclaimed. The reference to Christ as King reminds us of the title used to describe the Messiah in the first reading at midnight mass from Isaiah (9:2–7), "king of kings." Significantly, this royal title is closely associated with a sacrificial component when it is applied to Jesus, the "Lamb" slain for our salvation. John's acclamation, "Look! There is the Lamb of God who takes away the sin of the world!" (Jn 1:29), is noted here as a most appropriate way to address the Lord whose incarnation led to his acceptance of death to free us from sin and death.

The opening prayer acknowledges our need to be delivered from our slavery to sin (better rendered as "our age-old bondage of sin"). As we come to acknowledge not only the evil we ourselves perform but the sinful condition we have inherited from Adam, we admit our need for a savior and grow in appreciation of the full meaning of the feast of Christmas.

Today's first reading from Jeremiah (23:5–8), chosen to coincide with the gospel of the events leading to Jesus' birth, fills out the important Old Testament background about the Messiah's lineage from the house of David. This "righteous shoot" (vs. 5) is acclaimed "king" because he will govern his people with justice and peace. It is he who will save Judah and assure Israel's security. So essential to his rule is the establishment of justice and peace that he is called "the Lord our justice" (vs. 6). The prophet saw the coming of the Just One as parallel to God's intervention for his people at the Exodus. Just as Israel could rely on this memory of God's intervention, so will Jeremiah's contemporaries affirm the significance of his approaching intervention by stating that the Lord brought "the descendants of the house of Israel up from the land of the north" (vs. 8). These examples of direct divine action serve as paradigms for followers of covenant religion to realize and experience anew God's kindness in every generation.

The responsorial psalm repeats the refrain and some of the verses used yesterday from Psalm 72. Royal titles and imagery are used here to acclaim the Lord who continually "governs [his] people with justice" and whose special care extends to the "afflicted" (vs. 2). It is especially the "poor" (vss. 12–13) and the "afflicted" (vss. 1, 12) who will receive the reward of God's justice. We who admit our spiritual poverty before God and the sins we have committed can use these verses to express our cry for God's help and the assurance of his grace and forgiveness. At the end of the psalm, we bless the "glorious name" of the Lord (vs. 19) because he has acted on behalf of his people.

The gospel proclaimed today is used on the Fourth Sunday of Advent, "A" cycle (see commentary above) and at the mass of the Christmas vigil. As a continuation of yesterday's text, this reading explores how the Messiah came to be born and notes that his lineage is from the house of David. Significantly, today's text includes verse 24 about naming him "Jesus." This title means that he who is with us as "Emmanuel" is the enfleshment of him who saves us from our sins. To call on the name "Jesus" is to call on the one who alone can free us from evil and sin. This title recalls the title "Lamb" used at the entrance today and the biblical imagery (especially the Genesis myth) used in the opening prayer.

The prayer over the gifts (taken from a combination of two texts from the Bergamo Sacramentary) points to Jesus' taking on our human condition and therefore being made subject to death. It was by dying our death that Jesus destroyed the limits which physical death places on us. Through his death and resurrection, reenacted in the liturgy, we gain access to our heavenly inheritance.

The communion antiphon, taken from verse 23 of today's gospel, reassures us of God's presence (as Emmanuel, the title used in the "O" antiphon on December 23). It is this abiding presence which becomes our spiritual food when we receive the eucharist.

In the prayer after communion, from the former Roman Missal, we ask that God would grant us his mercy to prepare us for the "coming feast of our redemption." This latter phrase already sounds paschal overtones of the paschal mystery as we await the birth of Mary's child.

Celebration of the Eucharist

The introduction to the liturgy could speak of the ways Emmanuel makes himself present among us. At the liturgy, he is present in the assembly, in the Word proclaimed, in the broken bread and the shared cup.

As a sign that we have not always responded to Christ among us, the use of the second form of the penitential rite with the simple acknowledgment, "Lord, we have sinned against you" and "grant us your salvation," would be appropriate.

The second "O" antiphon as the alleluia verse (Lect., no. 202), about the leader of Israel, would be appropriate since it draws on salient features of salvation history, which achieves its fulfillment in the coming of Emmanuel, as stated in the gospel that follows.

Petitions about justice and peace in our world, about being aware of the many modes of God's presence in our lives, about moderation in food and drink in Advent and about a special urgency to prepare spiritually for Christmas would fit in well with the readings and this latter phase of the season.

The second Advent preface is assigned for proclamation today. The use of the Roman Canon with its references to "Mary, the ever-virgin mother of Jesus Christ our Lord and God" and to "Joseph, her husband" would reflect their roles in the incarnation, and reiterate the relationship of Joseph to Mary as mentioned in today's gospel.

A comment about doing God's will as Mary and Joseph did would suitably introduce the Lord's Prayer with its important petition, "thy will be done."

The third formula of dismissal, "Go in peace to love and serve the Lord," would help draw out the implications of the eucharist since it is always oriented to helping us live life on God's terms not just to celebrating in his memory.

Should a prayer over the people be used as part of the dismissal, number 11, in which we ask God to "make us ready to do [his] will," would underscore the concepts just mentioned.

Liturgy of the Hours

The first reading from Isaiah (46:1–13) in the office of readings continues the "comfort" message of Deutero-Isaiah. Here the author states that the worship of Babylonian (or other) gods is futile (vss. 1–2). The Lord God alone has done great things for his chosen people; it is he alone "who will continue and . . . who will carry you to safety" (vs. 4). The God we revere is a jealous God: "I am God, there is no other; I am God, there is none like me" (vs. 9). As God once saved Israel, he now promises to remain true to his promises to them: "Yes, I have spoken, and I will accomplish it, I have planned it, and I will do it" (vs. 11). He will establish "salvation within Zion, and give Israel my glory" (vs. 13). These verses gain greater significance when one recalls the troubles that afflicted Israel at the time this prophecy was proclaimed. Then Israel needed to hear that the Lord reaffirmed his commitment to his people. During Advent, we acknowledge our own personal exile and distance from God. Hence, it is fitting that we hear this reaffirmation of the Lord's presence with us and of the hope he gives us.

The second- (or third-) century letter to Diognetus is the source for the second reading at this hour about the incarnation. In a particularly moving section, the author relates our need for salvation to the wonder of the incarnation and its perduring effects. Reflecting on these phrases can help us prepare for the coming of the Lord among us at Christmas.

At morning prayer, the antiphon to Zechariah's canticle is particularly strong in urging resolute and determined preparation for Christmas: "Let everything within you watch and wait, for the Lord draws near."

The intercessions (repeated from the Second Sunday) use familiar Advent themes as they refer to the Lord's coming in judgment (introduction and second petition) and to our joyful longing for his coming (third and fourth petitions). Thus, both eschatological and incarnational aspects of the season are present.

At evening prayer, the "O" antiphon acclaims the God of the covenant, a contrast to yesterday's which emphasized the God of creation and redemption. The reference to God revealing himself to Moses in the burning but unconsumed bush and in the law at Sinai emphasize the enduring significance of the covenant for us who use these images in the liturgy. With reverence and awe, we await our Lord's coming and his gift of freeing us from sin.

In the first petition of the intercessions (repeated from the Second Sunday), we acknowledge our need to share in Christ's life that comes through the incarnation; in the second, we ask for his mercy whose acceptance of our human condition involved being weak and in need. The third and fifth petitions speak of the two comings of Christ; in the meantime, he intercedes for us at the Father's right hand.

Celebration of the Hours

The invitatory assigned to this second part of Advent could be repeated today with Psalm 95 as a sign that the emphasis has shifted to more urgent preparation for Christmas.

The intercessions at morning and evening prayer could be added to or adjusted should the community want to particularize what is reflected in them. Intercessions are general by their nature, hence applications that are too specific hinder their impact as universal prayers.

Some additional solemnity could be added by reverencing the scriptures or by dimming electric lighting at evening prayer (as suggested yesterday).

Reflection—"Silent Joseph, A Mighty Voice"

The scriptures contain no words spoken by Joseph, hence the title "silent Joseph." However, this is not to suggest that Joseph left us no legacy. Today's gospel proves the contrary. This quiet man is the model disciple because he did as the angel requested—he took Mary into his home despite his fears. Joseph obeyed without counting the cost once he knew that this was the Lord's will for him. One of Joseph's lasting legacies to us lies in witness, not in words.

What about us? Do we "talk a good game" and fall down in performance? The example of Joseph tells us that words have lost their value if they mask disobedience to God. Obeying God's word and accepting God's will for us is what really matters. The issue is whether, like Joseph, in our silence we come to know God and to obey him.

DECEMBER 19

Liturgical Context

The liturgy today continues a more intense preparation for Christmas. The gospel begins a series of stories demonstrating how God acts in very unlikely circumstances to accomplish his plan. The liturgy also contains subtle references to light and darkness, a motif which will become more dominant as the start of winter approaches. The natural phenomenon of shorter days and longer nights provides the context in nature that almost demands that we acknowledge Christ as the light who came to shatter the darkness of sin.

Liturgy of the Eucharist

Today's entrance antiphon affirms that the Lord is soon to come and "will not delay." Because "he is our Savior," there will no longer by any "fear in our lands"—he is among us as saving Lord.

The opening prayer, from the Leonine Sacramentary, asks that the world may see the splendor of God's glory in Christ's virginal birth. We pray for deeper faith and love so that we can more fittingly celebrate the astounding mystery of the incarnation (which phrase is more reflective of the Latin original).

The selection of the first reading from Judges (13:2–7, 24–25) is to prepare for the gospel. There are striking parallels between the announcement to Manoah of the birth of Samson and the announcement to Zechariah about the birth of John. Manoah was married to a barren wife; yet, she heeded the angel's message that she would bear a son (vs. 3). That Samson was destined for the Lord's service is reflected in his simple lifestyle (vs. 4). As a sign of his consecration to the Lord, no razor shall touch his head "for this boy is to be consecrated to God from the womb" (vs. 5). Samson's special mission is to begin the deliverance of Israel from the Philistines (vs. 5); throughout his life, the Lord blessed him and "the spirit of the Lord began to be with him" (vs. 25).

Psalm 71, as the responsorial psalm, can be understood (in an accommodated way) to reflect the first reading by its reference in verse 6 to dependence from birth on the Lord as strength ("from my mother's womb you are my strength"). Also the reference in verse 17 to being taught from youth and proclaiming the Lord's deeds indicates a lifelong commitment to do the Lord's work as exemplified in Samson and John the Baptist. As we pray this psalm, we draw strength from the images it uses to describe God—stronghold, rock, fortress, and hope.

The gospel of Luke (1:5–25) is a highly stylized text filled with references to Old Testament precedents and examples of God's acting in such an unexpected way that a barren and elderly woman, Elizabeth, would bear a son who would be special to the Lord. It is also important to note the stylistic traits that Luke uses to deepen our appreciation of these events. For example, Luke states that Elizabeth and Zechariah "were just in the eyes of God, blamelessly following all the commandments and ordinances of the Lord" (vs. 6). This shows that they stood firmly in line with other Jews who observed the Law faithfully, hoping in the promised Messiah. From among the more likely candidates who could have been chosen, God selected this couple to begin the fulfillment of the "old" covenant. All the rituals Zechariah observed as a member of the priestly class (vss. 8–10) would soon come to an end in Christ, the high priest of the "new" covenant. It was God's plan that Elizabeth's son would be the last of the prophets to prepare for the Lord. The "joy and gladness" (vs. 14) they would experience at the birth of John would only be a shadow, Luke says, of the joy the disciples would experience at Christ's resurrection from the dead (Lk 24:41 and Acts 2:26). As a prophet "filled with the Holy Spirit from his mother's womb" (vs. 15), John was "to prepare for the Lord a people well disposed" (vs. 17).

Despite the authority of Gabriel's message, Zechariah was obviously not prepared to receive it. He questioned the angel and was therefore struck dumb until the child had been born (vss. 18–20). Because he did not trust the angel's message, Zechariah had to suffer the ignominy of being a speechless priest, a pray-er who could no longer utter words of praise and thanks to God. Zechariah's example warns the truly faithful believer to listen to and obey the Lord's word.

The prayer over the gifts asks that despite our unworthiness (or "weakness" as stated here), as we bring our gifts before the Lord, he make them holy.

The prayer after communion asks that we might be purified by the sacrament we celebrate and so welcome Christ as savior with minds and hearts renewed.

The communion antiphon reiterates the light/darkness theme today by quoting the canticle Zechariah utters, that "the dawn from on high shall break upon us, to guide our feet on the road of peace" (Lk 1:78–79).

Celebration of the Eucharist

The introduction to the liturgy could mention Zechariah's fear at receiving the angel's message and point out that despite our own reluctance at accepting God's will for us, we can draw strength from the eucharist we celebrate.

The second set of sample invocations for the third form of the penitential rite could help reiterate the three comings of Christ commemorated in Advent.

For the alleluia verse, the third "O" antiphon would serve well (Lect., no. 202), especially because it recalls the house of David and the stem of Jesse from which will come the promised Messiah.

Among the petitions today, prayers for a deeper and freer response to the word in our lives, about being faithful to liturgy and prayer (as were Zechariah and Elizabeth), about the elderly being revered and respected, and about those who are confined to nursing homes would all reflect some of the concerns found in the scriptures.

The use of the third eucharistic prayer with the second Advent preface would be appropriate, especially because of the petition to "strengthen in faith and love your pilgrim church on earth." The use of the second memorial acclamation with the plea, "Lord Jesus come in glory," would be most fitting to reiterate the heightened sense of pleading for the Lord's coming in the "O" antiphons.

To introduce the Lord's Prayer, the former usage of the Roman rite would be effective: "Taught by our Savior's command and formed by the word of God we dare to say."

An introduction to the sign of peace, speaking about our support and concern for each other expressed in this sign, would be appropriate.

As a conclusion to the liturgy, the use of number 13 of the prayers over the people would be fitting since it is about the Lord helping us to seek him with all our hearts and so deserve what he promised for all eternity.

Liturgy of the Hours

The first reading at the office of readings continues from second Isaiah (47:1, 3b–15) and contains an ironic song over the defeat of Babylon. The first verse paints a scene of devastation for even though the people still enjoy material prosperity, the prophet sees and decries their interior corruption. The example of Babylon offers the very antithesis of the life of a true believer. The message for Israel in her exile (and for us today) is that she should not emulate Babylon and aim for passing and futile pleasures; she should seek justice and salvation from God alone (vs. 15).

The message of Advent is that so much of what we strive for in this life will ultimately be taken away and that what really matters is life lived in union with God, with an ever deeper commitment to him in faith and love.

The second reading from Ireaneus' *Against Heresies* deals with God's plan of salvation through the incarnation. It is precisely through Christ who took on our human nature that we have access to the God we cannot see. Christ becomes the means for us to come to the vision of God; the instrument of this is his humanity.

At morning prayer, the antiphon to Zechariah's canticle (which reflects the gospel recounting the annunciation to Zechariah of John's birth) uses the nature symbolism of light and darkness when it states: "like the sun in the morning sky, the Savior of this world will dawn." Through him, we can see the brilliance and fullness of the Father's love in Christ. This light descends "to rest in the womb of the Virgin" who "bore him in her womb with love beyond all telling" (Advent preface II).

At evening prayer the third "O" antiphon draws on the fact that Jesus is born of the house of David, whose father is the Jesse noted at its beginning, "flower of Jesse's stem." This antiphon is based on a reference in Isaiah 11:10 about Jesse's lineage; from what was apparently a barren tribe would now come the Messiah. The "sign for all the peoples" before whom kings and all nations worship is the incarnate Word of God whose death and resurrection reconcile us with the Father. The paschal nature of the Messiah's vocation should not be forgotten even as we legitimately reflect on the universality of his rule "for all peoples" as he comes to us in human flesh at Christmas and as the manifestation of God's infinite love for all at Epiphany. At the end of the antiphon, we plead "come, let nothing keep you from coming to our aid." We pray that we will put nothing in the way that God chooses to reveal himself to us.

Celebration of the Hours

The invitatory to the hours today: "the Lord is close at hand; come let us worship him," is particularly appropriate especially if the verse before the readings ("Lord, show us your mercy and love. . . .") has been used on Advent Mondays. To accompany the invitatory, Psalm 67 offers verses which subtly reiterate Advent themes such as: God's graciousness and blessing (vs. 2), the Lord's ways being known upon earth for all nations (vs. 3), who rules by justice and guides nations on earth (vs. 5).

Since the intercessions at morning and evening prayer are taken from those used on Monday of the second week of Advent, the suggestions made above should be consulted. In addition, however, some reference to the darkness/light symbolism should be made to echo other references in the liturgy.

Reflection—"When We Get What We Want"

It has been said that two things frustrate us in life—when we don't get what we want and when we get what we want. In either case, our expectation (generally inflated beyond imagining) exceeds reality. Hence, we are frustrated. Obviously, when we don't get what we think we need or would like to have, we are frustrated and sense incompleteness and unfairness at the way we are treated.

But, the other (more serious) cause of frustration comes when we get what we want and then find out that there are strings attached or challenges implied in our accepting it. Such is the plight of Zechariah and Elizabeth in today's gospel. They had prayed for a child and had been careful in observing religious customs to be found worthy before God. But, just when what they had asked for was promised through the angel's message, Zechariah doubted whether this could be true. He was about to get what he wanted and yet he could not accept this on God's terms. Hence, he was struck dumb and could not announce or explain the coming birth to others.

It is when we submit to God and surrender to his plans for us, whether they are or are not what we expect or want, that we are able to achieve contentment and happiness. Real happiness comes from God's ways, not our designs. Deep contentment should come from knowing that we are part of God's people and that his plan involves our salvation. Nothing we could want on earth could ever substitute for the one thing that really matters—the life of God within and among us as we yearn for complete union with God in eternity.

DECEMBER 20

Liturgical Context

Today's readings at the eucharist continue the annunciation stories begun yesterday, while the gospel emphasizes Mary's role in the incarnation. The fourth "O" antiphon speaks of the "key of David" whose birth and paschal mystery unlocks the bondage of sin and death that resulted from Adam's fall.

Liturgy of the Eucharist

Yesterday's "O" antiphon about the "flower of Jesse's stem" should be recalled as we consider the entrance antiphon today. This text speaks of the shoot to come from "Jesse's stock" through whom all nations will experience "the saving power of God." Taken from Isaiah (11:1; 40:5) and Luke (3:6), the antiphon points to the significance of the birth of the Messiah. The other aspect of this astounding event is reflected in the opening prayer where the Blessed Virgin is the model believer who was "always ready" to do the Father's will. This text, taken from the Leonine Sacramentary, coincides with the gospel as it speaks of Mary welcoming the angel's message. Then, in theologically nuanced language, the text goes on to say that she was "filled with the light of your Spirit," and "became the temple of your Word." It was by the Holy Spirit that Mary conceived Jesus, and it was her divine motherhood that makes us able to acclaim her the "temple" of the "Word." In being the temple of God's Son, Mary fulfills the purposes which temple worship had in Judaism and leads us to a renewed appreciation of the place of worship through Christ, the new temple.

The first reading today is the familiar text of Isaiah 7:10–14 discussed on the Fourth Sunday of Advent, "A" cycle. When proclaimed in the Christian liturgy, this text reminds us that when things seem to be coming apart and destruction is assured, it is then that God intervenes for his people. It is especially at such times that we come to know God as savior.

The response to the reading from Psalm 24 combines two of the psalm's verses in which we pray that the Lord will truly be our Lord and King: "let the Lord enter; he is the king of glory" (vss. 7, 10). We praise him in this psalm for the wonders of creation (vss. 1–2), for inviting us to stand in his holy place with sinless hands (vss. 3–4) and for the fact that, like Israel, we continually seek "the face of the God of Jacob" (vs. 6) as we live and work here on earth destined for eternal union with God in heaven.

The gospel of the annunciation to Mary is the central scripture reading today from Luke (1:26–38) (see commentary above, Fourth Sunday, "B" cycle). Once again, the liturgy stresses the role of the Virgin Mary in giving birth to Jesus and, therefore, for her role in our salvation.

Both the prayer over the gifts (from the old Gelasian Sacramentary) and the prayer after communion (from the Leonine) speak of the importance of the eucharist: to nourish us now (prayer after communion) and to lead us to the fullness of what it promises in eternal life (prayer over the gifts). The notion of Advent as a journey to the fullness of the kingdom is noted in the prayer over the gifts where we pray that this sacrifice may lead us to "eternal life we seek in faith and hope."

The communion antiphon is taken from today's gospel and reiterates the angel's message that Mary will conceive and bear Jesus. It is Christ as savior whom we receive in the eucharist.

Celebration of the Eucharist

The introduction to the liturgy could deal with our receptivity to the revealed word of God and to the Word Incarnate. Using the following Christological titles with the third form of the penitential rite would avoid any overly sentimental notion of the incarnation: only-begotten Son of the Father, Son of Man and Son of God, the Word made flesh, and the splendor of the Father's glory.

The use of the fourth "O" antiphon as the gospel verse (Lect., no. 202) states that he will "free . . . prisoners from darkness," referring to the prevailing darkness in nature and to the Lord as the one who rescues us from spiritual darkness and sin.

Among the intercessions today, appropriate petitions would be for all nations to receive the revelation of God made flesh, for all Christians to be ever more receptive to the word of God, and for peoples at war to put aside their strife and seek reconciliation. Also, prayers for mothers about to give birth to children and for families to cherish the love of God revealed among them would also be appropriate.

The use of the second eucharistic prayer with the text, "make us worthy to share eternal life with Mary, the virgin Mother of God, with the apostles, and with all the saints who have done your will throughout the ages," would reiterate Mary's willingness to accept God's will for her.

A comment about doing God's will could introduce the Lord's Prayer, the prayer Jesus himself taught us, and whose obedience we are to imitate.

The use of number 11 of the prayers over the people would be an appropriate dismissal today because it refers to the Lord blessing us with his heavenly gifts and to "make us ready to do [his] will."

Liturgy of the Hours

Today's first reading at the office of readings, Isaiah 48:1–11, offers a summary of much of what is contained in Isaiah 40–48. The author states that Jerusalem symbolizes all the hopes and promises God made to his chosen ones (vss. 1–2). When these were invoked, however, Israel was to have only the purest of motives and intentions. The Lord shows special concern for his people when he states, "for the sake of my name I restrain my anger, lest I should destroy you" (vs. 9). Even though Israel was experiencing affliction and exile, the Lord assures them that he is with them in their trial and that he will not give his special favor to any other nation (vs. 11). This passage is an example of the way God deals with all who profess faith and commit themselves to him. As God was ever faithful to this people (and to all he had created), so will he be faithful and kind to us who profess faith in the fullness of his love revealed in Christ.

The second reading from St. Bernard's homily about the Blessed Virgin fits in very well with today's gospel. Here, Bernard deals with Mary's response to the angel's message, for from the newborn Christ would come the world's hope of salvation. Just as Mary responded to God by saying, "your will be done," so the son born from her womb would say, "thy will be done," when he faced the passion. So are we to mean the words we say in the Lord's Prayer, "thy will be done."

At morning prayer, the antiphon to Zechariah's canticle is taken from the gospel of the day: "the angel Gabriel was sent to the Virgin Mary, who was engaged to be married to Joseph."

The fourth "O" antiphon about the coming "key of David," who will "break down the prison walls of death for those who dwell in darkness," is used at evening prayer. This statement reminds us to Jesus' statement at Nazareth, that he came "to proclaim liberty to captives . . . and release to prisoners" (Lk 4:18).

Celebration of the Hours

The verse and response at the office of readings, about making ready the way of the Lord, would be an appropriate invitatory verse to begin the hours today since it sums up John's role at the end of this season in which he figured so prominently. The use of Psalm 95 to accompany it would recall significant times in Israel's history when she heard the word but did not obey it. Using these texts challenges us to respond as fully as we can to the Lord who gathers us for worship today.

The intercessions at morning and evening prayer repeat those offered on Tuesday of the Second Week (see above for comments). The use of light symbolism at morning prayer should be especially noted and capitalized on today. At both morning and evening prayer (if this has not already become the custom), the singing of Zechariah's and Mary's canticles would be a most effective way of emphasizing their role in the incarnation.

Reflection—"Private and Public Morality"

Politicians often make a distinction between what they hold personally and what they hold as matters of public policy. Unfortunately, this dichotomy can all too easily affect the way we believers deal with moral issues. For example, sometimes we say in private that we favor human rights for all peoples, but when those rights infringe on our "rights" (or luxuries), then we often back down in public and say nothing. We may well believe privately that some things are wrong, but instead of speaking our convictions, we bend to popular opinion and say nothing.

The examples of Mary in today's gospel and of Jesus throughout his life indicate no separation between private and public morality or between what each professed with their lips and what they believed in their hearts.

As we come to the liturgy today, we are challenged by the silent yet forceful examples of Jesus and Mary to live what we believe and to put our lives in the service of God's plan. There is no room for two moralities, private and public.

DECEMBER 21

Liturgical Context

Today is the "shortest day of the year," the dark of winter has set in. This phenomenon accounts for many of the texts chosen for the liturgy which refer to the light to come and which has already dawned on us in Jesus. The gospel describes Mary's visitation to Elizabeth; thus, it reflects the design of the Lectionary to review events that led to Jesus' birth.

Liturgy of the Eucharist

Today's entrance antiphon recalls yesterday's first reading and expressed a familiar Advent notion—the Lord will come and we will call him Emmanuel because "God is with us." The Lord who came in human flesh has never abandoned his people; he will show himself in a special sacramental way when he comes to us at Christmas.

Today's liturgy of the word provides a choice of two Old Testament readings: one from the Song of Songs and the other from the prophet Zephaniah. Both texts mark the end of times of hardship and speak lyrically of the presence of God with his people.

The text from the Song of Songs (2:8–14) draws on the important nuptial imagery that describes the intimate union between God and his chosen. When read in the Christian liturgy, this intimacy is understood to have been manifest in Jesus' taking on the flesh of our humanity. We join in the joy and exuberance of the lovers who rise to welcome each other as we welcome the Lord on Christmas day (vs. 10). A certain irony marks the next two verses which present what has yet to happen—the end of winter and the flowering of the earth (vs. 11). Yet, when understood as a sign of things to come (as Advent stands in relation to Christmas), this text is a sign of what occurs with the onset of winter since spring follows. The hopefulness of Advent draws on the hopefulness of the changing seasons and the promise that light follows darkness. Just as sure and reliable as are the cycles of nature, so sure and reliable are the manifestations of God in our lives as light and as the beloved.

The text from Zephaniah (3:14–18) is a hymn about the remnant who will be restored to Zion. When read at the Christian liturgy, this hymn can refer to the joy and enthusiasm with which we welcome the Lord in our midst at Christmas. The biblical themes which the text employs have clearly influenced our Advent prayer, for the text states: "the Lord has removed the judgment against you" (vs. 15), "the King of Israel, the Lord, is in your midst" (vs. 15). Just as the remnant rejoiced, so can we rejoice in the knowledge that the Lord will renew us in his love (vs. 17).

It is with confidence and joy that we join in the responsorial refrain, "cry out with joy in the Lord, you holy ones; sing a new song to him" (Ps 33:1, 3).

The gospel of the visitation tells of Elizabeth greeting Mary, her cousin, with the words: "Blessed are you among women. . . ." The quiet joy of Advent reaches a certain high point in this meeting of two specially chosen women who put their lives at God's service. As they rejoiced in the birth of their sons, so do we rejoice because they were God's chosen instruments in granting us salvation.

Both the prayer over the gifts and the prayer after communion, taken from the Leonine Sacramentary, offer appropriate reflections of the theology of Advent and of the importance of the eucharist in our lives. The prayer over the gifts emphasizes one of the results of celebrating the eucharist—that we might derive from it a share in the salvation Christ accomplished. The prayer after communion notes that the eucharist is a "constant protection" for us as we make our way to the kingdom.

Celebration of the Eucharist

The introduction to the liturgy could speak about the rejoicing that marked the meeting of Mary and Elizabeth who would soon give birth to sons. That same joy is ours as we gather for the celebration of this Advent eucharist and as we look forward to the commemoration of the birth of Christ and our rebirth in him.

For the third form of the penitential rite, the use of titles from today's readings and other Advent images would be useful, such as: you are the promised of ages and the flower of Jesse's stem, you are the sun of justice and the splendor of eternal light, you are Emmanuel, God with us forever.

The use of the fifth "O" antiphon as the alleluia verse (Lect., no. 202), acclaiming the "radiant dawn," could help underscore the light symbolism which undergirds much of the liturgy today.

Suitable petitions in the prayer of the faithful would concern those lost in the darkness of sin that they would come to the light of Christ, those weighed down with the burden of old age that they might receive comfort from other Christians, and those who mourn recently deceased loved ones that they might gain comfort from Christ whose eternal light shines on those who die in him.

If the Lamb of God is extended beyond three strophes, titles of Christ taken from the scriptures or names found in the Advent liturgy would be suitable additions.

The last verse of the gospel is assigned as the communion antiphon, emphasizing Mary as a model of one who trusted "that the promises of the Lord would be fulfilled" (vs. 45).

The use of number 1 of the prayers over the people would be a fitting conclusion to the liturgy today with its reference to "the everlasting life you prepare for us." This would reaffirm the eschatological aspect of Advent, an emphasis that might tend to be lost at this point just before Christmas.

Liturgy of the Hours

The first reading at the office of readings contains two distinct sections. The first section, Isaiah 48:12–21, is a continuation of yesterday's text. In it Yahweh is revealed as the first and last, the origin and destiny of the chosen people. Just as God acted in creation (vs. 13) and in their history (vs. 17), so will he act through the Lord's friend, Cyrus (a foreigner), to care for them. Despite the strangeness of having a foreigner intervene, Israel is reminded that it is "the Lord, your redeemer" (vs. 17) who is their liberator. The Exodus motif of refreshing them with water is recalled to sustain them as they leave Babylon and make a new Exodus (vs. 20).

The second section, Isaiah 49:9b–13, uses the image of a shepherd leading his flock so "they shall find pasture." Exodus motifs recur here (vs. 10) and on this basis the contemporary community is urged to rejoice because "the Lord comforts his people and shows mercy to his afflicted" (vs. 13). When read for our instruction and consolation in Advent, this text offers important instruction on the ways the Lord dealt with his covenanted people. He has acted in the same way with us, his new chosen people, but now the mediation is through his own son who leads, nourishes, and strengthens his pilgrim people on their way to the kingdom.

The second reading from St. Ambrose stresses the parallelism between Mary/Elizabeth and between Jesus/John. In a particularly moving section, Ambrose shows how Mary's response should be our own:

"Let Mary's soul be in each of you to proclaim the greatness of the Lord. Let her spirit be in each to rejoice in the Lord. Christ has only one mother in the flesh, but we all bring forth Christ in faith."

The antiphon to Zechariah's canticle reflects the nearness of Christmas when it states: "In five days our Lord will come to us." This instance of counting the days until Christmas is unique in the liturgy; it is a way of saying that despite the fact that the darkness/light symbolism is apparent, we must still wait for the birth of the Son of God, the light of the world, among us.

At evening prayer, the light symbolism is emphasized in the "O" antiphon text: "O Radiant Dawn, splendor of eternal light, sun of justice: come, shine on those who dwell in darkness and the shadow of death." This text is filled with scriptural echoes, not the least of which are the last lines of the Benedictus (Lk 1:78–79), recalling the rising sun of justice in Malachi 4:2 (and in Isaiah 9:2).

It should be noted that the "O" antiphons originally accompanied the morning office not evening prayer. Hence, referring to the "radiant dawn" becomes all the more significant since it would have been sung at the rising of the sun, a daily reminder that as certain as day follows night, so certain are we that the Lord who once came in innocence in human history will come again as Lord and King at the end of time. Just when we would expect greater emphasis on Christ's first coming because of the proximity of Christmas, the liturgy reminds us that the Lord for whom we wait has yet to come again as Lord of all.

At both morning and evening prayer, the intercessions are taken from Wednesday of the second week. The second petition at morning prayer refers to the two comings of Christ and the fourth petition asks that the Lord "lead us into light." At evening prayer, the introduction speaks of the Lord to whom we address our prayers: "Christ, who rescues us from the darkness of sin."

Celebration of the Hours

The use of the verse and response as an invitatory today would be appropriate since this text speaks of the "Lord, our God," and in it we ask that he "show us [his] face and we shall be saved." The use of Psalm 95 would be especially appropriate if this invitatory precedes the office of readings, whose first reading recalls many examples of God's intervention in history. After the second reading from St. Ambrose, the suggested responsory might well be sung or recited because it uses Luke 1:45, which verse is found in the gospel at the eucharist today.

Especially today, the psalm prayers at morning and evening prayer could be adjusted to underscore the light/darkness motif.

Reflection—"Hardships Will End"

Hardships are not only meant to be gone through (or even gotten rid of); they are meant to be faced. When faced and accepted, they can become the means of deeper reliance on the Lord. This is seen in today's gospel. Elizabeth had to accept her infertility year after year. It was only very late in life that she received the good news that she was to bear a son. This son was to begin the process of bringing covenant religion to its fulfillment. She did not despair, but constantly trusted in the Lord. It was she who was ultimately chosen to bear a mighty son.

This pattern repeats itself in the scriptures and even extends to Jesus' acceptance of his Father's will in the agony in the garden. Jesus' victory there was not because of a tough stance. It was his surrender to God's will that mattered. His "tough times" did finally end, but they ended not because he avoided betrayal and death. They ended because he accepted death on a cross in obedience to his Father.

When we realize that we are not our own masters and that no amount of self-help can guarantee happiness, then we will come to the peace and serenity that marked the pregnancy of the aged Elizabeth and the peaceful way Jesus accepted the cross.

Hardships do come to an end, but for believers, the important thing is whether we allow God to carry us through tough times to life lived on God's terms.

DECEMBER 22

Liturgical Context

The liturgy over the next four days recounts what occurred before and at the births of Jesus and John the Baptist. The liturgy is concerned to draw us into the reality of the kingdom begun and made manifest through these men. Today's gospel containing the *Magnificat* is a statement of the values of the kingdom which Jesus' birth inaugurated, and which are celebrated in the liturgy and are central to the Christian life.

The "O" antiphon today addresses the "king" and "keystone" of our lives, Christ the Lord.

Liturgy of the Eucharist

The entrance antiphon (Psalm 24:7) refers to the imminence of the coming Messiah by commanding the gates to "lift up your heads . . . and let in the King of glory." In acclaiming Christ as the king of glory for whom we long, we affirm his lordship over our lives.

The mystery of the incarnation is referred to in the opening prayer (taken from the Bergamo Sacramentary). We admit our fallen condition and need for Christ in the opening lines, which text recalls the Adam/Christ parallel. Just as we have inherited our weakened condition through Adam, so now through Christ are we drawn into "his divine life."

The first reading from 1 Samuel (1:24–28) tells of Hannah, who had been sterile, but upon praying to the Lord for a son, she bore Samuel. She now brings the child to the temple and says: "as long as he lives, he shall be dedicated to the Lord" (vs. 28).

Portions of Hannah's song appear in today's responsorial psalm. Most exegetes cite this hymn as the basis for the *Magnificat*, hence its appropriateness, along with that of the first reading to introduce today's gospel.

The gospel text, Luke 1:45–56, containing Mary's Magnificat, can be divided into two sections: the first reflecting Mary's own situation before God (vss. 46–49) and the second describing how God dealt with Israel and then the people of God redeemed in Christ (vss. 50–55).

In Luke it is Mary, the "servant in her lowliness" (vs. 48) who is thus exalted, not a person whom the world would judge worthy of special note. It is the "lowly" ones who know their need for God. As was true throughout Israel's history, God intervenes on their behalf performing "great things" (vs. 49)—here that Mary would bear a son. Yet, what is even more interesting is the way Luke expands on this incident to allow all believers to identify with Mary, since the remaining verses provide a gloss on his version of the beatitudes (Lk 6:20–23). Here, it is the coming of God's kingdom in Christ through Mary that will confuse the proud, depose the mighty, and raise the lowly to high places (vss. 51–53). The promise made as far back as Abraham and reiterated to Israel (vss. 54–55) is recalled so that believing Jews would realize that Jesus' birth fulfilled this promise. As he had acted in the past to lead and sustain Israel, so now will he act to lead all nations to experience the saving power of God in Christ.

What is carefully crafted here is a series of verses which summarize salvation history and the overturning of accepted cultural standards. This canticle leads us to ponder the implications of the incarnation and the values of the kingdom Jesus came to establish. This model Christian prayer reveals that it is fidelity to God's ways that really matters and that it is this saving Lord who sustains us as we long for the day we will reach the promised kingdom.

Both the prayer over the gifts and the prayer after communion, taken from the Leonine Sacramentary, recall the importance of the eucharist as the sacrament that purifies, renews, and strengthens us so we may be prepared for the coming of our Savior at Christmas and ultimately be called to share eternal life with him forever.

Celebration of the Eucharist

The introductory comment today could address the importance of the values of the kingdom reflected in the gospel.

Invocations of Christ to use with the third penitential rite could include his coming among us in human flesh, his dying and rising to reconcile us with his Father, and his interceding for us at the Father's right hand.

The use of today's "O" antiphon as the alleluia verse (Lect., no. 202) would reaffirm images of Christ as the "king of all nations" and as "source of the church's unity and faith," whom we beg to come to "save all mankind."

A comment before the gospel about this familiar text could help the community to listen attentively to a passage whose meaning goes far beyond the incident of the visitation.

It would be useful to include petitions today for the poor and oppressed, for those suffering economic hardship, for the Jews who first shared in God's covenant, and for a greater witness to gospel values in our lives.

The use of the second eucharistic prayer with the second Advent preface when proclaimed slowly and prayerfully can help to continue the simplicity and sobriety of Advent as compared with the splendor of Christmas.

If the invocations at the Lamb of God exceed the three traditional acclamations, the addition of titles reflecting Jesus' lordship would reaffirm these important images as compared with those associated only with Christ's birth or infancy.

Liturgy of the Hours

The first reading at the office of readings, Isaiah 49:14–50:1, continues and deepens that read yesterday. The questioning and self-doubt expressed in verse 14 is countered immediately (vss. 15ff.) with a message of tenderness, intimacy, and lasting relatedness to God. The promise made to Abraham is recalled (vs. 19); Zion will be too small to contain the great numbers of the people of all nations who will be called together by the Lord. All of this, however, is given to God's chosen, who are willing to respond to his covenant by obedience to his commands (50:1).

The use of Isaiah 49:15 as the response to the reading (about a mother never forgetting her child) is itself a dramatic conclusion, for it exemplifies God's fidelity to his people.

The second reading from Venerable Bede is a commentary on the *Magnificat*. The author emphasizes our need to be humble in order to welcome Christ and to perceive reality through the eyes of faith. This same deepened faith enables us to appropriate and live the values which this canticle so lyrically and joyfully proclaims.

The antiphon to Zechariah's canticle refers back to yesterday's gospel when Elizabeth stated that when she heard Mary's greeting, "the child within my womb leapt for joy." (While this text would seem to have been more appropriate to use yesterday, the revised liturgy retained the traditional antiphon, noting that in five days what we have longed to celebrate will be accomplished.)

At evening prayer, the "O" antiphon emphasizes Christ as the king of all nations and the lord of our lives. The mission of Christ as keystone (referring to Is 28:16) of the "mighty arch of man" (referring to Eph 2:14ff.) and our cry that he would "come and save the creature you fashioned from the dust" (referring to Gn 2:7) is a complex but striking statement that our former "selves" estranged through Adam's sin are now reconciled through Christ. Thus, the text points to the centrality of the whole redemptive work of the Messiah.

Celebration of the Hours

The invitatory verse assigned for this part of Advent about the Lord being "close at hand" would be an appropriate introduction to the hours. When accompanied by Psalm 24 about the coming of the king of glory (vs. 7) and our accepting him with "clean hands and pure hearts," this invitatory reflects the mood of these last days of Advent.

At morning and evening prayer, appropriate Advent hymns to introduce the hour are important, as are adapted psalm prayers reflecting the many titles of Christ whose coming we await. The singing of both New Testament canticles would be especially appropriate these days.

At morning prayer, the intercessions from Friday of the Second Week are prescribed; additional (or substitute) petitions reflecting the urgency of preparing for the coming Christmas feast would be fitting. The same is true for petitions at evening prayer, which are repeated from Thursday of the Second Week.

Reflection—"True Riches"

The birth of a child is certainly a pivotal time in the life of a mother and in the relationship of husband and wife. It is a time of unique emotional intensity and of heightened awareness of how God works among us. To give birth is to share life with another whose very life is the result of human intimacy and love. For a believer to give birth is to share in God's plan for the human race, that it increase and multiply, and that it come to know God the Lord of all life and the source of all love.

Yet, it seems that this faith-filled vision of a natural and beautiful human phenomenon fades into the background as Mary offers her song of thanksgiving in today's gospel. While she certainly begins by acclaiming the mighty deeds of God for her, she continues by emphasizing how her son will affect the way generations of believers will come to see that human prestige, power, and influence are nothing compared with true riches that come from God. These true riches are a share in his life, grace, and peace. Mary affirms in her hymn what it means to give birth to the reality of the kingdom, not just to welcome a child into the world.

What we prepare for in these last Advent days is the coming of God among us. We await the rebirth among us of Mary's insight into what is really important in life. We await the rebirth of God's love among us, a renewal of his peace and care for us and a renewed establishment of the values of his kingdom.

In Mary's canticle, we find a mixture of motherly happiness and firm commitment to the kingdom of God. It is by affirming our commitment to the kingdom of God among us, brought about through

Mary's openness to the Holy Spirit, that we truly can be said to prepare for Christmas. Mary's hymn reminds us that Christmas is about the values of God's kingdom among us. These are true riches, far beyond human imagining.

Liturgical Context

This is the last full day of Advent, hence the "O" antiphons end today with the familiar "Come, Emmanuel." The gospels today and tomorrow form a unity as do the first readings at the office of readings. At the eucharist today, we read of the birth of John the Baptist followed tomorrow by Zechariah's canticle. At the office of readings, sections from Isaiah 51–52 are read to summarize the progress of salvation to that point and to reiterate the good news that Jerusalem would ultimately be victorious.

Liturgy of the Eucharist

Today's entrance antiphon is taken from the first reading from midnight mass (Isaiah 9:6) and a psalm frequently used between Epiphany and the Baptism of our Lord (Psalm 71). This antiphon reminds us of Christ's saving role: "a little child is born for us, and he shall be called the mighty God; every race on earth shall be blessed in him."

The opening prayer elaborates on this theme by speaking about the birth of Christ (seen more clearly in the Latin original) and our sharing in his forgiveness and mercy.

The first reading from Malachi (3:1–4, 23–24) is also assigned as the first reading in the Advent penance service proposed in the revised rite (see Appendix II, Rite of Penance). Chosen to reflect the gospel about the birth of John, the first verse offers a clear instruction about the prophet's role as the Lord's messenger to prepare the way before him (vs. 1). The seriousness of his role is demonstrated in his being compared to "the refiner's fire" and "the fuller's lye" (vs. 2). Yet, the last verses of this same text are comforting when understood that they signify God's care in sending the prophet (Elijah) to bring his people to conversion. When their hearts are turned to the Lord and to each other, they will know that their salvation is about to appear (vss. 23–24).

The refrain to the responsorial psalm (Lk 21:28) strikes an urgent, eschatological note: "Lift up your heads and see; your redemption is near at hand." In Psalm 25 itself, we pray that the Lord will make known his ways (vs. 4) and that he would guide us in his truth (vs. 5), aware as we are of our need for a savior. The psalm states explicitly that it is sinners and the humble who will be guided in the ways of the Lord (vs. 9). An appropriate sense of awe and fear should mark the Christian community as it looks for the Lord's coming: "the friendship of the Lord is with those who fear him" (vs. 14).

The continuation of the gospel of Luke recounts the birth of John the Baptist (1:57–66). The text states (implicitly) that Elizabeth and Zechariah were observers of the law for on the eighth day they had the child circumcised, the custom for any Jewish male child. Yet, to show the uniqueness of this particular newborn, Elizabeth and Zechariah affirm that he will not inherit a familiar family name. They state that his name will be John (vss. 59, 63). The overturning of cultural expectation in naming the child and the crowd's reaction (vs. 65) signal the important role which John would later play as the final prophetic voice to prepare for the Lord.

The urgency of these Advent days is reflected in the first part of the communion antiphon: "I stand at the door and knock, says the Lord" (Rv 3:20); the second part refers to hearing the Lord's word. When we prepare well for the Lord's coming here and now, we will one day be called to the eschatological banquet in the kingdom.

Fittingly, the prayer after communion refers to our being nourished with the bread of life, with receiving the peace of Christ, and asking that the Lord would "prepare us to welcome your Son with ardent faith." (Interestingly, the Latin original refers to having our lamps burning as did the five wise virgins. Hence, the eschatological demands of accepting Christ are very strong as Advent draws to a close.)

Celebration of the Eucharist

The tone of the eucharist today and tomorrow should be quiet and simple. These appropriate characteristics of the Advent season should be reflected in the liturgies immediately prior to the joy and festivity of Christmas. The introduction to the liturgy could mention the seriousness of these final days of Advent. The use of the second penitential rite would be a subtle acknowledgment of our sin ("we have sinned against you") and our need for a Savior ("and grant us your salvation").

The final "O" antiphon about the coming of Emmanuel as the alleluia verse (Lect., no. 202) would complete the use of these seven important texts.

Among the intercessions today, prayers for an end to hostility and terrorism in the world, for a full response to the message of John the Baptist, and for the right (nonmaterial) attitude toward Christmas would be appropriate.

The use of the third eucharistic prayer with John the Baptist's name inserted at the intercession of the saints would be fitting.

To introduce the Lord's Prayer, the fourth invitation, "Let us pray for the coming of the kingdom," would show the urgency of the close of Advent.

To conclude the liturgy, number 1 of the prayers over the people, about receiving what will lead us to everlasting life, would help reiterate how Advent and Christmas are not primarily about the birth of a baby so much as they are about our receiving Christ's redemption here and now and the fullness of his risen life in the kingdom.

Liturgy of the Hours

The first reading at the office of readings today and tomorrow (from Isaiah 51–52) is from the "great Zion" poem of Deutero-Isaiah. This text summarizes how God has dealt with his chosen people. When such events were recounted (for example, the Exodus tradition in verse 9), Israel drew hope and strength to rely more deeply on the Lord who promised to be ever present with them.

The second reading from Hippolytus deals with the importance of the word proclaimed and effective among us. The author associates the act of creation in Genesis with the incarnation of the Word made flesh in John 1. Like other partistic commentators, Hippolytus sees John's prologue as based on Genesis 1; in Christ, creation is brought to completion. This reference to the prologue is particularly appropriate today because John 1:1–14 will be proclaimed at the eucharist on Christmas day. Hippolytus emphasizes how our lives are recreated and renewed in Christ. He who made us out of nothing remakes us according to the divine image. In Advent, we are drawn into the mystery of God's creative love manifest especially at Christmas. Significantly, the responsory combines Isaiah 9:6, 7 and John 1:14, verses which are parts of texts to be read at masses on Christmas day.

The antiphon to Zechariah's canticle contains a sense of completion: "All that God promised to the virgin through the message of the angel has been accomplished." Through the liturgy, we continually experience God's gifts through Christ and so experience the fullness of salvation.

At evening prayer, the antiphon to Mary's canticle is the familiar text, "O Emmanuel, king and lawgiver, desire of the nations, Savior of all people, come and set us free, Lord our God." By combining a number of Old Testament texts, this brief antiphon points beyond the infancy of Jesus to his work as our Lord and Redeemer. "Emmanuel" has already been used on the Fourth Sunday of Advent to relate a characteristic element of God's enduring presence with his people. Because of our need for redemption and to be freed from our sins, we pray, "come and set us free." As is stated daily in the canticle at morning prayer, we know that our salvation is from God himself: "to give his people knowledge of salvation by the forgiveness of their sins" (Lk 1:77).

Celebration of the Hours

Since this is the last day on which the invitatory, "The Lord is close at hand; come let us worship him," can be used, it would be a fitting option to begin the hours today. It contains the note of urgency explicit in today's texts. The use of Psalm 95 as the invitatory psalm would itself recall many Old Testament images and examples of how God dealt with his people.

Hymns at the beginning of the hours should reflect Advent themes.

The intercessions at morning and evening prayer are taken from those seen earlier (morning prayer on Thursday of the second week and evening prayer on Friday of the second week). The sense of urgency in preparing for Christmas reflected in the texts of the hours should also be prominent in planning additional or substitute prayers today. The response, "come, Lord Jesus," would help to reiterate this urgency.

Reflection—"Full Stop"

By now, the atmosphere is filled with Christmas festivity and final preparations. News items record the huge numbers of people traveling home for the holidays and note how busy stores have been. The atmosphere in offices, town squares, and homes is filled with Christmas anticipation. For many, this is the last day of work or school before Christmas, hence partying and celebration may well be the order of the day.

However, the liturgy does not celebrate this unbridled festivity. While not as somber as it was at the beginning of Advent, the liturgy invites us to quiet reflection on the uniqueness of what is to occur. Are we to mark the birth of Jesus by parties, overeating, and noise? Is that the kind of welcome Christ deserves? Does such activity really welcome Christ?

The liturgy calls us to a full stop, to a time of quiet and serious reflection on God's dealings with his people in ages past, and how this same God will be present with us as Savior and Lord this Christmas. For the Word to take flesh in our hearts, we need to silence our hearts and calm our spirits to recognize Christ when he comes this Christmas.

DECEMBER 24

Liturgical Context

Advent ends today. The liturgy serves as a bridge between Advent and Christmas (which begins at Evening Prayer I). Just as John the Baptist foretold the coming of Christ the light, so we hear the Canticle of Zechariah at the eucharist to remind us of our need for this light which shatters the darkness of sin and draws us into life with God.

Liturgy of the Eucharist

The liturgy begins with an adaptation of a verse that is part of the second reading on the Solemnity of Mary, Mother of God. The text states that the "appointed time has come" and that "God has sent his Son into the world" (Gal 4:4). Thus, from the very beginning of the liturgy, we sense the immediacy of Christ's birth.

The style of the opening prayer is unique. It begins with the plea, "Come, Lord Jesus," a cry often used in the intercessions during Advent. We beg the Lord not to delay his coming to console us with his love. When we apply this text to ourselves, we open ourselves to God and admit our need for a savior.

The first reading from 2 Samuel (7:1–5, 8–11, 16) was already discussed on the Fourth Sunday of Advent, "B" cycle. One phrase of this text, however, applies directly to our situation just before Christmas because it notes that the "ark of God dwells in a tent" (vs. 2). This reference underscores the Lord's presence to his people in the ark of the covenant housed in a temporary shelter as they wandered in the desert. The ark was portable because Israel was a people on the move. This biblical background supports the statement in John 1:14 (used at the gospel on Christmas day) that Jesus pitched his tent among us (literally) when the Word became flesh and he dwelt among us.

The responsorial psalm expands the theme of the goodness of the Lord present with his people (Ps 89:2) and reiterates the covenant relationship (vss. 4–5).

The gospel today, Luke 1:67–79, contines to recount scenes from the early days of the life of John the Baptist. Zechariah's first utterance after receiving back his speech is also the canticle at daily morning prayer. Luke emphasizes the continuity between the old and new covenants by showing the important link established by the ministry of John the Baptist. All that the prophetic tradition foretold about the Messiah is to be fulfilled in Jesus (vs. 70). The covenants made with Israel through Abraham and his descendants will now be fulfilled (vss. 72–73). Zechariah's canticle speaks of the "dayspring" who will visit us in his mercy (vs. 78) "to shine on those who sit in darkness and in the shadow of death, to guide our feet into the way of peace" (vs. 79). These references to sun and light should be emphasized today because the intersection of light and darkness, so evident at this time of year, makes us especially aware of Christ's incarnation as the light of the world in contrast to the darkness of sin.

The prayer over the gifts refers to the eucharist as a sacrament that frees us from sin and that enables us to look forward to the coming of Christ in glory, that is, at the end of time.

The communion antiphon reiterates the importance of today's gospel by quoting the first verse of Zechariah's canticle, blessing God for visiting and redeeming his people (Lk 1:68).

The prayer after communion asks that we who look forward to Christ's birth may rejoice not only now but forever in the wonder of his love. Like so many other references in today's liturgy, this text serves as a bridge between Advent and Christmas.

Celebration of the Eucharist

Today's morning liturgy should be simple and reflective, especially because the liturgy of tonight's Vigil Mass as well as that of Christmas tomorrow deserve grand solemnity and festivity. The introduction to the liturgy could be a brief comment about watching and waiting for the coming feast, and of our need for the Messiah. The communal recitation of the "I confess" formula and a sung "Lord have mercy" (in a simple setting) could help emphasize our sinfulness and our acknowledgment that Jesus is our only Lord.

To repeat yesterday's alleluia verse (Lect., no. 202) would be appropriate since it acclaims the Lord as "Emmanuel."

For the general intercessions, the model provided for Advent could guide the formulation of prayers which touch on appropriate Advent themes.

The prayerful and measured proclamation of the second eucharistic prayer and second Advent preface could add to the reverence and simplicity of this celebration. The choice of the third memorial acclamation, with its reference to proclaiming the death of the Lord, "until you come in glory," would reflect the important Advent theme of provisionality and expectation.

Similarly, to introduce the Lord's Prayer with the last sample introduction, "Let us pray for the coming of the kingdom," would reiterate this important Advent theme.

Liturgy of the Hours

The first reading at the office of readings today is a continuation of the poem begun yesterday from Isaiah 51–52. This text is the last in a series of continuous readings from Isaiah proclaimed during Advent. (The last part of Isaiah will recur again between Epiphany and the Baptism of our Lord.)

Today's text can be divided into two parts, the first of which (51: 17–23) recalls the Babylonian invasion of Jerusalem and the beseiged state of the holy city. Yet, even here, the prophet assures the chosen of God's care for them (vs. 22). The Lord promises to reverse Jerusalem's fortunes and to remove their oppression. This hopeful message coincides with the central theme of Advent that the Lord always sustains his chosen ones.

The second part of the text (52:2, 7–10) is an exhortation and invitation to come into the Lord's presence. Like the original audience of this text, we are invited (figuratively) to "loose the bonds from your neck [and] ascend the throne" to God's presence (vs. 2). The major part of this text (which is also assigned as the first reading on Christmas day, verses 7–10) is a moving personification of God's intervention for his people, symbolized in a move from terror to the peace of Jerusalem freed from violence. The text begins by referring to the one who announces this important turn of events and invites them to acclaim, "Your God is King." The Lord comforts his people (vs. 9) and thereby fulfills his commitment to be with them always. But, the text ends with a verse that is explored fully in the Epiphany feast—"all the ends of the earth will behold the salvation of our God" (vs. 10). This verse is used as the response on Christmas day and often throughout the season. The joy and unbridled exhilaration of this text should be understood especially today as the liturgy shifts from Advent to Christmas.

The second reading is from a sermon of St. Augustine about the implications of the incarnation. At the beginning of the passage, he offers a summary of the important points he will draw out:

"You would have suffered eternal death, had he not been born in time. Never would you have been freed from sinful flesh, had he not taken on himself the likeness of sinful flesh. . . . You would have perished had he not come."

But the Lord has come and will come again this Christmas to draw us into his life and love more fully.

At morning prayer, special antiphons accompany the psalms. The first deals with the birth at Bethlehem of him whom we acclaim as king and ruler of God's chosen. The second refers to the urgency associated with this part of the season by stating, "your redemption is now at hand." The third text fittingly expresses our need this morning: "the day has come at last when Mary will bring forth her firstborn Son." This mystery will be recalled again through the liturgy during the Christmas season.

The response to the short scripture reading (Isaiah 11:1–3a, which has been used on Advent Saturdays) has been changed to reflect the nearness of Christmas: "Tomorrow is the day of your Salvation."

Celebration of the Hours

Today's special invitatory, "Today you will know that the Lord is coming,—in the morning you will see his glory," could be utilized effectively with Psalm 100. The verses of the psalm can be understood as our welcome of the Lord for we "cry out to the Lord, all the earth" (vs. 1) and at the end we acclaim him as "faithful from age to age" (vs. 5).

At morning prayer, the suggested intercessions are from Saturday of the second week. Since they contain references to the second coming of Christ, a theme which fully accords with a primary Advent theme, they reflect the theology of this season. Additional petitions could reflect the nearness of Christmas and our need for the coming Messiah. An introduction to the Lord's Prayer, referring to doing the will of God as Christ came to do the will of the Father, would be appropriate.

A chant-like hymn at the beginning of this hour and even the sung *Kyrie, eleison* as a response to the intercessions would fittingly conclude this season of joyful expectation for the coming of the Lord.

Reflection—"The Coming of God"

In her recent book, *The Coming of God*, Maria Boulding writes almost poetically about the importance of God taking on human flesh for our salvation. Time and again, she applies the incarnation mystery to ourselves, and at times she compares our situation to that of Israel in the Exile. While far distant from all that symbolized nearness to God (including worship at Jerusalem), Israel was invited to trust that the Lord would in fact come to be with his people and lead them home to a completely renewed situation.

We are like exiled Israel about to be brought back into God's gracious embrace. Like the chosen of old, we have many needs that can only be met by the Lord. We reflect Israel's need for God when we admit the poverty and emptiness of our lives without God.

As a final preparation for the coming of God among us, we

should think about the areas in our life that beg for God's intervention and love. It is only by admitting our poverty, our fear, our barrenness, our emptiness, our disappointments, and our lack of integration that we can truly make ready the way for the Lord. In so doing, we allow Jesus to be who he truly is, Savior and Lord of all. We only know what light is when we have experienced darkness; we only know what salvation is when we admit our sin. On this final Advent day, may we come before the Lord with our hands empty and our heads bowed in supplication so that when he comes at Christmas, we will be ready to receive him into our lives. He alone can forgive us and save us—the Lord, Emmanuel.

Chapter Five

Christmas Season: First Week

SOLEMNITY OF CHRISTMAS

Liturgical Context

Liturgical commemoration of the mystery of the incarnation focuses on our being incorporated into Christ; it is less concerned with details of his birth. However, it uses these mysterious events as the means to disclose how God came once in human flesh to redeem all peoples for all times. The season inaugurated at Christmas extends through the commemoration of the Baptism of the Lord as is stated in the *General Norms* for the Liturgical Year:

"Next to the yearly celebration of the paschal mystery, the Church holds most sacred the memorial of Christ's birth and early manifestations. This is the purpose of the Christmas season.

"The Christmas season runs from Evening Prayer I of Christmas until the Sunday after Epiphany or after 6 January, inclusive.

"Epiphany is celebrated on 6 January, unless . . . it has been assigned to the Sunday occurring between 2 January and 8 January.

"The Sunday falling after 6 January is the feast of the Baptism of the Lord." (nos. 32–38, *passim.*)

(Since it is the present custom in the United States to commemorate the solemnity of the Epiphany on the Sunday between January 2 and January 8 this will be assumed in the commentary that follows. Hence, there will be no commentary for the Second Sunday after Christmas.)

The separate commemorations of Jesus' birth at Christmas, his manifestation to the "astrologers from the East" at Epiphany, and the inauguration of his mission at his baptism are to be understood as inseparable parts of one mystery—the coming of God among us for our salvation. The earliest Eastern Liturgical evidence, for the first days of January, emphasizes the unity of this mystery commemorating the ways Christ was manifested to the Magi, at his baptism, and at the wedding feast at Cana. In the West, however, things were different. As a way of countering the year-end festival of Saturnalia at Rome (a vestige of which is the "twelve days"), the church took over a pagan feast in honor of the unconquered sun on December 25 and made it the day to commemorate Jesus' birth. The hope seen in his birth is likened to the hope which sun worshipers had in the sun now growing in brilliance because the year's shortest day is over (December 21).

The first of the Christmas masses to evolve was that celebrated on Christmas morning (the "day" mass). The Christologically significant texts of John 1:1–14 and Hebrews 1:1–6, traditionally assigned to this liturgy, indicate how the liturgy commemorates the incarnation. Furthermore, the unity established in Christ between God and humankind and about the interchange through which we humans become divine is reflected in the Christmas prefaces:

"Christ is [God's] Son before all ages,
yet now he is born in time.
He has come to lift up all things to himself,
to restore unity to creation,
and to lead mankind from exile into your heavenly kingdom."
   (Christmas Preface II, from a sermon of St. Leo the Great)

"Your eternal Word has taken upon himself our human weakness,
giving our mortal nature immortal value.
So marvelous is this oneness between God and man
that in Christ man restores to man the gift of everlasting life."
   (Christmas Preface III, from the Leonine Sacramentary)

These themes dominate liturgical texts through the Christmas-Epiphany cycle as they express our incorporation into the community redeemed by Christ, the mediator of the new covenant. The Christmas liturgy is concerned with drawing out the implications of the incarnation; it is not simply a chronicle about Jesus' birth. The Christmas liturgy is about Christ's coming among us and remaining with us still so that we can be drawn to the Father through him.

As the church reflected on this great mystery, certain events in Rome caused the evolution of three other masses in addition to the day mass. What we call the "vigil mass" was originally a simple eucharist that concluded the vigil office on Christmas eve. What we call "midnight mass" was originally celebrated for a small gathering at the church of St. Mary Major in a crypt chapel dedicated to the Bethlehem manger. The "dawn mass" evolved in Rome from a commemoration by a Byzantine community of the martyrdom of St. Anastasia at a church named for her. This long-standing commemoration was changed to commemorate the incarnation for this small (and select) community. Thus, one can see why the "day mass" retained priority theologically and liturgically in the Roman rite.

As popular spirituality sought to commemorate the events connected with the incarnation as exactly as possible, the mass at midnight grew in importance. Midnight was the earliest possible time when the church could commemorate the day when Jesus was born (although it is clear that we do not know the exact date and that December 25 was not chosen as an anniversary) and the darkness of night harmonized well with the gospel (Lk 2:1–14) read at this mass. Hence, the growth of midnight mass as the first mass of Christmas.

With the demise of the liturgy of the hours as popular liturgy, it was a short step to making the vigil mass less important in popular piety. Also, in recent centuries the dawn mass tended to be a "private mass" said by a priest as one of the three he could celebrate on Christmas. The texts and readings of the vigil and midnight mass in the present reform should be interpreted carefully to avoid the urge to dramatize the events surrounding Jesus' birth—an approach not supported by these texts. The core of the Christmas liturgy is found in the very important text from the Leonine Sacramentary now restored to the Christmas liturgy as the opening prayer of the mass during Christmas Day:

"Lord God,
we praise you for creating man,
and still more for restoring him in Christ.
Your Son shared our weakness:
may we share his glory. . . ."

Vigil Mass

The traditional entrance antiphon from Exodus 16:6–7 originally referred to the daily gift of manna found each morning. Used this evening, it invites us to be grateful for the Lord's gifts and to look to

Christ as their fulfillment. It states that "today you will know that the Lord is coming to save us," but that it is only "in the morning [when] you will see his glory."

The Glory to God returns to the liturgy at the vigil mass with its quotation of the angels' words: "Glory to God in the highest, and peace to his people on earth" (Lk 2:14). The traditional opening prayer at this mass notes some aspects of the Christmas mystery by stating that this is a feast "of our salvation," and asks that we may "meet [Christ] with confidence when he comes to be our judge." The image of "Christ as our Redeemer" is particularly striking because it sets up this evening's readings, for even when the gospel speaks about how Jesus was born, it points out implications of this event for our redemption.

The first reading from Isaiah 62:1–5 is a hymn-like praise of Jerusalem. The "new name" (vs. 2) is a new condition established by God for his people. Like the covenant relationship established with Abraham and his descendants, or like Peter's new vocation and mission reflected in his name change, so the term "new name" means that Israel will no longer be "forsaken" and "desolate" (vs. 4). The new condition resulting from divine intervention is that she shall be called the Lord's "delight" and "espoused," reiterating nuptial imagery to show the intimate union of God and his people.

The use of Psalm 89 with the refrain, "Forever I will sing the goodness of the Lord," refers to the establishment of the "covenant with my chosen one" (vs. 4) and to David's posterity (vss. 4–5). The notion of God's continued intervention for us is also seen in the text: "At your name they rejoice all the day; and through your justice they are exalted" (vs. 17). We have been blessed forever by God through the names "Jesus" and "Emmanuel" (used in tonight's gospel). Other important titles in this psalm are "father," "God," "Rock," and "savior" (vs. 27). These images remind us of God's action on our behalf through Christ, which continues in the liturgy.

The text from Acts (13:16–17, 22–25) is taken from Paul's speech at Antioch Pisidia, and refers to the Exodus (vss. 17–18), to King David and the son of Jesse (vs. 22), and to the fulfillment of Old Testament prophecies (vs. 23). This summary of salvation history culminates in the statement that from "this man's descendants [has come] Jesus, a savior for Israel" (vs. 23). The juncture between Israel's expectation and the proximate coming of Jesus is the ministry of John the Baptizer (vss. 24–25) whose mission was so clearly emphasized in Advent.

The gospel acclamation this evening, like the entrance antiphon, reflects the vigil character of this liturgy since it refers to "tomorrow" when wickedness will be destroyed because "the Savior of the world will be our king." As we keep vigil this evening (even with a Christmas eucharist), we look to tomorrow as the "day" of salvation.

The gospel this evening is the traditional text assigned in the Roman rite, Matthew 1:1–25, which was already used in two sections on December 17 and 18. It is also used on the feast of the Birth of Mary (vss. 1–16, 18–25) and the solemnity of Joseph, Husband of Mary (vss. 16, 18–21, 24). When read this evening, two themes from its latter verses emerge as important: calling the child "Jesus," and the fulfillment of the prophecy of Isaiah 7:14 that through Christ we experience "God with us." In the incarnation, God acts through human instrumentality to save us from sin, hence the name "Jesus." (For additional comments, see above for December 17 and 18.)

The custom of genuflecting during the creed at the words "and became man" is followed at all Christmas liturgies. This gesture should not be overlooked for it serves to reinforce the central theological notion stated so clearly in John 1:14 that the Word became flesh. The use of this gesture today helps to highlight the reason why we bow at these words every Sunday—the awe and reverence we show to God who took on our human condition.

The prayer over the gifts contains a particularly important reference which emphasizes the relationship between the incarnation and the paschal mystery. The statement that this liturgy "marks the beginning of our redemption" reflects how in the Christmas eucharist we experience the mystery of the incarnation and of redemption. By sharing the gifts of the earth, bread and wine, we reverence all of creation now graced through Christ's incarnation; by our communion in these blessed gifts now become Christ's body and blood, we become partakers in the dying and rising of Jesus.

The communion antiphon, Isaiah 40:5, refers to the comfort we receive because of the glory of the Lord revealed in Christ, through whom all will see God's saving power. The fact that the verse retains the future tense of the original text subtly reaffirms the fact that we are celebrating a vigil which looks for its completion in the liturgy tomorrow.

The prayer after communion links the feast of the incarnation with the eucharist; we ask God to let us begin a new life as we commemorate the birth of his Son who gives us food and drink in this sacrament.

Celebration of the Vigil Mass

In many pastoral situations, large numbers of families with small children attend this liturgy. Hence, planning it according to the third form of liturgy suggested in the *Directory for Masses with Children* would be appropriate. The comments that follow accord with the *Directory*.

With regard to environment, it should be recalled that the creche is an extra-liturgical addition (even though popular piety gives it great significance). Those planning the liturgy should evaluate the location of the creche, to make sure it does not draw attention away from the primary symbols of the altar, lectern, and chair. Placing the creche in too prominent a location would make the liturgy appear as merely a reminiscence of Christ's birth instead of a commemoration of the incarnation by which Christ came to accomplish our redemption through the paschal mystery.

The *Directory* permits the use of either the "Lord, have mercy" or the "Glory to God" after an introductory comment to begin the liturgy. Since the "Lord, have mercy" was emphasized in Advent and the "Glory to God" was not used since the solemnity of Christ the King, it would be good to sing it this evening. An appropriate setting might use, "Glory to God in the highest and peace to his people on earth," as a refrain that can also be used as a continuing acclamation during the third eucharistic prayer for masses with children.

For the liturgy of the word, only one of the first two readings need be proclaimed. The choice of the Acts text (13:16–17, 22–25) would be appropriate, since it summarizes much of the Advent liturgy, particularly the ministry of John the Baptizer.

Either the responsorial psalm or the alleluia verse can be used between the readings, with the preference given to the alleluia since it introduces the proclamation of the gospel of how Jesus came to be born. A procession with candles and incense can be an important gestural way to emphasize this proclamation. The procession should be timed so that the movement is accompanied by music that is neither too brief nor too long.

The intercessions this evening should be straightforward and simply phrased so all (especially the young people) can understand them.

The use of the third eucharistic prayer for masses with children can be chosen because of the nature of the congregation. The acclamations used throughout help sustain attention (especially when sung). The fourth memorial acclamation would be most appropriate because it ends by acclaiming Christ as the "Savior of the world." A sung "Great Amen" should be particularly strong at this festive eucharist.

If the Lamb of God is extended, then the use of titles of Jesus such as "son of man," "son of David," "savior of the world," "redeemer of all," and "Lord Jesus Christ" would all appropriately reflect the Christmas feast.

Mass at Midnight

The natural symbolism of darkness in which we celebrate this liturgy is reflected in many of the texts of the liturgy. Through them we understand the coming of Christ among us as a light shining in the darkness of our world and of our own hearts. The entrance antiphon, however, continues the custom of the former Roman rite by using verse 7 from Psalm 2: "You are my Son; this day I have begotten you"—obviously chosen because of its Messianic application. The alternate antiphon emphasizes the reason why the Lord came in human flesh—to bring us peace, which is only possible because of the birth of the savior.

The light symbolism is reflected in the (traditional) opening prayer. We affirm that God makes the darkness of night "radiant with true light," Christ, the light of the world. We pray that we might come to know the light of Christ more fully through the liturgy; yet, we also pray that we might experience eternal joy in the kingdom forever.

The first reading from Isaiah (9:1–6) can be understood in an accommodated sense to refer to the light of Christ coming into the world's darkness and gloom. We believe that the light that has shone (vs. 1) is Christ who leads us from the shadows of confusion to the light of his truth. We acknowledge that the "child . . . born to us" and the "son . . . given us" (vs. 5) is the one who judges justly (vs. 6) from "David's throne." His dominion is vast, yet it is

178   *Solemnity of Christmas*

forever blessed with his peace and joy. Using the titles of this reading, we can legitimately acclaim the Lord as "Wonder-Counselor," "God-Hero," "Father-Forever," and "Prince of Peace" (vs. 5).

The responsorial psalm, Psalm 96, is interspersed with the refrain from Luke 2:11 (part of tonight's gospel): "Today is born our Savior, Christ the Lord." The psalm invites us to "announce his salvation, day after day" (vs. 2) and to "tell his glory among the nations" (vs. 3). Because the Advent liturgy has prepared us, we "exult before the Lord, for he comes" to us (vs. 13). Yet, coupled with joy is our submission to him for "he comes to rule the earth" (vs. 13). To accept the Christ child is to accept his lordship, dominion, and sovereignty over our lives.

The second reading from Titus 2:11–14 is the traditional passage used to unite the mystery of God's grace made manifest in Christ (vs. 11) and the response we are required to give him in witness and mission. This grace of God appeared "offering salvation to all" (vs. 11), which grace empowers us and challenges us "to live temperately" (vs. 13) "as we await our blessed hope . . . ," that is, the second coming of our Savior Christ Jesus (vs. 13). It was "he who sacrificed himself for us, to redeem us" (vs. 14). Because he freely gave himself for us, "to cleanse for himself a people of his own" (vs. 14), we should be willing to fulfill the challenge to be "eager to do what is right."

The gospel acclamation repeats the refrain in the responsorial psalm, "today is born our Savior, Christ the Lord," and adds a reference both to the incarnation and to the gospel to be proclaimed in the words: "Good News and great joy to all the world."

The gospel from Luke (2:1–14) is the traditional text recounting the birth of Jesus. When interpreting it, we should recall the theological perspective of the Word made flesh (seen in John's prologue) and of Jesus' lifelong obedience to the will of his Father as essential elements of the Christmas mystery. "Messiah," "Lord," and "Savior" are used to refer to this child. Our willingness to submit to him under these titles is a challenge offered in this proclamation. Another concerns our appreciation of the astounding miracle that took place in the incarnation, first announced to simple shepherds. In reviewing this familiar text, we should allow Luke's editorial design to challenge us to see in this birth the inauguration of God's reign over our lives.

When Jesus was least Solemnity of Christmas 179
Power we have him – BIRTH/CROSS
– WHAT THIS SAYS Re: our Power

Luke's account contains the curious reference to Bethlehem as the "city of David," a term usually associated with Jerusalem. However, this change brings out even more clearly the lineage and association of Jesus' birth with the family of David (vs. 4). The statement about the actual birth, referring to the "swaddling clothes" and to the "manger" (vs. 7), is significant, not because of the heartlessness of innkeepers who turned away the holy family (as is commonly thought), but rather because of a reference to Isaiah 1:3. Previously, Israel did not know the ways of God, symbolized by their not knowing their "master's manger" (vs. 8).

It is the marginal shepherds who are the first to receive word of Christ's birth, a factor which coincides well with Luke's editorial plan where the humble are exalted and the mighty are deposed.

The titles of Jesus used by the angel offer important insight into the full implications of this event—he comes as Savior, Messiah, and Lord (vs. 11). The fact that these titles are commonly associated with post-resurrection summaries about the life and mission of Jesus (for example, in Acts 2:32, 36; 5:31) is significant since it means that Luke has taken these titles and placed them early on in the gospel to indicate that this child is God's extraordinary revelation to us. This child will redeem Israel from her sins and be the anointed one for all peoples; his lordship will extend to the ends of the earth. This gospel is thus a theologically sophisticated text whose style and editing bring out essential facets of Jesus' mission.

The prayer over the gifts is the traditional text from the Roman rite containing the significant notion of interchange or exchange of the divine and the human in Christ. We pray that the eucharist will enable us to "become more like [Jesus]."

The communion antiphon is adapted from the gospel of the Christmas day mass. This text is pivotal for an understanding of John's prologue and for appreciating the feast of Christmas: "the Word became flesh . . . and we have seen his glory" (Jn 1:14).

The prayer after communion is the traditional text of the Roman rite. We pray that we might live as Jesus taught and so fulfill what is implied in every eucharist—that the liturgy lead us to serve God through loving and serving each other. The addition of the phrase "the birth of the savior" is another subtle reiteration of the relationship between Christmas and the paschal mystery.

Celebration of the Mass at Midnight

Of all the Christmas masses, this one most obviously displays the light/darkness symbolism of this feast. While no special light symbols are added to the liturgy (as at Easter with the paschal candle and the new fire), Christ is seen as the prime analogue of all light.

Because "anticipated masses" are common and since the former restriction of the first mass to "midnight" is no longer in effect, this mass might well be celebrated at any time after nightfall so that the light symbolism can be evident.

If the church is kept in semidarkness for the first part of the liturgy, the procession of ministers carrying candles to be placed at the lectern for the liturgy of the Word and around the altar for the eucharist would be all the more striking. In addition to candles, the use of incense for the gospel procession and the presentation of the gifts is a nonverbal way of emphasizing the centrality of the lectern for the word and of the table for the eucharist. In preparing the liturgy, those responsible should review who will be ministering to be sure that there are readers for each reading and for the petitions of the prayer of the faithful (if there is no deacon) as well as sufficient servers to facilitate the celebration but no extras for show.

Since the liturgy is composed of a series of processions, the timing and pace of the entrance procession, the gospel procession, the presentation of the gifts, and the recession should be coordinated with the accompanying music. Flexibility in the music to accompany the breaking of bread and for the communion procession is important so that music covers these actions but does not dominate by being too long or distract by being too brief.

The issue of appropriate liturgical music should be addressed because too frequently the selection of a few carols to "fill in" during the mass is thought sufficient. In fact, the music chosen today (as at every liturgy) should primarily enhance the texts of the liturgy rather than overshadow them. The use of carols during the liturgy should not replace strong, solemn acclamations during the eucharistic prayer and at the gospel procession. Singing the responsorial psalm and the "Glory to God" would also be appropriate, as would an assembly/choir arrangement to accompany the communion procession.

Whatever the choice of eucharistic acclamations, they should be different from those used during Advent and should be used from now through the Baptism of the Lord. Since choirs usually want to do something special for Christmas, appropriate times are during the presentation of the gifts or before or after mass (as a prelude or postlude). Also, the choir can sing the invocations to a sung "Lord, have mercy," or a descant line to give well-known carols (or acclamations) depth and richness.

For the introductory rites, the question of a sung "Lord have mercy" and/or a sung "Glory to God" should be determined on the basis of how much solemnity is desirable. Should the third form of the penitential rite be used (whether sung or spoken), the use of the third set of invocations about Christ as "mighty God and prince of peace," "Son of God and Son of Mary," and as "Word made flesh and splendor of the Father" correspond well with the theology of Christmas.

The gospel procession should take place this evening with slow and reverent pace from the altar (where the gospel book is placed during the entrance procession) to the lectern accompanied by a sung alleluia and verse. After the gospel is proclaimed, the peoples' response could be a repetition of the sung alleluia verse. At the profession of faith, all kneel at the words "and became man."

The Sacramentary appendix contains a set of sample intercessions for the Christmas season which could help in composing original ones.

The third Christmas preface, with its references to the "oneness between God and man" and "a new light has dawned upon the world," make it particularly apt for this celebration. The proper section for Christmas is used with the Roman Canon.

If the "Lamb of God" is extended beyond three invocations, the use of the titles Savior, Lord, and Messiah found in the gospel this evening would be appropriate additions.

Because of the number receiving the eucharist on Christmas, an extended "Lamb of God" would seem warranted to accompany the distribution of consecrated bread onto patens and the pouring of consecrated wine into the chalices of the ministers.

The solemn blessing for Christmas, found in the mass formula, is an appropriate conclusion to the liturgy.

Mass at Dawn

Many of the themes found in the sacramentary texts for midnight mass are also found in the dawn mass. The opening prayer draws on the light/darkness theme and the prayer over the gifts emphasizes the importance of the gift of divine life.

The entrance antiphon is taken from the first reading at midnight mass, Isaiah 9:2, and from the gospel of Luke (1:33), about the light shining on us through the Lord who "is born for us." It should be noted that the phrase "for us" is more fully developed when it refers to Christ's sacrificial death and resurrection for the forgiveness of sins. The body given "for you" and the blood shed "for all" are shared at the eucharist because Christ first emptied himself, divested himself of all claim to dominion with the Father and was "born for us."

The opening prayer is traditional in the Roman rite and refers to the incarnate Word filling us with a new light, that "the light of faith shine in our words and actions." Thus, we pray for the harmony between our acts of liturgy and our lives in faith, a harmony established and exemplified in the life of the Word made flesh.

The first reading from Isaiah (62:11–12) will also be assigned for morning prayer on Thursday between Epiphany and the Baptism of our Lord; verses 1–12 of this chapter are assigned to the office of readings the preceding Tuesday, thus establishing it as an important text for the Christmas-Epiphany cycle. We acclaim the coming of the "savior" (vs. 11) whom we now acknowledge to be born today. We who accept the savior and receive his salvation are called "holy people, the redeemed of the Lord" (vs. 12). Our task is to live as those who have been freed from sin and redeemed by Christ's death and resurrection.

The responsorial psalm reflects the light symbolism of early morning by using the refrain, "a light will shine on us this day: the Lord is born for us." The verses of Psalm 97 articulate our gratitude at the birth of Jesus among us for like the psalmist, we are "glad in the Lord" (vs. 12) because "Light dawns for the just; and gladness for the upright of heart" (vs. 11).

The second reading from Titus 3:4–7 is traditional in the Roman rite, which used this text to relate the birth of Jesus to our justification by grace. "The kindness and love of God our Savior appeared" (vs. 4) in the birth of the Messiah; yet, it is through "the baptism of new birth and [the] renewal of the Holy Spirit" (vs. 5) that we become full sharers in this mystery. Through faith and baptism, we become "heirs, in hope, of eternal life" (vs. 7).

The gospel acclamation, "Glory to God in Heaven, peace and grace to his people on earth," recalls the gospel proclaimed at midnight (Lk 2:14). The gospel at this mass (Lk 2:15–20) is filled with important theological themes reflected in the way Luke recounts the announcement to the shepherds that Christ is born and the reaction of Mary to all that had come to pass. The shepherds haste to go and find the child (vs. 15), and their appreciation of what this birth meant ("once they saw, they understood," vs. 17) reflects back to Luke 2:10 and to Isaiah 62. These socially marginal and indigent shepherds are the ones who comprehend the significance of the birth of Jesus as opposed to the religious leaders Herod will consult about Jesus' identity. Just as Luke's gospel exalts the poor and reveals salvation to them (as seen in the Canticles of Mary and Zechariah), so this text shows how the birth of the Messiah overturns human expectations and invites us to reassess what we value in this world.

Mary is given as the model for all believers, for she treasured all these things and reflected on them in her heart (vs. 19). Throughout Jesus' public life, Mary is the model believer and faithful disciple even when it costs her suffering and pain for she knows how important it is to submit to God's will in faith and love.

The prayer over the gifts reflects the important Christmas theme of the divine/human interchange. We ask that the divinity of Christ would sanctify us once again and make us worthy of the mystery we commemorate today. This prayer fittingly reflects what occurs through the liturgy—our sharing in the divine life through the eucharist.

The communion antiphon speaks of the coming of a "King . . . the Holy One, the Savior of the world" (see Zec 9:9). Jesus is that King whom we acclaim as that Savior foretold by the prophets and whose birth we commemorate today.

In the prayer after communion, we pray that we might grow in the fullness of love incarnate made available to us through Christ, especially today as we celebrate and commemorate his incarnation.

Celebration of the Mass at Dawn

It would be appropriate to use this mass formula and readings at one or two early morning Christmas masses; but this mass should not derogate from the primary Christmas texts assigned to the day mass. Such a "dawn" or early morning liturgy should be kept simple. The music at this mass could begin softly and simply at the entrance procession. Should the third form of the penitential rite be used, appropriate (spoken or sung) invocations of Christ are those found in the third sample formula. Other invocations could be composed using the titles of Christ from this liturgy: "savior," "Lord," "Word," and "Son of God."

The "Glory to God" and the eucharistic acclamations deserve special emphasis; the refrain from the "Glory to God" could also be used to introduce the gospel.

The first Christmas preface would be a good choice because it can be thought of as reflecting the shepherds' reaction in the gospel: "Your eternal Word has brought to the eyes of faith a new and radiant vision of your glory." If the Roman Canon is used, the proper section about Christmas is proclaimed.

A special introduction to the sign of peace could be based on the second reading (Titus), which reminds us of our being heirs together of Christ's justifying grace.

Mass During the Day

The entrance antiphon is taken from the last line of the first reading from midnight mass (Is 9:6) about the titles and dominion of the "child . . . born for us." From the outset, the liturgy points to the full implications of the birth of Jesus among us—to be our savior and lord.

The opening prayer is a very important text taken from the Leonine Sacramentary. In it we acknowledge the Lord of creation and the restoration of all things in Christ; through Christ who shared our weakness, we hope to share the fullness of his glory. This glory is celebrated and experienced through the liturgy; its consummation will be achieved in the kingdom of heaven.

The first reading from Isaiah (52:7–10) is also the reading for morning prayer on the Epiphany. It recalls how God led his people from Babylon to Zion and restored their privileged status as God's chosen. The advent of "salvation" and "peace" through the "glad tidings" announced by the prophet can easily be applied to our experience of hearing the good news that the Messiah is born. The comfort which the Lord gives (vs. 9) as he redeems Jerusalem is offered so that "the ends of the earth will behold the salvation of our God" (vs. 10). This extension of salvation to all nations is a dominant theme of the days surrounding Epiphany; its presence on Christmas reminds us that the Messiah's birth is for the salvation of all peoples.

The responsorial psalm, Psalm 98, contains many words and phrases common to the Advent-Christmas cycle. We acclaim the Lord because his "right hand has won victory for him" (vs. 1), a reference to the First Sunday of Advent when the just are called to the Lord's right side in heaven. We acknowledge the Lord's "salvation" for "he has revealed his justice" (vs. 2) first to Israel and then to all nations on earth. The remembrance of the Lord's "kindness and faithfulness toward the house of Israel" (vs. 3) is experienced whenever the church celebrates the liturgy.

The second reading is the traditional and theologically rich passage from the opening verses of the letter to the Hebrews (1:1–6). It begins by referring to creation and to the care God has shown to Israel (vss. 1–3); it then explores the superiority of Christ to any other revelation. He alone "cleansed us from our sins" (vs. 3) and is now seated at the right hand of the Majesty in heaven (vs. 3). In contrasting Jesus' superiority to the angels, the author uses Psalm 2:7, "you are my son; today I have begotten you." As Christ was the only begotten of the Father, so we are newly graced (and in that sense begotten again) by God. In addition to the important phrase "only-begotten," the author draws on the equally significant term "firstborn" referring to Christ. He is the first to be born into the kingdom of heaven by his death and resurrection; so we follow him through this life in order to die and rise with him to true life in the kingdom.

The gospel acclamation is an important introduction to the Johannine gospel: "A holy day has dawned upon us. Come, you nations, and adore the Lord. Today a great light has come upon the earth." The reference to "light" is especially significant; with the passing of the dawn and the rising of the sun, we experience a symbol of God's love, his Son, called light and life in John's gospel.

While the Johannine prologue may seem to be abstract, it should be obvious by now that its richness and theological significance make it the dominant scriptural text today. (In fact, it is so important that it is read again on December 31 and on the second Sunday after Christmas in countries where the Epiphany is not celebrated in its place.).

The opening verses recalls the opening verses of Genesis about creation by the word of God. Here the Word was "in God's presence . . . in the beginning" (vs. 1). The work of creation is ascribed to the Word (vs. 3): through him "whatever came to be . . . found life . . . [and] light" (vs. 4). The light that overcame darkness in Genesis now pales in comparison with him who is light and life incarnate. Through him and because of him, we can say that "the light shines on in the darkness, a darkness that did not overcome it" (vs. 4). The daily cycle of light and darkness obviously marks time for us; with Christ as our light, there is but one eternal day in his presence.

The following verses remind us of what was so clearly proclaimed during Advent, that John the Baptizer came as a witness to Christ, but himself was not the light (vs. 7). Like all Israel, he looked for the light to come into the world (vs. 8). Using a play on the word "world," John relates that he who created the physical world came in human flesh so that the world (in the sense of the people in it) would believe in him as their creator and savior (vs. 10). That the Lord's coming demands choices in the way we order our lives is clear in the statement, "to his own he came, yet his own did not accept him." Those who did (and do) accept him "become children of God" (vs. 12). The next verse is pivotal:

"The Word became flesh
and made his dwelling among us,
and we have seen his glory:
the glory of an only Son coming from the Father,
filled with enduring love." (vs. 14)

The coeternal Son of God thus accepted the necessary humiliation of taking on human flesh so that we in our human condition might share the life of God in Christ. This is at the heart of what we have repeatedly seen in the prayers of the liturgy—the divine/human interchange in Christ. Jesus' "dwelling among us" recalls God's sustaining presence to Israel in the Exodus where he pitched his tent among the people as they journeyed (Ex 33:7–11; 18–23). In the new covenant, the Lord creates an abiding dwelling place with us through the human flesh of his Son (see 2 Cor 3:13, 15, 18). The "glory" of God that was revealed in the Old Testament was awesome; before it Israel bowed in adoration. In Jesus, the glory is revealed through his humanity so that through him we might experience the fullness of God's glory. It is "of his fullness [that] we have all had a share" (vs. 16). It is only in Christ (as opposed to the law) that we can share in God's "enduring love" (vs. 14).

These verses emphasize our present participation in the incarnation; it is Christ present with us now who fills us with God's life and love. This Johannine text thus discloses our appropriation of the incarnation through faith in Christ; through him "we see our God made visible and so are caught up in love of the God we cannot see" (Christmas Preface I).

The prayer over the gifts states that the eucharist renews in us the reconciliation Christ accomplished between God and humankind.

The prayer after communion speaks of the birth of the "Savior of the world" who made us children of the Father, and asks that he may welcome us into his kingdom.

Celebration of the Mass During the Day

The Christmas masses should be solemn and festive celebrations. Choir and/or organ preludes and postludes can establish a festive and solemn atmosphere for the liturgy. A well-paced entrance procession with all the ministers can help solemnize the celebration, especially when there are lectors for each reading and the intercessions (when a deacon is not present). The mix of the assembly, older and young people, men and women, should be reflected as fully as possible in the selection of ministers.

The gospel book carried in procession should be very decorative and the gospel procession emphasized.

The choice of special vesture (matching for concelebrants and deacon) should itself reflect the festivity of this day.

The use of incense at the entrance and the gospel processions and during the presentation of the gifts could enhance the celebration.

The third Christmas preface, which refers to the eternal Word taking on our human weakness, reflects the gospel today.

The proclamation of the Roman Canon with the special section about Christmas would be appropriate.

The eucharistic acclamations could be enhanced with harmonized choir parts and musical instruments along with the organ.

The choice of music other than the texts of the liturgy should reflect our share in the incarnation; it should not merely recount the story of how Jesus was born. Any "traditional" customs surrounding the use of the Christmas creche during the liturgy should be reviewed lest these popular devotions derogate from the liturgy itself. Care should be taken when composing the introduction to the liturgy and the intercessions (any any other comments) to avoid an overemphasis on Christ's childhood. Titles reflecting his adult life and ministry should be used as much as possible, for example, those found in the third set of sample invocations to the penitential rite. Other sources include the liturgy of the word today (especially Christ as the "Word" made flesh) and the solemn blessing of Christmas, which would form a fitting conclusion to the liturgy.

Liturgy of the Hours

The Christmas season begins with Evening Prayer I, containing proper psalms as well as special antiphons and intercessions. These texts inaugurate the commemoration of the coming among us of the Word made flesh. The first antiphon accompanying Psalm 113 acclaims the "King who is our peace," the One we have longed to see. The second text affirms the might and power of the Lord, who "sends forth his word to the earth, and his command spreads swiftly through the land." Just as God's powerful deeds in the old covenant (recounted in Psalm 147 to follow) reflected his Lordship and might, so we acclaim the Lord's power in Jesus, the enfleshed word and abiding presence of God among us. He comes to save and free us from sin and death. The "eternal Word, born of the Father" is acclaimed in the antiphon to accompany the Christ hymn from Philippians (2:6–11). This text should be noted especially this evening. It refers to Christ's act of humiliation in taking on our human condition and his free acceptance of death on the cross (vs. 8). The balance in this hymn, acclaiming the incarnate and suffering Lord, guides our appreciation of today's feast. When we commemorate the birth of Jesus among us, we also commemorate the paschal mystery through which we have been redeemed.

The scripture reading from Galatians (4:4–5) is also assigned for Evening Prayer I and II on the Solemnity of Mary, Mother of God

(January 1) and as the second reading at mass that day (vss. 4–7). This text asserts that at "a designated time," Christ was born of a woman, whose birth was to renew all people of every time and place. We do not believe in a vague, timeless divinity. Our God took time and history so seriously that he redeemed it through his Son's birth in time.

The antiphon to the Canticle of the Blessed Virgin contains many images that were used in the Advent liturgy to designate the significance of Christ's coming and our intimate union with God through Christ: "When the sun rises in the morning sky, you will see the King of kings coming forth from the Father like a radiant bridegroom from the bridal chamber." The Canticle of the Blessed Virgin this evening takes on special meaning since it reviews the implications of the incarnation and the ramifications of the Kingdom established through Christ's birth.

The introduction to the intercessions reflects the Philippian hymn to show how we can draw strength from Christ's example of being fully human yet not giving into temptation and sin. The intercessions themselves recall Jesus' humanity, weakness, poverty, and birth and ask that we may accept the limitations of the human condition to grow in the likeness of Christ. This hour ends with the collect used at the vigil mass drawing on the images of Christ as judge and redeemer, whose second coming will fulfill the redemption we celebrate at Christmas.

The invitatory to the liturgy of the hours combines the notions of Christ's sacrifice with our act of homage as we pray, "Christ has been born for us: come let us adore him." The sacrificial overtones associated with "for us" noted above should be recalled as we begin the hours this morning. Christ was born to die for us so that in him we might die to sin and live for one another.

The first reading at the office of readings from Isaiah (11:1–10) is the same text used at the eucharist on the Second Sunday of Advent ("A" cycle) and on Tuesday of the first week of Advent (see commentary for that Tuesday). When proclaimed on Christmas morning, this text is basic to the theology of the incarnation commemorated today. Its universal application and effect should be underscored; the child born for us today is the Lord of all the earth. The responsory points to our need for the incarnation when it refers to Christ's birth "for our sake" in order "to reclaim lost men." Once again, we are reminded that it is the redemption Christ accomplished for us that matters in today's commemoration of the incarnation.

The second reading from St. Leo's sermon on the nativity skillfully applies the effects of Christ's incarnation to our situation and need. Through Christ we have been redeemed, therefore, Leo encourages us to live the dignity granted us in Christ and to lead sinless lives until he comes again: "Christian, remember your dignity, and now that you share in God's own nature, do not return by sin to your former base condition. Bear in mind who is your head and of whose body you are a member." The darkness/light motif (seen above in the masses at midnight and at dawn) is expanded here to refer to baptism. We who have been baptized are to put aside deeds of darkness, our sins, and to walk in the light of Christ. "Do not forget that you have been rescued from the power of darkness and brought into the light of God's kingdom." The celebration of the incarnation gives us the hope and confidence we need to take up this challenge anew; graced in Christ, we are to perform deeds of light. In the words of the responsory, "today a new day dawns . . ." in us through Christ's human birth.

The antiphons and psalms are specially chosen for this hour. The use of Psalm 2 is significant since in Christian liturgical usage we can appreciate the Messianic overtones of verse 7: "you are my Son. It is I who have begotten you this day." Psalm 19, about cosmic praise of the glory of God, is introduced by an antiphon whose nuptial imagery once again demonstrates the intimate union between creator and creature in Christ: "The Lord comes forth, the bridegroom from his bridal chamber." The third antiphon recalls that in Christ God has blessed us forever. In Psalm 45, we find images used in Advent to refer to the coming of our King and Lord:

"Your throne, O God, shall endure forever.
A scepter of justice is the scepter of your kingdom.
Your love is for justice; your hatred for evil.

"Therefore God, your God, has anointed you
   with the oil of gladness above other kings:
your robes are fragrant with aloes and myrrh." (vss. 7–9)

This hour concludes with the ancient and theologically significant prayer from the Christmas day mass about Christ through whom our weakness and estrangement from God is overcome.

At morning prayer, the psalms from week I are used along with specially selected antiphons. The first antiphon reflects the morning hour and the gospel from the dawn mass containing the shepherds' reaction to what they have seen: "We have seen a newborn infant and a choir of angels praising the Lord, alleluia." The addition of "alleluia" to all three antiphons increases our appreciation that the Lord's birth led to his paschal triumph. The second antiphon continues this motif by repeating the announcement that "the Savior of the world" has been born. The third antiphon draws out the meaning of this child's birth for we acclaim him "mighty God." These antiphons function as ways of approaching the psalms so we can pray them in the light of the incarnation.

The reading assigned for morning prayer is taken from the first verses of the letter to the Hebrews (1:1–2); the same text is used as the second reading at the day mass (1:1–6). Fittingly, it stresses the supremacy of God's revelation through his son.

The antiphon to Zechariah's canticle is the angels' announcement from Luke (2:14): "Glory to God in the highest . . ." with the addition of "alleluia." This particular antiphon functions as a way of recalling the gospel from the mass at midnight (Luke 2:1–14), the gospel acclamation at the mass at dawn, and the "Glory to God" hymn restored to the eucharist today.

The introduction to the intercessions takes up the theme of the preexistence of the Word now born in time, thus fusing themes so clearly stated in the gospel of the day mass (Jn 1:1–14) and in the reading at Evening Prayer I from Galatians (4:4–5). He who is now born in time himself has no beginning or end; his incarnation was for our sake and for the salvation of the world. The intercessions use images of Christ the Messiah from the gospels as the bases on which we offer our prayers: "word of God," "savior of all," "king of heaven," and "true vine." Once again, this last title brings out the paschal overtones of the incarnation since this image from the gospel of John (15:1) is more commonly associated with the Easter season. The hour concludes with the collect from the dawn mass.

At Evening Prayer II, the first antiphon (accompanying Ps 110:1–5, 7) focuses on Christ's preexistence and his birth in time. We acclaim him as the one "endowed from your birth with princely gifts" and who was begotten "in eternal splendor." This adaptation of verse 3 of the psalm helps to bring out some Messianic overtones proper to the feast of Christmas. The second antiphon, introducing Psalm 130, speaks about Christ as savior for it affirms "the unfailing love of the Lord" and how "great is his power to save." This is particularly important when we consider the last verses of the psalm:

"Because with the Lord there is mercy
and fullness of redemption,
Israel indeed he will redeem
from all its iniquity." (vss. 7–8)

What the psalmist declared of God is now experienced in the church this Christmas through the birth of Christ among us. The third antiphon recalls the gospel of the day mass: "In the beginning, before time began, the Word was God; today he is born, the Savior of the world." This capsule review points to the cosmic significance of the incarnation and to the active presence of God with us now through the birth of his coeternal son. The choice of the Christ hymn from Colossians (1:12–20) is especially appropriate today because of the reference to "darkness" and being forgiven our sins (vss. 13–14) through Christ. This day of new beginnings in Christ's human birth is reflected when we acclaim:

"It is he who is head of the body, the church!
he who is the beginning,
the firstborn of the dead,
so that primacy may be his in everything." (vs. 18)

Christ's mission to reconcile us with God and with one another through the paschal mystery is emphasized in the hymn's final verses:

". . . to reconcile everything in his person,
both on earth and in the heavens,
making peace through the blood of his cross." (vss. 19–20)

The reading of 1 John 1:1–3 at evening prayer is a fitting complement to the Johannine prologue read at the day mass. What has come to pass in Christ and in history is testified to and affirmed as the unique moment of salvation (vs. 1). The author stresses our participation in this salvation when he states:

"What we have seen and heard
we proclaim in turn to you
so that you may share life with us.
This fellowship of ours is with the Father
and with his Son, Jesus Christ." (vs. 3)

We experience this fellowship and unity through the liturgy of
Christmas day.

Our experience of God with us in and through Christ is expressed
fully in the antiphon to the Canticle of the Blessed Virgin Mary:

"Christ the Lord is born today; today, the Savior has appeared.
Earth echoes songs of angel choirs, archangels' joyful praise. Today
on earth his friends exult: Glory to God in the highest, alleluia."

This text is especially striking when one considers the texts of the
"O" antiphons used in the latter part of Advent. All those images
have now been fulfilled; through the liturgy "today," we experience
the presence of God with us under his many titles.

The intercessions bring out our experience of the incarnation and
our need for Christ's presence in our lives. He who is "king from all
eternity," "chief shepherd and guardian of our lives," and the one
"awaited from the beginning of the world" intercedes for us at his
Father's right hand. Where he has ascended (to the kingdom of
heaven) is where we hope to be reunited with him. In the meantime,
we gather to pray through Christ, not a helpless infant, but a mediator and Messiah born for us and for our salvation. The concluding
prayer is the collect from the day mass (which was also used at the
office of readings).

Celebration of the Hours

The selection of the hymn to introduce these hours is important to
set the proper tone and theological perspective with which to celebrate Christmas. The traditional chant adaptation of the text *Corde
Natus Ex Parentis* summarizes our need for a savior and the love of
God now incarnate in Jesus (hence, a reflection of John 1). It would
be especially fitting at evening prayer to sing it in the popular translation "Of the Father's Love Begotten."

The fact that no proper psalm prayers are offered at the hours today affords the opportunity to compose texts that reflect the incarna-

tion (using ideas taken from the day's scripture readings and titles of Christ used in the liturgy). The prayers provided for morning prayer are those assigned to the Sunday psalter, hence they should be changed to suit the feast celebrated.

At each of the hours, the scripture readings assigned are specially selected. Extending each beyond the few verses chosen, however, can help enhance the celebration. At each of the hours, the intercessions provided are well constructed even though they are a bit wordy. Using a simple response for the congregation, such as "Lord, hear us," or "Lord, have mercy," can curb excess wordiness. If the intercessions themselves are edited, their structure should be kept because of their theological nuance.

For the invitatory, the use of the assigned text and Psalm 95 would be a most fitting beginning to the hours today. The choice of what elements of each hour to be sung will depend on the rest of the liturgy as celebrated by each community. However, in addition to the Canticles of Mary and Zechariah, singing some (or all) of the psalms and the Lord's Prayer would help to add solemnity to the hours. The use of the solemn blessing for Christmas as a conclusion at the main hours would be appropriate.

Reflection—"Why There Was a Christmas"

Christmas is a very special time. At times like these, most usual words don't fit the magic of the moment, the wonder of the occasion. Part of the reason is that the *what* and *how* of Christmas are readily known and all of us could tell the story with every detail.

But, the *why* of Christmas, why it all had to happen is the story not so often told. The *why* of Christmas needs special words . . . the words of a story . . . a story for children of all ages . . . for all of us are children at Christmas.

"Once upon a time" . . . or so the saying goes . . . long, long ago, . . . so long ago that it was "once upon eternity" that it all began . . . , there was a man named Adam. Now Adam lived in a garden with his wife Eve, and Adam and Eve had a friend, a very close friend indeed. . . . Adam and Eve's friend was God.

Now one day God told Adam that this garden was a kingdom . . . the peaceable kingdom we call it. . . . God was the King and he needed a gardener for his garden, the kingdom. And so, Adam became God's gardener. Things went very well indeed for Adam,

Eve, for God and for all the people and the animals who lived in the garden.

Now God wasn't a bossy king . . . just one rule had he . . . just one "don't" among all the dos, cans, shoulds, woulds, and maybes . . . just one *don't*, that's all. And all went very well, very well indeed for Adam, Eve, and all in the garden.

But, then came the day, that terrible day, when Adam and Eve did the *don't* God wanted them not to do . . . and that was the beginning of the trouble. Adam and Eve had to leave the garden . . . and things weren't very good at all.

But, all was not lost; Adam's friend, God the King, made a promise. He said they could return, not right away but when he would send his son to bring back the peaceable kingdom. . . . His Son would be the one, perfect gardener . . . the only true gardener. And so, once upon eternity . . . God made a promise.

And so it was, that Adam and Eve and their sons and daughters lived outside the garden . . . and their sons and daughters had more sons and daughters. They were all gardeners waiting for the promise to come true.

Some got tired and said, "No promises for me." "I want it now." "I can't wait for God," and things went from bad to worse outside the garden.

But then, once upon historical time . . . or so the saying goes, there was a new gardener, not the one perfect one, but a gardener like all the rest. His name was John. He told them, "remember the promise," "well, it's coming true," "get ready." He said that once again lions and lambs, cobras and children, enemies and friends would soon be back in God's garden and the one true gardener was to do it all. The promise would come true.

And so it was that one silent, holy night, the Son of God came . . . the promise finally came true. . . . God kept his promise. His son came and brought a new kingdom . . . a new peaceable kingdom. . . . He was and is the one true gardener.

All went very well, very well indeed and things were good for all the Son's friends . . . for other gardeners too. But, not for very long . . . just like before some got tired and went their way . . . they did not believe, that was the problem . . . the peaceable kingdom was not everywhere . . . it would now have to be made . . . and to be made everywhere and anywhere any man and every man, any woman and every woman . . . would let the garden come to be.

But, not just any and every person . . . just those who chose to believe that God kept his promise and that he had sent his son . . . the perfect gardener . . . the true son of God the king.

And so, the last part of the why of Christmas is once upon tomorrow . . . and tomorrow, and tomorrow . . . it's up to us, who believe that he has come . . . it's up to us to build his new kingdom here. We have to make a promise this Christmas to be good gardeners . . . to build the new and peaceable kingdom . . . now and always. And the only way we can is to believe in the perfect gardener who helps us live as good and better gardeners.

At Christmas God kept his promise. This Christmas let us make and keep a promise to live as he would have us live . . . to love as he would have us love . . . and to garden the way he taught us to garden. . . . After all, God kept his promise. . . .

It all started once upon eternity . . . it came true once upon historical time . . . it's now up to us to make it come true again and again . . . once upon tomorrow.

That's the why there had to be a Christmas.

DECEMBER 26—STEPHEN, FIRST MARTYR

Liturgical Context

The *General Norms* for the Liturgical Year state:

"Christmas has its own octave, arranged as follows:
  Sunday within the octave is the feast of the Holy Family;
  26 December is the feast of Saint Stephen, First Martyr;
  27 December is the feast of Saint John, Apostle and Evangelist;
  28 December is the feast of the Holy Innocents;
  29, 30, and 31 December are days within the octave." (no. 35)

The octave of Christmas is second only to the octave of Easter in importance. The first three days celebrate feasts while the remaining days refer back to Christmas. This somewhat curious arrangement is hinted at in Gregory of Nyssa's (fourth-century) list of those who have some connection with the Christ child; he names Stephen first along with Peter, James, John, Paul, and Basil. Stephen's designation as the "first martyr" in the title of today's feast obviously singles him out for special attention.

The connection between Christmas and the feast of Stephen is derived from the paschal overtones of Christmas. Just as Jesus became incarnate to save us by his passion, death, and resurrection, so his followers most closely imitate him by giving their lives in death to attest their belief in him. Stephen is the first who gave his life for the sake of Christ, hence, the place of honor given him in the calendar right after Christmas.

The specific connection between Christ and Stephen is reflected in the responsory to the second reading at the office of readings:

"Yesterday the Lord was born on earth that Stephen might be born
    in heaven;
—the Lord entered into our world that Stephen might enter into
    heaven.
Yesterday our King, clothed in flesh, came forth from the virgin's
    womb to dwell among us."

As Jesus became mediator because he was a victim and high priest because of his sacrifice, this "feast of Stephen" reminds us that like Jesus and the saint, we must offer ourselves in sacrifice and thus become pleasing to the Father.

Liturgy of the Eucharist

The entrance antiphon asserts that the "gates of heaven opened for Stephen, the first of the martyrs; in heaven, he wears the crown of victory." The opening prayer (taken from the former Roman Missal) states that today we commemorate Stephen's "entrance into eternal glory," a phrase which interprets the Latin word for "birthday." Liturgical commemorations of saints occur (most generally) on the anniversaries of their death, of their passage from this life to eternal union with God. In the second part of the prayer, we ask that we might imitate Stephen by loving our enemies.

The first reading from Acts (6:8–10; 7:54–59) is traditional in the Roman rite; it is part of a longer text which is used at the office of readings. Here Stephen is described as one who carried on the work of Christ in the primitive Christian community through "wonders and signs" (vs. 8) and whose debating skill overshadowed that of any of his opponents (vs. 10). In the lengthy speech that follows,

Stephen summarizes the Christian faith as the fulfillment of the history of salvation. While Stephen is still speaking, his opponents grow angry (vs. 54), yet Stephen, "filled with the Holy Spirit" (vs. 55), affirms his faith in Jesus at the Father's right hand in glory (vss. 55–56). As his opponents begin to stone him, Stephen cries aloud, "Lord Jesus receive my spirit" (vs. 59), as an act of faith, and he asks God not to "hold this sin against them" (vs. 59), a final sign of how he lived the teachings of Jesus. The similarity between these texts and the crucifixion scene in Luke 23:34, 46 is clear where Jesus asks his Father to "forgive them; they do not know what they are doing" (vs. 34) and Jesus' final statement, "Father, into your hand I commend my spirit" (vs. 46).

A certain irony is introduced by the fact that as Stephen was being stoned Saul (Paul) had cloaks piled before him in homage (vs. 58)—the very time when the church experienced its first martyrdom. The irony is deepened when the scene of Jesus' Messianic entry into Jerusalem is recalled where crowds "spread their cloaks on the roadway as he moved along" (Lk 19:36). The acclaim of the crowd for Saul and the derision of the crowd for Stephen is combined in Jesus' experience when the acclaim of the crowd at his Messianic entrance is overturned by the time of his trial when they will cry, "crucify him" (Lk 23:21). These references to the passion confirm the thesis that the liturgy sees a close connection between Jesus' human birth and saving death, as well as between his paschal victory and Stephen's death so he can enter into God's glory.

The response to the responsorial psalm likens Stephen's faith-filled statement to Jesus' tranquil surrender to his Father; "Into your hand, O Lord, I entrust my spirit" (Ps 31:6). The verses of Psalm 31 reiterate this pivotal statement about surrender to God, a fitting prayer for the Christian community on the day after the commemoration of the birth of him who spent his life doing the will of the Father.

The paschal overtones of today's feast are not lost in the gospel verse, especially its first part, Psalm 118:26: "Blessed is he who comes in the name of the Lord." The Lord who appeared to us in human flesh at Christmas is here affirmed as "the Lord God [who] shines upon us."

The gospel asserts that persecution will accompany anyone who witnesses to faith in Christ (Mt 10:17–22); and yet it contains Jesus' reassuring promise that in such situations "the Spirit of your Father will be speaking in you" (vs. 20). The text forthrightly asserts that we will be persecuted if we hold fast to faith in Christ (vs. 22); such persecution may even come from within our own families (vs. 21). While bloody martyrdom will not be expected of many Christians, a daily unbloody but no less real martyrdom is often required of each of us.

The prayer over the gifts asks that the Father be pleased with the gifts we offer to worship God and to remember Stephen.

With confidence we pray the words of the communion antiphon, "Lord Jesus, receive my spirit."

Jesus' birth is linked to Stephen's martyrdom in the prayer after communion. God saves us by the birth of his Son, and gives us joy as we honor Stephen the martyr.

Celebration of the Eucharist

In a brief introduction, the presider (or other minister) could apply Stephen's martyrdom to the suffering we endure in witnessing to Christ in our world (an unbloody martyrdom). The use of the third set of sample invocations to the third form of the penitential rite would subtly recall the Christmas season as the context for this feast. Since the Glory to God is used during this octave, it will be important to plan whether it will be sung (in unison or with a schola alternating strophes with the assembly) or will be recited.

The sample intercessions for Christmas provide a good model for adding additional intentions for present-day martyrs for the faith, for this assembly to be more committed to the gospel, and for those who, like Stephen, "have gone before us marked with the sign of faith."

The second Christmas preface would serve well today since it refers to our destiny to live with Christ forever.

The Roman Canon with the special Christmas section would be appropriate today because it mentions Stephen in the section about "fellowship of your apostles and martyrs, with John the Baptist, Stephen, Matthias, Barnabas . . ." The third memorial acclamation with the phrase, "you are the Savior of the world," would bring out the paschal and redemptive overtones of the Christmas season.

Should the liturgy conclude with a prayer over the people, number 18, referring to reliving "the mystery of the eucharist and so be reborn to lead a new life," would be an appropriate choice. If the carol "Good King Wenceslaus" is sung today (because of its reference to "the feast of Stephen"), be sure to sing all the verses, otherwise the story is incomplete.

Liturgy of the Hours

The invitatory to the hours combines the Christmas season with today's feast by praying: "Come, let us worship the newborn Christ—who has given the glorious crown to St. Stephen." Stephen the martyr shed his blood as a witness to Christ; like him our lives must witness to the Lord we worship.

The first reading at the office of readings is the longer section of Acts from which the first reading is taken at the eucharist (Acts 6: 8–7:2a, 44–59).

The second reading from Fulgentius of Ruspe shows the parallel between Christ's birth and Stephen's death. Both Christ and Stephen served the Father on earth; their passage to eternal life confirmed all they witnessed to while on earth. The path to eternal life has been opened by Christ who seeks to draw us to himself for all eternity. For the Christian, therefore, death is not an end but the beginning of eternal happiness with God forever.

The antiphons to the psalmody at this hour are taken from the Acts text, referring to Stephen's vision, his forgiving his attackers, and the Spirit who spoke through him. The selection of psalms (for the common of one martyr) is particularly instructive since Psalm 2 was also used yesterday at the office of readings to emphasize Christ's Messianic role. Today it helps to connect Christ's birth and Stephen's martyrdom. Psalm 11 reflects the martyr's faith in the face of suffering for it states: "In the Lord I have taken my refuge" (vs. 1). Psalm 17 reflects the feast of a martyr by asking for protection from the wicked (vs. 9) and being filled with the Lord's glory (vs. 15).

At morning prayer, the antiphons emphasize Stephen's martyrdom. They speak of his death by stoning (first), his vision of and entrance into heaven (second), and his vision of Jesus standing at God's right hand (third). The psalms for this hour are taken from the Sunday psalmody (indicating the importance of this feast). The scripture reading is from the beginning of Acts 6 concerning the appointment of deacons (vss. 2b–5a). The antiphon to Zechariah's canticle reiterates Stephen's vision of the opened gates of heaven and his entrance through them to be crowned the first martyr.

The introduction to the intercessions points to the importance of fidelity in witnessing to God as Stephen did. The petitions speak of the martyr's profession of faith, the necessity of bearing our cross, and of witnessing to Christ.

At evening prayer today (and on December 27 and 28), the antiphons, psalms, and canticle are taken from Evening Prayer II of Christmas, reiterating the context of the Christmas season. The reading assigned for this evening is 1 John 1:5b–7, reflecting the darkness/light theme so clearly emphasized in the latter part of Advent and on Christmas. The antiphon to the Canticle of the Blessed Virgin emphasizes the incarnation of the Word by stating: "While earth was rapt in silence and night only half through its course, your almighty Word, O Lord, came down from his royal throne, alleluia."

In the intercessions, we ask that our lives be lived in dedication to the Father, that we might labor on behalf of sinners and that we might be delivered from evil through the paschal mystery of Jesus. In the final prayer (emphasizing the incarnation), we ask that Jesus' birth "free us from our former slavery to sin and bring us new life." The new life we have from Christ is only partial until we meet him in the kingdom, a destiny achieved by Stephen the martyr.

Celebration of the Hours

The invitatory today could be emphasized by singing both the verse and Psalm 100, the joyful song of those entering God's temple. The option of not using any psalm prayers and extending the periods of silence after the psalms could help establish a reflective atmosphere after yesterday's festivity.

The fact that the Latin Breviary assigns a hymn about Stephen's martyrdom at morning prayer instead of a Christmas hymn directs attention to the importance of emphasizing martyrdom in the hymn chosen to begin this hour. The use of psalms from a Sunday other than week I at morning prayer would provide variety, especially since these same psalms are also assigned for December 27 and 28.

At morning prayer, the expanded account of the assignment of deacons (Acts 6:1–7) would provide a more logical scripture reading. The same is true of the reading at evening prayer, which could be expanded to 1 John 1:1–10, thus including many of the themes already seen yesterday when the prologue to John's gospel is read at the Christmas Day Mass.

Reflection—"Reminiscence and Reality"

The death of Stephen reminds us of what real life is all about and what it means to be born anew in Christ. Like the martyr, we are to witness to Christ even when this means suffering rejection, betrayal, or misunderstanding. There is a high price involved in this kind of witnessing; it is the price Stephen paid with his blood. While the "martyrdom" expected of each of us may not mean shedding blood, it may involve our being rejected for the sake of Christ. Yet the feast should also give us hope for as Stephen was sustained by his vision of Christ with him, so should we be sustained by the vision of God with us at Christmas through his incarnate Word. At the liturgy, we commemorate Christ's paschal sacrifice which draws us to a deeper commitment to the Father whom we worship through, with, and in Christ.

DECEMBER 27—JOHN, APOSTLE AND EVANGELIST

Liturgical Context

Today's feast continues the triduum of special feast days following Christmas: Stephen, John, and the Holy Innocents. Keeping these feasts right after Christmas attests to their importance both in the early evolution of the Roman liturgy and in present Christian observance since the *Lutheran Book of Worship* and the *Prayer Book* of the Episcopal Church in America celebrate these same feasts after Christmas. In early liturgical commentaries, this feast of John was said to be closer to Christmas than the feast of any other apostle because John was the "beloved disciple."

With today's feast, the post-Christmas liturgy begins a continuous reading of the whole of 1 John which will run until the last weekday before the feast of the Baptism of our Lord. Today's gospel text was chosen to reflect the feast, not the Christmas season.

Liturgy of the Eucharist

The Sacramentary contains two entrance antiphons. The first is the traditional text for this feast, Sirach 15:5, about the "spirit of wisdom and understanding" that fills the just, and the "robe of glory" with which such a person clothed. "Glory" may be understood to refer to the glory theme so dominant in the gospel of John and which was emphasized on Christmas day (Jn 1:14). The glory revealed through Christ was the glory of the Father, once veiled and protected in the Old Testament but now revealed through Christ and experienced in the church, especially through the liturgy.

The second antiphon refers to the Last Supper where John "reclined close to the Lord" as a sign of their deep relationship. This text acknowledges our dependence on the apostles who received the Lord's revelation and told it to the first generation of Christian believers.

The opening prayer, taken from the former Roman Missal, refers to the evangelist who opened the hidden treasures of the "Word," a reference that includes both the Incarnate Word in Jesus and the word of the scriptures. We pray that we might come to a deeper understanding and appropriation of the message John proclaimed.

The first reading from 1 John (1:1–4), already used at Evening Prayer II on Christmas day (vss. 1–3) and which will be used at the office of readings today (1:1–2:3), can be considered the prologue to a letter whose main concern is to refute certain errors. These verses parallel the gospel of John (1:1–6). They speak about the beginning of time when we first experienced the power of the "word of life" (vs. 1) and the presence of the "eternal life that was present to the Father and became visible to us" (vs. 2). The reality of the incarnation is what John proclaims to his hearers so they may share the life of God (vs. 3). He is concerned that they have fellowship "with the Father and with his Son Jesus Christ" (vs. 3), a bond that is possible only through faith.

Psalm 97 as the responsorial psalm uses many terms that characterize Johannine writings. In it we praise the Lord as "King" (vs. 1), the title John uses to describe the inscription placed on the cross, "Jesus the Nazorean, The King of The Jews" (Jn 19:19). This psalm also prays that "all peoples see his glory" (vs. 6), a theme that is already implicit this season but which will be emphasized in the Epiphany cycle. In addition, the statement that "light dawns for the just" (vs. 11) recalls the important use of light and darkness in John's treatment of the coming of the Word into our world and the darkness that is overcome by his passion, death, and resurrection.

The gospel from John (20:2–8) is introduced by a variation on an excerpt from the *Te Deum*, referring to the "glorious band of apostles." This selection clearly links the incarnation with the resurrection, a unity seen through the Christmas cycle. It was the apostle Peter who ran in haste to the tomb accompanied by John, the disciple Jesus loved. John outruns Peter (vs. 8), and it is John who "saw and believed" (vs. 8). Later, in this same chapter (vss. 24–29), we read of Thomas' slowness to believe. Unlike John, who did not see the body of Jesus (only cloths and trappings), Thomas insists on seeing the body of the glorified Christ before he will believe. John, therefore, becomes the model disciple and the model believer.

The prayer over the gifts uses such Johannine terms as the "eternal Word," which is revealed in words and in action at the eucharist. The fact that so many post-resurrection accounts have eucharistic overtones should not be forgotten when reflecting on this text.

The communion antiphon continues the use of Johannine texts, John 1:14, 16. By stating that "we have all received" "of his riches," it shows how the sacraments function as continuing in the revelation of God's Word in Christ. This is also reflected in the prayer after communion which refers to the Word made flesh "for our salvation," which salvation is experienced through the liturgy just celebrated.

Celebration of the Eucharist

The introduction to the liturgy today could address the importance of the apostles' testimony to the paschal death and resurrection of Jesus, whose words and shared experience draw us into a real communion with the Lord in the word and sacrament of the eucharist. If the third form of the penitential rite is used, the seventh set of sample invocations taken from John's gospel would be most suitable: "way to the Father," "consolation of the truth," and the "Good Shepherd leading us into everlasting life." Once again, part of the entrance rite today is the "Glory to God," which should continue to receive special emphasis (by singing perhaps) because it is part of the octave of Christmas.

Among the general intercessions, prayers for the church to be an effective sign of God with us, for the Christian community to be faithful to the testimony of the apostles by word and deed, and for local communities to continue to evangelize and perform the works of the apostolate with the faith and zeal of John would be appropriate. In addition, prayers for the sick could ask that they might draw strength from the risen Christ. Prayers for the dead might ask that they may be united with all the apostles and saints at the heavenly banquet in the kingdom of heaven.

The first Christmas preface would be the most appropriate today because it uses Johannine terminology: "Your eternal Word brought to the eyes of faith a new and radiant vision of your glory." The use of the Roman Canon may well be used today because of its explicit reference to John and because of its special commemoration of Christmas (used throughout the octave).

The first introduction to the Lord's Prayer could be effective because of its simple reference to prayer with confidence to the Father in the words "our Savior" gave us. Should the "Lamb of God" be extended, the titles from John used in the penitential rite or other Johannine titles could be included. The solemn blessing for the apostles would provide a fitting conclusion to the liturgy.

Liturgy of the Hours

Today's invitatory verse from the common of the apostles: "Come, let us worship the Lord, the King of apostles," appropriately introduces the hours commemorating John. (Yet the Christmas octave is not neglected since evening prayer is largely taken from that of Christmas.)

The first reading at the office of readings is 1 John 1:1–2:3 (the first part of which was commented upon above and the balance of which will be reviewed in conjunction with its proclamation at the eucharist tomorrow). The special significance of this text as noted in the responsory deals with "the eternal life" that "has been revealed to us"; what is contained in the epistle was written "that you may believe that Jesus is the Christ, the Son of God, and believing you may have life in his name." These typically Johannine themes invite us to deeper trust in the Lord's incarnation and presence among us at the liturgy.

The second reading is from St. Augustine's tractate on 1 John. In it the author emphasizes that what the apostles saw with their eyes and believed to be the revelation of God in their midst is what we put our faith in as we celebrate this feast: "for the Word is visible to the heart alone, while flesh is visible to bodily eyes as well." By the incarnation we are saved and brought near to God.

The psalmody at this hour is introduced by antiphons reflecting the person and work of the apostle. John is the one who "gave testimony to the Word of God: [and] witness to Jesus Christ whom he had seen" (first antiphon). This disciple whom Jesus loved (second) is the one "to whom the mysteries of heaven were revealed" (third).

Similarly, the psalmody at morning prayer (from Sunday morning prayer) is introduced by references to John, who was "loved by the Lord above all others" (first), who was the one to whom Jesus entrusted his mother (second), and who recognized and acclaimed, "it is the Lord" (third). This last text is particularly important because it reflects the post-resurrection scene in Galilee (21:7); once again, it is through the apostles' experience of the risen Lord that we can come to experience him through the scriptures and the eucharist.

This transmission function of the apostles is described explicitly in the text from Acts (4:19–20), used as the scripture reading at morning prayer. This short section from Peter and John's major address notes that they recounted "what we have heard and seen." Our task is similar in that we are to witness to what we see and know to be true: that the risen Lord is among us and that through him we have access to the Father.

The antiphon to Zechariah's canticle reflects the pivotal verse of the Johannine prologue (1:14) by stating that the Word became flesh, that he "lived among us and we have seen his glory."

The intercessions at this hour are general in that they refer to the "foundation of the apostles." We ask for a deeper share in the apostles' vision of Christ after his resurrection so we can live the good news Jesus came to preach and foster reconciliation and peace, gifts of the risen Lord.

Evening prayer is largely taken from that for Christmas day. The reading from Romans 8:3–4 is a Pauline affirmation of the reality of Christ's human birth. This theme will occupy a major portion of 1 John, hence this alternate source provides a helpful nuance.

The Canticle of the Blessed Virgin refers to Mary's place in the incarnation, for while remaining a virgin she was chosen to give birth to Jesus. The intercessions that follow reflect both the context established by Christmas and the feast in honor of John; they draw on the theme of darkness/light and of the Lord Jesus as the source of true peace.

Celebration of the Hours

The invitatory verse could be accompanied by Psalm 24 whose reiteration of the "king of glory" (vss. 7, 8, 9, 10) could be understood to refer to the Lord Jesus in Johannine terminology and language. With no psalm prayers offered at any of the hours, the composition of texts which join together these ancient songs with the feast of John would be appropriate.

At morning prayer, the use of a set of Sunday morning prayer psalms other than those assigned for week I would be an appropriate option. Since the psalm prayers provided with Sunday prayer often refer to the day of the resurrection, it would be especially important to substitute texts which refer to today's feast. The scripture reading could easily be expanded to include a longer section from the testimony of Peter and John in Acts 4:13–22.

At evening prayer, the use of a Christmas hymn is noted in the Latin Breviary. (This contrasts with a hymn for apostles to be used at morning prayer.) This variety should be kept in the celebration to show the fusion of both themes in the liturgy today. At evening prayer, the text from Romans 8 could easily be expanded beyond the two verses assigned if a longer reading is desired.

Reflection—"John or Thomas?"

There is an ironical note in today's gospel. The evangelist records how John went to the tomb where Jesus was laid and that "he saw and believed." All he "saw" were the cloths that had been wound around the dead body of Jesus. He did not see the risen Lord at all, yet he "believed."

A few verses later, the evangelist will describe another apostle, Thomas, who refused to "believe" until he not only had seen the risen body of Jesus but had also touched his wounded hands and sides. Thomas' hesitation to believe gained him the unhappy nickname of "doubting Thomas." The author extols the faith of John and invites us to imitate him in trusting in the reality of the resurrection even though we have not seen the body of the risen Lord.

Both John and Thomas had heard Jesus teach, they both had been called to be apostles, they witnessed the Lord's miracles and healings. One was the model believer, the other the proverbial doubter.

Is it so different in our lives of faith? Are we sometimes like Thomas? Are we more like him than we would want to admit? Perhaps one of the reasons the church puts the feast of John right after Christmas and proclaims the story of Thomas the doubter on the Sunday after Easter is to remind us that especially at these pivotal times we need to deepen our faith and to sharpen our perception of reality when viewed in faith. Perhaps it is the church's way of making us ask the uneasy question: Who are we more like, John or Thomas? Or, perhaps it would be better to phrase the question: Who are we more like this year, this Christmas?

What really matters is whether we have struggled like both of them and in the end have come to believe as each of them did that Jesus is truly risen and it is through him that we have access to real life—life eternal.

DECEMBER 28—HOLY INNOCENTS, MARTYRS

Liturgical Context

Today's is the last of the special feasts that follow Christmas; like that of St. Stephen, it points to the connection between the incarnation and witnessing to Christ in martyrdom. While an elaborate ceremonial developed around this feast in the early Roman liturgy, the texts today reflect on how our witnessing to the Lord requires heroic deeds and not just words.

Liturgy of the Eucharist

The entrance antiphon today speaks of the martyrdom of the sinless who followed the spotless Lamb. In their perfect imitation of Christ who was led to slaughter, they give us an example of what it means to be disciples of Christ. The reality of Christ's incarnation challenges us to live our lives in witness to him.

The opening prayer, traditional in the Roman liturgy, couples the example of the death of the holy innocents with our living as witnesses to the faith we profess.

The first reading from 1 John (1:5–2:2) explores the light theme stated in the first verse (vs. 5) and emphasizes other typical Johannine themes such as "truth" (vs. 6) and being cleansed from sin by the "blood" of Jesus (vs. 7). The author is very realistic, however, since he notes that despite our high calling, we may and do sin (2:1), at which time it is especially important to realize how precious is our calling and how important is Jesus' role as "an intercessor who is just" (vs. 1) and whose self-offering is "for our sins" (vs. 2). As we receive the Lord's forgiveness and cleansing, we are to extend his mercy and love to others.

The responsorial psalm, Psalm 124, is a hymn of thanksgiving in time of crisis. It reflects a confident trust by those who witness to the Lord despite difficulties. Verses of this psalm articulate our experience as witnesses before each other of our faith in God: "Had not the Lord been with us—when men rose up against us, then would they have swallowed us alive" (vss. 2–3).

Today's gospel verse is a continuation of that portion of the *Te Deum* used yesterday, citing "the radiant army of martyrs" who acclaim God. The martyrs are "radiant" because the life of God they shared on earth now fills them completely in the kingdom.

The gospel from Matthew (2:13–18) continues the infancy chapters and recounts the massacre Herod ordered of every male child two years old or younger (vs. 16). Drawing on the dreams sequence and the Joseph cycle in the book of Exodus, the author likens Mary's husband to the youngest son in Exodus, Joseph. Joseph fulfilled God's command, took the child and his mother and fled to Egypt (vs. 14). On another level, Joseph's action here reproduces salient features of salvation history since it was from Egypt that Israel was called, and it is Hosea's use of this place that Matthew uses in a way that can refer to Christ (verse 15 from Hosea 11:1). In this sense, Joseph's obedience reproduces the experience of the patriarchal family in the Exodus, and Jesus' life and work reproduce events in the history of Israel's life with God (vs. 18). The virtue of obedience characterizes those parents who gave their sons' lives as witnesses to Christ. What is commemorated today, therefore, is not merely the event of the slaughter of the innocents, but the faith and virtue that led believers to offer what was most precious to the Lord.

The prayer over the gifts, taken from the Leonine Sacramentary (thus attesting to the primitive nature of this feast), refers to the priority of God's gift of his life (grace) to us even before we are aware of its operation in our lives. It is this grace on which we rely when we ask that we be freed from sin by the eucharist we celebrate.

The communion antiphon (taken from the first reading for today in the former Roman Missal) contains a wealth of theology despite its brevity. The text refers to being "ransomed for God" and points to the Lamb who was slain as our savior and Lord. Like those who have died in the Lord, we hope to "follow the Lamb wherever he goes" (Rv 14:4) because he is the firstborn of all creation and the first-fruits of salvation.

The prayer after communion emphasizes the importance of the "wordless profession of faith" offered by the innocents and the full-ness of life they received because of their death. By our share in the eucharist, we pray that we might receive a "share in the fullness of salvation" now enjoyed by those who, like the innocents, live in the kingdom of heaven.

Celebration of the Eucharist

The introduction to today's liturgy could mention the importance of witnessing to our faith in Christ even when that means suffering rejection for the sake of the kingdom of God. The children who of-fered their lives in silence can be an example for us that remaining silent in the face of injustice may be part of the suffering we must endure.

If the third form of the penitential rite is chosen, the third set of invocations (iii), clearly associated with the Christmas season, would be appropriate. If the "I confess" form is used today, it could be un-derstood as an admission of our failure to witness to the faith and to admit our sinfulness as referred to in the first reading. The section of the "Glory to God" that is particularly significant today, in the light of the feast and of the text of the communion antiphon, acclaims Je-sus as the "Lamb of God," who takes away the sin of the world.

Among today's intercessions, petitions for missioners, evangeliz-ers, and those who suffer physical persecution for the faith would be fitting. In addition, it would be appropriate to pray for children with terminal illness because these can be contemporary examples of in-nocents whose sufferings lead to dependence and trust in God alone.

Of the Christmas prefaces, the third would be particularly appro-priate today because it refers to the light/darkness symbolism stated in the first reading.

SUFFERING FR
+ CHILD ABUSE

For the sake of variety and brevity, the second eucharistic prayer would be a fitting option, especially since it refers to Christ freely giving up his life for us and to all the saints, "who have done your will throughout the ages."

The "Lamb of God" might well be emphasized by singing today since it is Christ's paschal sacrifice that the innocents shared in and it is this sacrifice that we commemorate at the eucharist.

Of the prayers over the people, number 11, which states, "in your mercy make us ready to do your will," would be a fitting conclusion to the liturgy. For the dismissal, the choice of "Go in peace to love and serve the Lord" would also reiterate the importance of witnessing to the faith.

Liturgy of the Hours

The invitatory refers explicitly to today's feast: "Come let us worship the newborn Christ who crowns with joy these children who died for him." The first reading at the office of readings from Exodus (1:8–16, 22) contains the Old Testament parallel to the slaughter of the innocents. Here, Pharoah is jealous of the increasing power of the Israelites in Egypt (vs. 9) and wants to "deal shrewdly with them to stop their increase" (vs. 10), hence, his severe command that all Hebrew boys be thrown into the river (vs. 22). While this text is fitting as a presagement of what will occur right after Jesus' birth, the responsory uses texts from Isaiah (65:19) and Revelation (21:4, 5) to encourage us: "I will take delight in my people.—Never again will weeping and crying be heard among them. Death shall be no more; grief, tears, and sorrow will be forgotten, for behold, I make all things new." It is this newness that we experience through the Christmas mystery and the Christmas liturgy.

The second reading from St. Quodvultdeus speaks of the way infants bear witness to Christ. The author states: "They cannot use their limbs to engage in battle, yet already they bear off the palm of victory." Can we expect to do less than engage in battle for the Lord, we whose limbs and very being were created in God's image and likeness and restored to union with God through Christ? Part of the reality of Christmas requires that we bear our share of suffering for the sake of him who gave us new life.

The antiphons to accompany the psalmody at the office of readings (taken from the common of martyrs) apply directly to today's feast. The first antiphon asserts that the innocents praise God because they have been set free from earthly cares and life in the world. Hence the lighthearted text: "These little ones praise you and skip with joy like lambs." The second states that they are the "first of mankind to be won for God and the Lamb," who "stand before the throne of God." Like them, we pray that we will be faithful witnesses to the Lord and join them before the throne of the Lamb of God. In the third text, it is with a certain seriousness yet deep joy that we can say of them that "joy and gladness will be their lot [for] they will never again know sorrow and pain." Unlike them, we must still endure sorrow and pain; foremost is the pain of still being separated from God.

The antiphons to the psalmody at morning prayer reflect the uniqueness of this feast by asserting the importance of the innocents' witnessing to Christ. "By their death they have proclaimed what they could not preach with their infant voices" (second), and, in an adaptation of the scriptural text, "from the mouths of children and babes at the breast you have found praise to foil your enemies" (third). In citing Revelation in the first text, we pray that we might join all those who are clothed in white robes and who walk with the Lord in the kingdom; it is they who are "worthy."

The scripture text assigned for morning prayer is Jeremiah 31:15, which is also quoted by Matthew in today's gospel. In its original setting, this verse forms part of Rachael's lament which will come to an end, says the prophet, for this sorrow "shall have its reward" (vs. 16). What we perceive with human understanding can well be a tragedy, but through the eyes of faith, even the loss of children to Rachael and the death of the innocents lead to what is real gain— union with God. We pray in the antiphon to Zechariah's canticle: "They died for Christ, and now in the glory of heaven as they follow him, the sinless Lamb, they sing forever: Glory to you, O Lord." At the intercessions, we acclaim their unique role as we pray that from them we might gain the strength to be witnesses in word and action to our faith in God, grow in hope, be cleansed from sin, and share in the kingdom where they live in union with Christ.

At evening prayer (the first part of which is taken from Evening Prayer II of Christmas), the text from Ephesians (2:3b–5a) speaks about being dead to sin and brought to life in Christ. This theme is also reflected in the Magnificat antiphon, referring to Mary's nursing the child Jesus at her breast, which child we now worship as "the Lord who comes to save us."

The intercessions pray that through this Christmas mystery we might renew our faith, that the weak and aged might be strengthened, that the imprisoned and aliens might not be forgotten, and that the faithful departed will join the heavenly host who praised God at the birth of Jesus.

Celebration of the Hours

The use of Psalm 100 to accompany the invitatory verse today would be appropriate since it refers to entrance into God's temple; in an accommodated sense, we can say that the holy innocents entered into God's dwelling in heaven through their death on earth. The use of psalm prayers at the office of readings would be especially useful today because the first psalm, Psalm 2, contains Messianic references which could easily apply to these martyrs. The recitation/singing of the two parts of Psalm 33 as one unit with a psalm prayer at its end would offer variety.

At morning prayer, the hymn should be chosen to reflect the theme of martyrdom and witness; at evening prayer, a Christmas hymn should be used. The scripture texts at both morning and evening prayer could easily be expanded, for example, Jeremiah 31:15–20 and Ephesians 2:1–10. At evening prayer, any emphasis given to the Canticle of Mary (singing, gestures) would be appropriate as a way of underscoring the implications of the incarnation and the values of the kingdom established in Christ. Especially at evening prayer, the intercessions today could be expanded and specified to reflect the needy in our communities.

Reflection—"Innocence Restored"

Human beings have to live with the fact that they are not perfect and that they are not God. Like our first parents, Adam and Eve, we are estranged from God. Our task in life is to recover the path to God and to make the journey home to him. Unlike the martyrs, we commemorate today, we are not innocent!

Yet, we also know that Christ has restored to us the possibility of coming near to God and of living in union with him even as we struggle with our lost innocence and our separation from him on earth. The gap between heaven and earth has been bridged by Christ. Through him alone we can receive the help we need to return to the state which God intends for us—union with him.

This is the purpose of our celebrating Christmas, and the purpose of all liturgy, prayer, and spirituality. Through Christ, we know that lost innocence has been restored. So we pray in joy and we rejoice in him.

Yet, what is equally clear is that despite the incarnation and despite the presence of Christ with us in prayer, we have no guarantee of being united fully with God in heaven and we have no guarantee that we will be assured a place in the banquet of the kingdom of heaven. The liturgy we celebrate is a pledge, it is not a foolproof guarantee. What is required is that we witness to and live our faith in our daily life. It is then that our faith should show forth and it is by this criterion that we shall be judged when Christ comes again.

DECEMBER 29—FIFTH DAY IN THE OCTAVE OF CHRISTMAS

Liturgical Context

The office of readings begins with a series of texts from Colossians dealing with creation and our re-creation in Christ. At the eucharist, the continuous reading of 1 John continues; the gospel today (and for the next few days) concerns Christ's manifestations after the incarnation.

Liturgy of the Eucharist

The entrance antiphon today is a central verse in the Nicodemus dialogue (Jn 3) about being reborn and born from above in Christ. We are reminded that God loved us so much that he gave his only Son "that all who believe in him might not perish, but might have eternal life" (Jn 3:16). It is our faith that makes the difference in the way we interpret and appropriate the fact of the incarnation; through faith in Christ as the unique mediator of God's love, we receive "life" eternal.

The opening prayer reflects the Johannine theme of "light" already so important in the Christmas liturgy. The shadows of this world vanished at the birth of God's own Son, who is the "light of the world."

The first reading from 1 John (2:3–11) applies the image of "light" to our daily lives and challenges us to live according to God's commands; this will lead us to Christ, the true light (vs. 8). The image of shadows and darkness already used in the opening prayer finds its source in this text:

"But the man who hates his brother is in darkness.
He walks in shadows, not knowing where he is going,
    since the dark has blinded his eyes." (vs. 11)

Hence, we need Christ the light. If we live according to his word, we show that we accept him as our light and yearn for a share in the "love of God made perfect in him" (vs. 5).

The responsorial psalm, Psalm 96, is particularly important because it will be used again tomorrow and on December 31 as the response to the first reading. We acclaim the Lord for his might and power reflected in creation (vss. 5–6) and for his "salvation" (vs. 2) revealed through Christ.

The presentation of Jesus in the temple is recounted in today's gospel (Lk 2:22–35). The importance of this text is shown by the fact that it is used again on the feast of the Presentation of Our Lord (February 2, formerly designated as the end of the Christmas season) and on the feast of the Holy Family, "B" cycle. Today's text deals with Simeon and tomorrow's with Anna (vss. 36–40). From a liturgical and spiritual point of view, the canticles recounted in these texts are important expressions of Jewish piety (vss. 29–32, 34–35). The Canticle of Simeon is especially important in the church's liturgy since it is prayed daily at night prayer. Simeon "blesses" God, that is, he praises and thanks God for what he has accomplished in the past and then shows how God is active in the presentation of Jesus and the purification of Mary.

Luke is careful to assert that what occurs in this scene is the result of the Spirit's activity (stated explicitly in verses 25, 26). Also, here we see a scene shift, the presentation takes place in Jerusalem (vs. 25). The fact that the presentation takes place here indicates its importance as the juncture between the old and the new covenants. Jesus will go to suffer and die there; from Jerusalem the early church will go forth to spread the good news of his resurrection to the ends of the earth.

The aged Simeon and Anna represent the tired and frail old covenant. They are so imbued with covenant religion that they are able to recognize the advent of the new covenant in this child. The contrast in images between aging and the newborn reflects the contrast between prophet/fulfillment, that is, Simeon/Christ.

Finally, it is the evangelist's perception of the paschal mystery that enables him to paint such a rich picture of what the birth of Jesus means. Mary and Joseph were obedient to the (old) law (vss. 22, 23, 27); yet, the law is fulfilled and transcended in this child offered to God. He will be offered to God once again as sacrificed victim on Calvary.

The prayer over the gifts today continues the theme of the exchange seen throughout this season. This text from the Leonine Sacramentary asks that the gifts we present "from all you have given us" may become the source of divine life through Christ. Christ's mediation is reflected here, a role that was only possible because he was born among us and was like us in all things but sin.

The communion antiphon, taken from Zechariah's canticle (Lk 1:78), extends the light symbolism by stating that "the dawn shall break upon us" because of the "tender compassion of our God." We experience this compassion and love of God at the eucharist.

The prayer after communion refers to the eucharist as we pray that our lives might be founded on the mysteries we celebrate.

Celebration of the Eucharist

The introduction to the liturgy could speak about the light of Christ and our responsibility to walk according to the light of his revealed word. If the third form of the penitential rite is used, invocations of Christ that would reflect images from the liturgy today include: you are the Word made flesh, you are the light of the world, you are the living bread come down from heaven.

Of the alleluia verses provided for the Christmas season before Epiphany (Lect., no. 212), number 2 (taken from Heb 1:1–2) about the uniqueness of Christ's mediatorship would reflect much of what is emphasized in the gospel.

Appropriate intercessions today would include petitions for the church as a light of salvation to the world, for believing Jews to receive the fullness of salvation, for the elderly in our society to be revered as a gift from God, and that our communities (local, family, business) would reflect the light of Christ by living in peace and harmony.

The third Christmas preface about light dawning on the world and our oneness with God in Christ would be appropriate. If the Roman Canon is proclaimed, the special Christmas section is used.

Since the first reading emphasizes harmony and living in the light, the rites preparing for communion should be specially noted today. An introduction to the Lord's Prayer and to the sign of peace should signify our dedication to live in Christ's light.

Liturgy of the Hours

With today's celebration of the hours, we return to a Christmas office with some modifications each day. Today's invitatory is from Christmas and speaks of Christ being "born for us" and of our coming together to adore him.

The first reading at the office of readings from Colossians (1:1–14) introduces this letter dealing with creation and our re-creation in Christ. After a characteristic introduction (vss. 1–2), the author uses the Jewish style of "blessing" (already seen in today's gospel) to praise the Colossians for the way they live the faith (vss. 3–4). He urges them to continue to "lead a life worthy of the Lord" (vs. 10), who "rescued us from the power of darkness and brought us to the kingdom of His beloved Son" (vs. 13). It is through him that "we have redemption, the forgiveness of our sins" (vs. 14). Paul here expounds the meaning of the coming of Christ as Savior and the reality of our need for his light to free us from the darkness of sin.

The second reading from St. Bernard's homily on the Epiphany speaks about the divinity of Christ and our participation in God's life through Christ's sufferings.

The antiphons at the office of readings are general and reflect this season. We who commemorate Christ's birth can draw on the text of Psalm 46 about God being with his people: "The Lord of hosts is with us: the God of Jacob is our stronghold" (vs. 4). The use of Psalm 72 is particularly significant because it is also used on Epiphany and on three days following it, underscoring the universality of salvation (see vss. 10, 11, 12, 18, 19). Its opening lines are important for our appreciation of Christmas: "O God, give your judgment to the king, to a king's son your justice" (vs. 1). The justice for which we longed in Advent has come in Christ. It is this mystery that is commemorated through these days of Christmas and Epiphany.

At morning and evening prayer, we use the texts assigned for Christmas day, with some exceptions. The reading at morning prayer is taken from the second reading at the eucharist on Christmas day, Hebrews 1:1–2. The reading from Christmas Evening Prayer II is repeated.

The antiphon to Zechariah's canticle speaks about the shepherds making their way to Bethlehem to see for themselves what the Lord has revealed to us. What Simeon saw revealed in Christ at the presentation was already seen by the shepherds on Christmas night. At evening prayer, the paradox of Christmas is recounted in the Magnificat antiphon: "The king of heaven humbled himself to be born of a virgin, that he might restore man to the kingdom he had lost." The power and might of God was in Christ from his birth; through the eyes of faith, we know that this power is at work in us through the Christmas season. Familiar images of Christmas are found in the intercessions at both morning and evening prayer, including references to the "wise men," to "shepherds," and to darkness/light.

Celebration of the Hours

The invitatory verse of Christmas and the use of Psalm 95 would be appropriate choices to begin the liturgy of the hours today, especially because of the explicit invitation in the verse, "Come, let us adore him."

Combining the two sections of Psalm 72 at the office of readings would allow for a significant period of silence between it and the readings to follow. The absence of psalm prayers would also help to establish an atmosphere of reflection and simplicity, fitting on this day in the Christmas octave.

The reading at morning prayer could be lengthened to consist of Hebrews 1:1–6. At evening prayer, a text other than 1 John could be substituted because it has been used repeatedly in the liturgy this season. A substitute could be made from the second readings from Christmas.

The intercessions and response at morning prayer are wordy; simplifying or rewriting them would be helpful. One way of adding some solemnity would be to use the solemn blessing of Christmas as a conclusion to the major hours.

Reflection—"All Beginnings Are Hard"

At this time of turning from the "old" year to the "new" year, the gospel today offers a story about new beginnings. The contrast in the cast of characters could not be more dramatic—a newborn child (a perennial symbol of the coming new year) and the aging pair (one half of which symbolizes the ending of the year with "Father time"). The aging Simeon and Anna symbolize the last breath of the old covenant with its laws and observances.

But for us, the covenant has not waned and we (like the Jews in Jesus' time) have to keep deciding that we will look on all things in a totally new way—through the vision of faith of Christ with us. As the Jewish commentary, the *Midrash*, says: "All beginnings are hard." It was hard for Israel to turn and believe in Jesus as the Messiah even though they waited for him and prayed for him to come. It was hard because Jesus challenged the people then as he challenges us today—to see everything in life from a new perspective.

What about us, today, this Christmas season, on the eve of a new year? Are we willing to make this new year a totally new reality by looking on each person as sister or brother who deserves our love? Are we willing to work for such a conversion of heart that we are continually aware of God's presence with us on earth? Are we willing to see our baptism as an initiation to service and a work of reconciling all people in harmony and peace because that was Christ's mission and his task for us?

Will we allow Christ to dawn in our hearts and illumine our way this "new" year? Perhaps the sage phrase of the *Midrash* is the sagest advice of all: "all beginnings are hard." In Christ, all beginnings are possible.

DECEMBER 30—SIXTH DAY IN THE OCTAVE OF CHRISTMAS

Liturgical Context

When no Sunday occurs within the octave of Christmas, the feast of the Holy Family is transferred to today. Otherwise, the liturgy assigned to this sixth day in the Christmas octave is used. At the eucharist, the readings continue from 1 John and Luke; at the office of readings, the letter to the Colossians continues.

Liturgy of the Eucharist

The entrance antiphon today is an accommodated use of Wisdom 18:4–5. Originally, this text was part of a section dealing with the death of the Egyptian firstborn and the sparing of the Israelite children. In its present context, the verses can be understood to refer to the night when Christ was born, in "silence" when the "night had run half of her swift course." The "all-powerful word" coming down from heaven can refer to the incarnation of the Word of God. The implication of the incarnation as freeing us "from our former slavery to sin" is noted in the opening prayer.

The first reading of 1 John 2:12–17 contains many familiar and theologically significant Johannine terms. The author instructs us to "have no love for the world, nor the things that the world affords" (vs. 15). The "world" refers to the complex of earthly concerns of men and women whose principles and attitudes go against what Christ came to teach. They have chosen not to believe and thus they do not profess faith in the power of the "Name" through which our sins have been forgiven (vs. 12). Our task is to witness to the life that comes through Christ to the world.

It is by doing God's will that we will attest to the supremacy of God by resisting those "carnal allurements, enticements for the eye, the life of empty show [which are] from the world" (vs. 16). Christianity is a community that witnesses to the values of the gospel in this fragile and sometimes hostile world.

The responsorial psalm continues Psalm 96 used yesterday, which reflects the joy and exultation of the Christmas season.

The gospel, Luke 2:36–40, continues the presentation scene described yesterday. Here, the prophetess Anna is specially noted for her virtue and perseverance in the faith despite disappointment and old age. Luke is particularly concerned to note that "she was constantly in the temple, worshiping day and night in fasting and prayer" (vs. 37). Significantly, this text relates to texts in Acts (2:42, 46) which present a picture of the early Jerusalem community (albeit in an idealized way) gathered in prayer. Anna serves as a prototype of the way believers should conduct themselves.

Like Simeon, she "gave thanks" (vs. 38) for the birth of the Messiah. Anna's thanksgiving reflects the thanksgiving of Elizabeth when she receives the news that she is going to bear John the Baptist. Israel is redeemed through the instrumentality of the law-abiding parents of Jesus and these women of courage and faith.

The prayer over the gifts asks the Father to accept "our gifts" which can be interpreted as the bread and wine, which, when transformed during the eucharistic prayer, become sources of supernatural nourishment and strength, hence giving us the grace we need "to live more fully the love we profess." The prayer after communion asks that the eucharist touch us deeply and have its effect in our lives. These ancient texts (both taken from the Leonine Sacramentary) succinctly combine the important notions of the goods of creation, nourishment, and the body and blood of Christ.

The communion antiphon, from the prologue to the gospel of John (1:16), recalls that what we have comes from what we have received from Christ—"grace for grace."

Celebration of the Eucharist

The introduction to the liturgy could speak about fidelity to the Lord through hearing his word and sharing in this banquet of salvation. These actions include not just hearing the word but living it; not just celebrating the liturgy of the Lord's supper but living holy and devout lives having been strengthened by it. Invocations to accompany the third form of the penitential rite that would reflect the liturgy today include the Word made flesh, the splendor of the Father's glory, and Christ as the Son of God and the Son of Mary.

For the alleluia verse (Lect., no. 212), the second option would be appropriate since it speaks about how God spoke in many ways in the past but now has spoken definitively through his own son (Heb 1:1–2). It is to this God-Man that Anna gives her testimony in the gospel reading that follows.

Among the intercessions, petitions about the church giving fitting witness to Christ in the world, our sense of support for each other in bearing one another's burdens in the community of the church, a deepened life of prayer that would direct us toward Christ and to witnessing to him more faithfully would be appropriate.

Of the Christmas prefaces, the second about Christ leading mankind from exile to the heavenly kingdom would be a subtle reflection of the instruction found in the first reading. If the Roman Canon is proclaimed today, the proper section for Christmas is used. ✗

The last verse of the first reading about doing God's will could inspire the invitation to the Lord's prayer since we say, "thy will be done." An invitation to the sign of peace, about the communal nature of Christianity, would also be helpful as a way of imitating the unity found in the early Jerusalem community and the fidelity seen in the prophetess Anna.

If the liturgy is to conclude with a prayer over the people, number 22 would be appropriate since it contains the petitions that God will "bless your people and fill them with zeal" and "strengthen them by your love to do your will."

Liturgy of the Hours

The first reading at the office of readings continues with Colossians 1:15–2:3. The first part of this text is the familiar Christ hymn (vss. 15–20) used in rotation at evening prayer. The absolute preeminence of Christ is stressed here (vs. 18); his primacy holds creation together and gathers us together as the church, his body on earth. Verses 21–23 speak about our being reconciled in Christ and the importance of holding fast to faith in Christ transmitted "by the gospel you have heard" (vs. 23). These verses are a transition to the next section of the letter (1:24–2:3), which speaks about the mystery of Christ present with us as our "hope of glory" (vs. 27). That Paul identifies Christ and the church so intimately and closely is seen in his willingness to suffer "for the sake of [Christ's] body, the church" (vs. 24) and thereby to "fill up what is lacking in the sufferings of Christ" (vs. 24). Paul's missionary concern extends to all Christian communities so that they may be united in love and themselves become even more vibrant examples of the mystery of Christ present in our world.

The second reading is from the third-century Roman theologian Hippolytus. In interpreting the meaning of the incarnation, the author states explicitly that Jesus' creaturehood was the same as ours so that we might pattern our human lives on his, even to the point of understanding suffering as an important part of life. Hippolytus offers words of comfort as he concludes: "God is not beggarly, and for the sake of his own glory he has given us a share in his divinity."

The scripture reading at morning prayer, Isaiah 9:6, reflects the text used at midnight mass and contains the important titles: "Wonder-Counselor, God-Hero, Father-Forever, Prince of Peace."

The antiphon to Zechariah's canticle uses some poetic license when it states that the angels sang at the birth of Jesus, "Blessed be our God enthroned as King and blessed by the Lamb." These phrases are nonetheless significant theological reflections of how the power and mercy of God were manifest in Christ's birth.

At evening prayer, the scripture text is 2 Peter 1:3–4, which refers to how the divine power of Christ freely bestowed on us everything necessary for a life of genuine piety (vs. 1) and that through this unique mediator we have "become sharers of the divine nature" (vs. 4).

The antiphon to the Canticle of the Blessed Virgin praises Mary who gave birth to the savior, and asks her "to watch over all who honor [her]."

Celebration of the Hours

The verse before the readings at the office of readings could be used as an appropriate invitatory to the hours today: "The Lord has made known, alleluia.—His saving power, alleluia." This would shift attention from the birth of Jesus to some of its implications. The use of Psalm 67 as the invitatory would complement this text since it refers to his "saving power."

At the office of readings, the praying of Psalms 85 and 89 (in two sections) could be enhanced by the addition of psalm prayers at their conclusion.

At morning and evening prayer, the scripture readings could easily be expanded, especially that assigned for morning prayer which could repeat the text from midnight mass, Isaiah 9:2–7. If the intercessions are adapted at morning prayer, the parallelism and contrast motif (seen in the first three petitions: Son/Father, poor/rich, darkness/[light]) could be retained. The singing of the Canticle of the Blessed Virgin at evening prayer would be especially appropriate because the antiphon is addressed to her.

Reflection—"Anna and Mary: Models of the Church"

The liturgy yesterday and today emphasizes two women who serve as model believers. The law-abiding Mary exemplifies obedient and humble submission to God's will.

Anna, the prophetess of the old covenant, fasted and prayed in the temple, "worshiping day and night" (vs. 37), waiting for the consolation of Israel in the birth of the Messiah. She "gave thanks" (vs. 38) for she realized that all she had hoped for and desired was accomplished in Jesus' birth.

Mary and Anna are true disciples of the Lord and function as examples for us who are the community of his disciples in our day. Like them, we ought to spend time in reflection and prayer, pondering the wonder of God made flesh in Christ. Anna's example is most forceful for she prayed "day and night." Our imitation of Mary takes on special acuteness when we realize that she lived what she commanded of table servers at Cana—she did whatever God wanted, she did whatever he told her. To know what God wants of us takes reflection and prayer; to do what he wants takes the courage and integrity of the Blessed Virgin.

The juncture of old and new covenant religion at the presentation in the temple should serve as a challenge to us this new year as we rededicate ourselves to the kind of prayer and action for which Anna and Mary were noted.

DECEMBER 31—SEVENTH DAY IN THE OCTAVE OF CHRISTMAS

Liturgical Context

Today's liturgy parallels yesterday's; the first reading at mass continues from 1 John and the letter to the Colossians continues at the office of readings. The gospel text repeats the prologue to John's gospel used on Christmas day. The use of John's gospel will continue through January 5.

Liturgy of the Eucharist

Today's entrance antiphon is the same used on Christmas Day, Isaiah 9:6. This child and son has been given "to" and "for" us. Through the liturgy, we share again in this mystery and are drawn into the sacrifice Christ endured "for us and for all so that sins may be forgiven."

All the prayers in the mass formula are from the Leonine Sacramentary. The opening prayer states that the origin of our religion and its perfect fulfillment comes from the birth of Christ. We pray that the Father would give us a share in the life of Christ for he is our salvation.

Today's first reading from 1 John recalls how the Advent liturgy emphasized our situation between the first and second comings of Christ. The author is concerned that this community stand firm against any manifestation of the Antichrist who led others of their group into apostasy (vs. 19). We who have been granted an endowment of Christ's love (a meaning for "anointing" in vs. 20) must continually conform ourselves to the "truth" (vs. 21) of the gospel. As used here "truth" can refer to the knowledge that comes from God and coming to know God himself. In knowing God, we are enabled to live our lives in his presence and to choose those things that will lead to eternal life in him. The believer must continually choose, however, for this text reminds us of how precarious our life of faith can be. John asserts that he is concerned with those who have left the Christian community ("it was from our ranks that they took their leave," vs. 19) not with those who have never heard of Christ. Fidelity to the truth of Christ means knowing it and living by it.

The responsorial psalm repeats Psalm 96 assigned for these last three days of the calendar year. Once again, this song of joy and thanksgiving reflects our rejoicing in the birth of Christ among us. (Since the gospel repeats the Christmas selection, refer to Christmas Day for a commentary.)

The prayer over the gifts and the prayer after communion refer to the central place the eucharist has in our appropriating the Christmas mystery. In the prayer over the gifts, we acknowledge that it is through our sharing in the eucharist that we are drawn more closely to God and to each other. This means that the liturgy is a unique source of strength and a cause of deepening commitment to God and his "truth."

The prayer after communion asks that we come to value all things in Christ and through him to come to the fullness of eternal life in the kingdom. Truly, the eucharist is a sacrament of "strength" as we seek to live in this world with our minds and hearts set on knowing God's truth and cherishing Christ as the revelation of God's truth to us.

Celebration of the Eucharist

Today's celebration should be simple in contrast to the celebration of the Solemnity of Mary to follow tomorrow. The introduction to the liturgy could refer to our share in the divine life through Christ, especially when we celebrate the eucharist. The third set of sample invocations for the third form of the penitential rite once again would reiterate titles of Christ that coincide well with the Christmas season.

The alleluia verse that most appropriately reflects the gospel is number 1 (Lect., no. 212), which cites John 1:14, 12. This links the incarnation with our present experience of God in faith (and through the liturgy); in it we assert that the Word of God became man and that those who have accepted him have "become the children of God."

Among the intercessions today, petitions reflective of the readings would be for the church that she be a sign of the light and life of Christ in our midst, for all preachers and teachers of the truth of Christ, for those alienated from the faith, and for those who suffer that they might know the presence of God with them.

Of the Christmas prefaces, the use of the first, containing clear Johannine language, would be most appropriate.

While the Roman Canon is an option today because of its special section on Christmas, the use of the shorter and simpler second eucharistic prayer would seem preferable.

The introduction to the Lord's Prayer and to the sign of peace could both refer to the essentially communal dimension of Christianity which is brought out in the first reading, addressed to a community that needs to grow in faith and to deepen its conviction in the truth of Christ.

Liturgy of the Hours

In the passage from the letter to the Colossians (2:4–15) at the office of readings, Paul instructs his audience to adhere to right teaching (as opposed to "specious argument," vs. 4) and to see in Christ a radically new way of relating to God (vs. 9ff.). Clearly, Paul is concerned (as is the author of 1 John) that false teachers are leading away some of the baptized who are now are wavering in their commitment. Paul compares circumcision with baptism, pointing out that baptism "strips off the carnal body completely," with the result that through baptism we are not only buried with Christ, but raised from the dead with him.

The second reading at this hour from a Christmas sermon by St. Leo the Great deals with an aspect of the Colossians text, namely our rebirth in Christ through baptism. He reiterates what patristic commentators repeatedly state: "For the birth of Christ is the origin of the Christian people; and the birthday of the head is also the birthday of the body." Hence, what we commemorate in this season is both the fact of Christ's assuming humanity and our being renewed by his divinity. Leo goes on to state that this occurs through baptism: "For every believer regenerated in Christ . . . breaks with that ancient way of life that derives from original sin, and by rebirth is transformed . . ." The balance of Leo's text goes on to describe the effects of Christ's birth for us, principally our share in the gift of God's peace through Christ. He is called "our peace" because he has reconciled us with the Father and redeemed our human condition.

The psalmody at this hour reflects the joy and thanksgiving of Christmas, seen especially in the choice of Psalm 96 (used these past three days). The antiphons help us focus on the coming of the Lord who is a "light [that has] dawned for the just" and "joy [for the] upright of heart." Through the incarnation, "the Lord has made known his saving power." This saving power is communicated to us at the liturgy.

Morning prayer retains the flavor of Christmas. The brief text from Isaiah (4:2–3) is about the coming of the "branch of the Lord" who will mark the remnant in Jerusalem as holy and belonging to God. The antiphon to Zechariah's canticle recalls the gospel of Christmas night about the angels' announcement, "Glory to God in the highest . . . peace to his people on earth." The gift of peace granted us in the incarnation becomes the final gift of the risen Christ to his church (Jn 21:21).

Significantly, the intercessions invoke Christ under various titles and images, reflecting important theological insight: "born of the Father before all ages," "consubstantial with the Father," "Lord of David and Son of David." These continue to direct our attention to Christ's Lordship and mediatorship, not just to his infancy or human birth.

Celebration of the Hours

Like the eucharist, the celebration of the hours today is best kept simple and direct. An alternate to the Christmas invitatory verse is the verse following the psalmody at the office of readings. It combines aspects about Christ that are proclaimed in the readings from Hebrews and the gospel of John on Christmas day: "In these last days God has spoken through his Son. The Word through whom he made all things." The use of Psalm 100 would provide variety and would draw on images of Christ's Lordship ana our relationship to God as "his people, the sheep of his flock" (vs. 3).

At the office of readings, the absence of psalm prayers provides the option of allowing more time for silent prayer between psalms. This would be a fitting contrast to the festivity tomorrow.

At morning prayer, a set of Sunday psalms other than those from the first week of the psalter would provide variety. The reading from Isaiah could easily be expanded to include 4:2–6. The petitions in the intercessions (though rather wordy) contain many important theological concepts about the mystery of the Word made flesh.

Reflection—"Resolutions"

By this time in this "holiday season," most Americans are doing two things—preparing for New Year's Eve and deciding on resolutions for the new year. The one will be over tomorrow; the other, one hopes, will last through at least a part of the year to come.

However, the liturgy reminds us that everything we do and all that we are comes from God in Christ and that self-help commitments at New Year's are not sufficient. We Christians live this human life in grace and under the guidance of the Lord we worship.

As we face a new year, what are our resolutions? Do they concern a new job, or a new health regimen only? Do any of our resolutions concern God and how we want to relate to him? If our list of resolutions does not include something about drawing nearer to God, we may miss the most important part of the new year. After all, even the title of what we celebrate is the beginning of the "year of our Lord."

SUNDAY IN THE OCTAVE OF CHRISTMAS—HOLY FAMILY

Liturgical Context

In the former Roman Missal, the feast of the Holy Family occurred on the Sunday after Epiphany. In the present reform, its place on the Sunday within the octave of Christmas (or on December 30 if Christmas is on a Sunday) allows for the commemoration of the Lord's baptism to follow on the Sunday after Epiphany, a feast which has stronger liturgical roots and deeper theological significance. The feast of the Holy Family as retained draws its significance more from the commemoration of the Incarnation than it does from Epiphany. Today's feast is not about childhood reminiscences of the boyhood of Jesus; it concerns the love and harmony which should characterize all the baptized as members of God's family in Christ.

The gospels today concern Jesus' childhood and the virtues of family life (Lectionary Introduction, no. 95). In the second edition of the Lectionary, we have three full sets of readings; this new arrangement adds a first and second reading for cycles "B" and "C". These passages elaborate on the demands of faith (Genesis and Hebrews, cycle "B"), the merging of the old and new covenants in the presentation ("B" cycle), the birth of Samuel to Hannah ("C" cycle), our identity as God's children ("B" cycle), and the finding of Jesus in the temple and his obeying Mary and Joseph in Nazareth ("C" cycle). These additional texts help to draw out the challenges of this feast and orient our attention to the concrete ways in which we live out the mystery of the incarnation.

Sacramentary Texts

The Christmas context of today's feast is clearly seen in the entrance and communion antiphons as well as in the use of the Christmas preface and proper section of the Roman Canon. In the entrance antiphon, we acclaim the child Jesus "lying in a manger (Lk 2:16), and in the communion antiphon, we accommodate the text of Baruch 3:38 to refer to the incarnation when we pray, "our God has appeared on earth, and lived among men."

The newly composed opening prayer offers the holy family as a model of fidelity which will be rewarded when we are called to our eternal home. At the liturgy, we offer the sacrifice by which we are redeemed (prayer over the gifts), and we pray that refreshed with this sacrament, we may both imitate the holy family on earth and, like them, be called to heaven, our eternal home (prayer after communion).

Cycle "A" — Pref- CHRISTMAS II

The first reading from Sirach (3:2–6, 12–14) is divided into two sections, the first about family life in general, and the second about how a child is to treat his aging parent.

The responsorial psalm, Psalm 128, states: "happy are you who fear the Lord, who walk in his ways" (vs. 1); it then goes on to describe family life with the wife compared to a "fruitful vine" and children compared to "olive plants around your table." Those who "fear the Lord" (vs. 4) are blessed and will enjoy the blessings of God for eternity.

The second reading from the letter to the Colossians (3:12–21) draws out the implications of the incarnation for Christian living. Here, both the life of the Christian community at large (vss. 12–17) and that of the Christian home (vss. 18–21) are considered. Because Christians are "in the Lord" and because they are baptized into Christ Jesus, they can "forgive as the Lord has forgiven" them. The love of God for us is to be evident in our love for one another. This text challenges us to understand what real love in families means. (Fittingly, verses 12–17 are offered as an option for the rite of marriage.) Another important aspect of our moral-spiritual life involves prayer. The author emphasizes dedicating ourselves to thankfulness, to singing hymns and songs to the Lord, and to doing all things in the name of the Lord Jesus.

The gospel acclamation for all three cycles is taken from this part of Colossians (3:15, 16): "May the peace of Christ rule in your hearts; and the fullness of his message live within you." While customarily the gospel verse refers to the text to be proclaimed, this text reiterates the foundation of Christ's peace as that which should fill our hearts and bind us together as his people.

The gospel from Matthew (2:13–15, 19–23) recalls the Joseph cycle in Exodus as background for the dream of Joseph, the husband of Mary. (Verses 13–18 are used as the gospel on December 28; see above for additional commentary.) The text relates that Herod's death causes the angel to tell Joseph to return to his home (vs. 19); in Exodus it was the death of Pharoah that allowed Israel to return home. Jesus returns to Nazareth (vs. 23). The only other place in Matthew where this location is associated with Jesus is at Peter's denial when he says he does not know Jesus of Nazareth (26:71). Matthew's skillful work here thus links this seemingly domestic scene with the passion of Jesus, another indication of how editorial work reveals theologically rich meanings. When we recount the return of the holy family to Nazareth, we recount a story with paschal overtones, reminding us that this child will become the mediator of the new covenant.

Cycle "B"

The example of Abraham ("our father in faith," Roman Canon) is offered in the first (Gn 15:1–6, 21:1–3) and second readings today

(Heb 11:8, 11–12, 17–19). Abraham's lack of offspring is remedied by God who says that his descendants will be as numerous as the stars in the sky (Gn 15:5) if only he puts his faith in the Lord. Abraham obeyed and this was "credited to him as an act of righteousness" (vs. 6). This example is important as we reflect on Mary and Joseph's faith response to God's commands. Furthermore, Abraham's willingness to sacrifice Isaac, his only son, expands the parallel even further. The sacrifice of Isaac and the death of Jesus show what the demands of faith really imply.

The responsorial psalm, Psalm 104, is the very significant review of salvation history, recounting God's fidelity to his people despite their infidelity. Like Israel, we can still confidently pray, "the Lord is our God/He remembers his covenant forever" (vss. 7a, 8a). Because of God's active fidelity to his promises, we gather to celebrate these sacred mysteries; through them, we are once more graced and strengthened to live his life on earth.

The second reading from Hebrews parallels the Genesis text about Abraham's faith (vs. 8). Whereas Isaac was given back to Abraham as a symbol of God's power to raise from the dead, at the liturgy we receive the reality of Christ's risen life through signs and symbols. Implicit here is the dynamic of faith: complete trust in God's promises, his sustaining Israel despite her infidelity, and the fulfillment of all the promises made to her in Christ. We commemorate this fulfillment at Christmas and we await its completion in heaven.

The gospel (Lk 2:22–40) is the same text used on December 29 and 30, hence those commentaries should be consulted. Because of the many references to the holy family, an appropriate theme to emphasize is that of the family in which Jesus grew physically, mentally, and spiritually. This theme need not be restricted to natural family units, however, since the first two readings refer to faith as that which unites us as the family of the people of God.

Cycle "C"

The second part of the first reading, 1 Sm 1:20–22, 24–28, has already been used on December 22 to recount the birth of Samuel, which text led to Hannah's song as the responsorial psalm (see above). Today's response exclaims: "They are happy who dwell in your house, O Lord" (Ps 83:5), clearly a reference to the unity of the family of those who call God father and Lord, as did Hannah and

Elkanah, the parents of Samuel, and Mary and Joseph, the natural parents of Jesus.

The second reading from 1 John (3:1–2, 21–24) deals with our identify as God's children (vs. 1). Because "God is with us" (vs. 21), we are to keep his commandments and to do what is pleasing in his sight (vs. 22). The chief command, "to believe in the name of [God's] son, Jesus Christ, and . . . to love one another as he commanded us" (vs. 23), is pivotal for our understanding today's celebration (and for leading the Christian life as seen in the Johannine writings). Hence, we are challenged to live with the same faith and love that marked the holy family. It is for this that we pray in the third eucharistic prayer: "strengthen in faith and love your pilgrim church on earth."

The gospel, Luke 2:41–52, recounts the familiar story of the holy family's journey to Jerusalem for the celebration of Passover. While the ending explicitly refers to Mary who "kept all these things in memory" (vs. 51), the fact that the Solemnity of Mary, Mother of God, is on January 1 would militate against using this as a major focus of attention this Sunday. Other important sections of this text deal with Jesus' growing in wisdom, age, and grace (vs. 52) and his obedience to Mary and Joseph at Nazareth (vss. 50–51). The fact that the holy family journeyed to Jerusalem for the feast of Passover (vs. 41) presages Jesus' final journey to Jerusalem, a motif carried through in the second part of Luke's gospel. The fact that he taught the elders in the Temple for three days (vs. 46) can be interpreted as a support for such a passion reference since the "three days" between his death and resurrection will be hallowed by the Christian church in the celebration of holy week. The fact that Luke adds the reference to Jesus being in his Father's house should also not be overlooked (vs. 49) since some exegetes see in this a reference to Jesus' divinity, which will not be clearly established and universally revealed until his resurrection.

Celebration of the Eucharist

In planning and celebrating the liturgy today, any kind of speculation on Jesus' boyhood in Nazareth that would invite musing about him and his parents should be avoided. We are concerned here with a feast within the Christmas octave, a week-long commemoration of Jesus' incarnation and our sanctification through him.

The humanity of Jesus can be stressed today to lead us to appreciate our sharing in his divinity, experienced through the liturgy.

The rite of blessing and sprinkling with holy water may be used as the introduction to the liturgy today with a statement about our being one family in Christ because of the faith that gathers us for worship. If the third form of the penitential rite is used, the third set of sample invocations containing titles proper to the Christmas season would be appropriate.

Since the alternate form of the opening prayer contains a wider notion of family (that is, of all human beings), it might well be used today, especially since any idealization of the family should be avoided lest separated or divorced couples or children in single-parent families feel unwelcome.

In the intercessions, petitions for ministry to the divorced and separated, for those preparing for marriage in the new year, for families with handicapped members, and for families caring for the elderly should be included along with prayers for family unity and harmony. Both the introduction and the concluding prayer taken from the sample intercessions of Christmas could help reiterate the incarnational context of this feast.

Any of the Christmas prefaces would be suitable today; if the Roman Canon is used, the special Christmas section is proclaimed.

The rites before communion could well be emphasized today as a way of drawing out the challenge of the liturgy. To introduce the Lord's Prayer and the sign of peace by referring to the peace of Christ and the kindness noted in the Colossians reading would be appropriate. If additional titles of Jesus are added to the "Lamb of God," they should refer to the adult Christ, not the child Jesus.

The use of the solemn Christmas blessing would be another way of emphasizing the Christmas context for today's feast.

The settings for the acclamations used at Christmas should be repeated today and, where possible, the music for the "Glory to God" as well. While Christmas carols will likely be a part of today's music program, these should reflect the significance of the incarnation and not overemphasize the birth of the child Jesus.

Liturgy of the Hours

The liturgy of the hours today combines elements from the Christmas season, from the office of the Blessed Virgin, and those proper to today's feast.

At Evening Prayer I, the psalmody is taken from that used for feasts of the Blessed Virgin, but the antiphons are proper to this feast. The first (Mt 1:16) is part of the genealogy used at the Christmas Vigil, noting Jacob as the father of Joseph, the husband of Mary, who gave birth to Jesus, called the Christ. The second is from verse 20, recounting the angel's message to Joseph not to be afraid of taking Mary as his wife. The third antiphon is from the infancy narrative in Luke (2:16), recounting the finding of the child Jesus by the shepherds. These details from the Christmas gospels find a focus and depth in the scripture reading from 2 Corinthians (8:9) where Paul relates how for our sake Jesus "made himself poor though he was rich, so that you might become rich by his poverty." The antiphon to Mary's canticle is taken from the gospel in the "C" cycle (Lk 2:43–44) about Jesus remaining in Jerusalem and Mary and Joseph looking for him. At Evening Prayer II, the conclusion of this text is found where Jesus replies, "Did you not know that I had to be in my Father's house" (Lk 2:49). Interestingly in these two texts, we have a summary of the familiar story of the holy family's visit to Jerusalem and the announcement of Jesus' identification and service of his Father's will.

This same gospel passage is used in the antiphons for the psalmody at Evening Prayer II about Jesus in the temple (first), about his being obedient to Mary and Joseph (second), and his growing in wisdom (third). The psalmody at this hour is also taken from the common of the Blessed Virgin. The reading here is from the familiar Christ-hymn of Philippians 2:6–7 about Jesus' self-emptying. Once again, the paradox of the incarnation and our share in the divine life through Jesus is clearly asserted.

The intercessions are the same for both celebrations of evening prayer. Drawing on the example and model of Jesus, the petitions ask that we grow in reverence and obedience, in mutual love and peace, that we might reverence God the Father, and seek the kingdom of God here on earth.

The invitatory today reflects the uniqueness of the feast by stating: "Come, let us worship Christ, the Son of God, who was obedient to Mary and Joseph." Hence, from the beginning of prayer today, it is Jesus' obedience and submission to his human parents and to the human condition that is emphasized.

At the office of readings, the first reading is from the familiar (and sometimes misunderstood) text of Ephesians (5:21–6:4). What makes this text puzzling for some is its seeming insistence on female submission; yet, when understood in context and as a whole, mutual love and respect comprise its central teaching. The author here drew on a preexisting code of conduct (not necessarily Christian) and used it for his own purpose to express the mystery of Christ's love for his church (vs. 32). When this is seen as the key, then mutual respect and deferring to each other (vs. 21) form a natural consequence of the message of the text. Wives are so exhorted (vss. 22–24) as are husbands (vss. 25–30; 6:4) and children (6:1–3). In fact, it is husbands who are to love and care for their wives in the same selfsacrificing way that "Christ cares for the church" (vs. 29).

The second reading is from a discourse of Pope Paul VI about Nazareth. Interestingly, the lessons the holy father draws from his visit there concern the importance of silence, the sanctity of family life, and the dignity of work. These implications of the incarnation are thus brought into clear focus today.

The psalmody at the office of readings is taken from the common of the Blessed Virgin with antiphons from the gospels. The first speaks of Simeon in the temple (from the "B" gospel), the second is about the Magi finding the child with his mother (from the Epiphany gospel), and the third shows Joseph's obedience when he "took the child and his mother into Egypt."

At morning prayer, the psalmody is from Sunday Week I. The first two antiphons reiterate important aspects of the "C" gospel: observing the law and going to Jerusalem for the Passover (first), and Jesus growing in wisdom, strength, and God's favor (second). The "wonder" experienced by Mary and Joseph at what was said of their child (third antiphon) should characterize our appreciation of the Christmas paradox of humanity being graced in divinity through Christ. The text from Deuteronomy (5:16) about honoring father and mother is from the decalogue. This privileged revelation held a special place in Jewish law and custom; thus, it is a fitting Old Testament backdrop for today's feast.

The antiphon to Zechariah's canticle recalls the last line of the canticle itself when it speaks about guiding "our feet into the way of peace" (Lk 1:79) which "way" has been illuminated by the "light" given us through the holy family's example.

In the intercessions, we pray that Christ will be our model in humility, in being attentive to the word, in working diligently, and in growing toward God as our source and destiny.

Celebration of the Hours

The hymns at all the hours should reflect Christmas as much as possible and should express our participation in the life of God through the incarnation. The reading at Evening Prayer I could easily be expanded to 2 Corinthians 8:8–15, and at Evening Prayer II to the whole Christ hymn in Philippians 2:5–10. The singing of the Canticles of Mary and of Zechariah could help add festivity especially because of the important role these hymns play in the gospels in this season. If the intercessions are adjusted at evening prayer (especially to avoid repeating one formula), the pattern in the original should be kept because it is concerned with the incarnation.

For the invitatory, Psalm 100 would be a good choice to accompany today's verse; Psalm 24 should be avoided because it will be used as the first psalm at the office of readings.

At morning prayer, the psalm prayers offered reflect the Lord's day, hence they should be rewritten or dropped (especially when this feast is celebrated on December 30 instead of Sunday). Reading from a longer section of the decalogue at morning prayer (Dt 5) would be useful provided that the introductory verses give the context for whatever is read (vss. 6–7). The use of the solemn blessing of Christmas at these hours would help to emphasize the Christmas context for today's feast.

Reflection—"Welcome Home"

Home has been described as the place where, when you show up, they have to take you in, or as a haven from the heartless world. Whatever one's definition, it is clear that what is meant by "home" is not a domicile or a "house." "Home" carries with it associations of relatedness, intimacy, acceptance, and belonging. To speak of home automatically triggers many (and varied) associations. It is not a neutral word. To idealize "home and hearth" can be part of the Christmas mystique; part of the Christmas reality involves being with family and loved ones.

Is it any wonder that many involved in evangelizing and outreach efforts in the church today speak of such programs as "welcome home" because without the alienated and estranged the church is without members of its family? Yet, such is the reality in the Catholic church in America today; outreach programs are one indication of how the church attempts to respond to this need.

An important challenge is to help people feel "at home." It is not just reaching the marginal and inviting them back that matters. It is welcoming them home and making them feel accepted, not judged. Such efforts are not the preserve of committees, much less of religious professionals and clergy. It is the task of all the baptized for we serve each other best when we realize and express the fact that together we form the body of Christ.

Such is the challenge of today's feast. It is not primarily concerned with domestic relations, self-help techniques for getting along, or being concerned with one's immediate family only. It means that we open our arms to embrace our brothers and sisters in the faith, and realize that when we gather for worship, it is at God's invitation.

Chapter Six

Christmas Season: Second Week

JANUARY 1—OCTVAVE OF CHRISTMAS;
SOLEMNITY OF MARY, MOTHER OF GOD

Liturgical Context

When the Julian reform of the calendar took place, New Year's Day, January 1, became a civil holiday of festivity and rejoicing, and was adapted by the Christian church as a Marian feast. It is the most primitive of Marian feasts indigenous to Rome. However, later tradition assigned other titles to it, including the circumcision of Jesus, the octave day of Christmas, and the holy name of Jesus.

With the increasing tensions among nations and the threat of nuclear war, the popes have used this first day of the new year to plead for world peace. While the liturgy remains the feast of Mary, this other additional concern should not be neglected.

Liturgy of the Eucharist

Both incarnation and Marian themes dominate the eucharist. Of the two entrance antiphons provided, the first acclaims Christ as the light "born for us," whose "kingship will never cease" (from Isaiah 9:2 and Luke 1:33). Thus, the familiar images of the incarnation recur to reestablish the Christmas context. The second text, however (from Sedulius), acclaims Mary specifically as "holy Mother" and Jesus as "king." In these texts and in the opening prayer, it is clear that we worship the Father through Christ. The opening prayer (in the Latin original) states that we receive the gift of eternal life from the fruitful virginity of Mary through whom we have received the author of life.

The readings for the feast are comparatively brief. The text from Numbers (6:22–27) contains the pronouncement of the Aaronic blessing, the text of which is used in the first of the solemn blessings in the Sacramentary. The reference to the "name" in the last verse is significant since in the Hebrew mentality, to invoke another's name was to indicate a relationship with that person. Furthermore, to "bless" means to praise, glorify, and extol someone; secondarily, it means that a thing or a person is consecrated. Therefore, we "bless" God at the eucharist by proclaiming (and thus entering into) the redemption he grants us through the name of his Son, Jesus. Hence the importance of invoking the name Jesus as we begin a new year, and the reason why so many liturgical prayers end "in the name of Jesus the Lord."

The responsorial psalm, Psalm 67, is among those used as the invitatory psalm at the liturgy of the hours. Through it we pray that God would "bless us in his mercy" (vs. 2) and that all the ends of the earth would fear him (vs. 8).

The second reading from Galatians (4:4–7) has already been used as the reading at Evening Prayer I on Christmas and is also assigned for Evening Prayer I and II today. This text about the birth of Jesus, the Son of God, speaks forcefully about our status in Christ as adopted children of God. The specificity of the incarnation is also central here since Jesus was born at a specific time, to a particular people, from a mother specially chosen. The specificity of the event of Jesus' birth thus expands to the whole world; the movement is from particularity to universality (which theme will dominate the Epiphany cycle).

The uniqueness of God's revelation through Jesus is noted in the gospel acclamation (from Hebrews 1:1–2, already reviewed as part of the second reading on Christmas day). The self-communication of God to humanity occurred in the old covenant through his word to the prophets; now he speaks to us through his Son, the Word made flesh.

The gospel today, Luke 2:16–21, speaks of the name "Jesus" given to the child and of the observance of the Jewish law of circumcision. Hence, the first reading emphasizing the "name" and the second about being "born under the law" (vs. 4) are complementary.

Two major themes emerge on this feast. The first is salvation in the name of Jesus (as in the first and the gospel readings) and what it means to invoke the name of God at our worship. The second theme is Mary's motherhood and her trust in God's plan (the second reading and the gospel).

In the prayer over the gifts, we acknowledge God as the beginning and the completion of all that is good and that Mary's giving birth to Jesus marks the beginning of our "salvation" (which recalls the reference in the prayer over the gifts at the Christmas vigil mass: "the beginning of our redemption"). The Christmas context is once again emphasized in the communion antiphon, Hebrews 13:8, "Jesus Christ is the same yesterday, today and for ever." The liturgy spans these separate times and places; through it, we share in the fullness of the mystery of Christ.

The prayer after communion acclaims the Blessed Virgin as the mother of God and the mother of the church.

Celebration of the Eucharist

The tone of the liturgy should be simpler than that of Christmas or the Sundays of the season. However, the settings for the acclamations used then should be repeated to show seasonal continuity. After an introduction to the liturgy about Mary as mother of God and of the church, the third form of the penitential rite, acclaiming Christ as the Son of God, the Son of Mary, the Word made flesh and the Splendor of the Father's glory, would be appropriate. The model intercessions for the Christmas season could be utilized when composing this prayer (especially the first petition noting that the Word who was born for us of the sinless Virgin and the concluding prayer referring to Mary). The first preface of the Blessed Virgin is preferable today because it emphasizes her motherhood and acclaims Christ as the light of the world.

If the Roman Canon is used, the special Christmas section is proclaimed. This would be especially fitting today because it speaks of Mary who "without loss of her virginity gave the world its savior. We honor Mary, the ever-virgin mother of Jesus Christ our Lord and God. . . ." The solemn blessing for the new year would be a fitting conclusion to the liturgy.

Liturgy of the Hours

From the first antiphon at Evening Prayer I, the Christmas context for this commemoration of Mary is clearly stated: "O marvelous exchange! Man's creator has become man, born of a virgin. We have been made sharers in the divinity of Christ who humbled himself to share in our humanity." We praise the God whose son came to save his people (second antiphon); we are in awe at the "blessed and fruitful virginity" of Mary on whose prayerful intercession we rely (third antiphon).

Both tonight and tomorrow at evening prayer, the text of Galatians 4:4–5 is assigned, the passage used as the second reading at mass (see above). That Jesus knew the limitations of this mortal life and submitted to the restraints of the prescriptions of the old covenant is clearly stated in the antiphon to the Canticle of Mary. At Evening Prayer II, this antiphon is taken from the first part of the important text of Luke 12:37: "Blest is the womb which bore you, O Christ, and the breast that nursed you." In joy and praise, we call on him as the "Lord and Savior of the world." (However, what is particularly striking is the elimination of the second part of this verse which, in Lukan theology, reflects why Mary is really blessed: she heard and kept the word of God ("rather . . . blest are they who hear the word of God and keep it"). This second part of the verse should be kept in mind whenever we reflect on Luke's infancy narrative since Luke portrays the true disciple and hearer of the word of God.)

The introduction to the intercessions at Evening Prayer I refers to Christ as our peace; in the alternate response, we ask the Lord to grant "peace to all." At Evening Prayer II, the second petition is for peace while the others deal with families, unity among nations, and the dead.

The invitatory to the hours is specially chosen for the feast: "Let us celebrate the motherhood of the Blessed Virgin Mary; let us worship her Son, Christ the Lord."

The first reading at the office of readings, Hebrews 2:9–18, emphasizes Jesus' full humanity; it acknowledges that through him redemption and salvation from sin is offered to all. Christ tasted death "for the sake of all men" (vs. 9); by experiencing death, he has robbed physical death of its power (vs. 14). Significantly, the author emphasizes that Christ was made perfect through suffering (vs. 10) and that he was like us in every way "to expiate the sins of the people." It is only in the response that Mary's role is noted; we acknowledge her as "full of grace" and as the one who "bore the creator of the world."

The second reading from a letter of St. Athanasius explores the humanity of the Word made flesh and emphasizes that our whole selves, bodies and souls, are redeemed in him. Christ's humanity thus becomes the means (the instrument) through which God has freed us from sin and has reestablished our communion with him.

This emphasis on the incarnation is also reflected in the antiphons at the office of readings about Christ, the king of glory (first) whom we acclaim as "begotten of the Father, before the daystar shone or time began, the Lord and Savior has humbled himself to be born for us today." The insertion of the phrase "born for us today" reflects the terminology often seen in liturgical texts during the octave of feasts. (Today the Christmas octave concludes.)

The single exception to the use of the psalms from the common of the Blessed Virgin Mary today is at morning prayer when we return to the psalms of Sunday Week I. The first antiphon refers to Christ as Savior, born from Jesse's stock, itself a significant reference to the human origins of Jesus, proclaimed in the Matthean genealogy at the Christmas Vigil Mass (Mt 1:1–25). The second antiphon also recalls our Advent preparation since it quotes the acclamation of John the Baptizer: "This is the Lamb of God, who takes away the sins of the world." Jesus' intercession and self-offering to the point of death is emphasized; through the liturgy, we join the intercession of the Lamb of God for our salvation. The last antiphon refers to Mary as the one who bore "a King whose name is everlasting." Both the incarnation of Jesus and the manner of his birth from a virgin mother are unique, thus they deserve the homage and reverence paid to them in today's liturgy.

The text from Micah (5:2–4a) assigned at morning prayer provides an Old Testament reference to the coming of the shepherd of Israel who will care for his flock and who shall be called peace. These images offer important insights about how we should worship the Father through Christ in the Christmas season. It is through Christ's mediatorship, not merely his birth as an infant, that we approach the Father in prayer.

The antiphon to Zechariah's canticle draws out some of the implications of the incarnation and Christ's identity (in language that is more theologically refined than that customarily used in the liturgy). We attest that our nature is made new because he who is God became man for our salvation.

Celebration of the Hours

The hymns used to begin the hours today should reflect Mary's motherhood. Yet, they should also reflect the balanced incarnational theology found in the texts of the liturgy so that these do not emphasize only the birth of Jesus. The use of adapted psalm prayers and significant pauses between psalms is an important option to consider today; this is especially true at morning prayer since the psalm prayers refer to the Lord's day. The use of a text other than Galatians 4:4–5 at evening prayer today would be an option since the longer version is used at mass. Singing the Canticle of the Blessed Virgin would be especially appropriate today, as would the use of the solemn blessing of the Blessed Virgin Mary to conclude the major hours.

For the invitatory, the use of the prescribed verse and Psalm 100 would provide an appropriately festive introduction to the hours. For the intercessions at morning and evening prayer, the models provided offer important guidance since they reflect a solid theology of the incarnation; any additional prayers should avoid overemphasizing Mary's role to the detriment of the unique mediatorship of Christ. However, an introduction to the Lord's Prayer about doing the Father's will as Mary did would appropriately reflect today's feast.

Reflection—"Hail Mary"

As we begin a new year, the liturgy directs our attention to Mary whom we greet as "full of grace." With Mary as our model, we look to the coming year as a time of grace to grow in understanding and appreciating Jesus Christ, the Word revealed through her. The concrete ways Mary followed the call of the Lord can be important reminders for us of the practical nature of Christianity and how practical our spirituality should be.

We often pray, "Hail Mary, full of grace." She was filled with grace because she opened her life—all aspects of her life to the Lord. He was able to fill her with grace because she hid nothing from him. What do we need to open to the Lord this year that we have kept tightly shut because of fear or embarrassment? The Lord who knows all wants us to acknowledge our need for his grace as Mary did.

"Holy Mary, mother of God" begins the second part of this familiar prayer. Holiness is for everyone: for mothers and fathers, sisters and brothers who, like Mary, accept the very human situations of everyday life as the setting for growth in holiness and sanctity. She became holy by offering her life, work and prayer to God humbly and sincerely. Do we accept the daily, often boring routine of life as the setting to grow in holiness as Mary did? Do we succumb to the temptation to look for the new, the different, and the escape to sense excitement as we grow in sanctity? Real holiness is borne in the ordinary and the everyday.

"Pray for us sinners" is an important, though humbling part of our prayer. We are sinners. That is why we needed Christ to come in the first place; it is why we need to celebrate Christmas every year. It is also why we need intercessors, like Mary, to pray to God for us. With Mary's help and her intercession, we can grow in holiness this year in the concrete, everyday situations of life. That is what she did. Having done that, we acclaim her as model and mother of us all in the church, even as we acknowledge her today as "mother of God."

WEEKDAYS, FROM JANUARY 2 TO THE SOLEMNITY OF THE EPIPHANY

The liturgy for these days is uniquely structured. At the liturgy of the eucharist, the entrance and communion antiphons, the opening prayer, prayer over the gifts, and the prayer after communion are assigned according to the day of the week whereas the scripture readings are assigned according to the date. Hence, the sacramentary texts (which are of a seasonal nature) do not reflect the specific readings proclaimed on a given day. Thus, the Lectionary texts are assigned to the date (e.g., January 2) and the mass formulas from the Sacramentary are assigned to the day of the week (e.g., Tuesday). Because of this, in the first section of the commentaries that follow, we will discuss the scripture readings for the eucharist and suggestions for celebration. (It should be noted that the entrance and communion antiphons assigned for the eucharist this week are the same ones that will be used next week. The prayers over the gifts and the prayers after communion used from December 29 to 31 are used again in succession this and next week (hence, Monday's prayers are used again on Thursday and were used on December 29, etc.), leaving the opening prayer the only variable each day. This week these reflect the Christmas season; next week they reflect the Epiphany. This week the Christmas prefaces are used; next week the Epiphany preface is used.)

The liturgy of the hours is structured so that the psalms are taken from the usual weekly psalter distribution and the scripture readings, prayers, and antiphons to the Canticles of Zechariah and Mary are proper to the weekday. Hence, in the commentaries that follow these proper parts of the hours will be discussed according to the day of the week for which they are assigned, along with suggestions for celebrations. Therefore, in reviewing this week, the following structure will be observed:

January 2 to January 7
Liturgy of the Eucharist
Celebration of the Eucharist
Reflection

Monday to Saturday January 2 to Epiphany
Liturgy of the Hours
Celebration of the Hours

JANUARY 2

Liturgy of the Eucharist
Today's first reading continues the first letter of John (read since December 27) and explains the reference in the preceding verses to the "Antichrist" (mentioned on December 31). Here the author explores the identity of Jesus as the Christ, totally equal with the Father (vss. 22–23). Some commentators point out that this direct assertion is meant to counter those Jews who cling to their religious practices (seen in the dialogue with the Samaritan woman, John 4) rather than to see in Jesus their fulfillment and completion. Jesus is the unique mediator and is God's own Son. Faith in the works that Jesus performed (his "signs") should lead to faith in his person and ultimately to union in him. We are meant to abide in him as he abides in the Father. The first step in this process is putting faith and trust in Christ alone. John states that this faith should so take over our hearts that God will remain with us and in us forever (vs. 24). This union in Christ will lead to our full share in the life of God in eternity (vs. 25). This theme extends to our communion with each other (vs. 28). However, before stating this, the author uses the familiar terms "anointing" and "true" to denote revelation. While some see a baptismal theme in the anointing reference, John's main concern is to show that the Spirit of God brings us to this revelation (whether by a literal baptismal anointing or by his power at work in our hearts). The reference to the Lord's "coming" (vs. 28) should not

be ignored. This prominent theme from the Advent liturgy coincidentally reappears here and should help our appreciation of the fullness of the mystery of Christ—for whom we longed in Advent, in whose fullness we now share through Christmas liturgy and which will be complete in the kingdom of heaven. In the meantime, through the liturgy, we come to "know" God through his Son.

The use of Psalm 98 as the response today recalls its usage on Christmas Day with the same response about the universality of salvation. (It also looks forward to the next two days when this same psalm and verse will be used.) This choice reflects liturgical tradition which has used this psalm to describe how God's "right hand" (vs. 1) has established his victory, to emphasize that his "salvation" and "justice" have appeared through Christ (vs. 2), and that his kindness and faithfulness toward the house of Israel now extends to all peoples.

The text of the gospel of John 1:19–28 proclaimed today has already been proclaimed on the Third Sundy of Advent "B" cycle (see above). By design, the Lectionary uses the gospel of John, chapter 1, from December 31 through to January 5. Today's text presents John's assertion that he is not the Messiah. Tomorrow's gospel contains his assertion that Jesus is the Messiah.

Celebration of the Eucharist

The celebration of the eucharist these days should be simple and direct, less festive and in contrast with that of Christmas, Holy Family, and Mary, Mother of God. The introduction could speak about the presence of God with us at the liturgy, especially the revelation of the Word of God through the scriptures and the eucharistic banquet. If the third form of the penitential rite is used, acclamations of Christ as the Word made flesh, Messiah and Lord, Son of God, and Son of Mary would be effective.

For the gospel, verse 12 (Lect., no. 212), quoting John 1:14, would be most appropriate since it reflects the challenge of John's gospel to accept the Word of God in faith and trust.

Among the intercessions, a petition for Jewish believers, the first to receive the revelation of God, should be made so that any subtle antisemitism derived from the Johannine writings would be tempered. Petitions for those who are marginal to the church or who no longer practice the faith would serve as an invitation to renew their belief in the incarnation.

The introduction to the Lord's prayer could mention our faith in the "Word made flesh" and our imitation of Christ as he prayed to his Father (thus reflecting the first verses of 1 John).

Reflection—"Anti-Christ"

What are the things in life that show that we are followers of Christ and what are those things that are anti-Christ? The question is deceptively simple; but its simplicity should not deceive us. Each of us has to face the fact that professing faith in the incarnation is more than mental affirmation or assent—it must touch our hearts. And, in touching our hearts, this assent must be reflected in our lives. Do we affirm our faith in Christ by every choice and act we perform? Is there a symptom or two that is anti-Christ in our hearts and reflected in our lives? Am I dependent on alcohol or drugs to the extent that I cannot function without my "fix?" Does such dependency harm the body, the very thing that God has so revered when he sent his Son in human form?

A new year has just begun. Perhaps this is the year to recommit ourselves to the faith we speak with our lips, "we believe in Jesus Christ," and to deny anything that is "anti-Christ."

JANUARY 3

Liturgy of the Eucharist

The author of 1 John (2:29–3:6) understands the union between believers and God so intimately that he uses the terms "begotten" by God and bearing God's "holiness" (vs. 29) to describe the baptized. At baptism, the Christian receives God's Spirit and becomes a member of his chosen ones. Through the Spirit, the believer becomes "holy" as God is holy. While holiness and a direct relationship with God may well be understood and welcomed by Christians, they may not be so welcomed or appreciated by society at large. Like Christ, the begotten of God may experience rejection, lack of recognition, and even betrayal. Such is the lot of one who believes and commits him/herself to the Father in Christ. Just as "the world" did not recognize God's Son, so it may not recognize us as God's children (3:1). The pain and suffering endured by Christ is a model for the kind of suffering we will likely endure if we are faithful to the Lord.

While we receive here on earth a share in God's own life (see verse 2 about being "children" of God), we are reminded that this is necessarily limited. When the darkness of this world is over and we are called to eternity, "we shall see him [God] as he is" (vs. 2) and

we shall be like him." Because we are still separated from God and are still sinners, we need his sustaining presence to "take away sins" (vs. 5) and to reconcile us with the Father. The paschal overtones of the Christmas season thus come through at the end of this text and are in today's gospel.

The repetition of yesterday's responsorial psalm, Psalm 98, strikes a note of special praise and joy today with the inclusion of verses 5 and 6 about God's saving work among us. Any exclusivity and special status accorded to the chosen (Israel) is transcended here so that "all the ends of the earth" are assured a place in God's kingdom.

The gospel from John (1:29–34) tells about the Baptist's positive identification of Jesus as the Messiah In acclaiming Jesus as the "Lamb of God" (vs. 29), John strikes to the core of the Hebrew scriptures and liturgy. Jesus is here associated with the suffering servant led like a lamb to slaughter (Is 53) and to the passover lamb slain and eaten at the feast commemorating Israel's passage through the Red Sea (Ex 12). This image also points to the eschatological lamb who will destroy all evil forever (Rv 17). Clearly, the title "Lamb" is unique and significant theologically. For us, this usage is all the more important because it describes the sacrificial banquet of the eucharist. The eucharist is the reenactment of Christ's sacrifice and those who partake in it necessarily commit themselves to offering themselves in sacrifice and victimhood. To share in the eucharist is to be willing to offer oneself in oblation and sacrifice. The pivotal nature of the term "Lamb" should, therefore, be understood as a way of understanding Jesus as the fulfillment of Old Testament images for sacrifice and as the unique victim whose blood has washed us clean and will bring us into the company of the martyrs.

The expiatory role of the Lamb of God in forgiving our sins ties in with our need for forgiveness (see today's first reading, verse 5). Such is a result of every celebration of the eucharist. That the evangelist wants to emphasize this role is clearly seen in the other title of Jesus found in the last verse of the gospel reading: "God's chosen One." This title is used in the gospels to describe Jesus' experience of God's Spirit at his baptism. When the Spirit came upon him at this mission-inaugurating scene (to be discussed below on the feast of the Baptism of our Lord), he was revealed as God's "chosen," a clear reference to the servant song in Isaiah 42:1. This text is repeatedly used in the liturgy to refer to the role of the Messiah in our salvation and sanctification. This text carries unmistakable sacrificial overtones as does "Lamb of God." Our "identification" with Christ, commemorated and emphasized during the Christmas season, is no cheap title or easily won status. Like Christ's privileged status at the Father's right hand, it can only come through humiliation and suffering. But the suffering is made light and the humiliation possible to endure because Christ is with us. The oblation of Christ is made real at the eucharist; through this oblation, we are able to bear our sufferings to attain complete and total identification with the Father in heaven.

Celebration of the Eucharist

The introduction to the liturgy could speak of our being members of God's household through Christ and being his chosen ones. In the penitential rite, the use of the titles "Lamb of God," "Chosen One of the Father," and "Messiah and Lord" would reflect names used in John's gospel. Once again the use of the first alleluia verse (Lect., no. 212) about the "Word of God" becoming man, the central Johannine revelation, would be appropriate.

Among the intercessions, petitions for the Jews who first shared in the covenant, for purity of intention at religious practices, for a sense of self-sacrifice, and for those who suffer physically, emotionally, and spiritually would be helpful.

A sung version of the "Lamb of God" with special emphasis on those words (repeated at least three times) would be especially appropriate today, as would a clearly stated and slowly paced invitation to communion: "This is the Lamb of God who takes away the sins of the world. . . ." If the sacrifice of Jesus is noted in the homily or is made the basis of today's celebration, number 17 of the prayers over the people would be appropriate as a dismissal.

Reflection—"Worthy Is the Lamb"

The final section of Handel's *Messiah* is the Revelation hymn, "worthy is the Lamb that was slain for our salvation," followed by the exuberant section, "and trumpets shall sound." This perennial favorite of Christmas musical fare is a summary of salvation history from promise to fulfillment—in the birth of Christ, to his passion, death, resurrection, and to his exaltation at the Father's right hand.

The key to understanding the major portions of the *Messiah* is the same key which unlocks our understanding of redemption, salvation, and the incarnation—each involves sacrifice. We acclaim Christ as "worthy" of all praise and thanksgiving because of what he endured for us. The deeper issue concerns how willingly we accept the suffering we must endure in following Christ.

Christmas should mean more than giving gifts to those who will reciprocate; it should mean turning the other cheek when we are rejected because of what we stand for. Christmas should mean more than entertaining the same people we will see at other parties; it should mean offering food, clothing, and shelter to the needy because doing it for them is doing it for Christ. Christmas should mean more than vacation days and feasting with family and friends; it should be a time for peacemaking and reconciliation with those who may have hurt us or whom we may have hurt. Christmas should mean more than going to the sacraments to have our sins taken away; it should be a time to forgive and to forget the sins others have committed against us.

When Christmas takes on this deeper meaning, then it is fitting that we acclaim the Lamb of God who takes away our sins and reconciles us with God and neighbor.

JANUARY 4

Liturgy of the Eucharist

Today's first reading, 1 John 3:7–10, expresses the contrast between holiness and sin. The contrast motif continues throughout these verses with Christ pitted against the devil (vss. 8, 9) and holiness contrasted with sin (vss. 7, 10). When placed in this dualistic framework, the reality of Christian truth stands out clearly—in Christ, we who have been saved from our sins are to lead holy lives, rejecting sin and abiding in Christ. This gift of salvation is therefore not an individual possession; it endures in the Christian community whose chief characteristic is love for each other. The holiness referred to in this reading (vs. 9) should not be understood as the moral perfection of each member of the body; the state of being like God is given to the church as a whole so that God's love and salvation can be experienced in the Christian community. This Christmas season is a time of annual renewal in love—of God's love for us in Christ and of our love for each other. Empowered with God's love, we must choose Christ over the allurements of the devil and holiness over attachment to sin.

The responsorial psalm is once again Psalm 98 with the addition of verses 7–9. The last verse is of particular interest since it acknowledges that the Lord comes to us "to rule the earth . . . with justice" and "the peoples with equity." This song is applied to Christ in its liturgical usage today; through Christ, we now experience the justice and Lordship of God.

The gospel readings for today and tomorrow, John 1:35–42 and 43–51, both deal with the call of the first disciples. Today's text singles out Andrew and Simon. The first verses join the ministry of John the Baptizer with the mission of Jesus since John (once again) points to Jesus as the "Lamb of God" (vs. 36). By pointing to Jesus as Messiah, he challenges the disciples to put their faith in Christ. The implication here is that such a profession of faith necessarily involves following the Lord and abiding with him. The fact that the evangelist states that they "followed Jesus" (vs. 37) indicates that they left everything behind to follow Christ's ways not their own. The disciples' faith in Jesus serves as a model for us of how we too are to follow along the road that leads to Jesus.

The second part of the text is a subtle wordplay on the names of the disciples and titles for Jesus. The first called to "come and see" (vs. 39) was Andrew; it is Andrew who then acclaims that Jesus is Messiah (the "Anointed"). In acclaiming Jesus as Messiah and the Anointed of God, Andrew states his conviction that Christ reveals God's plan of salvation for all the world. Andrew then invites his brother to come to Jesus who changes his name to "Cephas," which is rendered "Peter" (vs. 42). This name change reflects the importance which affirming faith in Christ has for the disciples. For us to be called by our name at baptism is a contemporary application of what occurred throughout the scriptures: God's call to his people and Jesus' call to his disciples to "follow" him in the ways of justice and salvation.

A minor point that is worth noting concerns the fact that this exchange occurred at four in the afternoon. Some commentators maintain that the reason the disciples went to Jesus' lodging was that it was time for the Jewish sabbath to begin. The disciples followed their "Rabbi" (so stated in vs. 38), but from the perspective of resurrection faith, they would regard him and the passover ritual in a different way. This ritual would now be infused with a new meaning, that Jesus was and is the Messiah, whose death and resurrection is the new passover, the new way to liberation and freedom from the bondage of sin. The liturgical application for us is clear. Through the eucharist, we share now in the fulfillment of all Old Testament rituals; through it we are made sharers in the salvation of Christ.

Celebration of the Eucharist

The introduction to the liturgy could address our new status in Christ as those who have been redeemed and yet as those who have to deepen their commitment to Christ through the liturgy. The titles used to acclaim Jesus in the gospels these days would be appropriately used in the third form of the penitential rite: Lamb of God, Messiah, and Lord.

The use of number 2 of the alleluia verses (Lect., no. 212) could be understood to reaffirm the uniqueness of the mediatorship and salvation we share through Christ (Heb 2:1–2). Among the intercessions today, petitions for those soon to be baptized (appropriately on the feast of the baptism of our Lord), for the vibrant witness of Christians in the world, and for God's justice to reign in human hearts so that violence can be overcome would be appropriate.

The use of the second Christmas preface would be appropriate today since it reflects our need for the Messiah who

"has come to lift up all things to himself,
to restore unity to creation,
and to lead mankind from exile into your
     heavenly kingdom."

The use of number 14 of the prayers over the people about rejoicing in the mystery of redemption (in the liturgy) and our hope "to win its reward" in the kingdom would be a fitting conclusion to the liturgy.

Reflection—"Called by Name"

Whether clothed in the eloquence of Shakespeare's question about what is in a name, or in the (corny) lyrics of Cohan's "grand old name" for the Marys among us, it is clear that a perennial theme in literature and life concerns finding the right name for people and things—one that "fits." Parents of newborn children agonize over the right name for their infant and artists often anguish over the right title for their latest creation. Naming takes on enormous significance.

In today's gospel, we hear about name-changing (Simon to Peter) and name-calling ("Messiah" and "Anointed"). For us Christians who were called by name from all eternity in God's divine plan to be his chosen ones, this relationship was concretized and ratified at baptism. Through the ceremony of initiation, we were named by our parents and claimed for Christ the "savior" by the sign of the cross by priest, parents, and godparents.

The custom of name-calling is continued whenever we celebrate the liturgy. In worship, we call on God—Father, Son, and Spirit—at its beginning and ending. To call on God in this way reaffirms our intimate relationship to him through Christ, who is acclaimed "Messiah" in today's gospel. We who once were anointed at baptism and confirmation to bear the name of Christ are thus reminded of our status as God's named and chosen people. The unique relationship between believer and Lord begun at baptism is renewed through the liturgy to enable us to witness to Christ's Lordship over us in all our lives.

JANUARY 5

The first part of the text from 1 John (3:11–21) recalls the section on fraternal love read on December 29, 1 John 2:3–11. The first verse here reiterates the central message, "love one another," as "heard from the beginning" (vs. 11). The author uses the story of Cain killing Abel (from Gn 4) to illustrate his point. Cain belonged to the "evil one" as opposed to Christ; unlike his brother whose deeds were "just," Cain's were "wicked" (vs. 12). The author's point is clear—we are to choose just deeds over wicked deeds to show that we belong to Christ not to "the evil one." This if forcefully brought out in verse 15 where the example of Cain's murderous act is applied to any act of hating by which we (in effect) kill others: "Anyone who hates his brother is a murderer, and you know that eternal life abides in no murderer's heart" (vs. 15). The disposition of our heart is revealed in the kind of works we do; they are to accord with Christ's command to love one another. When proclaimed during the Christmas season, this text draws our attention to the simple ways in which God is made known in our world—in the undramatic but often very demanding love we show to others. This is particularly evident when we love those in need (vs. 17) and when our affection is demonstrated in deeds, not in words only (vs. 18).

The last verses of the text (vss. 19–21) shift from exhortation to reflection on the kind of quiet hope we experience who believe in the coming of God in Christ. The Lord's abiding presence with us (in the Johannine idiom) gives us confidence when we choose love over hate, just deeds over wicked deeds. Through all of this, "we can be sure that God is with us" (vs. 20).

The use of Psalm 100 as the responsorial psalm reflects the joy and exaltation of the Christmas season. Used as one of the options for the invitatory psalm in the liturgy of the hours, this text emphasizes our communion with God through Christ:

"Know that the Lord is God;
  he made us, his we are;
  his people, the flock he tends." (vs. 3)

When used in the Christmas season, this psalm helps us to reflect on Jesus' role as shepherd and Lord rather than on his infancy.

The gospel of the calling of Philip and Nathaniel, John 1:43–51, continues the section on calling the disciples begun yesterday. Here we see Jesus' initiative in calling followers ("follow me," verse 43) and the first one inviting a second to join him (here it is Philip who encourages Nathaniel, verse 45). Nathaniel's reaction was to look down upon Jesus' origins, but when he came and saw Jesus he became his follower. Direct contact with the Lord, not a review of his lineage or where his family lived, made all the difference.

Interestingly, Jesus states that Nathaniel has "no guile in him" (vs. 47), a text which may well suggest that Nathaniel personifies the faith of Israel ready to burst into its full flowering at the sight of Jesus, the Messiah and Lord. The heritage of God's revelation leads the true Israelite to put faith in Jesus who fulfills the covenant. Another indication of transcending the old covenant comes in the reference to ascending and descending (vs. 51), referring back to "Jacob's ladder" (Gn 28:12) on which "God's messengers" went up and down to intercede and to receive God's revelation. This traditional usage would not have been lost on the Johannine audience who would see Jesus as he who fulfills and transcends any other (lesser) messengers. Jesus is the unique revelation and manifestation of God among us (vs. 49).

The reference to "Son of Man" in verse 51 is its first appearance in John's gospel. For John it refers to Christ's mission and his mediation. Jacob's ladder has been transcended through Christ, yet it offers a helpful way to understand the role of mediatorship and liturgy in our lives. Through Christ, we can ascend to the Father; from him, we receive the revelation of the Father.

Celebration of the Liturgy

The introduction to the liturgy could refer to our call to follow Christ (as did Philip and Nathaniel) and the kind of conduct that characterizes true disciples. The use of the titles Son of God, Son of Man, Messiah, and Lord would appropriately reflect today's gospel.

The use of number 2 of the alleluia verses (Lect., no. 212) would reflect the gospel since it refers to the way God speaks "through his Son" (Heb 1:2). Among the petitions today, prayers that Christians truly love as Christ loved, that deeds of committed service reflect the Christian church as it witnesses to Christ, and that we would experience the active presence of Christ for us through the liturgy would be appropriate. Of the Christmas prefaces, the second would be appropriate since it is the only one that refers to Christ with the title "Son before all ages."

Reflection—"Where God Is"

In common parlance, we often refer to God as the one "upstairs" in heaven or as the one we find in church. While such associations reflect a certain awe and reverence for God and are thus appropriate in themselves, these are much too limiting for the Christian understanding of where God is. Unlike the rites and beliefs of Israel, which more usually reflect the otherness of God, the Christian understands God's presence as wide and expansive.

God is known when and where we love each other as he loves us. He is present where we offer water to the thirsty, a sandwich to the hungry, a shirt to the needy, and comfort to the troubled. It's that simple. Yet, so often we can miss these manifestations of God in our midst because we are looking for a "thunder and lightning" revelation or the kind of miracles Jesus worked while on earth. To do so is to misread the scriptures and to misunderstand the meaning of the Christian faith. God is not limited to the astounding, to the miraculous, or to the cult. He is found in the ordinary, the everyday, the noise and the silence of daily living. Jesus' message to his disciples is that he is found in the ordinary more often than in the extraordinary; he is found in the simple, not the complex.

He asks us to live on in his love. To help another is to help Jesus. To love others is to love Christ. To wash another's feet is to care for the God-man. This is where God is. Have we seen him lately?

JANUARY 6

The continuous reading from 1 John skips to chapter 5 (the continuous reading from chapter 3 begins again on Monday after Epiphany). The readings assigned for today and tomorrow reappear next week on the Friday and Saturday before Epiphany. Today's text, verses 5–13, begins by connecting the notion of conquering the world through belief in Jesus the "Son of God" (vs. 5) with true testimony. False teaching had obviously plagued the community. The author repeatedly emphasizes the true and honest "testimony" that Jesus, the Son of God is the source of salvation. We are to believe the truth of this testimony and are to commit ourselves in faith to Jesus as Son of God who invites us to share eternal life.

The text reiterates that Jesus came "through water and blood" (vs. 6), that is, as the central witness to the Father whose revelation and atonement are uniquely linked and cannot be separated. To understand Jesus as revealer is to understand him as redeemer. He began his mission as he was baptized by John and he completed it by his death on the cross when blood and water flowed from his side.

That this death is the source of "eternal life" (vs. 11) is clearly affirmed; that Jesus is the source of this "life" for us is equally clear. We are to believe this on the testimony God gave on his Son's behalf; this firm testimony compels us to put our faith and trust in Jesus.

Some commentators have seen here an oblique reference to the church's sacramental life as that which continues to manifest the presence of God with us through Jesus. The reference to "water" and "blood" is thus applied to baptism and eucharist as sacraments of initiation into the mystery that is Christ. Alternatively, the reference to "water and the blood" could itself be a reference to the eucharist through which we share in the divinity of Christ who came to share our humanity. The eucharist is the actualization of the whole paschal mystery, including the sufferings and death of Jesus. Hence, it is fitting that our belief in the eucharist contain the aspects emphasized in this passage—the entirety of Jesus' revelation and the mystery of his cross and resurrection. We who believe these mysteries of faith are given a share in "eternal life" (vs. 13) through liturgy; through belief "in the name of the Son of God" (vs. 13) and all it implies, we gain access to the Father and therefore share his "life."

The responsorial psalm, Psalm 147, praises God's revelation to Israel in choosing them and in revealing his "statutes and ordinances" to them (vss. 9–10). We identify with the uniqueness of Israel revealed here when we "praise the Lord" since through the proclaimed word of God at the liturgy we are drawn again and again into a unique relationship with God through Christ.

The gospel passage today breaks with the continuous reading of John to recount Jesus' baptism from Mark 1:7–11. This same text is used in the "B" cycle on the feast of the Baptism of the Lord (made all the clearer since the alleluia verse, Mark 9:6, from that liturgy can be used today). This passage recounts a most significant manifestation of Jesus for it marks the beginning of his mission—a mission preordained by God, which is the consequence of the incarnation. Actually, this text has two units: the first refers to John the Baptist's testimony to Jesus (verses 7–8, already seen as part of the gospel on the Second Sunday of Advent, "B" cycle) and the second refers to the baptism itself. John's self-effacement and role as the one who prepares for Jesus' coming is reaffirmed here as it was described during Advent. The baptism that Jesus will bring is performed by the power of the Holy Spirit (vs. 8) unlike John's which was a cleansing rite that looked to its fulfillment in the coming Messiah. John's ministry should not be downplayed, however, for even Jesus submitted to baptism in the waters of the Jordan (vs. 9). The fact that the Spirit descended on Jesus immediately after he came out of the water (vs. 10) is a parallel to the creation story in Genesis. Just as it was a "mighty wind [that] swept over the waters" in Genesis 1:2, so here it is God's spirit descending on Jesus to inaugurate a new creation, the result of his mission on earth. Similarly, the church relies on the continual action of the Holy Spirit so that she might remain faithful to a new creation in Christ (begun in baptism).

The meaning of the Greek text should be noted: the spirit came "into him" it did not merely come around or envelop him. This indicates a new life principle just as baptism is a new principle of life for the believer. The statement from the heavens: "You are my beloved Son. On you my favor rests" (vs. 11), draws on the familiar usage from Psalm 2:7 about sonship (which was already seen in Hebrews 1:5, the second reading on Christmas day) and on the usage of Isaiah 42:1 about the servant in whom God is well pleased. This skillful joining of texts points to Jesus as God's son and servant—in him these roles are joined; through him they are revealed to any who believe in him. From the perspective of a community that has celebrated Advent and Christmas with the book of Isaiah as a major focus, the usage of Isaiah 42:1 here and the reference to Isaiah 63:19 whereby the sky was rent in two (vs. 10) combine to emphasize the person and work of Jesus. We who have prayed in Advent, "that you would rend the heavens and come down" (Is 63:19), are to see in Jesus' baptism the fulfillment of our prayers and the beginning of his ministry among us as God's Son.

Celebration of the Eucharist

The introduction to the liturgy could note the importance of the liturgy as the means for our coming into and experiencing God's presence begun at baptism and continually renewed at the eucharist.

The second set of sample invocations for the third form of the penitential rite would serve well today since it refers to Christ's ministry, his presence at the eucharist, and his coming again with salvation for his people.

The option of using the text adapted from Mark 9:6 (from the feast of the Baptism of the Lord) as the alleluia verse (Lect., no. 21) would be an appropriate choice today.

Petitions for a deeper sense of our dignity as God's sons and daughters because of our baptism, for a commitment to knowing and living according to the truths of our Christian faith, and for all baptized Christians that the Spirit would make us one family in faith would be appropriate today.

Of the Christmas prefaces, the second about Christ restoring unity to creation would be appropriate since the gospel recounts the event that began Jesus' public ministry.

Number 20 of the prayers over the people about the gifts we receive in Christ and the riches of his grace would be an appropriate conclusion to this liturgy in which we have been endowed once more with God's Spirit, through word and sacrament.

Reflection—"Baptized into Mission"

Today's gospel reminds us of an important aspect of Jesus' and of our baptism: when we are baptized, we were initiated into the task and mission of witnessing to God in the world. At our baptism, we received the same Spirit for the same reason. At the end of the eucharist, we are often challenged to "go in peace to love and serve the Lord," reminding us of the mission and witness aspects of the liturgy. No Christian prayer is ever self-contained; all Christian prayer should have its effect in the lives of those who participate. The gift of the Spirit at baptism is a gift to be shared and made manifest throughout our lives.

The gift of being related to God as sons and daughters endowed with the Spirit carries with it a heavy responsibility. Yet, precisely because we are endowed with the Spirit, we are able to face this challenge as did Jesus. Like him we are "baptized into mission."

JANUARY 7

Today's first reading is the conclusion of 1 John. The passage (5:14–21) can be divided into two parts, the first dealing with confidence in God who hears our prayer (vss. 14–17) and the reality of sin in the early Christian community (vss. 18–21). While the first section is not limited to intercessory prayer, certainly this text was among those which the early fathers often used to draw out the Christian application of the prayer of petition found in Jewish liturgical prayer. We ask because we are in need, and asking is an act of faith in the God who cares for all he has created. However, there is more in intercessory prayer than an act of humility. It is a sign of trust that God's ways are right and that what we request will be granted only if it accords with God's will (vs. 14). The example of Jesus whose complete trust in the Father led him to death on a cross is the model of the Christian who prays. In addition, it is clear that the author here emphasizes prayer for one another in the Christian community, especially for those in sin (vs. 16). Thus, there is an efficacy in prayer that we cannot determine and which relies on the confidence we have placed in God when we join in the act of praying. Christian prayer is thus an act of submission to God's will. It involves the needs of all people with whom we pray. It is not self-concerned or self-serving.

In the second part of the text, the author treats the importance of remaining true to our faith in Jesus and to refrain from any kind of idol worship (which apparently has crept in to the Christian community, see verse 21). The author repeats the theme of avoiding the "world" and of remaining faithful to our identity as those "begotten of God" (vs. 18). He then reiterates that the Lord Jesus is truly the Son of God, through whom we have access to the Father. He repeats (from verse 13) that Jesus "is true God and eternal life" (vs. 20). This enables us to pray to the Father as we ought; through Christ, we are truly God's daughters and sons. The author challenges us once more to live this identity in faith and prayer.

This identification with God is reflected in the psalm response that follows: "The Lord takes delight in his people" (Ps 149:4). As God's people, we gather to pray and to grow in committing ourselves to continue the incarnation of God among us by the ways we manifest his love in our lives.

The gospel of the wedding feast at Cana (Jn 2:1–11) has traditionally been interpreted as Christ's first "manifestation" in John's gospel. Like yesterday's text about the baptism of Jesus, this text about his first "sign" must be understood as the evangelist's way of revealing the public aspect of Jesus' ministry. John's main point is noted at the end where he states that through this "sign" Jesus revealed "his glory," and "his disciples believed in him" (vs. 11). These are key concepts for John. By using them in this early chapter, he invites our reflection on how we view the miracle as a sign of God's power and the extent to which we believe in the reality of the Word made flesh and share in his glory.

The fact that Jesus first states that his "hour" had not yet come (vs. 5) but then performs the miracle shows that John associates this "sign" with Jesus' death and resurrection, the definitive sign of God's power and glory. The disclaimer heightens our awareness that we ought to look toward this other central act as the key to understanding Jesus' mission. Another indication that this miracle looks beyond itself for its understanding is the simple fact that water becomes wine; what is nature's gift (water) becomes a rich symbol of human productivity (wine), which is a familiar sign of abundance in the scriptures. What Jesus provides for Cana's guests is thus a sign of what he will provide in his kingdom—the abundance of eternal life with the Father forever.

At this point in the liturgical year, the text should be associated with the manifestations of Christ's presence on earth, with the inauguration of his ministry, with his death and resurrection, and with the superabundant life shared by those who believe in him. It is one thing to recount this manifestation story—it is another to believe in the Lord who accomplished it. This same Lord continues to give us food and drink at the eucharist until we share in the eternal banquet in the kingdom of heaven.

Celebration of the Eucharist

The introduction to the liturgy could point to the Cana miracle as a manifestation of God's power which is operative among us especially when we gather for the liturgy. As a way of acknowledging our sin (consonant with the first reading), the first form of the penitential rite ("I confess") would be an appropriate option today.

For the alleluia verse, the use of number 1 of the choices (Lect., no. 212) quoting John 1 would be suitable today. Appropriate petitions today would involve those who are marginal to the church, those involved in prayer movements, those who work with basic Christian communities, and those who live the contemplative life in monasteries.

The third Christmas preface would be a good selection because of its reference to receiving "the gift of everlasting life," referred to at the end of the first reading. The paced and careful proclamation of the second eucharistic prayer today could serve as a way of making this liturgy simple in comparison with the expected festivity tomorrow, the Solemnity of the Epiphany.

An introduction to the Lord's Prayer that emphasizes its communal nature would serve to reiterate an important part of the lessons contained in the reading from 1 John.

Reflection—"Needs, Not Wants"

How often do we pray for what we want rather than for what we need? When I pray the prayer of petition do I ask for things to possess or for a break so I can get what I want, or for a situation to present itself so I can achieve what I think is my fondest desire? Are these things I really need?

That we pray for what we want is human; that we get what we need is from God. Today's instruction from the first letter of John assumes that divine grace is more important than mere human motivation. The author states clearly that we do get what we need, what is in accord with God's will. It's that simple. Today's challenge concerns how we react to this instruction. Will it affect my prayer? Will I begin to look at life from the perspective of God's grace and will? When and if I (finally) choose to do so, then I will be able to subordinate my wants to my needs as I rely on God's decisions.

There is no guarantee that we will get what we want, especially because some of our wants can get in the way of what is really important in life. We are assured, however, that we will receive what we need to grow closer to God and to one another.

MONDAY, FROM JANUARY 2 TO THE EPIPHANY

Liturgy of the Hours

The scriptures at the office of readings from Monday through Thursday this week continue from the letter to the Colossians (begun on December 29). Today's text, 2:16–3:4, concludes the doctrinal section with verses 16–19 closely connected with the argument from 2:1ff. about false teaching. Here Paul confronts practices that are contrary to Christian belief (vs. 16) and which are of no avail (vs. 17). The source of growth and union with God for the Christian comes from Christ through whose paschal sacrifice we gain access to the Father. While repudiating false worship, the author does not imply that Christian worship and ascetical practices are of no avail; when done with proper motivation and when they influence the rest of our lives (see Romans 12:1ff.), they are important means (not ends in themselves) for experiencing the presence of Christ.

The last part of this passage (3:1–4) begins the exhortation section of the letter. The statement in 3:1 is an important link: "Since you have been raised up in company with Christ, set your heart on what pertains to higher realms where Christ is seated at God's right hand." The glory and honor which Christ shares with the Father is offered to us through the liturgy. To celebrate the liturgy implies a commitment to putting aside anything that leads us from Christ for if we have died in him (vs. 3) then we judge the things of this earth to be of no avail. We should "be intent on things above rather than on things of earth" (vs. 2). By continuing to choose what leads only to God, we will become more and more like him and one day be called to sit at his right hand in glory (vs. 4). In pleading for ethical conduct and proper judgment, Paul offers us hope and encouragement from the fact that we share in Christ's paschal sacrifice. Significantly, the pivotal verses joining doctrine and ethics are also used as the responsory to this text (3:1–2).

The patristic text from St. Basil's work on the Holy Spirit explores the meaning and implications of leading the Christian life. The author unites our actions, prayer, and common life as three elements which rely on the presence of the Spirit within and among us. Then, he explores the more theological question of the relationship among the Father, Son, and Spirit. This text helps to draw out the Trinitarian aspects of what is celebrated in this season of the Incarnation. What we share through Christ was ordained by the Father and is made possible through the power and instrumentality of the Spirit.

The short reading at morning prayer from Isaiah (49:8–9) uses the strong image of being freed from bondage and imprisonment as a way of appreciating the power of God manifest to Israel. When read for our instruction in this season, it invites us to acknowledge the bondage in our own lives and the things that prevent us from experiencing the fullness of God's presence.

The paradox of Christmas is recalled in the antiphon to Zechariah's canticle by the careful juxtaposition of the helpless/glorious, humbled on earth/eternal in heaven. The intercessions use significant titles of Christ, such as new Adam and Sun of justice, which help draw out the implications of the incarnation and our identification with the Christ.

The collect (used at all the hours and at mass today) is a combination of a text from the Leonine and the Old Gelasian Sacramentaries. It establishes our union with God in glory through Christ, and it asks that we experience this mystery here on earth.

At evening prayer, the reading from Colossians (1:13–15) deals with the effects of the incarnation for it assures us that God has rescued us from darkness and has granted the fullness of redemption in his Son. This text (with its responsory about the Word becoming flesh) is juxtaposed with the antiphon to Mary's canticle, addressing Christ as the "radiant child" who brought "healing to human life."

Celebration of the Hours

The invitatory of the season, "Christ is born for us; come let us adore him," would be a fitting introduction to the hours today. The use of Psalm 24 to accompany it would be a reminder that we have to put aside sinful ways if we are to receive the fullness of God's grace through the incarnation.

If a longer text is desired at morning prayer, extending the reading to include Isaiah 49:8–13 (or to 19) would be suitable. If the morning prayer intercessions are adapted, the Christological titles should be retained, especially the significant title "new Adam" found in the introduction and in the fourth petition. The Lord's Prayer could well be introduced by that formerly used at mass, itself containing important titles for Christ: "Taught by our Savior's command and formed by the Word of God we dare to say. . . ."

At evening prayer, the extension of the 1 Colossians reading to include verses 13–20 would form a logical unit. Since the intercessions are relatively brief and the alternate response is the theologically significant *Kyrie, eleison,* these can be used as presented with additional (brief) petitions for more needs.

TUESDAY, FROM JANUARY 2 TO THE EPIPHANY

Liturgy of the Hours

The first reading at the office of readings continues from Colossians (3:5–16) concerning the Christian life. The foundation of moral living is baptism. When listing the things that the baptized should do to reflect their relationship with God in Christ, Paul emphasizes baptism: "what you have done is put aside your old self with its past deeds and put on a new man" (vss. 9–10). In characteristic Pauline fashion, we are reminded that our new life principle is Christ, not our "natural" inclinations or our "flesh" (vss. 5–9). All impurity or greed must be put aside. The center of our lives is Christ.

The second part of the text (vss. 12–16) concerns the practice of virtues (as has been seen in the commentary for this text on the feast of the Holy Family) and is introduced by verse 11 about our unity in Christ that is so profound that it eliminates any divisions in the community. The familiar Pauline metaphor of the body may be understood here (as is clearly stated in 1 Corinthians 12, and as is implied in Romans 12 and Ephesians 4) where there is no longer Jew or Greek, slave or free—familiar ways of symbolizing differences in the community. Now any differences reflect the variety inherent in the body of Christ; they need not cause separation, jealousy or a stratified society. With Christ as the center, all are equally dependent on him and equally redeemed by him.

The patristic text from St. Augustine's treatise on John deals with the relationship between love of God and love of neighbor. In Augustine's words, "love of God is the first to be commanded, but love of neighbor is the first to be put into practice." Until we meet God face to face in the kingdom, it is our neighbor who (for better or worse) reveals God to us and who deserves our love and respect. As we journey through life with each other, the saint urges us to "support, then, this companion of your pilgrimage if you want to come into the presence of the one with whom you desire to remain forever." This passage draws out some of the important implications of how God reveals himself to us in daily life especially through other people.

At morning prayer, the scripture text from Isaiah (62:11–12a) concerns the restoration of Zion. When read at this season, it reminds us that our savior has come in Jesus and that it is through the paschal mystery that we can be called the "holy people, the redeemed of the Lord." The antiphon to Zechariah's canticle recalls the important place which the Johannine prologue plays in our appreciating the incarnation. The incarnation of the Word among us makes us sharers in God's "grace and truth" for it is from Christ's fullness that we have received the gift of God's love. This gift is to be shared in love for each other (as Augustine notes so carefully in the text at the office of readings).

The intercessions at morning prayer continue the practice of using the various titles of Christ as ways to acclaim him and to ask him to intercede for us. The alternate response, "Be with us, Emmanuel," reminds us that we must be attentive to Christ with us especially at the liturgy.

Today's collect, from the Leonine Sacramentary, recalls the reality of Christ's having become "like us in all things but sin." In this prayer, we ask that "we who have been reborn in him [may] be free from our sinful ways."

At evening prayer, the reading from 1 John (1:5b–7) recalls and reiterates the light symbolism so central to the celebration of the Christmas liturgy. The challenge John puts before us is to walk in the light of Christ and thereby to reflect God's presence in our world.

The antiphon to the Canticle of the Blessed Virgin is a particularly exuberant text (referring to dancing and rejoicing in the presence of the Lord) because "eternal salvation has appeared on the earth." This serves as a reminder that it is not so much the birth of the infant Jesus but the birth of the savior that we commemorate at Christmas. Through this commemoration, we experience his salvation. This is reflected in the introduction to the intercessions at this hour.

Celebration of the Hours

The use of the verse before the readings at the office of readings would serve as an appropriate invitatory today: "The Son of God has come to give us understanding—That we might know the true God." When accompanied by Psalm 100, this unit provides a particularly joyful and theologically significant introduction to the hours.

Should a longer reading be desired at morning prayer, the text provided can be expanded to Isaiah 62:6–12a. If the intercessions are rewritten, the Christological titles provided should be kept where possible since each of them affords significant insight about who the Lord is who was made flesh in the incarnation. The alternate response would likely be easier to use if the order is reversed to read "Emmanuel, be with us."

At evening prayer, the suggested reading could be expanded to include 1 John 1:5b–10 as a more logical unit; however, if this is thought to be too close to the reading assigned for the feast of the Holy Innocents, 1 John 1:5–22, then an alternate might be chosen.

Because of the particularly joyful antiphon to Mary's canticle, an especially festive setting for singing the Magnificat should be chosen.

The balance established in the intercessions about Christ as the head of the church, the union of the human and divine in him, his role of mediation, and the new era of salvation begun in him should be retained even when the intercessions are adapted.

Tuesday, from January 2 to the Epiphany   267

Liturgy of the Hours

The scripture reading at the office of readings continues from Colossians (3:17–4:1), and concerns "the life of the Christian family" (subtitle). The first section was used on the feast of the Holy Family (see above for commentary on verses 17–21) and concerns the deference family members should show one another. The next section (vss. 22–4:1) deals with the social institution of slavery which Paul accepts but to which he gives limited endorsement. That slaves should be subservient is clearly asserted; but Paul contends that this obedience is due out of respect for the Lord not just to please their masters. The work slaves do is to be endured for the sake of God, not for the sake of their masters. In fact (as stated in verse 11), Paul understands that all people, including slaves, share the dignity of being freed by Christ and subject only to his laws. The author deftly shifts metaphors in verse 24 and asserts that we are all slaves of Christ, bound to his will. We lead our lives in submission to him and in deference to one another. In the last verse, Paul specifically asks slave owners to "deal justly and fairly with your slaves" (vs. 1) lest the situation of slavery become an excuse for subjection and abuse.

The second reading from Maximus the Confessor is one of the few by this seventh-century author in the office of readings. A proponent of orthodox Christian beliefs in the face of the Monothelite heresy (about Christ's human will), Maximus emphasizes our share in the life of Christ and the importance of deepening our faith in this mystery. He states: "The Word of God, born once in the flesh . . . is always willing to be born spiritually in those who desire him." Hence, we who are graced by his incarnation are to live the virtuous life of Christ so he is manifest through us. Through faith, we know that God has acted in Christ. Hence, the importance of the conclusion to the reading: "Faith alone grasps these mysteries. Faith alone is truly the substance and foundation of all that exceeds knowledge and understanding." Through faith, we come to know and understand the infinite love of God made flesh in Christ.

The scripture reading assigned for morning prayer from Deutero-Isaiah (45:22–23) recalls God's promised salvation to Israel despite their bondage and exile. What the Lord promises in this text has been fulfilled in Christ; we are drawn into this mystery through the liturgy.

Christ's mediatorship is recalled and given careful expression in the antiphon to Zechariah's canticle, which states that Christ "took upon himself our wounded nature and became the first new man." We share in the new creation established in Christ despite the fact that we remain "in the flesh" of our human nature. Through Christ, our human nature takes on immortal value. The patristic adage that the flesh is the instrument of salvation is important to recall here. We were redeemed because Christ took on our human nature, not because he disdained it for a spiritualist redemption. When we live according to God's will and in his grace, we come to share his divinity even now as we live in the body and have human needs and desires. These can all be transformed through Christ and made new in his grace.

Today's collect, taken from the Hadrianum Sacramentary, draws on the light symbolism of the prologue to John's gospel. Here we acknowledge Christ as our light and the enlightenment (received in baptism) received anew in this Christmas season.

Celebration of the Hours

The use of the alternate verse from the office of readings would be a fitting invitatory verse today because of its reference to the Johannine prologue and its brevity: "In Christ was life.—And that life was the light of mankind." The use of Psalm 95, the traditional invitatory psalm, would be fitting today.

At morning prayer, the text from Isaiah could be expanded to 45: 18–25, thereby exploring more fully the meaning of the Lord as savior and restorer of wounded Israel. The intercessions at morning prayer could use some adjustment, specifically the awkward phrasing in the second petition ("uncreated justice") and in the fourth petition ("worthy of your companionship").

At evening prayer, a longer section from Romans 8 would help explore the full meaning of what is implied in the text presented. The use of the alternate response to the petitions ("Lord, have mercy") could aid in focusing attention on the petitions spoken by the leader. A sung response to this English text or *Kyrie, eleison* (as was suggested on Monday evening) would add a degree of solemnity without adding to the length of the liturgy.

Liturgy of the Hours

The last part of the letter to the Colossians (4:2–18) is the first reading at the office of readings today. The first section deals with prayer, especially the prayer of petition (vss. 2–4), the second section deals with the virtue of prudence (vss. 5–6), and the third section is Paul's farewell message to individuals and to the community (vss. 7–18). The author speaks of the importance of the prayer of petition, especially prayer for him as he witnesses from prison to the power of Christ (4:3–4).

He concludes by urging them to be prudent in dealing with "outsiders" (vss. 5–6) and he sends greetings to coworkers in the community at Colossae. Despite his imprisonment for the sake of Christ (vs. 3), Paul maintains a strong sense of hope, the same hope which he noted above as a virtue that should mark the lives of Christians (3:4).

The second reading from a sermon of St. Augustine concerns the paradox of the incarnation and the importance of our annual commemoration of Christmas. Augustine stresses the importance of the paradox of Christ's taking on human flesh to show that we, in our human nature, experience the life of God with us in Christ. Despite this mystery of the human-divine interchange and of our participation in this mystery, the author clearly reiterates what is repeatedly expressed in the Advent liturgy—all is yet to be fulfilled at Christ's second coming.

Augustine reminds us that "we are not yet ready for the banquet of our Father, so let us contemplate the manger of Jesus Christ our Lord." Our celebration of Christmas is thus an important means to participate in God's life. Only in heaven will we be at rest in God; through the earthly liturgy, we come as closely as we can to the mystery of God revealed in Christ.

A certain allegorical interpretation of the reading from Wisdom (7:26–27) assigned for morning prayer would relate wisdom to Christ, whom we acknowledge as the "refulgence of eternal light, [and] the spotless mirror of the power of God" (vs. 26). Through wisdom, we come to experience God's life among us. Hence, the importance of the reference to creation in this text, the renewal of which is granted us through the Christmas celebrations.

The important notion of Christ's coming to redeem us and to reconcile us with each other is asserted in the antiphon to Zechariah's canticle: "The Lord has come to his people and set them free," and in the intercessions. This is also reaffirmed in the collect, taken from the old Gelasian Sacramentary, in which we pray that we might be brought to the glory promised by the Father.

At evening prayer, the scripture reading from 1 John (5:20) repeats the text from the first reading at the eucharist on January 7, about Christ, the Son of God and about our participation in the life of God through him. The reality of Christ's human birth and life among us is emphasized in the Magnificat antiphon and in the intercessions which use the details of Christ's childhood and birth as ways of describing our need for God.

Celebration of the Hours

The verse before the readings at the office of readings provides a fitting alternate invitatory today with its reference to Christ as the "true light" who "gives light to all people." The use of Psalm 24 as the invitatory psalm would be appropriate since it refers to the "king of glory," the "Lord," and the "God who saves" us.

At morning prayer, should a longer text from the book of Wisdom be desired, the use of 7:24–30 would be suitable. The use of the alternate response to the intercessions, "Lord, save us by your birth," is a significant formula and recalls the prayers at the final commendation of the funeral liturgy where our prayer is based on the events of Jesus' life, death, and resurrection. Fittingly, the emphasis here is on our experience of salvation through Christ's incarnation.

At evening prayer, the longer text, 1 John 5:14–20, can provide a context in which to situate the important verse assigned to this hour. The introduction to the intercessions could be rewritten to eliminate any awkward phrasing. An introduction to the Lord's Prayer that mentions the "Son of God" as found in the reading from 1 John would be a subtle way of reiterating this title and its importance throughout this season.

FRIDAY, FROM JANUARY 2 TO THE EPIPHANY

Liturgy of the Hours

The selection of Isaiah 42:1–8 as the scripture text for the office of readings helps to set the context for the Solemnity of the Epiphany next Sunday. This first servant song will be repeated in the office of readings on the feast of the Baptism of the Lord. While in its original setting, this poem referred to a prophet or to the whole of Israel; in its Christian liturgical usage, it clearly refers to Christ, his attributes, and mission. The use of "my servant" and "my spirit" in the first verse recalls the mission of Jesus as the one who did his Father's will and as one endowed with God's spirit (seen clearly at his baptism) so that he could do his Father's will. The universality of Christ's mission is noted in the reference to the nations receiving his justice. This servant will execute his role quietly and humbly (vss. 2–3).

The act of creation and re-creation by God is noted in verse 5, where the prophet explicitly recalls the scene in Genesis when God's spirit brought order to chaos on the earth. This same life-giving power will re-create and reform Israel according to the word spoken by his prophets. The power of this creative word is noted in the examples that follow (vs. 7): it will open the eyes of the blind and the ears of the deaf and it will bring prisoners out of confinement. To allow this to occur, however, those who receive the word must be open to it and allow it to challenge every aspect of their lives.

The second reading from a sermon of St. Gregory of Nazianzus will also be used on the feast of the Baptism of the Lord. In it the parallel between John the Baptizer and Jesus is set up, the one doing God's will by administering baptism, the other equally responsive to God's will by accepting baptism to inaugurate his mission. The parallel is then extended to refer to Jesus and all the baptized who, like him, have come forth from these life-giving waters as a new creation freed from sin and enabled to bear witness to the Lord. The author makes the direct application to all Christians, that radiant in the light of Christ, and freed from sin, they should imitate their Lord.

The choice of these two readings points to the church's concern to lead us to appreciate what will occur in the liturgy on the Epiphany and on the Baptism of the Lord.

This same servant motif is seen in the passage selected for reading at morning prayer from Isaiah (61:1–2a) (which text is used tomorrow at the office of readings, Isaiah 61:1–11). Luke's use of this text in the scene in the synagogue at Nazareth (Lk 4:18–19) shows how the evangelists relied on such texts to emphasize the beginning of Jesus' ministry.

The antiphon to Zechariah's canticle acclaims Jesus as the one who came "through blood and water"—a reference to the text of

1 John 5 about the three witnesses of spirit, water, and blood. The reality of Jesus' incarnation and sacrificial death is thus alluded to here.

As the introduction to the intercessions states, we acknowledge that the Word of God "existed before the creation of the universe yet was born in time." Aware of the sustaining presence of God with us through the liturgy, we make our needs known to him and ask his guidance as we seek to do his will.

The collect today from the Hadrianum Sacramentary uses light imagery to remind us of our dignity as the baptized (who have been brought from darkness into the light of Christ) and of how we seek to share more fully in the glory and splendor of Christ our savior.

At evening prayer, the selection of Acts 10:37–38 once again reminds us of the centrality of Jesus' baptism as the event that inaugurated his public ministry. It also reminds us of the responsibilities placed on all who share Christian baptism to continue his work of witnessing to the Father on earth—to continue "doing good works" and aiding all who are tempted to follow the devil rather than the Lord's ways.

The divine sonship which identifies Jesus as the unique revelation of the Father is noted in the antiphon to the Magnificat. By extension, we can say that all the baptized share in this unique status as God's sons and daughters through Christ. Baptism in his name frees us from sin; where God is there can be no sin.

Celebration of the Hours

The use of the alternate verse, "sing to the Lord and bless his name.—Proclaim his saving love day by day," would be a fitting introduction to the hours today, especially when understood as referring to the name of the Lord implanted within us at baptism, the "saving love" which sustains us throughout our lives. The use of Psalm 24 as the invitatory psalm would reiterate the importance of putting aside evil so that we may join the blameless who enter God's presence.

If a longer reading is desired at morning prayer, any or all of Isaiah 61:1–11 can be used. However, communities that celebrate the office of readings in common should be aware that this is the first reading at morning prayer tomorrow, hence another of the servant songs might be preferable, such as Isaiah 49:1–6 or 50:4–9. The use of a simpler response to the petitions at morning prayer, such as "Lord, hear us," would make this section of the liturgy shorter.

The use of a special introduction to the Lord's Prayer referring to this assembly as the baptized and chosen people of God would be appropriate. The use of number 14 of the prayers over the people as a conclusion to this hour would reiterate the fact that through baptism we share in the "mystery of redemption" and that through the liturgy we are confirmed in this mystery.

At evening prayer, the whole of Peter's speech, Acts 10:34–43, could be proclaimed if a longer reading is desired.

SATURDAY, FROM JANUARY 2 TO THE EPIPHANY

Liturgy of the Hours

Today's first reading at the office of readings from Isaiah (61:1–11) recalls the many times during Advent when Messianic prophecies were proclaimed to help us appreciate the mystery of Christ's incarnation in the flesh and his mission on earth. The universality of Christ's mission (emphasized in the Epiphany tomorrow) is amply set up by the reference in verse 4 to the new dwelling for Israel rising from the old, the "ancient ruins." From these ashes will come the full flowering of God's presence with his people, the new Israel, the community of all the baptized. The fact that the Lord will accomplish this extension of salvation (see verse 8, the covenant formula, "I, the Lord, love what is right . . . a lasting covenant I will make with them"), exemplifies what was promised to Abraham and his descendants (see verse 9). Through Christ, this privilege of being among God's chosen is granted to all who come to faith and are baptized. Hence, the importance of the acclamation with which the text ends: "As the earth brings forth its plants, and a garden makes its growth spring up, so will the Lord God make justice and praise spring up before all the nations" (vs. 11).

The responsory confirms the Christological interpretation of this passage by referring to John 8:42, "I have come forth from God and have come into the world." Christ's coming and ministry enables all peoples to share in the life of God.

The second reading from a sermon of St. Augustine recalls the very significant notion reiterated by many Church Fathers—that God became incarnate in Jesus so that all might become like God in

Christ. The paradox and utter gratuitousness of the intervention of God in human history is once again reaffirmed here. The reality of the incarnation is stressed by reference to the details of Jesus' human birth. These remind us that in whatever situation we find ourselves, Christ's presence enables us to act in a Godlike way and thus to reveal to all peoples the presence of God in our midst.

At morning prayer, the text of Isaiah 9:5, used at Christmas midnight mass, is repeated. It was the birth of the child Jesus, acclaimed under the titles mentioned here, that unites us with each other under the common fatherhood of God. We experience the saving power of God among us through the liturgical commemoration of the incarnation. We acclaim him in the antiphon to Zechariah's canticle as the one "whose kingdom will last forever." Through baptism, we are made members of his kingdom and we are governed by his rule.

The universality of Christ's salvation is noted in the introduction to the intercessions today with its citation of Psalm 98:3, "All the ends of the earth have seen the saving power of God." The intended unity of all peoples, the many presences of Christ with us, the importance of our actions as revealing God's presence with us and the power of God to transform all creation are all parts of the intercessions today. The alternate response, "Glory be to you, Lord Jesus Christ," appropriately reflects the acclamation of joy which the community of the baptized offers because of Christ's revelation in our midst.

The collect, taken from the Bergamo Sacramentary, is a fine example of a liturgical prayer. In it we are reminded of the "coming of Christ" among us born of the Virgin Mary, and of the destiny we share through him in sharing in the glory of the kingdom. The balance here between the fact of the human birth of Jesus and his eternal union with the Father offers a paradigm for us as we celebrate the Epiphany liturgy.

Celebration of the Hours

Since this is the last day for the Christmas seasonal invitatory, "Christ is born for us; come let us adore him," and because this text reflects what is found in the patristic text from Augustine and in today's collect, it would be a fitting introduction to the hours today. The use of Psalm 100 as the invitatory psalm would add an exuberant tone without adding to the length of the hours (which should be kept simple in comparison with the festivity to come tomorrow).

At morning prayer, Isaiah 9:1–6 could well serve as a longer reading. The use of the alternate response to the (proposed or adapted) petitions would be an important acclamation and affirmation of faith in Christ as Lord. If the petitions are rewritten, the formula established here should be held to so that aspects of Christ's life are used as the bases for our prayer. When clearly spoken (or sung), the collect today invites attention to the central mystery we commemorate through the Christmas liturgy—God taking on human flesh in a given time and place so that all times and places can be redeemed in him.

Chapter Seven

Christmas Season: Third Week

SOLEMNITY OF THE EPIPHANY

Liturgical Context

Liturgical tradition has emphasized three events that comprise the full manifestation ("epiphany") of Christ; "Today the star leads the Magi to the infant Christ; today water is changed into wine for the wedding feast; today Christ wills to be baptized by John in the river Jordan to bring us salvation" (Magnificat antiphon, Evening Prayer II). The reformed liturgy has separated these three events. Today the visit of the Magi is emphasized. Next Sunday is the commemoration of the baptism of the Lord. On the Second Sunday in Ordinary Time, "C" cycle, the gospel text is of the wedding feast at Cana.

Trying to discover the exact origins of the Epiphany feast presents historical and liturgical problems. In ancient Egypt, the time of the winter solstice was celebrated as the turning of the year and a time of new beginnings. This pagan background forms part of what we still commemorate on Epiphany—new beginnings through the incarnation. In Eastern liturgical tradition, this day was the commemoration of the Lord's baptism and his manifestation as Son of God. In its early evolution, it was an important festival for the celebration of baptisms everywhere except at Rome. Also part of this feast concerned the visit of the Magi to the infant Jesus.

The themes for the feast from liturgical tradition include the nativity of Jesus, the baptism of Christ, the commemoration of the Cana miracle, and the transfiguration (as itself a turning point in Jesus' life after which he set forth for Jerusalem to suffer and die). This richness is reflected in today's readings and prayers. It should be recalled so that the visit of the Magi is understood to be only part of what is celebrated today.

The assigning of Epiphany to a Sunday (instead of January 6) has been debated. Some maintain that this derogates from the primary emphasis of Sunday as the day of the Lord's resurrection, but this arrangement gives the majority of Christians an opportunity to experience the fuller meaning of the incarnation commemorated today. The manifestation of Christ to Eastern astrologers is highly symbolic—all peoples are now numbered among God's chosen. Those who respond form the body of Christ, the communion of the baptized. Notions of universality, incorporation into the church by baptism, and continuing to search for God are important aspects of today's feast. The glory of God has appeared in Christ. His light illumines our way to God and his grace makes us God's daughters and sons.

Liturgy of the Eucharist

Much of today's mass formula is retained from the former usage of the Roman rite. Malachi 3:1 is adapted at the beginning of the liturgy to acclaim the "Lord" and "ruler" whose kingship we revere and whose power is manifest in Christ.

In the opening prayer, the extension of salvation to all peoples is reflected in the first phrase (of the Latin original) which speaks of the revelation of Christ as the light of all nations. We pray that we who know God by faith in Christ may come to the fullness of sharing his glory in the kingdom forever. In faith, we acknowledge Christ as the Messiah who has reconciled us with the Father.

Isaiah 60 is the source for the first reading at mass (vss. 1–6) and at the office of readings today (vss. 1–22). This chapter is very much in the spirit of those which immediately precede it in Deutero-Isaiah. The author knew of the destruction of Jerusalem and offered a message of hope. This text has been an important part of the church's liturgical tradition surrounding Epiphany because of its many possible applications to the incarnation. These begin in the first verse with the reference to the "light" that shines for all the peoples (vs. 2). All nations will walk by the brilliance of this light (vs. 3), a possible reference to the universality of salvation, and "kings [shall walk] by your shining radiance" (vs. 3), a possible application to the Magi whose journey to adore the infant Christ makes them radiant with the light they thus experience. While the central focus of the envisioned unity of all peoples is Jerusalem (vs. 4), a Christian interpretation would make Christ the source of all unity and the fullness of life. Where the "wealth of nations" formerly was brought to the holy city, the Magi bring the wealth of the world to Christ, the source of all true wealth and salvation.

By using characteristic Isaian paradox and contrast, the author notes that the violence Israel experiences will be changed into peace (vs. 18) because of the light that overcomes the darkness of this world (vs. 20). The true origin of this peace and light is the Lord who will visit his people. For the Christian church to celebrate the Epiphany is to commemorate the end of violence, darkness, and hatred and the inauguration of God's reign of peace, light, and harmony.

The responsorial psalm today, Psalm 72, will be used on Tuesday, Wednesday, and Thursday of this week to emphasize the wide expanse of God's mercy through his Son. In the Lord, we acknowledge that "justice" and "peace" (vs. 7) have been established on the earth. The visit of the Magi can be understood in the reference to the kings offering gifts (vs. 10) and in the acclamation that "all kings shall pay him homage, all nations shall serve him" (vs. 11).

The second reading from the letter to the Ephesians (3:2–3, 5–6) deals with what the author calls the "mystery" of God's secret plan, that both Gentile and Jew are now co-heirs of the promise once reserved to Israel (vs. 6). That Paul's ministry is both unique and essential is clearly attested in the beginning verses (vss. 2–3). His place is unique since he was a militant law observer who came to believe that Christ is the fulfillment of all such external observances and the source of true life.

The gospel acclamation, taken from the text to follow (Mt 2:2), draws on the light symbolism of this time of year. For the Magi to have seen the "star" in the East and to have followed it implies their faith in this mysterious way that God reveals himself to us. For us to follow this star means that we commit ourselves to following and to living according to the light of Christ.

The gospel account of the Magi's visit, Matthew 2:1–12, parallels the shepherds' visit recounted in Luke's gospel. Each evangelist shows that these visitors come and pay homage to Jesus, and then return home. They receive the vision of God manifest in Christ and return home changed and charged to live by his light. By following the brightness of a star, these astrologers find Jesus; but that light pales in comparison with the light who is Christ himself. To the eyes of faith, no illumination or brilliance can compare with the illumination and brightness we share through Christ's manifestation in human flesh.

What is almost shocking—thereby making it an essential part of this story—is the fact that those who come to adore Christ are foreigners, untrained in the word of God or in the law. Those "prepared" for the coming of the Messiah are unprepared to surrender to him; those who were unprepared are drawn to him in faith. This makes the comparison between the Magi and Herod (vss. 3–10) all the more poignant. These astrologers inquired of Herod's associates where the Messiah was to be born so they could worship him, when it should have been those schooled in the law who knew well the path to the newborn king. One application is clear. Religious observance or understanding of the law is itself no guarantee that our faith is as strong as it should be or that we truly believe in the presence of God with us. Knowledge should lead to submission to God. Herod and his associates did not have this humility. Paradoxically, it is the foreign kings who submit to the Lord and come to acknowledge him as the promised Messiah.

What is noted briefly in the gospel about the kings offering gifts (vs. 11) has often been used in the liturgy to specify the homage paid to Jesus. It is used in the prayer over the gifts to draw a parallel between the Magi's homage and the eucharistic sacrifice. Through the eucharist, we offer to the Father the very same sacrifice that Christ offered while on earth—his obedient life, submission to death on a cross, and his resurrection to new life. Hence, we acknowledge that while we do not offer gold, incense, and myrrh as did the Magi, our offering is the perfect sacrifice of Christ to the Father. As Messiah and Lord, we acknowledge him in faith; as sacrifice and spiritual food, we receive him at the eucharist.

The proper preface for the Epiphany is assigned for proclamation today, a text taken from the Leonine and Old Gelasian Sacramentaries. This traditional text draws on the light symbolism of the feast and states simply;

"Today you revealed in Christ your eternal plan of salvation
and showed him as the light of all peoples.
Now that his glory has shone among us
you have renewed humanity in his immortal image."

We receive the light and glory of God through Christ; through him we are renewed and remade in God's image and likeness.

The proper section of the Roman Canon for today reiterates the "glory" aspects of this feast by stating: "we celebrate that day when your only Son, sharing your eternal glory, showed himself in a human body." The paradox of the incarnation is thus reaffirmed.

The light symbolism already seen in the gospel acclamation is reiterated in the communion antiphon, again quoting Matthew 2:2 about seeing the star and coming to worship the Lord. This same symbolism is found in the prayer after communion (the traditional text of the Roman liturgy) in which we ask that the light from heaven shine on us so that we may grow in knowledge and love of the sacred mysteries we have just celebrated. Like the prayer over the gifts, this text capitalizes on the relationship between themes of this feast and the eucharist. Through the eucharist, we share in the light and life of Christ, manifest today to all nations in the person of the astrologers from the East.

Celebration of the Eucharist

Because this solemnity and next Sunday's feast of the Baptism of the Lord are essential parts of the Christmas cycle, the decor used since Christmas should be retained through next Sunday, even though Christmas decorations are already disappearing from stores and homes.

The use of incense is always an option for the entrance, the gospel procession, and the presentation of the gifts. It would be appropriate to use incense at these places today to demonstrate symbolically what is expressed in the gospel about showing reverence for Christ by offering incense to him.

The action of presenting the bread and wine at the procession of the gifts should be emphasized today as a way of recalling the reverence the Magi showed to Christ by offering him gifts. Inviting a newly baptized adult or a newly arrived family to be part of this procession would demonstrate the wide embrace of the Christian community as it welcomes new members to the parish community.

The festive music from Christmas for the acclamations, and the "Glory to God," etc., should be used again today to help unify the liturgies of the whole season.

Since the feast of the Baptism will be celebrated next Sunday, to-day's introductory rites could be the third form of the penance rite with the same invocations of Christ used on Christmas instead of the blessing and sprinkling with holy water.

The gospel procession should be timed especially carefully today if incense will be used. A more elaborate musical setting for the gospel acclamation may well be needed to cover the action. A sung acclamation (brief) after the proclamation of the gospel would give more emphasis to the gospel and would help cover the movement of ministers back to their places for the homily.

If the sample intercessions of the Christmas season are used today, the introduction and concluding prayer should be rewritten since these apply more directly to Christmas itself. The universal nature of this prayer could be demonstrated by offering petitions in various languages (by a number of different people), reflecting the ethnic diversity of the community. The use of the Epiphany preface is prescribed today, as is the special section of the Roman Canon if it is proclaimed.

An introduction to the Lord's Prayer that emphasizes the gathering of all peoples into one body in Christ would reflect the universality of this feast. Titles of Jesus, such as Messiah, Lord, Son of God, Light of the nations, etc., would be fitting additions to the "Lamb of God" today. The use of the solemn blessing for Epiphany would be a fitting conclusion to the liturgy today, especially since it draws out the important light symbolism of the feast. Its last prayer, "May you too find the Lord when your pilgrimage is ended," recalls the journey of the Magi and the journey in faith of all who see in the infant Jesus the Messiah and Lord of all the nations.

Liturgy of the Hours

The antiphons at Evening Prayer I reflect Epiphany themes—the appearance of the Lord in human flesh (first) and as the King of kings whose light was manifested by a shining star (third). The use of the canticle from 1 Timothy (3:16) offers a succinct summary of the implications of the incarnation, that Christ was "manifested in the flesh" and that he who is now exalted in glory was "proclaimed to the pagans" and "believed in the world." These simple phrases underscore dominant themes of Epiphany, as do the verses from 2 Timothy (1:9–10) assigned as the reading. By the grace of God "made manifest by the appearance of our Savior," we are brought to life and share in eternal life with God. The antiphon to the Magnificat from Matthew 2 (to be proclaimed at the eucharist tomorrow) notes the light symbolism and gift-giving associated with this feast. The intercessions provided (which are also used tomorrow evening) draw on important titles of Christ: savior and king of the nations whose glory and justice are manifest to us today.

Today's special invitatory introduces the hours very simply: "Christ has appeared to us; come let us adore him." The first reading at the office of readings, Isaiah 60:1–22, was reviewed above as the first reading at the eucharist. The second reading from a sermon of St. Leo the Great contains a characteristic patristic way of using scripture quotations (especially Isaiah 60) to illuminate the meaning of today's feast. The gospel reference to the star that led the Magi is linked to Abraham's progeny who were to be as numerous as the stars in the heavens. This promise passed from the patriarch to Israel and then to all who believe in Jesus as the Messiah and Lord. St. Leo captures the full meaning of the feast by drawing on scriptural texts, from Abraham to the Magi. Through the brilliance of the shining star, all peoples will be called forth from their own darkness and sin to union with God through Christ, the light of the world.

The second part of the responsory states: "The Magi saw his star and rejoiced to lay their treasures at his feet. God's holy day has dawned for us at last; come, all you peoples, and adore the Lord."

These same sentiments are found in the psalmody at this hour, especially in the antiphons which invite us to adore and worship the Lord (second and third). The selection of Psalms 72, 96, and 97 is significant since the first is the responsorial psalm at the eucharist, the second speaks of the glory of the Lord's name, and the third speaks of the light shining forth for the just. Hence, these are clearly applicable to this feast of exaltation at the manifestation of Christ to all peoples.

Some of the same ideas are found in the antiphons at morning prayer, specifically the mention of the wise men offering their gifts (first), and the light and glory of the Lord coming through Christ (third). The Lord's kingship and triumph over the most adverse of circumstances is reflected in the scripture reading at morning prayer from Isaiah (52:7–10) (the same text proclaimed as the first reading on Christmas day). The antiphon to the Canticle of Zechariah is a most significant text since it adds a nuptial symbolism and intimacy to the feast: "Today the Bridegroom claims his bride, the Church, since Christ has washed her sins away in the Jordan's waters; the Magi hasten with their gifts to the royal wedding; and the wedding guests rejoice, for Christ has changed water into wine, alleluia." We the church are drawn into an intimate union with God through Christ, as intimate as bride and bridegroom. The nuptial imagery found in the Advent liturgy should be recalled here.

At Evening Prayer II, the themes of Christ's kingship establishing his reign of peace on the earth, and his coming as a light for all nations on earth are noted in the antiphons to the psalmody. Just as the scripture reading at morning prayer repeats a Christmas text, so the text assigned for evening prayer, Titus 3:4–5, is first proclaimed at the Christmas dawn mass. Significantly, verse 5 speaks of "the baptism of new birth and renewal by the Holy Spirit" that makes us children of God. As noted above, the text of the Magnificat antiphon brings together the three dominant themes that have marked the commemoration of the Epiphany in the Roman rite.

Celebration of the Hours

The text of the hymn that begins the hours should not limit the understanding of the Epiphany to the visit of the Magi. Themes of light, glory, and Christ's kingship should be reflected in the hymnody chosen.

If a longer reading is desired at Evening Prayer I, the text of 2 Timothy 1:6–14 (or vss. 9–14) would be suitable, as would the text of Titus 3:4–7 at Evening Prayer II. Since the intercessions provided are the same for Evening Prayer I and II, an adaptation at either hour would avoid unnecessary repetition. The use of a simpler response (such as "Lord, hear us") would be appropriate. The singing of the Canticle of the Blessed Virgin Mary would be appropriate because of the richness found in its antiphons today.

An introduction to the Lord's Prayer that addresses the universal aspects of this feast would be appropriate. As part of the dismissal, the use of the solemn blessing for the Epiphany would emphasize the solemnity of today's feast. Because of its traditional nature and because it summarizes much of Israel's experience of waiting for redemption, Psalm 95 would be a fitting invitatory psalm. At morning prayer, the psalms of Week I are assigned; however, another set of Sunday psalms can be chosen instead.

Since incense is mentioned in the gospel and since its use demonstrates reverence and honor during the liturgy, it might well be used at evening prayer during the Canticle of the Blessed Virgin (its traditional place) to add a certain solemnity.

Reflection—"The Work of Christmas"

Today's feast of the Epiphany and next Sunday's of the Baptism of the Lord stretch out the Christmas celebration, not to prolong the telling of the story, but to expand on the implications of the mystery of Christmas. What does it mean to celebrate and commemorate our new status as bearers of God's very life among us? What does it mean to be a co-heir, as Ephesians says, or a bearer of light, as Isaiah declares, or to take the place of kings to adore and bear the gift of Love Incarnate to each other? What has happened to the Christmas mystery even as we put aside trees, gifts, mangers, and holiday displays?

It is up to us to echo the *glory* song of the angel in the real life situations in which we live—to raise our voice in simple, direct affirmation of the values of life together, love enfleshed in our families, peace in this troubled world, and in gentle rebuke when life and love are so attacked as to be unrecognizable.

What happens when the light of God's love is unseen by so many? What about turning the beams of his love toward others, especially those "who sit in darkness/or the shadow of death"—the lonely, the aged, the troubled? It is there and then that we are to be beacons of the light of Christmas.

How many times in Christmas displays are we affected by the image of a shepherd and his simple life for his sheep? And how often do we like to hear that the Lord himself is a shepherd we call Good? What about our shepherding of each other—the marginal, the one lost, and not the ninety-nine already saved? Many do not feel the embrace of Christ's love. Is there something we are not doing, saying or being that discourages others who stand in need of the peace of Christ?

Amid all the "wisdom" of this age, there is still the need for affirming and proclaiming God's wisdom—that humility leads to true riches in him. That peacemaking is the message of our faith, not violent strategies to preserve man-made territories.

No, Christmas is not a one-day or even a twelve-day celebration. The dawn follows the silent night to remind us that every day and age needs to experience his redemption.

MONDAY AFTER EPIPHANY

Liturgical Context

The liturgy for the weekdays between Epiphany and the Baptism of the Lord continues to explore the meaning of the incarnation. At the eucharist, the chants and orations (except for the opening prayers) repeat texts that have already been used since Christmas. The readings at mass continue from 1 John and from selected passages relating the initial manifestations of Christ (gospel). At the office of readings, the continuous reading from the latter sections of Isaiah resumes; at morning and evening prayer, most selections repeat those used last week.

Liturgy of the Eucharist

The opening prayer, taken from the Old Gelasian Sacramentary, reflects motifs already seen in the Christmas-Epiphany cycle. The first part of the text reflects words especially emphasized on Epiphany—splendor, glory, and majesty. We ask that these, made flesh in Jesus, will shine on us and lead us through the darkness of this world to the "radiant joy of our eternal home." Johannine motifs are present here with the important eschatological note so dominant through Advent.

The first reading from 1 John 3:22–4:6 continues the text read on Jan. 5th and deals with three essential aspects of Christian living—keeping Christ's commandment to love, experiencing the Spirit in community and holding to correct teaching in the face of the anti-Christ. Some commentators state that testing the spirits (4:1) must be understood in light of a liturgical context where believers make a public declaration of their faith before the community and thus "confess" and "acknowledge" their belief in God. Since "every spirit who fails to acknowledge [Christ] does not belong to God" (vs. 3), the true Christian uses the liturgy as a prime occasion to declare allegiance to Christ and submission to his rule. This reading requires the two-pronged response to the revelation of God in Christ—love for one another and right belief in the God made visible, Christ the Lord.

The use of Psalm 2 as the responsorial psalm today continues the use of this important text in its Messianic sense. The statement about sonship (vs. 7) is all the more significant today when we understand the references to paying homage to the Lord (vs. 8) and all nations sharing in the heritage of God (vs. 8) through Christ as being essential parts of what Epiphany is all about.

According to some exegetes, today's gospel, Matthew 4:12–17, 23–25, should be understood as the real beginning of the gospel proper since it is the beginning of Jesus' preaching. Yet, an important point made by the evangelist is that Jesus' ministry involves both preaching and healing—words and deeds. To emphasize one without the other would not adequately reflect Jesus who established the kingdom through words and actions.

The shift in location from Nazareth to Capernaum (vs. 13) is significant as a way of setting the stage for Jesus' public ministry. Also, the citation of Isaiah 9:1 implies that Jesus is now to fulfill this prophecy and will bring light to those who wait in darkness for his redemption. The description of Jesus teaching in the synagogue and preaching about God's kingdom (vs. 23) is an especially important statement for a Jewish-Christian audience who would immediately identify Jesus as the one who ushers in the reign of God. Similarly, the cures noted (vs. 24) recall the Messianic prophecies read in Advent; these healings usher in the kingdom, they are not just individual physical healings. The reign of God has come in Jesus; it continues to be manifested where disciples love each other and act in his name.

Celebration of the Eucharist

The introduction to today's liturgy could relate the words and deeds of Jesus in his public ministry to our hearing his Word and sharing in the bread and cup of this eucharist as sources of healing and strength. Appropriate invocations for the third form of the penitential rite include "you raised the dead to new life," "you cured the sick and healed the infirm," and "you bring pardon and peace to the sinner."

For the alleluia verse, either number 1 or 2 of the options (Lect., no. 219) is fitting since each is taken from the text of the gospel (Mt 4:16, 23). The first concerns the light/darkness motif and is therefore more seasonal in nature; the second refers more specifically to Jesus' preaching and healing.

Appropriate intercessions would be that those who proclaim the one gospel might be united as one church, that those who suffer might have the faith to see this as a share in the sufferings of Christ, and that those who care for the sick and terminally ill might draw strength from the Lord Jesus.

The use of the Epiphany preface is suitable for celebration all week (although the Christmas prefaces are also permitted).The use of the second eucharistic prayer, proclaimed clearly and distinctly with appropriate (slight) pauses would be a good choice today (especially since the Roman Canon with its special Epiphany section was optional yesterday).

The use of number 7 of the prayers over the people, referring to receiving light, and asking for protection as we seek to live the mysteries just celebrated in devoting ourselves to doing good would be an appropriate choice.

Liturgy of the Hours

The first reading at the office of readings, Isaiah 61:1–11, repeats that assigned for Saturday before the Epiphany (see above). The second reading from St. Peter Chrysologus, a preacher contemporary with Leo the Great, offers his reflections on the three mysteries that mark the Epiphany: the Magi, the baptism of Jesus, and the Cana miracle. Regarding the gifts, he states: "As they [the Magi] look, they believe and do not question, as their symbolic gifts bear witness: incense for God, gold for a king, myrrh for one who is to die." What is especially significant is the author's treatment of and emphasis on the role of the Spirit in Jesus' baptism and the sacramental application of the Cana miracle to the eucharist. True to patristic interpretation and style, the author interprets these events that manifest the presence of the Lord Jesus as having enduring power and value. This enduring effect is properly understood as experienced in and through the liturgy.

At morning prayer, the Magi are cited in the antiphon to Zechariah's canticle as offering symbolic gifts to adore the Lord (recall the interpretation given them in the office of readings). The introduction to the intercessions uses the familiar text, Psalm 98:6, and applies it to Jesus: "All ends of the earth have seen Jesus Christ, the saving power of God." Themes reflective of Epiphany are reiterated in the petitions about unity, the presence of God in our midst, the revelation of God to us, and the power of God at work transforming all creation. The second petition is particularly significant since it brings together the presence of Christ in the Church and in its members, an indication of the important unity between the Church and the world accomplished in the incarnation.

At evening prayer, the reading is from 2 Peter (1:3–4) about our being "sharers in the divine nature" (vs. 4) through Christ; thus, it is a most appropriate selection on this day after Epiphany.

The antiphon to the Magnificat returns to the role of the Magi as those who followed the star and were filled with joy at seeing the Lord. The light of the star mentioned here is cited in the introduction to the intercessions and in the alternate response, evidence of the importance of the light symbolism throughout this season.

Celebration of the Hours

The invitatory verse today could be the verse before the readings at the office of readings since it specifies much of the theology of Epiphany: "The heavens proclaim the justice of God.—All nations shall see his glory."

It would be important to review the texts of the hymns to be sung at the beginning of the hours to see how well they reflect the Epiphany themes of light, glory, splendor, unity, as well as the manifestations of Christ at the visit of the Magi, at Cana, and at his baptism in the Jordan. To restrict these texts to the event of the Magi's visit is to limit the theology of these days after Epiphany.

At morning prayer, the scripture reading from Isaiah (9:5) repeats that used on Saturday; the extended text noted above or an alternate text would offer variety. The alternate response to the petitions at morning prayer, "Glory be to you, Lord Jesus Christ," leaves out the intercessory aspect of this prayer; hence, it might be replaced by another (such as "Lord, have mercy" whether sung or recited).

At evening prayer, the text of 2 Peter 1 could be expanded to include verses 3–11 if a longer text is desired. Among the intercessions provided, the fourth is about consecrated virgins. To help local communities specify its meaning, mention might be made of religious communities of men and women who serve in or are known in the area.

An introduction to the Lord's prayer that mentions Christ as our "light" would carry through on this theme as seen in the antiphon to the Magnificat and in the intercessions.

Reflection—"Presence, Action, and Prayer"

As the liturgy of this Christmas-Epiphany season takes a turn today toward emphasizing Jesus' public ministry, it is clear that he is actively engaged in teaching and healing—he speaks and his words have effect. By word and deed, he reveals the reign of God. But this is only part of the story. The same gospel that presents his message and that recounts his activity also recounts that he spent whole nights in prayer, and that he withdrew to quiet places to commune with his Father in heaven.

Even this Messiah-Lord had to have quiet times on earth so that he could experience the tranquility of spirit necessary for his deeds, actions, and activity. This offers a paradigm and model for us. Like Jesus, we must witness to the reality of God among us both by actions and by presence, as well as by personal prayer. Without regular recourse to personal prayer, our deeds can become self-centered philanthropy. Without regular acts of charity and service, our prayer can become a symptom of withdrawal and denial. Appropriately understood, our common witness to Christ must include presence, action, and prayer. Does it?

TUESDAY AFTER EPIPHANY

Liturgy of the Eucharist

The opening prayer is a brief but full expression of the mystery of the incarnation. We acknowledge that Jesus, the only-begotten of the Father, revealed himself in the flesh and thus became one of us. His miraculous act of humiliation and complete identification with our humanity enables us to have the confidence to ask that he transform and remake us according to his divine nature. The interrelationship between the divine and the human in Christ offers us the means whereby our human nature is graced and sanctified.

The first reading from 1 John (4:7–10) is a deceptively brief summary of our responsibility toward each other in love. The pivotal verse is the last where the author reminds his audience that love for each other is founded on God's prior and sustaining love for us. Christ, as the only begotten of the Father is the final and definitive revelation of God; in him and through his grace, we experience his love and are enabled to love each other. To love each other is possible only because God continues to reveal his love for us through his son. We are "begotten of God" as was Christ. In this relationship with God, we have received his infinite love and have been made a new creation in him. Christ came that we might have life (vs. 9); our response to this new life is to share Christ's love with each other.

The responsorial psalm repeats Psalm 72 used yesterday (also used tomorrow). It is an important reminder of the epiphany when we acknowledge Christ as our king who governs us with his justice.

The text of Mark 6:34-44 is another manifestation of the power of God at work in Jesus. A first level of interpretation reveals this as a miracle story, the feeding of the crowds with bread and fish. It is through faith that we understand this act of food multiplication as a sign of the reign of God and that God is manifest in this deed. Unlike the disciples who did not understand what was occurring (vs. 37), we are to believe in the miracle and put our trust in the Lord who thus showed his love for his people.

A second level of interpretation concerns the food given to Jesus' followers. Just as Israel relied on God for food and drink (manna and water) in the desert, so does the new people of God. The reference to this miracle taking place in a "deserted place" (vs. 35) can be taken to refer back to the Exodus. This text also has the additional significant detail that the bread left over filled twelve baskets (vss. 43-44) symbolic of the twelve tribes of Israel and twelve apostles. The Lord who provides is here depicted as one who supplies an overabundance. As the texts of Deutero-Isaiah reiterate, the Lord in whom we trust will more than supply our needs, he will give us an oversupply to show his great love.

The third level of interpretation concerns unmistakable eucharistic overtones. The use of bread and fish recalls the postresurrection meals of Jesus with his disciples, which meals continue in the church at the eucharist. The highly symbolic use of bread and fish, meaning sustenance and the presence of the Son of God would not have been lost on the primitive Christian community. The stylized language in verse 41 about Jesus raising his eyes to heaven, blessing, breaking, and giving the food recalls Jewish ceremonial meals (especially the Passover) and the primitive shape of the eucharist. These actions are recounted in the institution narrative in the eucharistic prayer. Hence, it can be asserted that this passage recounting Jesus' instructing his followers with his words (vs. 34) and with this food continues in the church's eucharistic practice.

Celebration of the Eucharist

The introduction to the liturgy could speak of how God feeds and nourishes us with his Word and sacrament at the eucharist as Jesus fed and nourished his followers in the gospel with his instruction and the meal of bread and fish.

The text of the second form of the penitential rite speaks about asking for the "mercy and love" of the Lord and a share in his salvation; this can be understood to mean that in the eucharist we find the Lord's grace, mercy, and love.

The use of number 2 for the alleluia verse (Lect., no. 219) would be appropriate since it speaks of Jesus preaching and healing. It can thus introduce the gospel about Jesus' teaching and feeding his followers.

The introduction to the intercessions could recall God's love for us in Christ; it is on this basis that we confidently pray for our needs, knowing that God will hear us. Petitions for the church, that she might always reflect the love of God to all peoples; for married couples, that they would grow stronger in their commitment to love; for the faith to perceive Christ present in all areas of our lives; and for the dead, who were once fed at the table of the Lord, that they might be seated at the banquet in the kingdom, would reflect today's scriptures.

Because of the eucharistic overtones of the gospel and specifically because of Jesus' taking bread, blessing it, breaking and sharing it, today would be a good time to review the customary way in which the eucharistic bread and wine are presented and how they are prepared for communion at the "Lamb of God." Reflecting on what ministers are involved in each, how they are chosen, and whether the same people perform these ministries each day might lead to inviting others to become involved in liturgical ministry.

The use of the Epiphany preface would be appropriate today because of its seasonal nature. At the dismissal, the use of number 1 of the prayers over the people, asking that God would "grant us in this life the good things that lead to the everlasting life you prepare for us," would be appropriate. The use of "Go in peace to love and serve the Lord" would itself be a subtle reiteration of the close connection between correct faith and sharing God's love reflected in the readings from 1 John.

Liturgy of the Hours

The first reading at the office of readings, Isaiah 62:1–12, has two parts (vss. 1–5, 6–12). The first deals with a "new name" (referred to in vs. 2), recalling the frequent use of a name change to indicate a new condition established by God (as in the cases of Abraham and Peter). Jerusalem had been called "forsaken" and "desolate" (vs. 4); from now on, it will be called God's "delight" and "espoused" (vs. 4). The bridal imagery is a significant indication of how God will overturn Israel's infidelity and bring her to union with himself (vs. 5).

The second section of the text is an exhortation to vigilance; Jerusalem will be rebuilt and the Lord will once again visit his people. The natural food and drink for which Israel toiled (vss. 8–9) will be kept in Jerusalem as a sign of God's favor and presence with them. The last verses (vss. 11–12) can be understood as providing background for the Christian affirmation that Christ is our savior. Just as the Lord came to dwell with his people to rebuild the holy city, so we acclaim the presence of the Lord to us so that we "shall be called the holy people, the redeemed of the Lord" (vs. 12).

The second reading from a sermon by St. Hippolytus once again draws out the baptismal implications of Epiphany. The Word himself is cleansed with water and the Holy Spirit as a model and example of how the Spirit endows us with life at baptism. The Spirit given to Jesus at his baptism is given to us at our baptism, enabling us to share Christ's dignity as begotten of God. The symbol of water becomes a rich symbol of rebirth for us just as it was through the water of the river Jordan that Jesus was cleansed and from which he emerged as source of life and light for all who believe in him.

This reference to immersion in water at baptism should not be missed; by imitating Jesus' descent into and emergence from the water, we are freed from our sins and are reborn to live his life on earth. Fittingly, the responsory capitalizes on the action of the Spirit and the relationship between John's baptism in water and Christian baptism in the Holy Spirit.

At morning prayer, the scripture reading from Isaiah (4:2–3) about the "branch of the Lord" can be interpreted to mean the survivors in Israel or the Messiah himself. When understood to mean the Messiah, this text offers us the hope (already affirmed during Advent) that we will receive a share in God's glory through Christ and thus become God's special possession.

The antiphon to the Canticle of Zechariah reiterates the gospel account of the wise men offering gifts to Christ. The intercessions begin with an important reference to the compassion of God (introduction) and the petitions contain important seasonal themes, such as being renewed through Christ's birth, the interchange between humanity and divinity, and the Word who was made flesh of the Virgin living in our hearts.

At evening prayer, the text of Ephesians 2:3b–5 reiterates that we have been freed from sin in Christ, our Lord.

The antiphon to the Magnificat draws on the familiar Christmas theme of light coming from light, and one of the petitions recalls the judgment theme frequently used in Advent. By sharing the light of Christ through baptism, we are initiated into the community that waits in joyful hope for the Lord's return when he will judge us according to how well we have lived out the implications of our baptism.

Celebration of the Hours

For the invitatory today, the use of the seasonal phrase, "Christ has appeared to us; come let us adore him," would be suitable. The use of Psalm 100 as the accompanying psalm would reflect the joy and festivity of this Epiphany week. Since Psalm 37 is arranged in three sections at the office of readings, one has the option of reciting it straight through with a significant pause at the beginning and (most especially) at the end.

If a longer reading is desired at morning prayer, the rest of Isaiah, chapter 4, could be proclaimed (Is 4:2–6). If the alternate response is used to accompany the intercessions, it might be better to change it to read, "by your birth, save us," a simpler version than the one offered.

At evening prayer, the use of Ephesians 2:1–10 as the reading would provide a fuller elaboration on what is stated in the text assigned about salvation through Christ. If the intercessions are rewritten, the third and fourth deserve better phrasing although the intentions themselves (for travelers and the deceased) are part of the church's traditional concerns in intercessory prayer.

Reflection—"Eucharist and Kingdom"

The liturgy of Christmas and Epiphany demonstrates clearly how Jesus is the fulfillment of all that Israel hoped for and dreamed of. All the signs that Isaiah prophesied to signal the inauguration of the kingdom of God are evident in Jesus' earthly ministry. But the promise-fulfillment motif leaves us with the question, "Where is the kingdom now?"

Today's gospel gives us more than a clue. It recounts a miracle story that Mark has edited to show us that the kingdom of God is among us here and now. The kingdom is present where communities share the Lord's banquet and grow in his grace. Like all indications of the kingdom while Jesus was on earth, this story uses signs—the signs of bread and fish. Viewed with the eyes of faith, these ordinary means of nourishment refer to Jesus' very body and blood shared at the eucharist.

It is for this reason that early liturgical tradition regarded the eucharist as the most important sign of the kingdom of God among us. Through the assembled community, the kingdom is present—where two or three are gathered God is with us. The hearing and preaching of the Word of God is a sign of God's kingdom—through it we learn of the values of the kingdom and the ways to establish it here on earth. Finally, the signs of bread broken and wine poured out give us life in Christ and in his kingdom. To the unbeliever these signs—people, word, and food—are what they merely seem to be: a gathering of individuals, a text proclaimed and food eaten. To the believer, however, these signs convey what they signify—the presence of God with us until the kingdom is finally complete at the end of time.

WEDNESDAY AFTER EPIPHANY

Liturgy of the Eucharist

The deceptively short opening prayer from the Old Gelasian Sacramentary is rich in theology. It opens by acknowledging God as the "light of all nations," a phrase that strongly emphasizes the theology of Epiphany. Just as our forefathers in the faith shared in the light of God through faith in Christ and sacramental initiation, so we baptized believers pray that we might share more completely in his "radiance" and "lasting peace." Implicit here is the understanding of eucharist as a renewal of baptism.

The first reading continues from 1 John (4:11–18), containing instruction and exhortation to the Johannine community. Jesus is the unique revelation of God; he is the "Son of God" and the savior of the world (vss. 15–16). We dwell in God when we confess our faith in Jesus as his Son. The second part of this text reminds us of the active presence of God with us: "God is love, and he who abides in love abides in God, and God in him" (vs. 16b). This abiding love gives us hope and confidence on the day of judgment; it casts out any fear in our relationship to God (vs. 18). This hopeful and confident text is all the more significant today as we look to the Lord's baptism on Sunday and the renewal of our identification with Christ in baptism.

The responsorial psalm is once more taken from Psalm 72. The inclusion of verse 10 is a particularly poignant reminder of the fact that Epiphany celebrates the unity of all peoples in Christ:

"The kings of Tarshish and the Isles shall offer gifts;
the kings of Arabia and Seba shall bring tribute."

These names and places take on a highly symbolic function at the liturgy as they represent all peoples now as members of God's family through Christ.

The gospel from Mark (6:45–52) continues the passage read yesterday. It is another manifestation story whose main point concerns the disciples' lack of comprehension about who Jesus is and his role as a Messiah who must first suffer before entering into his glory. That this is a "manifestation" story is clear from the reference in verse 48 to walking on water, referring back to Old Testament theophanies. This text is an appropriate choice for these days when the liturgy explores the many manifestations of Christ.

The most telling statement about the disciples, that their "minds were completely closed to the meaning of the events" (vs. 52), is a poignant reminder that we ourselves may sometimes close our minds to the full meaning of the incarnation. The liturgy of the

Christmas season repeatedly explores this full meaning by emphasizing that the birth of Jesus led to humiliation, suffering and the cross as well as to being raised from the dead to the glory of resurrection.

Celebration of the Eucharist

The introduction to the liturgy could deal with our love of God and love for each other. By coming to the eucharist, we acknowledge it to be the way we grow in God's love; at its beginning, we should pray that it will bring us to love others more deeply. The use of the "I confess" formula recited in common would subtly reiterate the connection between loving God and each other by acknowledging that in thought, word, or action, we have not always shown love to others. The sung *Kyrie, eleison* would emphasize the Lordship of Christ.

Of the alleluia verses, number 5 (Lect., no. 219) taken from 1 Timothy (3:16) would be an appropriate choice especially because it emphasizes the importance of faith and giving glory to God in contrast to the disciples' lack of full commitment in the gospel text.

The introduction to the prayer of the faithful could briefly note that God's love for us gives us the confidence to call on him in prayer. Petitions for the church to be a true sign of Christ's reconciling love in the world, for an end to hostility among nations, for a deeper faith through the liturgy this season, and for those who love and support the sick and dying would be appropriate today.

The use of Christmas Preface II with the reference to "Christ as the revelation of your love" would be a fitting choice based on the first reading today.

Introductions to the Lord's Prayer and the sign of peace could emphasize that in loving others we show our love for God. The use of number 9 of the prayers over the people about enjoying the gift of God's love and sharing it with others would also reiterate the message of 1 John.

Liturgy of the Hours

The first reading at the office of readings from Isaiah (63:7–19) recalls Israel's experience of being abandoned by God as exemplified in the destruction surrounding Jerusalem. The hopelessness of the situation can only be overcome by God's intervention. Hence, the appeals to the Lord "their savior in their every affliction" (vss. 8–9), based on "all he has done for [them]" in the past. Despite their rebellion (vs. 10), God has constantly intervened for them (vs. 9). These verses recall Exodus and Moses' leadership as prime examples of God's direct intervention on behalf of the chosen people (vss. 11–13). The prophet states: "Thus you led your people, bringing glory to your name . . ." (vs. 14). He asks why God allows his people to distance themselves from him (vss. 17–18); and he pleads that God will again intervene for his chosen ones by rending the heavens and causing the mountains to quake before him (verse 19, used in Mark 1:10). The God who acted in the Exodus will act again in these latter days; this same God has intervened to change the course of human history in the birth of his Son. He who was faithful to Israel at its most trying times is ever faithful to us through the liturgy commemorating Christ's birth and saving paschal mystery.

The second reading from St. Proclus of Constantinople considers the baptism of the Lord part of the Epiphany commemoration. The author reviews many scriptural texts referring to the incarnation and discusses the symbolism of water. While in Noah's time water was the means of destroying the human race, "now the water of baptism has recalled the dead to life by the power of the one who was baptized." Hence, the renewal of the covenant of baptism at the eucharist (especially this coming Sunday) shows that what was a symbol of destruction in Noah's time is now a symbol of salvation through Christ.

Our use of holy water at church entrances, the rite of blessing and sprinkling with holy water, and the sprinkling with holy water at the end of night prayer all attest to the church's use of this as a rich symbol of grace and sanctification.

The scripture text at morning prayer, Isaiah 49:8–9, was already reviewed above (Monday, from January 2 to the Epiphany). The intercessions at this hour once more draw on significant Christological titles: "Word begotten by the Father," "Son of the living God," and "Sun of justice." Each of these carries with it an aspect of the many and varied facets of Christ's incarnation and so should be retained in liturgical use.

At evening prayer, the reading of Colossians 1:13–15 was also used last Monday. The antiphon to the Canticle of the Virgin Mary refs to the "sign" of the "brilliant star in the heavens." The redemptive aspects of the incarnation are implied in the introduction to the intercessions about our sins being cast out by Christ. There is a strong tradition that evening prayer is a sin-forgiving, purgative act, hence the appropriateness of this reference.

Celebration of the Hours

The Epiphany invitatory verse would be appropriate today: "Christ has appeared to us; come, let us adore him." The use of Psalm 24 to accompany it would reiterate our need for forgiveness and continual purification.

At evening prayer, another text should replace Colossians 1:13–15, which is part of the Christ canticle before the reading this evening. The proclamation of one of the other Christ canticles (so often used at evening prayer) would help draw attention to its meaning without repeating these same verses (e.g., Rv 11–12 or Phil 2). The petitions at evening prayer are particularly wordy. Keeping the same ideas but shortening the prayers would be useful. The use of a shorter response would also be an option this evening.

Reflection—"Why We Prefer Nostalgia"

At holiday times, people seem to prefer traditional celebrations, customs, and festivity. Time-honored or family traditions are part of the Christmas-New Years expectation. Deviating from them often gives rise to endless heartache because "we never did it that way before." Nostalgia can make us close-minded.

Sometimes we prefer nostalgia simply because it is familiar. It doesn't demand very much from us. But when we face reality as Jesus wanted his disciples to face it, we are confronted with the unknown, the unfamiliar, the uncontrollable. Then we realize why we prefer nostalgia—it makes no demands. It repeats "the way we were." Faith in the future makes demands. Christian faith demands that we choose the future with God's help and in his grace.

Faith demands that we accept the challenge the disciples often avoided in the gospel. They chose not to see that suffering and death in this life are required for the life of Christ to grow in us. They preferred nostalgic reminiscences of Jesus the wonder worker.

Will we accept the challenge of faith or luxuriate in nostalgia?

Liturgy of the Eucharist

The opening prayer today from the Old Gelasian Sacramentary contains familiar Epiphany themes of light and glory. Through Christ, we share in God's very light and life; hence, we ask that by his grace, we will experience the full splendor of the Redeemer and come to everlasting light in his kingdom. The darkness and expectation motif of Advent has once again come full circle.

The first reading from 1 John (4:19–5:4) contains a summary of themes already seen: God's initiative in loving us (vs. 19), the command to love others (vss. 20–21), and the importance of showing our love for God by obeying the commandments (5:2–3). Other Johannine themes have synoptic parallels: the dual command to love God and neighbor (see Mark 12:28–34) and the statement that his commands are not burdensome (see Matthew 11:30). We who are begotten of God (5:1) are to "do what he has commanded" (vs. 2)— to believe in him and to love him as he loved us. This exhortation is especially appropriate as we look to commemorate the Baptism of the Lord. By the sacrament of baptism, we are made members of God's family and experience his light and life for the first time.

The reponsorial psalm is once again taken from Psalm 72, thus underscoring the Epiphany motif of these days.

The gospel of Luke 4:14–22 recounts the important event of Jesus beginning his teaching in Nazareth, clearly manifesting him as God's Son. That Jesus is said to be "in the power of the Spirit" (vs. 14) is a technical Lukan assertion, reflecting his concern to emphasize how the Spirit directs the present Christian community as it directed Jesus himself following his baptism. The fact that the synagogue (vs. 15) is the setting for this event is important since it connotes the traditional place for authoritative teaching in the Law and in the ways of God (vss. 20–21). The quotation from Isaiah (vs. 18) reflects the important themes of the Spirit, anointing, preaching the good news, and society's outcasts being the first to receive this revelation. For Luke, this event clearly inaugurates the Messianic era.

Celebration of the Eucharist

The introduction to the liturgy could address the importance of the Word of God as a source of spiritual growth as it is proclaimed in the liturgy (as it was in the synagogue at Nazareth in the gospel).

The invocations that accompany the third penitential rite could address Christ as the Word made flesh, the fulfillment of the hopes of Israel, and as the Lord who proclaimed the gospel to the poor. The alleluia verse that would coincide well with the text read today is number 3 of the choices provided (Lect., no. 219) taken from two verses of the gospel, Luke 4:18–19.

Appropriate petitions among the intercessions today could be for the Jewish people who were the first to receive God's revealed word, for preachers and teachers of the gospel, for the marginal in society, and for the physically ill, especially those with permanent disabilities such as blindness, deafness, or impaired mobility.

The use of Christmas Preface III containing the text, "Your eternal Word has taken upon himself our human weakness," would be an indirect reiteration of the emphasis given to the word in today's gospel. The traditional invitation to the Lord's Prayer in the Roman rite would emphasize the importance of the word in coming to know God ("Taught by our Savior's command and formed by the word of God, we dare to say . . .").

Since the gospel gives such detail about the ceremony of taking and reading from the scroll, it might be helpful to review the way the gospel book is (or is not) carried in procession to the lectern for proclamation. The present reform of the liturgy assumes that there is one book for the gospel and one for the other readings.

Liturgy of the Hours

The reading from Isaiah (63:19b–64:11) at the office of readings continues yesterday's text, including the repetition of verse 19b, where the prophet pleads that God would rend the heavens and come down to intervene for his people. That the God of the scriptures is a God who acts on behalf of his people is clearly stated in the acclamation of faith in verse 3: "No ear has ever heard, no eye ever seen, any God but you doing such deeds for those who wait for him."

The astounding fact that God intervenes for Israel despite her infidelity (stated clearly in verses 4–6) is acknowledged in the conclusion (vss. 7–11), an appeal to God and to the prophet's hearers that each be more faithful to the covenant. Israel is to submit to God who is the potter who will shape them as he wants (vs. 7). He asks God to forget their guilt (not hold it against them) and to sustain them with his mercy. This appeal to God reflects our own situation. We need to experience the Lord's grace with us so that we can remain faithful to his word and be steadfast in faith. Like Israel, we are to be like clay, allowing God to be the potter to mold us as he wills. For this to occur requires that we have the same humility Jesus had when he submitted himself to our human condition.

The text from St. Cyril of Alexandria deals with the seasonal context about the baptism of Jesus and the "gift of the Holy Spirit on all mankind." Cyril speaks of Jesus as the first to receive the Spirit and that he is the "firstfruits of our restored nature." We who have been baptized are incorporated into this restored relationship with God because we too have received the Spirit at our baptism. This text draws out the meaning of Christ's baptism and our incorporation into Christ.

The scripture readings at morning and evening prayer are the same as those assigned for last Tuesday (see above). The antiphons to the New Testament canticles continue the custom seen this week of referring to the Magi offering gifts to the Christ child. The content and structure of the intercessions at morning prayer (more oriented to praise and thanksgiving than to intercession properly speaking) is significant. These are partially drawn from the *Te Deum* (used at the end of the office of readings); the last two concern self-sacrifice in imitation of the "martyrs" and "holy witnesses" who put God above all other things in life.

At the intercessions at evening prayer, the first two petitions show the importance of appreciating the revealed nature of our faith and that we know God through reason and revelation. The last petition refers to the dead whom we pray will be clothed "in the glory of your chosen people."

Celebration of the Hours

For today's invitatory, the verse before the readings would be fitting: "The Son of God has come to give us understanding.—That we might know the true God." The use of Psalm 100 to accompany it would provide variety and sustain the sense of joy and festivity of these final days of the Christmas cycle.

Since the feast of the Lord's baptism is to be celebrated this Sunday, the hymns used to begin the hours these days might well refer to the place of the Spirit in our lives (as is carefully described in the reading from Cyril.) At morning prayer, the petitions might be re-written to be more intercessory in nature. At evening prayer, the awkward structure in the fourth petition about seeing God more clearly might be rephrased.

Reflection—"The Spiritual Life"

Today's gospel shows Jesus as one led by and empowered by the Spirit. Jesus, "in the power of the Spirit" and anointed by the Spirit, lived a fully human life on earth. He was the integrated human being whose humanity and divinity were perfectly fused. The key to this unity and harmony is the Spirit. The same Spirit who guided Jesus is the Spirit who dwells among us, the baptized. Our lives can be called "spiritual" to the extent that the Spirit takes over as the principal of our life, fostering a union of mind and heart which gives our body, flesh and matter a proper place in functioning and living this human life. Christianity does not seek to do away with the body or the flesh; it seeks to enliven our bodies and flesh through the Holy Spirit, the presence of God with us.

While our human nature continually needs the grace and mercy of God to guide and direct us in life, this grace and mercy do not exempt us from dealing with the real issues that human life presents us with, or the needs of our brothers and sisters. We do not live in "two different worlds;" we live in one world graced by the Spirit. Bringing any polarities into harmony in the Spirit is a good description of the spiritual life.

FRIDAY AFTER EPIPHANY

Liturgy of the Eucharist

Today's opening prayer from the Hadrianum Sacramentary recalls the important and familiar themes of light and salvation in Christ. We acknowledge God's revelation "by the light of a star" which led the Magi to the infant Jesus, which light reveals Christ as Savior of the world. We ask that the Father continue to "guide us with his light."

The first reading today, 1 John 5:5–13, was used last Friday (see above for commentary) and is assigned as an alternate reading in the "B" cycle on the feast of the Baptism of the Lord. The responsorial psalm shifts today from the universality expressed in Psalm 72 to the praise of God by "Jerusalem" in Psalm 147 (used on January 6). "Jerusalem" in this text can be understood to refer to all the baptized who now share the heritage of being God's chosen in Christ.

The gospel from Luke (5:12–16) is another miracle story told to emphasize how the power of God is manifested in Jesus healing the leper. This man was a social and religious outcast, whose status was far worse than other marginal persons with whom Jesus associates in the Lukan gospel (such as Pharisees and tax collectors, see Luke 15:1ff.). A leper's sores and contagion would make him/her socially unacceptable in any society. Yet, in the religious society of the old covenant, the detailed prescriptions in Leviticus 13:3ff. would not be forgotten by those who heard this story. After examination, the priest would declare a leper "unclean" (vs. 3). The unclean were to have no social relations with the rest of society. Anyone touching such persons would become ritually unclean. This explains the reference to the Levite's passing the half-dead man in the parable of the Good Samaritan (Lk 10:30–32); if the "clean" priest touched the "unclean," he would not be able to officiate at religious ceremonies.

Jesus' attitude toward the outcasts and his touching the leper in this story (vs. 13) show Jesus' concern for all peoples, especially those ostracized by the prescriptions of the Mosaic Law.

The note at the end of the story adds a typical Lukan motif—Jesus "often retired to distant places" to pray (vs. 16). Luke shows Jesus' behavior as a model for his followers, who themselves should spend time in communion with the Father in private (as well as in liturgical) prayer.

Celebration of the Eucharist

The introduction to the liturgy could unite the healing miracle of Jesus with his healing and sustaining presence at the eucharist. The invocations from the sixth set of sample invocations for the third form of the penitential rite about Jesus raising us to new life, forgiving our sins, and feeding us with the eucharist would be suitable today. The use of number 4 of the alleluia verses (Lect., no. 219), taken from Luke 7:16, would reiterate the fact that through this miracle "God has visited his people."

Petitions that the church might spur rich nations to help the poor, that we might grow in reliance on God through prayer, that the physically handicapped or mentally ill might not suffer isolation because of their illness, and that Christian health care professionals might help the terminally ill prepare for eternal life would reflect some of the concerns of the gospel.

The use of the Epiphany preface would continue to reiterate the context for this eucharist within the Epiphany-Baptism cycle. The use of number 16 of the prayers over the people, about the Lord caring for his people and purifying them, would echo Jesus' care for the leper.

Liturgy of the Hours

The Isaiah text at the office of readings can be divided into two sections. The first, Isaiah 65:13–16, deals with the distinction between the faithful and the unfaithful based on the servant's response to God. The true servant will then be called by a new name, an indication of a new identity not bound to Israel (vs. 15). This looking beyond Israel leads to the second section (vss. 17–25) about the universality of redemption. The "new heavens and a new earth" (vs. 17) usher in a time when "the things of the past" will be forgotten and wiped away forever (vs. 17). The point made here is that God intervenes in our lives by remaking us inwardly by his unfailing love. Those who have remained faithful will receive a long and fruitful life (vss. 20–22). At the end (vs. 25), the peaceable kingdom of Isaiah 11:6–9 is recalled, again denoting God's intervention in their lives.

When proclaimed during this season, the text can refer to the incarnation of God in our lives and in the real situation of the world in which we live. His reign is already present among us in the salvation Christ accomplished. Like Israel, we are dependent on God to intervene in our lives and to sustain us. As we look for the full manifestation of his kingdom (see responsory from Revelations 21:1, 3, 4), we are made aware of the presence of God already in our midst through the liturgy.

The second reading from St. Maximus of Turin once again concerns the Lord's baptism, which he calls "the feast of his birthday." Maximus relates that despite the years intervening between Jesus' birth and baptism, through the liturgy we commemorate these events in the same season. The liturgy is not a biography; it is the means through which we commemorate and thus share in the events of redemption in their power and fullness. He regards the baptism as the Lord's birthday because he who was born in mystery is now revealed to all nations as the Son of God. Through the water of baptism, we are similarly reborn and made new.

The scripture readings at morning and evening prayer were used on Wednesday of last week (see above for commentary and for celebration options).

The antiphons to the New Testament canticles deal with bowing down in worship before Christ (Zechariah) and of the Magi being warned by an angel to return home by a different route (Mary). The intercessions at morning prayer draw on the humanity/divinity paradox of the incarnation and of Christ's human birth from the Virgin Mary. At evening prayer, the unity of all peoples in Christ is noted, a motif that is clear throughout the whole Epiphany cycle.

Celebration of the Hours

The verse before the readings at the office of readings draws on the important Johannine prologue: "In Christ was life.—And that life was the light of mankind." Psalm 67 would function well as the invitatory psalm since its verses point to the universality of salvation for "all nations." This is repeated in the refrains, "let all nations learn your saving help," "let all the peoples praise you."

The use of Psalm 38 in three sections as the psalmody at the office of readings provides the opportunity for reciting/singing this psalm straight through with an appropriate psalm prayer and silence at the end. Since the psalm prayers offered are general in theme, one could be composed that would speak of the light of Christ leading us through the darkness and sin of this world.

The intercessions at morning prayer are wordy and could easily be condensed. The first petition should more correctly refer to our share in the liturgy (not just the eucharist); the alternate response is better rendered "by your birth, renew our lives." The alternate response, "Father, hear our prayer," would serve well at evening prayer.

Reflection—"Birthdays"

Part of any culture's annual family rites surround the birth dates of its members. Planning and celebrating with appropriate festivity mark these anniversaries. We commemorate the event of human birth by celebrating because this day is unique to the individual honored—the day he or she saw the light of day.

The day of our baptism can also be regarded as a day of our birth. It is unique because it is the day on which we became members of God's family—a family that traces its origin and source to God.

The day of our baptism was the day we first "put on Christ" and we live our lives in Christ until he comes again in glory. In the meantime, we grow in his divine image and likeness through grace, especially in and through the liturgy.

Even if we do not commemorate the date of our actual baptism, this coming Sunday's commemoration of Christ's baptism invites us to renew and deepen our commitment to the Lord, begun at the waters of the baptismal font and sustained whenever we gather for the liturgy. In this sense, we can say that this Sunday is a day of birthdays—Christ's and ours in him.

SATURDAY AFTER EPIPHANY

Liturgy of the Eucharist

The opening prayer, taken from the old Gelasian Sacramentary, affirms our identity as a new creation through Christ who has formed us in his divine image and likeness. With confidence, we pray that he would join us more intimately to him since through him our human nature is made divine. This text recalls St. Augustine's adage that God became one of us so that we could become like God.

The first reading, 1 John 5:14–21, and its accompanying responsorial psalm, Psalm 149, have already been commented upon above on January 7.

The gospel from John (3:22–30) is very fitting today since it ends the Christmas season by recalling John the Baptist's important role. His ministry as precursor dominated Advent; his role as the baptizer of Jesus (commemorated tomorrow) concludes the Christmas season. That John baptized to prepare for the coming of Jesus is reaffirmed here (vss. 22–23), but it is John's admission that he is not the Messiah (vs. 28) that dominates today. John states humbly, "He must increase, while I must decrease" (vs. 30). The nuptial imagery affirming that Jesus is the bridegroom should be noted since this imagery is very significant in the liturgy of the whole Advent-Christmas season. The intimacy reflected in a marriage union is the human paradigm for the intimacy between Christ and his Church.

Celebration of the Eucharist

The introduction to the liturgy could concern our communal submission to Jesus as Messiah and Lord, just as John submitted to him as the one who must increase. The third set of sample invocations from the third penitential rite could be used as a kind of summary of the Christmas season in which we acclaim Jesus as "mighty God," "prince of peace," "God of God, Son of Mary," "Word made flesh," and "splendor of the Father." The use of the fifth alleluia verse (Lect., no. 219) would be appropriate since it offers: "glory to Christ . . . from all who believe in him." Those who so believe must imitate John and submit to him as Messiah and Lord.

Among the intercessions, petitions for the church, that she witness in word and deed to Christ as Messiah; for newly married couples, that they may reflect God's love by loving each other and all people in Christ; for those who will be baptized tomorrow (and their families and sponsors), that they will grow in the likeness of Christ; and for the dead who were buried with Christ in baptism, that they will come to share the fullness of eternal life with him forever would be appropriate.

The use of the Epiphany preface and the second eucharistic prayer would be appropriate today because of the seasonal nature of the preface and the brevity of the eucharistic prayer.

The introduction to the Lord's Prayer could speak of our waiting for the coming of the kingdom in and through Christ, the kingdom we first shared in through the waters of baptism.

Liturgy of the Hours

The first reading in the office of readings is the last section of Isaiah (66:10–14, 18–23), completing the continuous reading of Isaiah begun on the first Sunday of Advent. The first verses today (vss. 10–14) are a poem rejoicing in the comfort Jerusalem receives from God (vss. 12–13). "As a mother comforts her son . . . so will I comfort you" (vs. 13), says the Lord; this same text can easily be applied to the comfort and peace we receive through Christ as Son of God and Word made flesh.

The second part of the text, verses 18–23, is a lyrical conclusion to the book. Here, the universality of God's will to save is expressed through the prophet's skillful reworking of the Babel story (Gn 11). The Lord will come "to gather nations of every language" (vs. 18), erasing differences between peoples and making individuals share in a unity and harmony willed by God—that in him all will become brothers and sisters. The source for this is the work God himself will do (vss. 22–23) when "all mankind shall come to worship before me" (vs. 23). When this happens, the self-glorification expressed in Babel and the resulting confusion of many languages will be overturned. This is part of what is commemorated at Pentecost, when we pray:

"Today we celebrate the great beginning of your Church
when the Holy Spirit made known to all peoples the one true God,
and created from the many languages of man
one voice to profess one faith." (Preface for Pentecost)

The second reading from a sermon by Faustus of Riez is an allegorical interpretation of the account of the wedding feast at Cana, the third of the manifestations commemorated on the Epiphany. The marriage celebrated is allegorized to signify the union between Christ and the Church. The water changed into wine illustrates the change that occurs in us by baptism, and is effected through the same symbol—water. Such an approach draws out what is implied when the church commemorates events of Jesus' life in the liturgy. We do not recall historical events primarily; rather, we participate (partake in) these events through the liturgy.

At the hour of readings, the use of Psalm 106 is a most significant summary of salvation history. On this last weekday of the Christmas season, it serves to recapture the high points of salvation history in which God remained ever faithful to Israel despite her faithlessness and lack of complete response to him.

The text of Wisdom 7:26–27 (used last Thursday) is assigned for morning prayer. The antiphon to Zechariah's canticle this morning is particularly interesting because it draws on the Cana miracle as a manifestation of Christ: "At Cana in Galilee, Jesus worked the first of the signs which revealed his glory." Once again, we see the importance of this incident as part of the Epiphany.

Celebration of the Hours

The use of the Epiphany invitatory would be a fitting introduction to the office today, especially because this is the last day when it can be used. Psalm 100 would be a fitting text to follow this refrain because it is joyful and acclaims the Lord who is "faithful from age to age" (vs. 5).

At the office of readings, the three sections of Psalm 106 can be combined into one text with a significant period of silence following the doxology.

The hymn to introduce morning prayer could emphasize the Cana miracle, which would coincide with the antiphon to Zechariah's canticle and help to emphasize this least emphasized of the Epiphany manifestations. If possible, the hymn chosen should demonstrate how we are brought into this mystery and share in the manifestation of the Lord to us. The use of the intercessions as presented with the alternate response, "Christ, Son of God, hear us," would be appropriate since these are (comparatively) short and direct. The tone of the hours today should be simple and restrained in contrast to tomorrow's festivity.

Reflection—"Bridesmaids and Best Men"

Today's gospel points to a practice common in our culture which was obviously practiced in Palestine at the time of Christ—best man and bridesmaid for a wedding. While the similarity between then and now cannot include details, it does include the basic role played by these assistants. These are the people who waited on their friends and who helped prepare the details of the wedding ceremony. They are singled out for special recognition by the very fact that they have been given this role. But they are number two. Number one is the couple—bride and groom. As the adage implies, no matter how often one is a bridesmaid or a best man, that does not make one a bride or a groom.

This is the point of John's use of this analogy in today's gospel. He was obviously an important prophet. In fact, he was the last and his act of baptizing was the final preparation for the coming of the Messiah. Yet, as important as John was, he was number two. Jesus was number one, the Messiah. He is the source of all unity and reconciliation. He alone is the only begotten of God. Like John, we must point to him and allow him to be number one.

And yet, in and through Christ, we share a dignity and status that unites us to God. That bond is baptism and that identity is as sons and daughters of the Father; thus are we brothers and sisters of each other. In this sense, we are each other's bridesmaids and best men. Such a status is due to God's grace; the attendant responsibilities remind us of the tasks which are ours as the beloved of God.

BAPTISM OF THE LORD

Liturgical Context

The commemoration of the baptism of the Lord marks the end of the Christmas season. Theologically, this is a most fitting conclusion to the season because the readings and prayers today help focus our attention on the implications of the event of Christ's birth and life among us. The feast is a fitting climax to the season of expectation and hope in the coming of the Lord in Advent and his manifestation to all the nations in Epiphany. This feast commemorates the inauguration of his earthly ministry and his role as servant of the Father.

The liturgy of the Eastern tradition emphasizes this feast as a theophany—God revealing himself to his people. A parallel is often drawn between the baptism of the Lord and his transfiguration since at both theophanies a voice from heaven declared Jesus to be God's Son and urged the witnesses to listen to his word of revelation.

The Eastern tradition also emphasizes the enlightenment and illumination today that occurs at our baptism and which are renewed at this feast. The state into which we were born, known as original sin, is thus overturned; we now share in the life of the new Adam, Christ.

The composition of a new mass formula for this feast in the revised liturgy and the recent addition of optional readings for the "B" and "C" cycles in the Lectionary attest to the importance which this feast now receives. It serves as an important hinge, disclosing the full meaning of the commemoration of his incarnation through the Christmas season, and pointing to the proclamation of his words and deeds on the Sundays through the rest of the liturgical year.

An important focus for the feast is the natural symbol water and its use in Christian worship. A glance at the blessing prayer for water in the rite of baptism or the prayers for blessing and sprinkling water at the beginning of Sunday eucharist shows how important water has been in the history of salvation and how central its use is in the sacrament of regeneration and rebirth. A theme that is seen repeatedly in the liturgy today notes that the waters of the Jordan become holy by Jesus' baptism. Despite these positive associations, the fact that water is the place where the forces of evil dwell should not be forgotten. In fact, this ambivalence—that it destroys as well as it gives life—makes Jesus' baptism in water a sign of his triumph over the forces of evil and sin symbolized in water itself. The scene of the first verses of Genesis should be recalled when reviewing the liturgy today (especially the gospels) because it was the Spirit hovering over the waters that brought order to creation. Many patristic commentaries on the parting of the Red Sea at the Exodus speak of this as an example of the way God used water to save his people; hence, it is all the more significant that Jesus is baptized in water and that we are reborn and saved through the life-giving waters of the baptismal font. The thirst for living water seen both in Isaiah and in John's gospel are also part of the church's liturgical tradition. We are urged to thirst for Christ, the living water, the source of all holiness. The most obvious and central symbol of the event of Jesus' baptism, the water of the Jordan river, should also figure into our appreciation of the liturgy's use of water and its full significance in celebration today.

Many of the themes associated with this feast in the tradition and in our present liturgy are summarized in the following prayer from the Byzantine liturgy:

"Today heaven and earth rejoice, watching the Lord being baptized and drowning in the water the great load of our sins.
The human soul is illuminated because, delivered from the shadow of sin, she puts on a divine and incorruptible garment.
The Kingdom of God is at hand. Christ, announced by the Law and the prophets, comes to regenerate us in his divine baptism.
You are a mighty torrent, you who have created the sea and the water springs; you come to these waters to wash us yourself, who are to everyone cleanliness and purification.
You are a gulf of truth, O Christ!
You, the undefiled water source! How could the Jordan hold you?
You are the sun that knows no twilight!
You have illuminated your sacred flesh as a torch in the midst of the Jordan.

You have found man's image soiled with passion and sin, and have washed it through your baptism."

Such a text shows how we are incorporated into this mystery and share in the life of God through Christ who himself underwent baptism for our sakes.

As the eighth-century *Missale Gothicum* states:

"For those who are baptized, who seek the chrism, who are crowned in Christ, to whom our Lord has been pleased to grant a new birth, let us beseech Almighty God that they may bear the baptism which they have received spotless unto the end."

Our baptism is the moment of incorporation into Christ, but as an initiation, it is the beginning of a lifelong process of conforming ourselves more and more deeply to Christ. Thus, the weekly celebration of the eucharist with its rite of water blessing and sprinkling and today's annual commemoration of the Lord's baptism invite us to renew our adoption as God's sons and daughters and to witness before the world the light of Christ granted us at baptism.

Cycle "A"

The first reading from Isaiah (42:1–4, 6–7) is the important first servant song of Deutero-Isaiah. It has already been used at the office of readings on Friday, from January 2 to the Epiphany (see above for commentary), and it forms half of the first reading at the office of readings today. The fact that this text also appears as the first reading at mass on Monday of Holy Week attests to the fact that the liturgy uses it to refer to Jesus as both the Father's servant (stressed today) and as suffering servant (stressed in Holy Week). While in its original setting, these verses likely referred to an individual or to the whole of Israel, its use today obviously invites our reflection on Christ's role as servant and our servanthood in him.

The responsorial psalm, Psalm 29, reflects the importance placed on water in today's liturgy (see verses 3–4) and how the Lord's voice over the waters was powerful and causative at creation. In the gospels, a voice from the heavens will declare Jesus as God's son, thus making the word of revelation an important source of our re-creation and renewal in the Lord. The last verse about the Lord being enthroned also applies to Jesus' status as God's son, a declaration made when he emerges from the water bath of baptism. We are declared and made daughters and sons of our Father through this same life-giving water bath.

The second reading from Acts (10:34–38) is interesting since it is the only New Testament writing, except for the gospels themselves, which speaks of the baptism of Jesus. It serves as a proper introduction to understanding Jesus' ministry since it indicates that he is anointed with the Holy Spirit, that he brings the good news of salvation to the poor, and that he heals those who are in the grip of the devil's power. Significantly, some of these same verses recur on Easter Sunday as the second reading, a fact that attests to the importance given to Peter's discourse. Today both at Evening Prayer I and II, verses 37–38 are assigned as the scripture reading.

The alleluia verse is particularly significant today because it is taken not from the gospel to be proclaimed but from the scene of Jesus' transfiguration (Mk 9:6). The text, "The heavens were opened and the Father's voice was heard: this is my beloved Son, hear him," reminds us that these same things occur at Jesus' baptism. The Lectionary editors here demonstrate the important continuity between the baptism and the transfiguration, both of which reveal the power of God revealed through Jesus who willingly submits himself to be the Father's servant. The humiliation Jesus experienced by submitting to baptism and the exaltation he received at the transfiguration indicate how Jesus' suffering and exaltation are combined to exemplify the life of all believers. This particular verse before the gospel urges us to be attentive to the revealed Word of God we hear in the gospel.

The text of Matthew 3:13–17 recounts the baptism of Jesus by John. Some scholars maintain that in placing emphasis on the baptism of Jesus at the beginning of the gospel, Matthew presents Jesus as the new Moses who has to submit to all "God's demands" (vs. 15), the law he reveals from God. This willing consent to baptism marks Jesus as the one who transcends the law and fulfills the prophets' warnings about the coming of a Savior. The "law and the prophets" are thus fulfilled and transcended by Jesus who will declare a new law and a new way of acting (especially in the beatitudes, Matthew 5). That there is an unmistakable reference to the Exodus in the verses that deal with Jesus' baptism is clear from Matthew 4:1–2, where Jesus is led into the desert for forty days and nights. The forty years' sojourn of Israel waiting for deliverance is thus recapitulated and exemplified in Jesus' earthly life. Hence, this additional reference back to the Old Testament confirms Jesus' role as the new Moses, leading his people by word and example. The Exodus and Exile of Israel have come to an end; they are recapitulated and fulfilled in the life of Jesus.

A final reference in today's gospel (vs. 17) points back to the book of Genesis where the "mighty wind" swept over the waters; here the Spirit hovers over the scene of Jesus' baptism to empower him to do the Father's work, now not of creation, but of redemption.

Cycle "B"

The first two readings (and the psalm and alleluia verse) have been added as optional readings in the second edition of the Lectionary. The first, Isaiah 55:1–11, is also used as a reading at the Easter Vigil. This usage plus the text itself points to the important symbolism of water as a sign of salvation. We are invited to "come to the water . . . all you who are thirsty" (vs. 1). Yet it is not just water that will satisfy our thirst for God, for the author clearly emphasizes that we are to come to the Lord "heedfully [to] listen, that you may have life" (vs. 3). It is the revealed word of God that satisfies and that should be pondered. This word "shall not return to me void, but shall do my will, achieve the end for which I sent it" (vs. 11). From the book of Genesis when it was by the word of the Lord that creation came into being, through the revelation of the Lord's word in the Law in Exodus, to this text about the all-powerful word of the Lord, the biblical tradition supports a notion of the word of the Lord as creative and as formative. Hence, this text fittingly leads to the gospel account of Jesus' baptism at which the word from heaven declared and effected Jesus' status as Son of God (see, Mk 1:11).

The response from Isaiah 12 (vss. 2–3, 4b–d, 5–6) is from the song of thanksgiving which also refers to water, to our exultation in acclaiming God as savior and our receiving strength and courage from the Lord. It is thus an appropriate complement to the first reading and serves to emphasize even more the life-giving properties of water.

The second reading from 1 John (5:1–9) has already been used on Thursday and Friday after Epiphany (see above for commentary). This text is a summary of many of the major themes of the letter about the command to love, our status as the begotten of God, and the importance of spirit, water and blood as witnesses to Christ. Once again, the water symbol is used to emphasize that the way we come to know God is through the water of baptism.

The alleluia verse from John (1:29) recalls the gospel text formerly used in the Roman rite today about John acclaiming Jesus as the "Lamb of God who takes away the sin of the world." This text reminds us that the testimony John offered on Jesus' behalf at the beginning of the gospels was also used through Advent to prepare us for the coming of the Lord as the savior of the world.

The gospel of Mark 1:17–11 has already been used on January 6 (the weekday, not the Solemnity of the Epiphany; see above for commentary). The apocalyptic image here of the heavens being torn apart indicates that Jesus is God's son. The image occurs again at the transfiguration (Mk 9:7) and at the death of Jesus (Mk 15:39). The present text is about God's son whose ministry is understood as a journey from his baptism, through his transfiguration, to enthronement at his crucifixion. At each state, he is acclaimed as Lord. In the first two of these, the manifestation is by a heavenly word accompanied by cosmic images. Hence, this text is to be seen both as the conclusion of the season of expectation and waiting and as the inauguration of a period of reflection on Jesus' ministry. The text of verse 11 about sonship can be applied to us in the sense that in baptism we are made God's true daughters and sons. The mention of the sky's being "rent in two" (vs. 10) recalls the entrance antiphon of the Fourth Sunday of Advent: "Let the clouds rain down the Just One, and the earth bring forth a Savior" (Is 45:8).

Cycle "C"

The optional first reading is the first part of Deutero-Isaiah (40:1–5, 9–10) that was used on the Second Sunday of Advent, "B" cycle (see above for commentary). Once again this significant "comfort" text reminds us of God's direct intervention to save and to protect us. Today, this is concretized in the baptism of Jesus; through this action, the waters of the earth are understood as life giving and life sustaining. This notion of renewal and recreation in water is noted in Psalm 103, whose verses are used as the response to this text.

The second reading from Titus (2:11–14; 3:4–7) combines the two texts used as the second readings on Christmas day (see above for commentary, the mass at midnight and the mass at dawn).

The alleluia verse is taken from the gospel, Luke 3:16, where John speaks of Jesus as the mightier one who is to come who will baptize in the Spirit and in fire. The gospel itself (Lk 3:15–16; 21–22) reminds us of the Third Sunday of Advent ("C" cycle) since it speaks of the self-effacement of John the Baptizer before the coming Messiah who is the "mightier" still to come. The first section of the reading (vss. 15–16) is part of the text of the Third Sunday of Advent, while the second section (vss. 21–22) speaks of the baptism of Jesus in the Jordan as the beginning of his ministry. The descent of the Spirit in the form of a dove, and the announcement, "You are my beloved Son; on you my favor rests," are important references to the mission of Jesus, the Servant, who fulfills the hopes described in the servant songs of Isaiah 42 and 49 (used at the office of readings today). The fact that Jesus was praying when the Spirit descended (vs. 21) should be noted. For Luke, this is important because the church is to imitate Jesus and the early disciples (see Acts 2) who receive the gift of the Spirit in a special way when they pray. The example of Jesus at prayer is used throughout the Lukan gospel (see 11:5ff., 18:1, 22:39) to instruct Jesus' disciples. The example of the primitive Christian community at prayer (see Acts 2:42ff.) also serves Luke's purpose of encouraging later generations to pray regularly and faithfully as did their Lord and his first witnesses.

(It should be recalled that in this "C" cycle of the Lectionary, the recounting of the miracle at Cana is the gospel to be read on the Second Sunday of the year, the Sunday following this feast. We again note that the liturgical cycles are connected rather than completely separated at this conclusion of the Christmas season, just as the First Sunday of Advent is connected with the preceding Sundays of the year, most especially the Solemnity of Christ the King.)

Sacramentary Texts

The entrance antiphon is taken from Matthew (3:16–17), part of the gospel in the "A" cycle. The cosmic sign of the heavens being torn apart, the descent of the Spirit on Jesus, and the voice declaring Jesus to be the Son of God are all significant references to the scriptural foundations for today's feast.

The newly composed opening prayer draws on the declaration of Jesus' sonship and applies this to our baptism in the sense that through this sacrament our relatedness to God through Jesus is declared and confirmed. We pray that we may be worthy of our calling as adopted children and heirs of eternal life.

The celebration of the eucharist itself reiterates the important place which the liturgy has in renewing and confirming our status as adopted children of God, reborn by water and the Spirit. The third text offered as an opening prayer (the second being the customary alternative opening prayer) is the traditional text of the Roman rite which is general in theme and concerns the interchange between humanity and divinity in Christ and through Christ in us.

The prayer over the gifts (especially in its Latin version) points to the importance of the theology of the eucharistic action. We pray that "our gifts" may become the sacrament of Christ's sacrifice by which he took away the sins of the world. This celebration does not add to the sacrifice of Christ; rather it is our present participation in that unique sacrifice.

The preface for the Baptism of the Lord combines the familiar images of the voice from heaven descending on Jesus in the Jordan, the Word made flesh in Jesus, the Spirit revealing Jesus as the servant of the Father, and the importance of Jesus' mission of preaching the good news to the poor. Thus, it is a helpful summary of many of the dominant scriptural themes proclaimed today.

The communion antiphon reiterates John's testimony that Jesus is the Son of God (Jn 1:34).

The prayer after communion, while brief and direct, contains important themes. We acknowledge that we who have been fed on the holy sacrament must not abuse what we have received. We pray that we will continue to hear the word of Jesus and put it into practice in our lives so that we may be and "become your children in name and in fact." Once again, the central importance of interior conversion and continual turning to the Lord are essential components in the lives of all, even of those who have received baptism and are members of the body of the church.

Celebration of the Eucharist

This feast is an obvious choice for a special celebration of infant baptism at a principal liturgy. (Infant baptism is noted since adult initiation is best reserved for the Easter Vigil.) However, the introduction to every liturgy this Sunday should contain the rite of blessing and sprinkling with holy water because of the obvious sense of renewal and recommitment celebrated today. For the celebration of baptism and the renewal of baptismal faith, the location and use of the baptismal font is of paramount importance. This should dominate part of the sanctuary area and it should be emphasized along with any Christmas decor. The retention of Christmas decorations in church through today is an important nonverbal suggestion of how the liturgy celebrates this season from Evening Prayer I of Christmas to Evening Prayer II today.

Whatever acclamations have been used since Christmas should be used again today with appropriate and festive accompaniment. Hymns about the Lord's baptism, ministry, service, or the identity of the church as the communion of the baptized should be used. These should draw us into the liturgy today of renewal and recommitment of our own baptism and service role in the church.

When planning this celebration a decision should be made whether to use the optional texts in the "B" and "C" cycles of the revised Lectionary.

Of the sacramentary texts, the first form of the opening prayer expresses well the main themes of today's liturgy.

Because of the emphasis placed on hearing the word, today would be a good opportunity to emphasize the proclamation of the word with a pause before and after each text proclaimed. Also, a fitting gospel procession (with candles and incense) would be a good way to emphasize the word.

Among the intercessions today, petitions for the church, that it might imitate Jesus the servant; for world leaders, that they might work toward harmony and peace; for those who do not practice their faith, that Christians might inspire them to return to the sacraments; and for those to be baptized today (and their families and sponsors), that they may grow in true knowledge and love of God would be fitting.

The proclamation of the special preface for today's feast with either the second or third eucharistic prayer would be appropriate. (While the Roman Canon may be used today, the fact that it has no proper section for today's feast, would militate against its repetition.

Also the fourth eucharistic prayer is only used with its own preface and hence would not be used today.)

If the invocations of the "Lamb of God" are to be extended beyond the three provided, the use of the titles of Christ which form the first part of the petitions at evening prayer today would be very appropriate. The conclusion of the liturgy could be the Epiphany solemn blessing preceded by the dismissal to "Go in peace to love and serve the Lord." This version of the blessing draws out the important light/darkness theme of the Epiphany.

Liturgy of the Hours

The psalms selected for Evening Prayer I and II are repeated from those used last week for the Epiphany. Hence, the parallel between these two commemorations is continued.

The antiphons for Evening Prayer I serve to direct attention to the feast by using the words of John the Baptizer as he prepared for Jesus. His baptism was for the forgiveness of sins (first antiphon), but Christ's would be in the Holy Spirit and in fire (second). It was only at the scene of Jesus' baptism by John that the heavens opened thus marking a definitive theophany (third).

The scripture reading assigned for both Evening Prayer I and II is from Acts (10:37–38), the same verses that form part of the second reading at the eucharist today in the "A" cycle (see above for comment).

The antiphon to the Canticle of the Blessed Virgin notes that we participate and share in Jesus' baptism. We experience new life in Christ, healing for our sinful nature and unfailing holiness through the "cleansing waters of [our] baptism."

The structure of the intercessions (used at both Evening Prayer I and II) is significant because the petitions refer to titles of Christ used in the liturgy and scripture readings today: "Servant of God," "Chosen One of God," "Son of God," and "Savior."

At Evening Prayer II, the antiphons to the psalmody deal more precisely with the Lord's baptism. They reiterate the importance of the declaration that Jesus is God's Son whose word we should listen to and obey (first), they assure us of our victory over Satan and sin by the cleansing waters of the Jordan (second), and they speak of the mystery of the creator of the universe having washed away our sins in the Jordan (third). Whereas the antiphons to the psalmody of

Evening Prayer I emphasized John's baptism and role, these texts explore the meaning of Jesus' baptism itself.

The antiphon to the Canticle of the Virgin at Evening Prayer II notes the importance of the paschal mystery when Christ poured out his blood and washed away our sins. This is a particularly important text because it demonstrates the close unity between Christ's baptism as the beginning of his ministry and his death and resurrection as its culmination.

The first reading at the office of readings from Isaiah (42:1–9; 49:1–9) presents the first two servant songs from Deutero-Isaiah. The first is also assigned as the first reading at the eucharist today in the "A" cycle (as it was for the Friday from January 2 to the Epiphany; see above for commentary). The second servant song, 49:1–9, contains many themes that reflect the liturgy of this part of the Christmas season. When proclaimed today, we understand Jesus as the servant through whom God will show forth his glory (vs. 3). We can say that Christ, like the original servant, was chosen "from the womb" (vs. 5) to do his Father's will, which included giving his life for our salvation and sanctification. While "Israel" and "Jacob" are noted as having shared in the salvation wrought through the servant, the universality so central to appreciating the Epiphany cycle is seen in the text: "I will make you a light to the nations, that my salvation may reach to the ends of the earth" (vs. 6). The light symbolism that had played such an important role in determining when to celebrate the birth of Christ and which dominates in the Christmas-Epiphany liturgy is once more recalled and used as a way of understanding the importance of Christ's mission for all peoples. That the liturgy wants to associate Jesus with the servant songs is made clear by the responsory which is taken from the Markan and Lukan accounts of the baptism of Jesus.

The second reading, from the fourth-century writings of St. Gregory Nazianzus, deals with the important notion of the illumination we experience through baptism. In characteristic patristic usage, the text begins: "Christ is bathed in light; let us also be bathed in light. Christ is baptized; let us also go down with him, and rise with him." The illumination and enlightenment we receive from water baptism and anointing with chrism is here assumed to be derived from Christ's own baptism and anointing with the Spirit of God. The waters in which Jesus was cleansed were life giving; we share in that life through the water used at our baptism. From this same water bath, we receive the light of Christ to illumine our way through the difficulties of life to final peace and tranquility in the kingdom of heaven.

At the office of readings, Psalms 29 and 66 are used with antiphons referring to the voice over the waters being the voice of the God of majesty and to the light which dawned for all ages through Christ's baptism. We are to be joyful and reassured by these images—word and light—as we renew the grace of our baptism through the liturgy today.

At morning prayer, the psalms of Sunday Week I are assigned along with antiphons that speak of the relationship between John and Jesus, the dove and voice attesting to the importance of the act of baptism (first), to the importance of water as the symbol which now symbolizes Christ who has "hallowed all creation" (second), and of praise for the forgiveness of sins by "fire and the Holy Spirit" (third).

The reading from Isaiah (61:1–2a) recalls the use of this text in Luke 4:18ff., referring to Christ's own ministry. The last part of this text recalls the verse in the Lukan account of the baptism read in the "C" cycle about how Jesus "preached the good news to the people" (Lk 3:18).

The antiphon to the Canticle of Zechariah speaks about the world being made holy and that in Jesus our sins have been taken away. The intercessions deal with how the baptism of Christ applies to us and how we participate in his humble service as well as share in his light and the dignity of being God's adopted sons and daughters through him.

Celebration of the Hours

The specially composed invitatory should be used today: "Come, let us worship Christ, the beloved Son in whom the Father was well pleased." The use of Psalm 95 to accompany this verse would be appropriate.

At the office of readings, Psalm 29 is recited as a unit and Psalm 66 is presented in two sections. The latter could easily be combined into one with the second antiphon used at its beginning and end. This would allow for a psalm prayer to relate this text to the feast celebrated and for a period of silence before the readings.

At morning and evening prayer, the choice of hymns is important (as was noted above under celebration of the eucharist). The application of Christ's baptism to our participation in the life of God should be reflected in the texts chosen. At both Evening Prayer I and II, the text of Acts could be changed to avoid repetition since it is used at mass; to use one of the second readings from the "B" and "C" cycles at this hour (when they are not used at mass) would avoid this problem. At morning prayer, the proclamation of the whole of chapter 61 of Isaiah (vss. 1–11) would not be overly long and would provide important Old Testament background for the feast.

The singing of the Canticles of Zechariah and Mary would add to the festivity of this feast, as would the singing of the Lord's Prayer. The use of the alternate response, "Lord, have mercy," at morning prayer could help to simplify praying the intercessions. If the intercessions at evening prayer are adjusted (to avoid duplication), a simpler form should be used at a simpler celebration of this hour (likely the evening before) and the full set as presented should be used at the more festive celebration (likely on the day itself).

The use of number 7 or 9 of the prayers over the people would be a fitting way to end those hours which are comparatively simple, while the use of the Epiphany solemn blessing would be an appropriate conclusion to the most festive of the hours celebrated today. The seventh prayer over the people is presented in the mass formula today and uses the light symbol as a focus; the ninth deals with enjoying Christ's love and spreading it among others. Either of these help to draw out the mission and witness aspects of this feast.

Reflection—"An End and a Beginning"

Today's feast is both an end and a beginning. It is the end of the Christmas season since "ordinary time" begins tomorrow. It is also a beginning because it commemorates the event inaugurating Jesus' earthly ministry. For us, today is a transition. On the one hand, we recall and renew our baptism into Christ, the beginning of our sharing the life of God and the beginning of living what baptism implies—witnessing to Christ in our world. On the other hand, it is an ending of Christmas festivity and of commemorating Christ's incarnation. We now focus on his mission on earth and our mission in him.

Today, we renew the vows of our baptism in sacred ceremony, realizing that tomorrow and the days and weeks that follow, we must live what we celebrate and witness to what we say. Just as Christ was baptized in the power of God to begin his public ministry, so we are baptized in the power of God to live lives in his service.

Just as baptism is a sign of God's work among us, so we who are baptized see in creation, in each other, and in the liturgy signs of God's presence with us. At baptism, we were chosen by God to be his special people. That choice carried with it the responsibility to live the life of God in a world whose values and standards are often very far from those of the gospel. The real message of the Christmas season now ending is that we continue to incarnate Christ in our world by the manner of our lives and the witness of our deeds.

In one sense, the celebration of Christmas ends today; in another, it never really ends because we incarnate Christ in our day and age. Christmas is only the beginning of our experiencing redemption. We continue to experience it and extend it through the rest of the year.

Today, we end a season and begin again to live what this season implies. We do this in response to the God who searches for us in Christ and calls us again and again into his very life. We shared that life first at baptism; we are challenged to share it with each other in "ordinary time."